Kindly Leave the Stage!

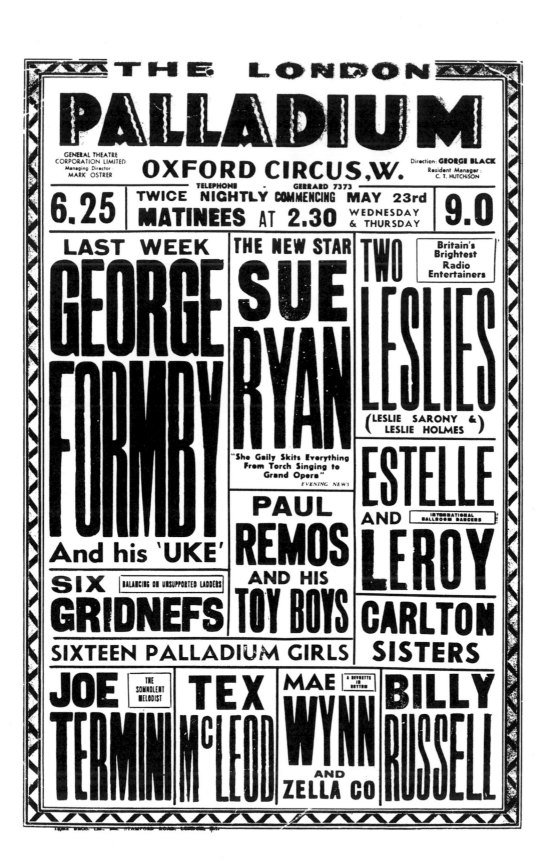

Kindly Leave the Stage!

The Story of Variety
1919–1960

ROGER WILMUT

METHUEN

By the same author

Tony Hancock 'Artiste'
From Fringe to Flying Circus
No More Curried Eggs For Me (editor)
Son of Curried Eggs (editor)

The Goon Show Companion (*Robson Books*)

First published in Great Britain in 1985
by Methuen London Ltd
11 New Fetter Lane, London EC4P 4EE

Copyright © 1985 Roger Wilmut

Made and printed in Great Britain
by BAS Printers Limited
Over Wallop, Stockbridge, Hampshire

British Library Cataloguing in Publication Data

Wilmut, Roger
    Kindly Leave the Stage!: the Story of Variety
    1919–1960.
    1. Music-halls (Variety-theatres, cabarets, etc.)
    – Great Britain – History – 20th century
    I. Title
    792.7'0941   PN1968.G7

    ISBN 0–413–48960–4

This book is dedicated

to every hopeful young comedian who ever played first house (i.e. the first of two evening performances) on a Monday at the Empire Ardwick or the Alhambra Bradford to a small audience of uninterested landladies; walked off the stage to the sound of his own footsteps; shrugged his shoulders, and said to the nearest stagehand: 'It'll go better second house'

Contents

Acknowledgements   9

List of Illustrations   10

PROLOGUE: 'Let's all go to the Music Hall'   13

INTERLUDE: 1919   18

1   'It'll go better second house'   21
Variety in the 1920s

2   'Ha! Ha! – Joke over!'   26
Stand-up comics: One (the 1920s)

3   'Do not sneeze at the microphone'   36
Broadcasting in the 1920s

4   'How's your father?'   40
Sketch comics: One (the 1920s)

5   18 Charing Cross Road: 49
The Variety Artistes' Federation, etc: One (1906–1939)

6   'Oi!'   53
Double-acts: One (the 1920s and 1930s)

7   Life is crazy   63
Variety in the 1930s

8   'Grammatical words to a British tune'   70
Musical acts

9   'We don't book acts with dirty shoes'   82
Running the business: One (1919–1939)

10   'Too lazy to learn a comic song'   90
Acrobats: One (straight acrobatic and adagio acts)

11   An Ass?   95
Variety and the Law

12   'Our 'Erbert's fell in the river'   99
Sketch comics: Two (the 1930s)

13   'A nice little act'   109
Speciality acts: One (dancers and animals)

14   'It's the way I tells 'em, lady'   116
Stand-up comics: Two (the 1930s)

15   'They get in for nothing and laugh at us'   126
Broadcasting in the 1930s

8 Contents

INTERLUDE: A week in Variety   133

16 'All dark and no petrol'   136
   Variety in World War Two

17 'Let's get *on* with it'   141
   Double-acts: Two (the 1930s and 1940s)

18 'From somewhere in Britain'   151
   Broadcasting in wartime

19 Americans and nudes   156
   The post-war boom, 1945–1952

20 'I'm proper poorly'   161
   Stand-up comics: Three (the 1940s and 1950s)

21 Couthy comedy   171
   Variety in Scotland (from the 1920s to the 1950s)

22 Magic and 'a gottle of geer'   175
   Speciality acts: Two (magicians and ventriloquists)

23 Falls – and decline   182
   Acrobats: Two (knockabout and balancing acts)

24 'Look behind you!'   186
   Variety and pantomime

25 Making the Grade   190
   Running the business: Two (1940–1960)

26 Negotiation and amalgamation   193
   The Variety Artistes' Federation, etc: Two (from 1945 onwards)

27 'Are you putting it around that I'm barmy?'   196
   Sketch comics: Three (the 1940s and 1950s)

28 The box in the corner   208
   Broadcasting 1953–1960

29 Nudes and rock 'n' roll   215
   Variety in decline, 1953–1960

INTERLUDE: Indian summer   220

FINALE   226

Glossary   227
Notes   229
Appendix 1: Books   233
Appendix 2: Records   235
Index   237

Acknowledgements

This book covers a very large field, and would have been quite impossible to write without the generous help of a large number of people. Firstly I should like to thank all those who gave me interviews; not all of them could be quoted directly, but all were extremely useful for background research, and my grateful thanks are due to: John Ammonds, Marée Authie, Louis Benjamin, Harold Berens, Alfred Black, the late Norah Blaney, the late George Bolton, Douglas Byng, James Casey, Roy Castle, Johnny Cooper, Florence Desmond, the late Reg Dixon, Vic Duncan, Ted Durante, Arthur English, Serge Ganjou, Joe Gladwin, Ted Gollop, Jimmy Grafton, Adelaide Hall, Harry Harbour, the late Sam Harbour, Jan Harding, Vernon Harris, Pat Hatton, Dickie Henderson, Pat Hillyard, Philip Hindin, the late Stanley Holloway, Pamela Howe, Nat Jackley, Nan Kenway, Peter King, Bob Konyot, Suma Lamonte, Jimmy Logan, Jack Marks, Billy Marsh, Horace Mashford, Charles Maxwell, Rikki and 'Copper' McCormick, Nat Mills, Norman Murray, Allan Newman, Audrey Payne, Bob and Alf Pearson, the late Sandy Powell, Paul Raymond, Marjorie Ristori, Cardew Robinson, Keith Salberg, the late Leslie Sarony, Victor Seaforth, Sir Harry Secombe, Dennis Selinger, the late Michael Standing, Reg Swinson, the late Ronnie Tate, Harold Taylor, Brenda Thomas, Wally Thomas, Peter Titheradge, Max Wall, Elsie Waters, Trafford Whitelock, Dennis Main Wilson and Chris Wortman.

The extracts from various acts which are included in the text are quoted by the kind permission of the copyright holders; all rights of reproduction and performance remain with the copyright holders, to whom I am most grateful for permission to use their material. My thanks are due: to Mrs Hallie Tate for 'Selling a Car', 'Running an Office' and 'Going Round the World' by Harry Tate; to Mrs Margaret Galletly for 'No Power On Earth', 'The League of Nations', and patter by Billy Bennett; to Dickie Henderson for patter by Dick Henderson; to Mr R. Constanduros for 'Mrs Buggins Makes the Christmas Pudding' by Mabel Constanduros; to Bryan Burdon for 'The Means Test Committee' by Albert Burdon; to Flanagan and Allen Ltd for 'The Cl"OI"sters' and 'Digging H"OI"les'; to Stoll-Moss Theatres Ltd for *The 6th London Palladium Crazy Show* and *O-Kay For Sound*; to Douglas Byng for 'Sex-Appeal Sarah' and 'A Christmas Pantomime'; to Betty Western for 'Keeping Up The Old Traditions' by the Western Brothers; to Mrs Betty Herriott for patter by Leon Cortez; to Billie Carlyle for patter by Claude Dampier and Billie Carlyle; to Mrs Kay Powell for 'The Lost Policeman' and 'The Ventriloquist' by Sandy Powell; to Norman Hemsley for patter by Harry Hemsley; to Mrs Sheila Chadwick for patter and 'Murgatroyd and Winterbottom' by Tommy Handley; to Robin Ray for patter by Ted Ray; to Mrs Ruth Harris for patter by Max Miller; to Mrs Marjorie Jamieson for patter by Gillie Potter; to Anthea Askey, Richard Murdoch and Vernon Harris for *Band Waggon*; to Jimmy Jewel for patter by Jewel and Warriss; to Nat Mills for patter; to Elsie Waters for 'Gert and Daisy' material; to P. J. Kavanagh for *ITMA*; to Mrs Mollie Warner for patter and 'Occupations' by Jack Warner; to Mrs D. M. Jenkins for patter by Suzette Tarri; to Frankie Howerd, Beryl Reid, Cardew Robinson, Arthur English and Reg Dixon for patter; to Billy Whittaker for patter by 'Coram'; to Peter Brough for patter; to Basil Boothroyd for 'The Photographer'; to James Casey for patter by Jimmy James; to Ray Galton and Alan Simpson for *The Hancock Show* and *Hancock's Half-Hour;* to Spike Milligan for *The Goon Show*; to Ken Dodd and Les Dawson for patter; and to Eddie Braben for *The Morecambe and Wise Show*. The extracts from 'Let's All Go To The Music-Hall' by Butler, Tilsley and Wright; 'Only A Few Of Us Left' by B. C. Hilliam ('Flotsam'); and 'When I'm Cleaning Windows' by Formby, Gifford & Cliffe, are quoted by permission of the publishers, Lawrence Wright Music. 'Out in the cold, cold snow' by Will E. Haines and Jimmy Harper: copyright © 1934 by Campbell Connelly and Co Ltd., used by permission, all rights reserved. The extracts from BBC internal memos are the copyright of the BBC and are quoted by permission; the extract from the book *Tommy Handley* by Ted Kavanagh is quoted by permission of P. J. Kavanagh.

Every effort has been made to trace copyright holders, but in some cases this has not been possible; apologies are due for any errors or omissions in the credits which, if more information comes to light, will be corrected in future editions.

Thanks are due to the following for help in the research: Morris Aza, Joan Davies, Anne Dent, Norma Farnes, Lew Lane, Tessa Le Bars, Dick James Music, Graham Newell, The Grand Order Of Water Rats, Mavis Quinault, D. Jeremy Stevenson, George Stone, the Westminster Library, The British Library Manuscript and Newspaper Collections, and BBC Copyright Department, Sound Archives, and Written Archives Centre at Caversham.

Special thanks are due to Mrs Hallie Tate; and to Roger Hancock for advice, encouragement and help.

Finally, thanks are due to Helen Baz for compiling the index; to Tim Smith for checking through the typescript; and to Peter Copeland for access to his record collection, for invaluable research assistance, and for criticism of the typescript as it progressed.

Roger Wilmut
March 1985

List of Illustrations

The illustrations for this book have been collected and their subjects identified as a result of much patient and generous help from many individuals and organizations. The author and publisher are especially grateful to Douglas Byng, Johnny Cooper, Vic Duncan, the Ganjou Brothers, the Konyots, Lew Lane, Suma Lamonte, Richard Leacroft, Horace Mashford, Bob and Alf Pearson, Rikki Del Oro, Mrs Hallie Tate and Billy Whittaker for their help with the illustrations; and to the Mander and Mitchenson Theatre Collection. Every effort has been made to describe the subjects and attribute picture sources correctly and trace copyright owners. Apologies are made for any errors or omissions.

Flanagan and Allen (BBC Hulton)   1
London Palladium bill 1938   2
Harry Tate   3
Holborn Empire bill 1918   12
Sir Oswald Stoll   15
Marie Lloyd (Mary Evans)   16
The Original Dixieland Jazz Band (Mander and Mitchenson)   16
Harry Tate   20
The Palace of Varieties, Leicester   22
Chaz Chase   23
Stanley Holloway   24
Norman and Forman   25
Dan Leno   26
George Robey (Mander and Mitchenson)   27
Florence Desmond (Warner Brothers – First National)   28
Stanley Holloway (Houston Rogers)   29
Tom Foy (Mander and Mitchenson)   30
Norman Evans   31
Billy Bennett (Mander and Mitchenson)   32
Dick Henderson (Mander and Mitchenson)   34
Robb Wilton (BBC copyright)   42
Harry Tate and Company   45
Harry and Ronnie Tate   47
from The Performer 27 May 1926   51
The Poluskis (Mander and Mitchenson)   54

Harry Mooney   56
Joe and Dave O'Gorman (Mander and Mitchenson)   57
Naughton and Gold (Mander and Mitchenson)   58
Clapham and Dwyer   59
Flanagan and Allen (BBC Hulton)   60
Flanagan and Allen (Topham)   61
George Black (Mander and Mitchenson)   63
The London Palladium (exterior) (Mander and Mitchenson)   64
The London Palladium (interior) (Victoria and Albert Theatre Museum)   64
Nervo and Knox (Mander and Mitchenson)   65
'Monsewer' Eddie Gray   65
The Crazy Gang   66
The Crazy Gang in 1948 (Popperfoto)   67
Adelaide Hall   70
Bob and Alf Pearson   71
Leslie Sarony and Leslie Holmes   73
The Western Brothers (Mander and Mitchenson)   76
Nellie Wallace   77
Lily Morris   78
George Formby (Mander and Mitchenson)   78
Gracie Fields   80
Bill 1930   83
from The Performer 2 May 1935   85
The Metropolitan Edgware Road   89
Rikki McCormick ('Del Oro')   91
Rikki and 'Copper' McCormick ('Del Oro')   91
The Ganjou Brothers   92
The Ganjou Brothers and Juanita   93
Horace Kenney (Mander and Mitchenson)   99
Claude Dampier   100
Sandy Powell and 'Little Peggy'   102
Will Hay (Rank)   106
Will Hay, Charles Hawtrey, John Clark and Billy Nicholls (BBC copyright)   107
Johnny Cooper   109
Wilson, Keppel and Betty   111
Horace and Edna Mashford   112
Duncan's Collies   114
Vic Duncan rehearsing the chair-back trick   115

Ted Ray   119

Tommy Trinder (Mander and Mitchenson)   120

Billy Russell   121

Max Miller at the Holborn Empire
(BBC Hulton)   122

Max Miller (Keystone)   124

Max Miller (BBC Hulton)   125

Michael Standing (BBC copyright)   127

Richard Murdoch and Arthur Askey (BBC
copyright)   130

from *The Performer* 14 October 1948   135

Phyllis Dixey   139

Harry Champion (Mander and Mitchenson)   139

Jimmy Jewel and Ben Warriss (Mander and
Mitchenson)   141

Arthur Lucan and Kitty McShane (Mander and
Mitchenson)   143

Nat Mills and Bobbie   145

Elsie and Doris Waters   149

Pat Hillyard and John Watt (BBC copyright)   151

ITMA: Tommy Handley, Dorothy Summers, Jean
Capra (BBC copyright)   152

Jack Warner and Joan Winters (BBC)   154

Val Parnell   156

Danny Kaye   157

bill from The Empire, Tonypandy, 1949   159

Jeanne de Casalis (BBC copyright)   161

Suzette Tarri and John Sharman (BBC
copyright)   162

Harry Secombe (by Jack Oakley)   162

Frankie Howerd (Mander and Mitchenson)   164

Issy Bonn   167

Reg Dixon   168

Harry Lauder   171

Will Fyffe   172

Harry Gordon (Mander and Mitchenson)   173

David Devant (Mander and Mitchenson)   175

Johnny Cooper   177

Fred Russell and 'Coster Joe' (Mander and
Mitchenson)   178

Coram and and 'Jerry Fisher'   178

Arthur Prince and 'Jim'   179

Peter Brough and 'Archie Andrews' (BBC
copyright)   180

Johnny and Suma Lamonte   183

Bob and Marion Konyot   184

Bob and Marion Konyot   185

George Robey (Mander and Mitchenson)   187

Douglas Byng   187

Dickie Henderson and Arthur Askey (Mander and
Mitchenson)   188

from *The Performer* 1 May 1952   192

from *The Performer* 1 Feb 1945   195

Nat Jackley (Mander and Mitchenson)   196

Frank Randle   197

Frank Randle (Mander and Mitchenson)   198

Dave Morris (BBC Hulton)   199

Sid Field   201

Sid Field and Jerry Desmonde (Rank)   203

Jimmy James (Mander and Mitchenson)   204

Jimmy James and 'Hutton Conyers' (BBC)   206

Tony Hancock, Bill Kerr, Sid James (BBC)   212

The Goon Show (BBC copyright)   213

Johnny Ray (Melody Maker)   216

Lonnie Donegan (Melody Maker)   217

Cliff Richard   217

Max Wall (Morris Newcombe)   220

Ken Dodd   222

Les Dawson (BBC copyright)   223

Eric Morecambe and Ernie Wise (BBC
copyright)   224

Will Hay (BBC Hulton)   227

Wilson, Keppel and Betty (Mander and
Mitchenson)   232

Tommy Trinder and Gracie Fields
(Topham)   236

HOLBORN EMPIRE

HIGH HOLBORN, W.C.

Licensee   Mr. CHAS. GULLIVER

Twice Nightly at 6.20 and 9.10
MONDAY, MARCH 3rd, 1913.

ARTHUR ROBERTS In "THE IMPORTANCE OF being ANOTHER MAN'S WIFE"	**AMERICAN RAG-TIME BAND**	**EVIE GREENE** By permission of G. Edwardes
JACK PLEASANTS	**TOM MOORE** THE BIOSCOPE	**REGAN & RYAN**
MAUD EDWARDS	Mr. Chas. GULLIVER Presents **PAUL J. RAINEY'S AFRICAN HUNT** Marvellous Moving Pictures Daily at 3. Prices, 6d. to 5s.	**HARRY RUSSON**
JACK & EVELYN	**LUDWIG AMANN**	**HARRY CHAMPION**

At the PALLADIUM. Daily at 2.30. Mr. MATHESON LANG and Miss HUTIN BRITTON, in "WESTWARD HO!"

BOXES. 10/6 & 15/6 To Seat Four Ex. Seats, 2/6, 3s.	ROYAL FAUTEUILS **2/-** Bookable, 2/3	Fauteuils & Gr. Clr. Faut. **1/6** Bookable 1/9 Tip-Up Arm Chairs	GR. CIRCLE **1/-** Bookable in advance, 1/3 Finest in London	Pit Stalls **6d.** Tip-up Seats	Balcony **4d.** A Magnificent Seat Beautifully Upholstered

Saturdays (2nd House only), Bank Holidays and Special Performances: Royal Fauteuils, 2/6—No Booking Fee; Fauteuils and Grand Circle Fauteuils, 2/.—Bookable in Advance, 2/3; Gr. Circle, 1/6— Bookable in Advance, 1/9; Pit Stalls, 9d; Balcony, 6d.

Seats can be booked by Telephone the number being HOLBORN 5367-8-9 (3 lines). The Management reserve the right to dispose of the same if they are not paid for by 6.30 & 8.30 in the first and second house respectively. Seats booked by letter should close remittance to cover also stamped addressed envelope. Right of Refusing Admission is reserved. No Money Refunded or Seats Guaranteed unless booked in advance

Seats Booked by Telephone for SATURDAY NIGHTS will not be retained after 6 o'clock for 1st House, & 6.20 for 2nd House.

PROLOGUE: 'Let's all go to the Music Hall'

Let's all go to the Music Hall
Where the show is gay and bright,
Let's all go to the Music Hall
Where the stars are twinkling twice a night.
Whether you sit in the gallery, the circle, or the pit
Or whether you sit in a red plush stall –
When the busy day is done
If you want to have some fun –
Let's all go to the Music Hall.

Radio and television are nowadays so much a part of our lives that it is difficult to visualize a period when they were not the main media of popular entertainment. In the second half of the nineteenth century the main form of amusement for what were called the 'working classes' – apart from drinking, of course – was music-hall: entertainment from a wide range of performers, presented theatrically but also with food and drink being available to the audience.

Using the term 'working class' presents problems of definition, because the term carries the stigma of snobbery – it was in any case a euphemism for 'lower classes', which is how the poorer-paid manual workers were referred to by the 'middle classes' (tradespeople, professional people, and the like) and the 'upper classes' (the rich – idle or otherwise). Until the 1950s this sort of class distinction was a normal part of British life; in this book the expression 'working classes' will be used (in lieu of a better one) but simply as a definition of a grouping of people.

Problems of definition also arise from the outset with the subject-matter of this book. The form of entertainment under examination was specifically a collection of separate and varied performances, as opposed to straight theatrical plays; and in the period before the 1914–18 War it was generally known as 'music-hall'. It was robust, unashamedly *popular* in the true sense; and distinctly British, for although America and European countries had their own equivalents they came from a different tradition and were different in style and atmosphere.

The pre-1914 tradition – which will be examined in outline in this prologue – provided the background to the subtly different style which characterized this sort of popular entertainment in the period from the end of the first World War to its virtual demise in the late 1950s. The

War, of course, made sweeping changes in the world as a whole. The pre-1914 period is now seen as part of history – quaint, colourful, and usually romanticized; from 1920 on we can see the beginnings of the modern world, and the styles and attitudes of the period seem much less alien. Inevitably, as society changed, music-hall changed with it. It altered its style, its pacing and broadened its appeal; and the years from the end of the War to 1960 are really a quite separate story from that of the old music-hall. It is this story which is the subject of this book, rather than the Victorian and Edwardian tradition which in some ways has retained a greater grip on the popular imagination and has tended to overshadow the later period; a story which has its own attractions and fascinations which deserve more attention than they have usually received.

Not only the style changed as the new post-War period moved on; the name 'music-hall' gradually gave way to the term 'Variety' – although they have usually been regarded as interchangeable; indeed it is not easy to provide a pat definition of the difference. 'Music-hall' conjures up the popular idea of the Victorian halls, with red plush seats and a somewhat rowdy working-class audience, a chairman to introduce the acts and lots of chorus songs – the sort of atmosphere suggested by the song quoted above. 'Variety' is less easy to define, except as simply what the term implies – a variety of acts. Both terms have been used since the earliest days – indeed the first recorded use of the expression 'Variety' in the context of an entertainment seems to have been on Easter Monday 1841, when Samuel Haycroft Lane, proprietor of the Britannia Theatre, Hoxton, presented a melodrama, an opera, a ballet, and six acts under the title 'A Variety of Artists'. This predates the opening of what is generally thought of as the first music hall proper, the Canterbury, by eleven years.

'Music-hall', remained, however, the more generally accepted term in the last century. Its beginnings were in the pubs and supper-rooms, where amateur talent would gather to drink and sing; gradually these performances developed into more organized entertainments by professional artists. In this period – the first half of the last century – these were entirely for the working classes. The middle classes were developing a severe attack of respectability which was to keep them out of the music halls until early in the twentieth century. Since the audiences were mostly male – the only women present would usually be prostitutes – the emphasis was often on lewdness; and the entertainment was regarded as of secondary importance to the food and drink.

The change from what was in effect public-house entertainment to classic music-hall was largely the work of one man: Charles Morton, born in 1819. In 1848 he bought the Canterbury Hall, at that time another glorified pub, offering food, drink, entertainment, skittles – but for men only. In 1852 he re-opened it, much rebuilt and improved, and presented a higher quality of entertainment; it was the first true music hall in the style that was to become widespread. He provided a high quality of refreshment and entertainment – he also ran a book on races until this practice was made illegal in 1853 – and he gradually introduced the idea that ladies might come to a music hall. This of course meant a toning-down of the bawdier aspects of the entertainment.

Shortly afterwards Morton changed from admission by a ticket which also entitled the purchaser to a drink, to a straightforward admission ticket, costing threepence. The Canterbury also became the first hall to admit ladies every night; the transition to music-hall was complete. Many other halls, both in London and the provinces, followed suit. Morton himself opened another London hall, the Oxford (on the corner of Oxford Street and Tottenham Court Road); other London halls included Gatti's; the Royal, Holborn (later the Holborn Empire); and the Metropolitan Edgware Road; while all over the country independent managers opened their own halls.

The popular image of the early halls – fostered by songs like the one quoted above and reconstructions for the cinema and, much later, television – is somewhat over-nostalgic. In the early days there was tremendous vitality, and indeed often strong social satire, in many of the performances. The prominent critic Max Beerbohm wrote that people flocked to the halls to be cheered up by seeing a life uglier and more sordid than their own. But gradually the increasing respectability of the halls toned down this element of social satire, and later performers – such as Ella Shields as 'Burlington Bertie from Bow' – seemed instead to preach ironic acceptance of a hard life.

The other popular conception of the halls – that the audiences were rowdy and difficult to control – seems on the whole not to have been true. The 'turns' were introduced by a chairman, part of whose function was to keep order (and another part of whose function was to be bought drinks by nearby members of the audience); and in any case extreme rowdyism would have been resented by those who had come to see their favourite artists. There were exceptions – The Varieties, Hoxton, was so notorious that it became known as 'The Sod's Opera'.

The legal position of music halls was rather odd. The early legal situation of theatres was complex in the extreme, but the Licensing Act of 1737[1] allowed only two theatres in the entire country to present straight plays, both in London – Covent Garden, and the Theatre Royal, Drury Lane. Other theatres had to be content with ballets, music, or 'burlettas' (speech, but with *continuous* music). The Theatres Act of 1843[2] regularized the position of other theatres, bringing them under the control of the Lord Chamberlain, whose licence was required before any drama could be presented. (His main function was to protect the monarch and God from any unseemly remarks in the course of a drama; only later did 'vulgarity' and obscenity become his main concerns. The tight censorship that this measure enabled continued until 1968.)

Theatres and entertainment rooms were faced with a choice – either to present plays, subject to the Lord

Chamberlain's censorship, but be forbidden to serve food and drink in the auditorium; or to be allowed to sell food and drink, but be forbidden to present performances which might be construed as plays. This meant anything involving more than one person speaking; monologues were allowed, and songs, and ballets, but not sketches, playlets, or what we now know as 'double-acts' (unless they were entirely mimed). Those premises which chose to become music halls became subject to an act of 1751 originally intended for the regulation of Disorderly Houses[3] (i.e. brothels).

The dubious origins of the music halls caused an atmosphere of disapproval by those in authority which lingered on well into the twentieth century, and was one of the reasons behind the Metropolis Management Act of 1878[4] which required the actual buildings to be licensed for suitability by the Metropolitan Board of Works (later the London County Council) in London, and by similar authorities in the provinces. This closed many of the older halls, and was another step towards the larger, plusher, more organized style of music-hall.

On the management side, the independent owner-managers were either building up a chain of halls, or being bought out by their more successful brethren. Sir Edward Moss founded the chain of 'Empires' – huge, ornate, and very professionally run; Sir Oswald Stoll had his own chain and in 1904 opened the Coliseum – a tribute to megalomania which still stands and perhaps makes a better opera house than ever it did a Variety hall.

The most popular music-hall artists at the end of the century were the comics, usually presenting a character study in song, or a song with patter; but the essence of music-hall was the wide range of entertainment it could provide. There were straight singers, of sentimental or stirring patriotic ballads; there were acrobatic acts, animal acts, dancers, 'speciality acts' such as conjurers or jugglers; there were juvenile acts, family acts with performers ranging from the youngest to the oldest members . . . and the audiences of those days had stamina; there could be anything up to thirty acts on a bill lasting some three or four hours.

Obviously such a long bill would be presented only once each evening, but the technique of two shorter performances each evening – 'twice-nightly', the second 'house' or performance being a repeat of the first – had been introduced in the north of England in the 1860s. Gradually it took over from the longer 'once-nightly' bills, and by 1914 it was the norm. (The expression 'once-nightly' became used in the business to differentiate straight plays from

Variety shows.) The construction and selection of acts for Variety bills was something of an art in itself (and will be examined in more detail in Chapter 9); but every bill

Sir Oswald Stoll

normally presented as wide a range of different acts as possible, with the most popular artist – the 'top of the bill' (so called because he or she was listed at the top of the printed publicity posters) – placed near the end of the programme. (Their act was usually followed by a small-time acrobatic or similar act as a 'chaser'.)

Two types of acts were conspicuously absent (to modern eyes) from most bills of the pre-first World War period – comics who simply told a string of unrelated jokes (the style had not yet been invented); and anything involving more than one speaker – double-acts, sketches, etc. These were still forbidden by law – not that that always stopped them appearing. Charles Morton – after fifty years in the business one of the most highly respected managers – was irritated by the anomalies in the law, and periodically presented sketches (the term at this time meant a one-act play) in a deliberate move to stir things up. He would promptly be reported by jealous managers of legitimate theatres (who did not see why he should be allowed to present plays but not be subject to the licensing regulations which controlled them), hauled into court and fined; and not long afterwards the whole silly game would start again. In the end an agreement was reached between the Variety managements and the Theatrical Managers Association (representing the managers of legitimate theatres), and from 1907 music halls were allowed to present sketches up to half-an-hour long without legal consequences following.

Meanwhile the halls were becoming big business. The top-grade Moss and Stoll circuits were emulated by smaller (and tattier) circuits run by MacNaghten, Broadhead, Barrasford and other entrepreneurs. Artists began to be represented by agents, who found them work for a commission (with varying degrees of efficiency and legality). Both the performers and the managers were becoming stronger and more organized. In 1907 a long-standing grievance about whether extra matinées should be paid for or included in the artists' weekly salary led to the Music Hall Strike; this in turn led to the first attempts to regularize contracts. Music-hall was becoming more respectable, and one of the reflections of this new respectability was the Royal Command Performance of 1912, when many of the most famous artists of the day appeared before King George V and a large royal party at the Palace Theatre (in Cambridge Circus, London – another former music hall which now does duty as a theatre for plays and musicals). One artist who was *not* commanded to appear was the queen of the saucy song, Marie Lloyd; she, at any rate, was not respectable enough.

This was the peak and at the same time the swan-song of the old Victorian music-hall; for in the same year the law on the licensing of theatres was amended to remove the anomalies between theatres and halls. Both were brought under the Lord Chamberlain; and food and drink finally disappeared from the auditorium (though not from bars elsewhere in the theatre). This, perhaps more than anything else, changed the style of music-hall; there was less of the everybody-sing-along type of act, less of a free-and-easy feel to the proceedings, and gradually the presentations – though still in a similar format – became more of a *theatrical* experience for the audience. The chairman, and his function as compère, had in most cases disappeared, to be replaced by a printed programme, and this had a further effect on the entertainment – perhaps placing the artists at a greater emotional distance from the audience.

Marie Lloyd

The classic text-book on the old music-hall is probably W. Macqueen-Pope's *The Melodies Linger On*,[5] and in it he offers his own definition of the difference between music-hall and Variety – 'Music Hall,' he says, 'was Variety (although Variety is not Music Hall)' – which is epigrammatic, but unhelpful. Perhaps pigeon-holing styles in this manner is ill-advised; but the present book regards music-hall proper as something that died, if not in 1912, at any rate by the end of that much more obvious influence, the first World War; and Variety as the equivalent entertainment medium in the post-1919 period.

By the time the War started in 1914, music-hall was already under threat from a new style of presentation called 'Revue'. In style, this tended to be something between music-hall and the spectacular musical comedies of the period (in which the costumes and scenery were often more impressive than the music); the artists appeared throughout in different scenes, rather than being confined to their own act, and there was sometimes a pretence for a plot. Although as time went on revues tended to become less spectacular (and by the 1940s were often only Variety bills in disguise) the term was used until the 1950s to indicate this cross between Variety and musical comedy – a competitor to Variety which for the most part must lie outside the scope of this book. It was just one of the newer forms of entertainment with which Variety had to compete after the first World War ended.

Almost every book on music-hall – *The Melodies Linger On* included – dismisses the period after 1919 as of no interest. Variety, they claim, was dying, just as music-hall itself was dead. Well, certainly Variety was dying – it went on dying for forty years, and it was not until 1960 that the corpse was truly cold (and even then manifestations of it – perhaps ghosts – continued to be observable). And in those forty years there were many fine artists, much excellent entertainment, and even a move into a new medium – broadcasting, which, though first seen as a threat, became a saviour. Variety appeared in some strange disguises from time to time, and occasionally in strange company; and this long and entertaining death-scene is the story told in this book.

It is of course a very complex story, and the first thing which needs to be said is that this book is not an encyclopaedia. There were several hundred premises in the country in 1919, and several *thousand* Variety performers; and an attempt to list them all would result in a very boring book. This is the story of the medium of Variety itself, told partly through the experiences of a (reasonably) representative selection of those who worked in it, partly through extracts from some of their acts, and partly from research into the surviving documents and records. With a few exceptions, those artists whose greatest fame was achieved in the pre-1919 days are not included; but since this is an attempt to illustrate the business from the inside there are agents, managers, and the backroom boys of broadcasting as well as a selection of the big stars of the time. There are also some of the small acts – the reliable people who never made it to the top, but whose presence on a Variety bill was an essential part of the atmosphere. Their names are not remembered today, but this is their story too.

In order to attempt to cover the ground with something approaching clarity, the structure of the book cannot be strictly chronological. Chapters looking at the overall pattern of Variety in the 1920s, the 1930s and so on, and others looking at broadcasting in those same periods, will be intermingled with 'subject chapters' covering aspects of the Variety world – sketch acts, double-acts, acrobatic acts, the people who ran the business, etc. In order to avoid, for example, discussing a 1950s comedian when the 'historical' sections of the narrative are still in the 1930s, most of these 'subject chapters' have been split into two or three sections which are placed in roughly their correct chronological position. Inevitably there are still some chronological absurdities; but then the world of Variety was itself a little absurd.

So as we begin our story of Variety, it is 1919; old-time music-hall is dead; and so is the safe Edwardian world it flourished in, for the War to end all wars has blown it away for ever. No longer a purely working-class entertainment, Variety is now halfway respectable, and even the moral middle-classes walk through the fancy doors into the ornate halls. For a short time, Variety is the principal entertainment of the people, for films are as yet in their infancy and radio is unheard-of as an entertainment medium. Perhaps already there are some in the business with the vision to see that Variety will have a finite life-span – leaving a cold and empty world for the performers who are its life-blood – but they still go onto the brightly-lit stages to do their acts in the eternal hope that 'It'll go better second house'.

INTERLUDE

1919

Besides being the first year of the long-hoped-for peace, 1919 had three points of special interest about it for the Variety world. The one which had the most immediate effect on the ordinary members of the profession was the Arbitration proceedings which took place in September to hammer out a proper contract for artists. The details of this will be dealt with in Chapter 11; but at this stage it is worth noting the strong stand by the performers – represented by Fred Russell of the Variety Artistes' Federation – against attempts by the managers to place severe restrictions on the appearances which artists who played their theatres might make subsequently. Indeed the majority of the proceedings was taken up with arguing about this particular point, which arose because the managers wanted to be sure that an artist could not follow an appearance at one of their halls with an immediate appearance at another hall in the same area. In the end a reasonable compromise was struck, and the contract as finally agreed by all parties gave Variety artists the most satisfactory terms of employment they had ever had. The '1919 Award Contract', as it became known, remained the standard, with only minor adjustments, until the end of the Variety period forty years later.

Performers were at last regarded as having a right to reasonable terms of employment; and although there was much improvement needed in the actual physical conditions in which they worked (many theatres were a disgrace backstage and remained so), the 1919 Award was the final step in the journey from the uncontrolled amateurism of the old century to the professionalism of the new.

A quite different event took place in 1919 which at the time cannot have seemed of much significance to members of the Variety profession. In April five young white American musicians came over to Britain to appear in the revue *Joy Bells* at the London Hippodrome; they were the Original Dixieland Jazz Band.

The dispute still continues among jazz fans whether the ODJB were innovators, or merely imitators of a black style of music who happened to get themselves onto gramophone records first. A good deal of fun can be had by reopening that discussion in the right company, but this book is not the place to do so. What is at any rate agreed by everybody is that they were the first to use the actual name 'Jazz' (or, in its original form, 'Jass' – apparently a slang word with obscene connotations; all previous bands in this field had used the term 'Ragtime') and that they were the first to come to the notice of the public through gramophone records. What is also certain is that nothing like them had ever been heard before on this side of the Atlantic. Many found them raucous, not to say actually frightening, and moralists and the press had a field day of disapproval – exactly the same sort of display later accorded to crooners, swing, rock-and-roll, skiffle and punk rock.

Despite all this, when the ODJB opened in *Joy Bells* on 7 April 1919, the audience (which included a fair proportion of American soldiers) was wildly enthusiastic – so much so that the star of the show, top music-hall comedian George Robey, insisted on the band's removal. They then played several top Variety theatres, including the Palladium, with great success before going on to dates in nightclubs.[1]

Their impact on British popular music was tremendous. It was perhaps more their presentation than the jazz itself that caught the public imagination – trombones played with the feet, funny hats, teddy bears on the drum kit and so on – and which set up an association between jazz and vacuous frivolity that was not dispelled for over forty years; but British dance bands thereafter were modelled on a toned-down version of the ODJB's style – the Savoy Orpheans were a classic example – and this change in the style of popular music was inevitably reflected in the world of Variety. From this time, even comic songs owed a debt to jazz, however distant the relationship; and with the rise of radio and the gramophone, dance bands and vocalists became a major part of popular entertainment.

The third major event of interest to the Variety world was the second (and last) Royal Command Variety Performance, given at the Coliseum on 28 July 1919 'in celebration of Peace'. The only other *Command* Performance (for Variety artists) had been in 1912; the series of annual shows which began in 1921 and continues today are simply Royal Variety Performances – there is no 'com-

The Original Dixieland Jazz Band

mand' involved. Most performers, however, seem to like the idea of being commanded royally, and continue to use the expression.

Once again, the show gave royal approval to the Variety profession – and thanks for the work done in raising money for various war funds – which more or less removed the stigma of the business's dubious beginnings. From this time onwards there was less reluctance on the part of the middle classes to go to the halls; and though there was perhaps a loss of frankness and social 'bite' in the comedy compared with the Victorian era, the wider appeal that Variety could now exercise placed it – for a while – in the forefront of entertainment.

The Royal Command Performance was, as might be expected, a suitably star-studded occasion. The cast included George Robey and Violet Lorraine, the stars of the revue *The Bing Boys Are Here* (whose hit song, 'If You Were The Only Girl In The World' remained popular for many years); Clarice Mayne and 'That' ('That' being her husband and accompanist in her comic songs); The Flying Banvards; Sam Barton; Ernest Hastings (who performed monologues in a northern accent); the great European clown Grock; and the ventriloquist Arthur Prince and his nautically-attired dummy Jim.

One of the funniest acts on the bill was that of Harry Tate – already a top star, and in the 1920s one of the best of all the comedy sketch acts. He and his company presented their sketch 'Selling A Car'. Although there was a lot of visual humour in the act – Tate's huge moustache twitching impossibly as each new annoyance presented itself, not to mention the ramshackle car itself – some idea of the sketch can be obtained from the following extract. Tate has hopes of selling his car, and his character's son (played by Tommy Tweedly, as he was for many years) is reading through the advertisement:

SON: 'For immediate sale.'

TATE: Well, I don't know that I like that word
        'immediate' – it looks as if we want to get rid
        of it, doesn't it? I think I should cut that out.

SON: 'Detachable wheels.'

TATE: Yes.

SON: *Are* they detachable?

TATE: Of course they are – didn't one come off
        yesterday?

SON: 'Tyres – Dunlop.'

TATE: That's wrong.

SON: That's how you told me.

TATE: No I didn't – I said . . . tyres *done-a-lot*.
        Alter that, it's misleading.

SON: 'Owner has good reason for selling.'

TATE: *Yes.*

SON: 'Perfect running order.'

TATE: 'Perfect' . . . well . . . what do you think?

SON: Well, it's . . . er . . .

TATE: That's what *I* think, too. I should alter that.

SON: 'Owner has only driven it 200 miles.'

TATE: That's right – I've *pushed* it the rest.

SON: 'Suitable for a clergyman.'

TATE: Y-yes.

SON: Why?

TATE: Because . . . he daren't tell you what he
        thinks of it.

SON: 'Self-starter.'

TATE: Well . . . down hills, yes.

SON: 'Three speeds.'

TATE: That's right – Faith, Hope and Charity.

SON: 'And reverse.'

TATE: And reverse – get out and push it back.

SON: 'Two cylinders . . .'

TATE: *One* cylinder.

SON: '*Two* cylinders in one piece.'

TATE: Oh, I thought it was one cylinder in two
        pieces. I'm glad you found that out.

SON: 'Streamlined body.'

TATE: Well, poet's licence, yes . . .

SON: 'Nothing cheap about it.'

TATE: No. I don't like the word 'cheap' – I know
        what you mean – there's nothing *shoddy* about
        it.

SON: 'It's *good*.'

TATE: It *is* – if we sell it.[2]

Harry Tate – 'Golfing' (*c.* 1925)

So the Royal Command Performance, the 1919 Award
Contract, and – in their own modest way – the Original
Dixieland Jazz Band, signalled the way ahead into the
1920s – a new acceptability to people who previously
would never have gone near a music hall; new, more
organized and professional working conditions; and the
beginning of the so-called Jazz age. As the 1920s began,
Variety was in the forefront; but the next ten years were to
turn its world upside-down yet again.

1 'It'll go better second house'
Variety in the 1920s

Think of the 1920s, and what is the image that comes to mind? Probably a colourful medley of wild parties, 'flappers', everyone driving about in vintage cars – the popular image of 'The Roaring Twenties'. This of course is the *American* image – partly a legend, partly a segment of the truth – as put about by the cinema, both at the time and since. In Britain it wasn't all like that. There were the high spots of the London night-life; and certainly young women had a freedom which would have seemed unbelievable only ten years earlier; and for those who were rich, life was as pleasant as it always is for those who are rich. But for the mass of ordinary men and women, life was much drabber. The servicemen who came back from the horrors of the War to 'A land fit for heroes to live in' found employment hard to get – the sight of ex-soldiers begging in the streets became too common to excite much interest – and life in general was hard and expensive. There were nearly a million unemployed by the beginning of the 1920s, and the general economic depression was not helped by an air of fiscal incompetence radiating from the corridors of the Government (who fixed the pound at far too high a value so that British goods were over-priced outside the Empire – Britain still had an Empire – and thus difficult to sell).

Despite the economic slump, Variety at first found itself in a boom period, for it provided escapism and did it for only a few pence. At first it had little competition. At the beginning of the 1920s the cinema – which was then of course silent – was only just coming into its first maturity; and radio, which began in 1922, had little practical effect for several years. By the end of the 1920s, silent films were to provide much more serious competition. The scratched, flickering, many-times-copied prints which are all too often seen today give little idea of the visual beauty of many films of the period, and the Hollywood star system had built up a huge following for idols such as Valentino, Garbo, Fairbanks and Pickford. Films and Variety co-existed to some extent in the form of 'cine-variety', whereby a film would have a supporting programme of several Variety acts; but, perhaps because the films, though popular, provided a totally different and rather unreal sort of experience, it was not until the coming of sound films at the very end of the 1920s that the competition became really serious. Variety could provide colour, music, and the personal performer-to-audience relationship that the silent films could never approach.

Real life, however, was not represented. The early music-hall had parodied the hard life of the period; but Variety in the 1920s attempted no such feat. Comic songs leaned towards the nonsensical rather than the satirical, and comedians towards the grotesque rather than the observant. The audiences were not interested in real life – they had just had four years of it, which threw a shadow over the whole period up to the next war, for few people had escaped the loss of several friends and relatives in the fighting.

Wally Thomas, who worked the halls as a boy in the early 1920s as 'Thomé, the young French violinist' (not being able to speak a word of French) thinks that audiences were already becoming more sophisticated.

'Better education, a broadening of views – they started to get more knowledge through newspapers and so on; there was a general trend towards better-class stuff, not the old knees-up Mother-Brown . . . looking more for the talented side of it.'

The War had had two particular effects on some sections of the audience. Whereas before 1914 few of them had been any further away from home than the seaside, there were now men who had fought in France, in Mesopotamia, and other far distant lands. There was also a new cynicism about the rulers of the country and the newspapers – particularly the newspapers, for men who, while retreating in bloody disorder, had read censored newspapers reporting splendid British successes in their campaign would never again have much trust in what they read in the press.

In the change from the old music-hall to the new Variety many old-fashioned stars found themselves out of favour. A young lady called Florence Dawson was just starting her career in Variety in 1920 at the age of fourteen; under her stage name of Florence Desmond she became one of the top artists of the 1930s (although in 1920 she was performing comic songs – none too well). One day she was with her agent, Walter Bentley, when the phone rang.

'He picked it up, and said "'Ullo – who's that? . . . Tom? . . . I've been onto the Gulliver circuit, Moss Empires, the Syndicate Circuit . . . they don't want you, Tom – I'm sorry . . . no, nothing." So he put the phone down, and I said, "Who was that?" He said, "That was T. E. Dunville" – who was quite a top-of-the-bill music-hall man. Two weeks later T. E. Dunville walked into the river Thames and drowned himself.'

There was always little enough room for sentiment in business, and Variety was certainly big business. There were sixty-nine halls playing Variety or revue in the London Metropolitan area alone in 1920,[1] and over 600 in the rest of the country (although these included some very small ones which probably did not operate all the time). Birmingham, for example, had the Alexandra, the Elite, the Empire, the Gaiety, the Grand Theatre of Varieties, the Hippodrome, and the New Palace. Leeds had the City Palace of Varieties, the Empire, the Hippodrome, and the Queen's Theatre. There were twelve in the Manchester area, eight in Liverpool, six in Sunderland; two in Leamington Spa, Peterborough and Swansea; and among the smaller towns that could still boast one Variety theatre were Carmarthen, Darlington, Limerick, Malvern . . .

The Palace of Varieties, Leicester

All the important halls were owned by the big circuits. Moss Empires, despite the death of its founder, Sir Edward Moss, in 1912, was generally considered the top-class circuit – it was the ambition of every rising star to work on it. In 1920 the circuit – or 'tour' as it was known, since its artists could work the various halls in succession – comprised twenty-four theatres,[2] rising to thirty by 1925. They provided traditional Variety of a high standard, together with the occasional revue.

The Stoll tour comprised seventeen halls in 1920,[3] with several theatres being dropped as the decade went on. The flagship of the circuit was of course the London Coliseum, the massive, ornate building which has been used as an opera house since 1968. Here Stoll adopted a policy of high-class Variety, mixing the more usual acts with spectaculars such as tennis tournaments or golf demonstrations on-stage. In earlier years he had even presented horse-races! (The Coliseum had a huge multiple revolving stage consisting of three concentric rings, the outer two each being 12 feet across and the middle section being 25 feet in diameter, and by running it in the opposite direction to the horses, the competitors would stay in the centre of the stage. This technique was also used for the chariot race in the stage version of *Ben-Hur*, and in 1929 for dog races.)

As well as these spectaculars, Stoll presented serious musical and dramatic performances at the Coliseum, among them the Russian Ballet under the direction of Diaghilev. In 1925, when they presented among their ballets the first appearance in Britain of the last act of *The Sleeping Beauty*, they found themselves sharing a bill with performers such as Nervo and Knox (a knockabout act), Hilda Ward's 'Lady Syncopators', several speciality acts, and a newsreel. Stoll also ran the Alhambra (where the Odeon Cinema, Leicester Square, now stands), and the Stoll Picture Theatre (where the Royalty Theatre now stands).

There were two circuits under the management of Charles Gulliver – the Variety Theatres Controlling Co Ltd, which ran several provincial theatres, and London Theatres of Variety Ltd ('LTV'), which ran the Holborn Empire and the London Palladium among others. The Palladium was always a premier Variety theatre – though difficult to run at a profit – but it did not really come into its own until the 1930s.

Another circuit dealing only with London was the Syndicate Halls, which owned among others the London Pavilion and the Metropolitan Edgware Road; while in the north of England there were a number of small circuits of varying degrees of tattiness. The foremost was the Broadhead tour, with seventeen theatres; others were the MacNaghten Circuit, and, later on, Howard and Wyndham. There were several other small circuits, and, even at this time, many independently run theatres.

There were mergers and takeovers as the 1920s went on, just as in any big business. Walter Gibbons – the man who originally built the Palladium and formed the LTV circuit, but had lost control of it – set up a new firm which in 1929 gained a majority shareholding in the old LTV and the Variety Theatres Controlling Co; this became the

General Theatres Corporation (GTC). Almost immediately he lost control again, being bought out by the Gaumont-British Picture Corporation. At the time of its formation, GTC controlled fifty-six theatres and cinemas, thus becoming one of the most powerful circuits in the business.

Throughout the 1920s Variety co-existed with other, related, forms of stage entertainment. Revue (as we saw on page 17) had been extremely popular during the War, but *The Stage* Yearbook for 1920 noted that the public demand for it had slackened since the War ended, and that musical comedies were becoming more popular. The dividing lines were a trifle blurred – many revues had a story line, for example *The Bing Boys Are Here* which starred George Robey – and some artists were able to work in both formats; but the majority of Variety artists appeared in revues only if they were closely related to Variety – by being more or less a fixed Variety bill which toured, for example.

Strictly speaking, Variety itself consisted of unconnected acts who appeared, then travelled to other locations and appeared with a totally different set of artists. However, it was quite common for what was in effect a normal Variety bill to tour as a package – often in later years mounted by the top act – under a flimsy title of some sort. From this it was only a step to revue proper, in which individual artists would appear in more than one spot and with the other artists on the bill – unlike Variety proper, where everyone stuck to their own spot. Many Variety artists played in both types of entertainment: Harry Tate, for example, had been in revue at the London Hippodrome for five years prior to the 1919 Royal Command Performance in which he appeared; he subsequently returned to touring the halls.

Despite the new respectability of the halls mentioned earlier, the posher sort of revue and musical comedies were generally considered a cut above ordinary Variety, and few artists made the step up to this type of show. One who did was Norah Blaney, whose career was a little odd altogether. She was with a small group of mostly classical musicians who had been taken to France to entertain the troops by the singer Gervase Elwes, when she first met her future co-star Gwen Farrar – a budding cellist who was supposedly still at school.

'Gwen was at school at Heathfield, Ascot – where all the grand girls go – and she ran away on the top of a Harrods' van and went and stayed with an aunt in London. So Lady Farrar said, "Oh, Gervase, do take Gwen – I can't do anything with her". So Gwen played the cello – she played the cello very well – and I was the comic relief, because I sang silly little songs at the piano.'

They came together because one of the other performers broke an ankle.

'We had no rehearsal or anything – I sang my silly little songs; and Gwen didn't know them, so she stood up at the piano and pulled faces at me! And I don't know why, but the soldiers loved it.'

From this unlikely beginning Farrar – who came from a rich family and didn't take any of this seriously – and Blaney – who had studied music at the Royal College and had no plans for a career in Variety – went straight to the top.

'We worked the Palladium, the Victoria Palace, and the Coliseum . . . only the West End – we were awful snobs! Gwen didn't want to go on tour – her father was a millionaire – it was top or nothing! So we were always top of the bill, or she wouldn't go.'

When the act broke up after four years, Norah Blaney went on into musical comedy, glamorous review, and eventually straight acting until she left the stage in 1932. Few artists – even those who managed to make their way into the posher sort of show – could boast that sort of career; but there was a sort of theatrical snobbery about

Chaz Chase at the Kingston Empire

the relationship between Variety and the other forms of entertainment.

On the whole Variety artists have always been a friendly lot amongst themselves, but there seems – particularly in these early days – to have been some sort of pecking order. Florence Desmond certainly found it so, although this may have been because she was very young at the time.

'I don't think anyone today would quite understand it – the music halls were very *proper*; the acrobats kept themselves to themselves – the top of the bill never mixed with the rest of the people – and as for a young person working, they were always very well chaperoned.'

She also came across snobbery about different forms of entertainment when looking for lodgings in Birmingham.

'She said, "Where are you from?" – I said, "I'm from the Hippodrome" – she said, "No, sorry – I only take them from the Theatre Royal." '

Oddly enough, the snobbery about Variety artists when appearing in Variety did not extend to their appearances in pantomimes. People who would never think of going to a Variety theatre were happy to take their children to the pantomimes which replaced Variety at many of the theatres for the few weeks after Christmas each year, and which provided a different show-case for the talents of many Variety performers. Famous comedians would appear as Dames, and there were plenty of parts for comics and double-acts as Broker's men, Buttons, etc. Here their stage personalities could be enjoyed by a wider audience. (Panto itself is too large a subject to be covered in detail in this book, but its relationship to Variety will be examined more closely in Chapter 24.)

Another relative of Variety which, being more genteel, was also accessible to a wider audience, was 'concert party'. Like revue, these were shows consisting of various turns in which the same artists would appear solo or in different groupings. The principal outlet for concert party was at seaside resorts during the summer – end-of-pier shows, shows at halls in the town, and even open-air performances on the sands. The standard of entertainment was nothing like as professional as that of the best Variety theatres, but it was more acceptable socially to those who looked down their noses at Variety – and in any case the holiday atmosphere helped to break down any remaining barriers.

Most concert parties worked in the traditional Pierrot costumes – all pom-poms and frills – and performed little sketches, monologues and light-hearted songs. If musical comedy and perhaps even revue were felt by Variety performers themselves to be a cut above them profession-

ally, then concert party was perhaps a cut below. Certainly it was a much smaller-time operation, and as such provided a starting point for many Variety artists – among them Stanley Holloway, who had studied singing in Milan before the War (he had a fine baritone voice).

Stanley Holloway in *The Co-Optimists*

Like many others, Holloway gained much of his early performing experience in the seaside concert parties; and he was one of the cast of the only concert party ever to play in a West End theatre – *The Co-Optimists*, which opened at the Royalty in 1921. Although the quality of performance and material was higher than any ordinary concert party (it would have had to be) the basic format was the same – songs and sketches performed by the cast in various teamings.

Holloway remembered: 'I was a sort of utility man, really – you see each member of *The Co-Optimists* held the audience on their own for five or ten minutes, and would then be prepared to muck in with the rest and form the chorus, and so on. I went out front and sung some rollicking baritone songs, and then I would play a policeman or something in the next sketch. It's real concert party – party got together to do single numbers, and then do chorus numbers and sketches and so forth.'

Revue, of course, was similar in format, but there was a distinct difference, as Holloway explained.

'If a concert party do sketches they should use very little make-up or costumes, whereas a revue can alter the whole thing to suit the number they're doing. With a concert party it's only suggested by a moustache pinned on, or a hat . . . still wearing the Pierrot costumes; in the second half we might change into a suit.'

There was also more in the way of scenery in a revue, and the bigger ones were often quite spectacular.

Concert parties were not limited to the seaside – there were many touring ones, playing the small theatres and halls; J. B. Priestley's novel *The Good Companions* gives a fair (if somewhat romanticized) idea of a concert party touring in the 1920s. The situation in which the concert party in the book finds itself to begin with – stranded because the manager has decamped with the money and the lady pianist – was certainly all too common. The problems of artists being let down and consequently stranded by dishonest and sometimes downright bogus managers was so serious that in 1925 the Theatrical Employers Registration Act[4] was passed by Parliament. This required all theatrical managers to be licensed, which helped the situation but did not offer a complete solution.

New regulations were also brought into force to tighten up conditions backstage; it was not unknown for dressing-rooms to contain an open drain, and one lady artist contracted diphtheria from such a drain.[5] Pressure from what would nowadays be called the Animal Rights Lobby was put on Parliament in 1921 to outlaw performing animals completely from theatres and circuses, but the bill was withdrawn before going through the entire process of becoming law. Despite continuing pressure animal acts were never banned, but in 1925 the Performing Animals (Regulation) Act[6] was passed which required all animal trainers to be licensed. (However, in the case of invertebrates the law remained spineless.)

A restriction which had caused the managers much annoyance was not lifted until 1926. The sale of alcohol had been tightly controlled since the first World War under the Defence Of The Realm Act – hours in which drinks might be sold were restricted as an emergency measure (which still applies today) – and local authorities licensed any premises where alcohol was sold. This included theatres; and though the London County Council was happy to grant licences to legitimate theatres, and many of the older Variety halls already had drinks licences, newer Variety halls had been unable to obtain them because of pressure from temperance organizations. (One can only suppose it was felt that no-one who went to a serious play could *possibly* be ill-mannered enough to get drunk; whereas people who frequented Variety halls . . .) Since drinks represented a significant part of the profits (even if they could not be taken into the auditorium) this was an important matter. In one or two cases managers even changed to straight drama in order to make the additional profits on alcohol, but by the end of the 1920s the restrictions on Variety theatres were lifted.

Greater threats to Variety came from the new wireless broadcasting (which will be dealt with in Chapter 3) and, later in the 1920s, talking pictures. 'Phono films' – short items, usually musical, with a soundtrack – ran at the Holborn Empire as part of the variety bills in August and September 1926; and by 1929, with the success of *The Jazz Singer* and the subsequent '100% All-Talking, All-Singing, All-Dancing' sound films, the threat was apparent. The Stoll circuit wired its halls for sound films – though more as a precaution than anything else – and even the powerful Moss circuit began to worry about the future of Variety. The 1920s had come in with a boom in the profession; they went out in an atmosphere of apprehension.

Norman and Forman – 'The Burglar and the Cop'

2 'Ha! Ha! – Joke over!'
Stand-up comics: One (the 1920s)

Today the expression 'stand-up comic' suggests a man who comes on-stage – usually wearing a smart suit – and tells a string of unrelated jokes. In the early 1920s both the expression and the style were unknown, and indeed this chapter might more accurately have been headed 'solo comics'.

In nineteenth-century music-hall the solo comics relied largely on comic songs, usually sung in a character costume and often telling a story. Most artists would have a small range of such songs, with appropriate costumes. By the turn of the century the style had developed into a mixture of patter and songs, exemplified by the greatest of that period's comics, Dan Leno. His style, which remained the standard for other comics for many years, was to appear as a particular character – a floor-walker, or an egg salesman, or a Beefeater – to sing a couple of verses of a song, do some patter, and finish with another verse. The humour arose entirely out of the character portrayed rather than in telling jokes as such. In this example he appeared as a lady talking about her sweetheart, but the main source of humour was the absent Mrs Kelly:

> But you know Jim's a totally different man – Jim does love me, you know, and he's lodging now with Mrs Kelly. You know, Mrs Kelly? . . . *You* know Mrs Kelly . . . don't you know Mrs Kelly? Her husband's that little stout man, always at the corner of the street in a greasy waistcoat . . . good life, don't look so stupid, don't – you must know Mrs Kelly! . . . *Don't* you know Mrs *Kelly?* . . . Well of course, if you don't, you don't – but I thought you *did*, because I thought everybody knew Mrs Kelly. Oh, and what a woman – perhaps it's as well you *don't* know her . . . oh, she's a mean woman. Greedy. I know for a fact – her little boy, who's got the sore eyes, he came over and told me – she had half a dozen oysters, and she ate them in front of a looking-glass, to make them look a dozen. Now that'll give you an idea what *she* is.[1]

Dan Leno

George Robey

difficult – as the Original Dixieland Jazz Band found out; and he was rather given to pontificating at length on various subjects, in particular 'smut'. He held himself to be an exponent of 'honest vulgarity', and hated the more suggestive forms of humour which were coming into the halls as time went on.

Like Leno, he could create a believable character in a short time; and, although he used more actual gag-lines, most of his humour grew out of the character. In this example – which in fact first appeared in the revue *Bits and Pieces* in 1926 but is in exactly the style of his Variety work – he portrayed a bride just after the wedding.

> I've flopped, never to flap again. Oh, and I do feel so fun-ny. . . . I feel as if all me past life was running down the back of me neck. I don't know whether to laugh or cry, or mix 'em both up like a Sedlitz powder. I feel like a potato – I want to be mashed.[2] . . . Mind you, I wasn't sure of him till the banns went up three weeks ago. They do say there's always three clear Sundays before the execution takes place. And I don't know whether he's got any money or not, but I *do* know that he pays Income Tax. I suppose that's why he's taken me on – to get a bit off. Of course, everything's so different now, and so strange. I have to be so careful what I say and do now . . . if ever I mention him to any of my friends I can refer to him as 'Mai Husbarnd!' . . . I can say 'Mai Husbarnd' without getting funny looks from people. And only a few weeks ago I didn't know whether to look upon him as a gift from heaven or a thundering liar. Mind you, girls, this wedding business is no joke. Oh, no. It's a very serious business is marriage, you know. There isn't a word for marriage . . . it's a sentence.[3]

Robey, and most comedians of his period imitated recognizable types; but some artists concentrated on imitating specific people. A surprising number of people

Leno died in 1904, but this style of comedy was still in use in the period covered by this chapter. Its principal exponent was George Robey, 'The Prime Minister of Mirth'. Robey made his name in the music halls before the first World War, but remained tremendously popular well into the 1940s.

His presentation – when working in music-hall – was essentially the same as Leno's; either patter-songs or character acts with a song surrounding some speech. By the 1920s he was working more in revue and musical comedy, eventually branching out into films and even Shakespeare (as Falstaff), but he continued to appear in Variety from time to time. Off-stage he could be extremely generous – he did a lot of work for charity – or extremely started their careers in this way, both in Victorian music-hall and in later Variety; for inexperienced artists it provided ready-made characters and, provided they could do moderately accurate impressions, an easy way of getting laughs. Most of them moved away into their own style after a time. Florence Desmond, however, became famous only after she started to do impressions. From her unpromising beginning in music-hall she had moved into C. B. Cochran's lavish musical revues as a chorus girl and understudy. She was by now much more experienced, but success still eluded her. In 1928 she was working with Noël Coward in *This Year of Grace*.

Florence Desmond impersonating Bette Davis (film: *Hoots Mon*)

'I said to Noël one day, "What is wrong with me? – I'm never out of work . . . always understudy – why don't the managers make me the star?" He said, "Possibly, darling, you're a jack-of-all-trades and master of none – specialize, dear, specialize." I started to do a cabaret act – I sang some songs, and I did some imitations; and *they* went so much

better than the songs – I thought, maybe this is the message. So then I specialized in doing imitations, and I don't think I ever looked back.'

Unlike the rather rough imitations presented by artists at the start of their careers, Desmond's performances were of a very high standard. She started with people she had worked with, such as Tallulah Bankhead and Gracie Fields; and then she had a break in an unexpected way. She needed some material for a broadcast, so she wrote a sketch called 'The Hollywood Party', in which she imitated Janet Gaynor as the hostess, and guests including Marie Dressler, Jimmy Durante, Gracie Fields, and Greta Garbo ('I vant to be alone').

'So I did this sketch, never expecting ever to use it or hear of it again. At this time I was rehearsing for my first lead part in London, in *Savoy Follies* at the Savoy Theatre; the producer said, "Everybody's talking about your broadcast – could you put it in the show?" I said, "No, I couldn't look like all those people – that was just sound, it's not visual", but I did it for him, and he said, "It's brilliant – I don't know how you did it", and it was put in the show.'

She recorded it for HMV on 25 July 1932.[4]

'It was a bestseller! Then Victor Records issued it in America – then it became a sort of funny-ha-ha in Hollywood!'

This led to an invitation to appear in American cabaret, and to a contract to make some films. She made only a few; in *Mr Skitch* (1933) she starred with Will Rogers and Zasu Pitts; in one scene she does a devastatingly accurate impression of Zasu Pitts while standing next to her – for a few seconds it really is quite difficult to tell which is which. These impressions of Hollywood stars became a regular part of her stage act.

'Strange things happened – I found that I could look like the people. . . . I never used a mirror or anything like that. . . . People used to say to me, "How do you look like everyone? – how can you turn round from the piano, before you even speak, and you get a round of applause?" I didn't use wigs, or props, like Mike Yarwood – it sounds like an exaggeration to say I went into a mental trance, but I did.'

The comic effect of her imitations depended entirely upon the wickedness of the observation – just enough exaggeration without becoming a caricature – combined with the almost alarming accuracy of the appearance; when interviewed at the age of seventy-six she could still do an imitation of Bette Davis which, from four feet away, was hilariously accurate in both voice and appearance.[5]

There have been few enough top-grade impersonators, and none with her range and accuracy.

Most comedians, however, relied on creating imaginary characters. Usually these existed only for the one song or act, but occasionally a character would be strong enough to appear in a succession of different acts. The best-known example of this is Stanley Holloway's 'Old Sam', who was the hero of a number of monologues which, although their style was by the end of the 1920s rather old-fashioned, became very popular. Holloway was perhaps the last major artist working in this sort of style, presenting rhyming narrative monologues spoken with a simple piano accompaniment. He borrowed the general style from an older comic called Ernest Hastings whom he had heard during the first World War in the north of England.

'He used to perform monologues, playing for himself at the piano, and one he did was "And Yet – I Don't Know". That was the first one I did as my party piece. Finding that was successful, Leslie Henson had told me a story about how a man's musket was knocked out of his hand, and he wouldn't pick it up until the Duke of Wellington asked him, and I wrote that idea up in verse form and did it at the Palladium to break up my songs.'

At Gracie Fields' suggestion he toured the Variety halls for a time in the early 1930s with Old Sam, to great success. He performed in costume, with a piano accompaniment which was very simple and merely underlined the words.

The first Old Sam monologue, 'Pick Up Tha' Musket', and its successors such as 'Marksman Sam' and 'One Each A-piece All Round' were immensely popular; the gramophone records sold widely and have been re-issued on LP several times, so that they are still very well known. Holloway also performed another set of monologues, written by Marriot Edgar, which began with 'Albert and the Lion'; this told the story of how young Albert Ramsbottom and his 'stick with the 'orse's 'ead 'andle' were eaten by a lion during an otherwise uneventful visit to the zoo; in 'Albert Comes Back' the boy returned just in time to prevent his father from receiving the insurance money from the 'man from the Prudential'.

All these monologues were spoken in a northern accent which became so identified with Holloway as to trap one respected film encyclopaedia into referring to him as a northern comedian (he was born in Manor Park, London). He chose this accent because he had been with a Yorkshire regiment in the War, and Ernest Hastings had performed with a Yorkshire accent.

'It's much more confidential, with the short "a". I did

Stanley Holloway as 'Old Sam'

all the monologues with a tinge of northern – especially up there – I often wondered why they didn't mind, because it was a hell of a nerve, really, for a southerner to go up there and do all this stuff.'

Holloway was also extremely popular in the south; but northern and southern comedy did not always mix too happily. The north of England had developed almost a separate tradition of comics, less brash and with their humour angled more against the performer. The traditional dim-witted 'Wet Willie' type of character was perhaps more difficult for southern audiences to adjust to – although it has also been suggested that northern comics coming south might actually exaggerate their regional characteristics in order to conform to the stereotypes that the southern audiences would expect.

Two comics who established the northern style in the pre-1914 period were Tom Foy and George Formby Senior. Foy specialized in spoken (as opposed to recited) monologues and sketches, where Formby worked in a sort of cross between monologues and songs. Both presented a helpless, woman-dominated 'gowk'.

Here Tom Foy illustrated a standard theme – the adolescent helplessness of the character in the presence of a young lady.

Tom Foy

> Listen – I just wanted to tell you summat while I'm here, but – ee, I do hope it doesn't go any farther. Listen . . . shhh! . . . you know, I'm going to tell you summat very private, and I don't want me mother or anybody else to know owt about it. I'm courtin'. It's reet! Aye, I am – I've started. . . . Eee, but she's a bonny lass, she is an' all. Better lookin' than me, any day. I'll never forget, I met her in t' park, I were having a walk one day, and she were sitting on a seat under a tree, you know; and I went walking past, like, and I put on a bit of style, you know – I can do, sometimes, when I like – and she did laugh at me. Well, you couldn't blame her. I'll bet I'd laugh if I met me. But I was a bit frightened, tha' knows, and I blushed up a bit when she kept looking at me . . . and she says, 'Come here' . . . I said, 'nay . . . ' – she said, 'Come on – come and sit down a bit, and let's whisper words of love or summat.' I says, 'What?' – she says, 'Let's whisper words of love.' I says, 'Ee – I don't know any.' Then she says, 'Come on, sit down' – I said, 'nay – I'd sooner stand here and throw mud at thee.'[6]

Norman Evans – 'Over the Garden Wall'

By the 1920s this sort of material was less common in the south, although much northern comedy continued to grow out of the same sort of character and situations. Whereas southern stand-up comics were tending towards more use of actual gags, even though usually presented in a character framework, northern comedians relied more upon observation of character. Norman Evans, who started in Variety around the end of the 1920s and did much of his work as a dame comedian, made good use of this sort of observation and exaggeration. In this example, 'Auntie Doleful' visits an (unseen) sick woman friend:

> You're not looking too well, are you? I brought some flowers – I thought if I was too late they'd come in handy, but I see you're still here. I tell you what – it's a very awkward bend at the top of t'stairs here to get a coffin down, isn't it? Scrape t'wallpaper a bit, won't they? Ah well, you'll have to try to look bright and cheerful, and keep on t'bright side, you know. I suppose you don't know that your Willie's on the millpond in a tub with another boy? Bottom looks as if it'll come out any minute – and if it does, there'll be a lot of bubbles, too. Oh, no, no – I know you can't get to them – you'll have to trust to providence to come along, you see. Yes – you what? You're feeling a lot better? Ah,

well, you never know – I mean, there was Mrs White – it were nobbut last Thursday, you know – she was doin' nicely, just like you are, you know – and all of a sudden she started with spasms round the heart – she went off like a flash of lightning on Friday. They're burying her today.[7]

Norman Evans went on to become widely known on television after the second World War for his 'Over the Garden Wall' act, which had started in Variety, and in which he impersonated a northern housewife of generous dimensions – with his false teeth removed for greater facial effect – having a conversation with the next-door neighbour.

Northern comedians made up the most important part of the area of dialect comedy – of course, for those working on home ground it was not regarded as dialect comedy anyway – and other dialects were relatively under-represented. There was a separate tradition of Scottish comics – see Chapter 21 – although few of them came south of the border; and, perhaps surprisingly, there were very few Welsh comics. One Welsh act was Ted Hopkins, usually working with his wife May, but their material was fairly primitive. Since Variety was essentially an urban entertainment, rural accents were not usually used.

There were a few Jewish comics in the 1920s, although the tradition of Jewish stand-up humour is more American – and indeed the best-remembered Jewish comedian of the period, Julian Rose, came from America originally. He made his home in Britain from the early years of the century, but his act – a character monologue telling a story well interspersed with gags – maintained its American atmosphere. The wedding celebrations which his Mr Levinsky attended were certainly more Lower East Side than East End.

> We had chicken and castor-oil, lobster à la Limberg, with tomato surprise – but that was no surprise to me, because I eat tomatoes long before that. Say, you know Abraham Cohen – he was there too, with his two daughters Rachel and Becky. And the oldest girl is over seventeen – a smart girl, oy oy oy, what a smart girl! She used words so big you couldn't understand her at all. She recite for the company a nice piece of poetry – 'Asleep by the ditch', by Ella Screamer Pillbox.[8] The other little girl played something on the piano – 'The Maiden's Prayer' by Sousa.

Billy Bennett

Cohen said, 'Say, Levinski – what do you think of her execution?' I said, 'I'm in favour of it.'[9]

A comedian who used both spoken patter and recited monologues was Billy Bennett. His outfit – large moustache, scruffy suit, and brown army-style boots – and the aggressive delivery of his often almost surreal material made him one of the most entertaining comics of the period, and one who is worth examining at greater length than the ones we have met so far. He performed prose routines, monologues and songs in his individually fruity manner which made him a top comic for twenty years – his trick of pointing the end of a joke by saying 'boom-boom' has entered the language – and much of his appeal lay in the strange images he could conjure up in the mind. His monologue 'The Green Tie of the Little Yellow Dog' is a surprisingly close parody of the then-famous melodramatic poem 'The Green Eye of the Little Yellow God', dragging in a reference to 'Gunga Din' (itself one of the most parodied poems in the English language).

In his song 'No Power on Earth' he made good use of the old 'suspended rhyme' technique, getting his effect by *failing* to use the title-phrase, 'No power on earth can pull it down'.

The man is sure to rise in life that sits down on
    a tack
But no power on earth can pull it down.
The undervest I'm wearing has slipped half-way
    up me back
And no power on earth can pull it down.
To all these grabbing profiteers a lesson we must
    teach
The price of food is out of every humble
    person's reach
Our chickens they are laying eggs at fourpence
    ha'penny each
And, er, no power on earth can make you buy
    them. . . .
    No power on earth can pull it down –
    Winston Churchill sold us all a pup
    He tries with might and main – but when it
        starts to rain
    He hasn't got the power to push it up.
    We still have women on the land that do the
        work of men
    They don't dress like the girls do in the
        town –
    Every country Mary Ann is wearing trousers

like a man . . .
(pause)
And the second house begins at nine-o'clock.[10]

Bennett's spoken patter was on a par with his monologues, usually given in the form of a semi-political address:

The trouble today is that the women are trying to rule the country. They say their place is at the polls. I think so myself. They can go either to the south or to the north pole, I don't care which. Fellow citizens and scroungers! . . . I want to say it may be all right to allow women to vote, but I certainly think it's wrong to allow them to serve on a jury. For instance – supposing there's a jury of six men and six women, and they're locked in a room to consider their verdict. Do you think anybody would believe them when they came out and said 'Not Guilty'?[11]

By the late 1930s his patter style had adapted slightly, and he was telling jokes in the framework of a personal approach:

I'm not feeling very well myself – I've been suffering with the Gathering of the Clans. I went up to the hospital the other day – the doctor was very very busy on a big case – there were only two bottles left. One of the doctors took my temperature – another one took my wristwatch –

he found there was something wrong with my heart. He said 'Have you had trouble with Angina Pectoris?' – I said, 'I've had a lot of trouble with her, but you haven't got the name right. I've had trouble with her ever since the day I married her.' Of course I walked into that wedding with both my eyes shut – her brother shut one and her father shut the other.[12]

His most-quoted monologue, 'The League of Nations' (a skit on the ineffectual and fractious predecessor to the United Nations) illustrated his particular talent for the surreal:

The League of Nations met at Marks and
    Woolworth's
And asked them if a discount they'd allow.
A farmer with his tanner said he wished to buy a
    spanner
He could use when he was milking of the cow.
A Turk said 'We want work and not much of
    it –
A job like giving gooseberries Marcel waves'.
A Zulu most courageous said 'Brothers, it's
    outrageous
Black puddings should be treated as white
    slaves.'
Shall we ever do so if we can't do?
Could we, would we, if we, p'raps we won't –
Admiral MacNestle of the Swiss Navy arose
Shouting 'Where would Turkey be without the
    Parson's Nose?'
The Rajah of Schemozzle got up and blew his
    nozzle
He had these few well-chosen words to say –
'Can a sausage keep its figure if its burberry is
    slack?
If a duck has had its tonsils out where does it
    keep its quack?
We know a hen can lay an egg but can it put it
    back?
That's what Levy and Franks are fighting for
    today.'[13]

As Billy Bennett's style bridged the gap between old-fashioned monologues and the later patter style, so the act of Yorkshire comedian Dick Henderson bridged the gap between character and gag comedians. Henderson's stage character – a bluff, rotund northerner with a cigar and a

Dick Henderson (1927)

bowler hat several sizes too small for him – was less exaggerated than previous character comics had been, and his use of jokes foreshadowed the more recent stand-up comic style. He also innovated in another way. His son, Dickie Henderson (a popular comedian of a later era in his own right) remembers:

'A lot of people have said that he was responsible for some dreadful acts, because he finished with a [straight] song . . . and then people came along afterwards and finished with a song, and *they* really couldn't sing, and so you had these awful comedian-singers; but there's no doubt that Dad was the first one. He used to start off-stage, singing 'No Rose in All the World' – he could sing so well that it filled the theatre when he was on the side of the stage – and then he used to walk on looking funny. He was a good stand-up comic – good, not average – he used to have a lovely opening line; he'd sing a song to open with, and then he'd say, "No, please, I don't want any applause, I'm strictly doing this for the money. And I've just been paid in advance, so I'm really flogging a dead horse. Don't expect too much." That was very advanced humour for those days – people used to say, "Oh, he's a rum bugger, isn't he", because they weren't ready for the idea of somebody saying don't applaud.'

Henderson's gags were always personalized – linked into a loose structure, and told in the first person, rather than presented as a string of isolated gags. When he included a particularly obvious joke, he would follow it with his catchphrase: 'Ha! Ha! – joke over!' His jokes, which were mostly of the usual domestic variety, make an interesting comparison with the style of Tom Foy quoted earlier; marriage is still a 'sentence', but the man he portrays is a resigned adult rather than Foy's helpless adolescent. Henderson's version of his first meeting with his wife is cynical from the start:

> She came right up to me and looked into both of my eyes – and I looked into her one – mind you, I didn't mind her only having one eye. What I really took exception to was her teeth. Not that I do in the ordinary course of events, but I did to hers because they belonged to her sister, and her sister has a bigger mouth than her . . . Ha! Ha! – joke over! But I'm not really grumbling about that – I don't like her being mean. She gets up in the morning and brings me a cup of tea – and drinks it herself – and when I come down to breakfast she boils me a couple of eggs, but gives me the gravy . . . but to give you an idea how really mean she is, she's too mean to shiver when it's cold. Believe me or believe me not, if you had the misfortune to be going to the workhouse, I don't believe she would show you the shortest way. And she's very short-sighted. Let me tell you how short-sighted she is – a rag and bone man came round this afternoon with a cartload of balloons, and she went out and asked him for a pound of grapes. But apart from that she has one very very good point – ee, by gum, she can cook. She's what one would call a religious cook – everything she sends up is either a sacrifice or a burnt offering.[14]

As Dickie Henderson says, his father's technique of using a straight ballad to finish on was copied by many later comedians – a good percentage of whom did not have the voice for it. Henderson's style of placing his gags in a framework produced a result which was faster in approach than the purely character work of Leno and Robey; but humour was speeding up generally, and the next step for stand-up comedy was into pure gags.

(The subject of stand-up comics is resumed in Chapter 14, page 116.)

3 'Do not sneeze at the microphone'
Broadcasting in the 1920s

No gags on Scotsmen, Welshmen, Clergymen, Drink, or Medical matters. Do not sneeze at the microphone.   (*Card handed to new Variety broadcasters in 1925*)

Before 1914 broadcasting was an experimental medium, the province of what would now be called radio 'hams' and professional experimenters. The World War showed the value of radio for military communications – so much so that the Armed Services, both in America and Britain, made every effort to prevent the emergence of radio for anything other than military use. In America, despite this opposition, small stations sprang up in many towns, offering entertainment on a largely amateur basis. In Britain, there were a few experimental broadcasts – most notably the one by Dame Nellie Melba from Chelmsford in 1920 – but it was not until the formation of the British Broadcasting Company in 1922 that there was a continuing regular broadcast service.

The Company was formed by a consortium of manufacturers of radio sets, who naturally enough wanted broadcasts for their sets to receive. From the start there was considerable control exercised over broadcasting, which was placed under the Postmaster-General. There was opposition from the press – who felt themselves threatened and obstructed by the broadcasting of news – and from various vested interests; and it was largely due to the strength of character of the BBC's first General Manager – later Director-General – John Reith that the BBC resisted attacks from all quarters, including various forms of political pressure.

In 1926 the BBC became a Public Corporation funded from the sale of receiving licences. The principles of public service broadcasting which Reith had formulated in the days of the Company became officially enshrined in its Charter. In the early years there was only one programme, with regional variations gradually coming in as new stations opened; in 1927 an experimental alternative programme started, broadcast from Daventry. Within a year of the beginning of the BBC, a fair range of programmes was being broadcast, although there remained a preponderance of the 'palm court' type of light music for many years.

Light entertainment and comedy was of course an important part of the programming; but from the beginning there was a deep distrust of broadcasting by the Variety profession. This is understandable when it is remembered that, for example, a comedian could work the Variety circuits for a lifetime on one or two acts; because he would appear in any one town only at intervals of several years, by which time the memory of his performance would have faded, there was no pressure on him to find new material. Rather the reverse, in fact; the audiences would be disappointed if he didn't perform the routines for which he was famous.

It was obvious that radio would be voracious for material, and the fear of 'giving their acts away' was the first objection raised by performers. It did not at this stage occur to anyone that broadcasts might encourage more people to go and see them; and though the fear of giving away material did arise from a genuine (though not insoluble) problem posed by radio, it is odd that no-one thought of the comparison with gramophone records. Many artists had been recording versions of their acts since the turn of the century, but there is no suggestion that the availability of these records had any adverse effect on the theatres.

Part of the difficulties arose because there was no-one at the BBC who had any experience of the entertainment industry. Variety and related programmes came under the Productions Director – in the late 1920s this was R. E. Jeffrey – who also dealt with drama productions; Variety was something of a sideline. The agents and managers who controlled the business flatly forbade their artists to broadcast. Those who were currently under contract had clauses inserted into their contracts forbidding any broadcast appearance; others were threatened that if they broadcast they would not be booked for theatrical appearances in future.

In this atmosphere the BBC had to find its own artists. Some came from the less organized world of concert-party; some were amateurs or small-time professional performers to whom radio meant a whole new career. Fred

Spencer presented a number of comic monologues as 'Mrs 'Arris' in 1923; Ronald Gourley, billed as an 'entertainer' made a large number of appearances in the early 1920s; and others at this period were 'Aerbert Parks', Philip Middlemiss and Jack Duncanson – small names who disappeared when broadcasting managed to attract bigger stars.

The most famous radio comedian from this period was John Henry, whose monologues and scenes with his radio wife 'Blossom', delivered in a mournful Yorkshire accent, were in the tradition of northern comedy but adapted to the radio audience. Part of his success was in his delivery, which was quiet and aimed at one person, rather than the more outgoing style adopted by theatrical artists who had to play to a large audience.

My pal Joe Murgatroyd comes from Yorkshire the same as I do. Of course, I *am* a Yorkshireman, you know. Oh, yes – a lot of people think by my accent that I'm an Oxford man, but I'm not. No, I'm a tyke. Joe comes from Heckmondwyke. That's in Yorkshire, you know – it's near Cleckheaton. Oh, he's a clever fellow, though, a very clever fellow. It was Joe that found out when you're hanging pictures it's a good thing to put a drop of oil on your thumbnail, and then the hammer slides off easier. He knows all about politics, too – he was telling me only the other day that there's only one man ever gone into the House of Commons with the right idea, and that was Guy Fawkes. Joe's a bit of a musician too, although he's not really highbrow – I went with him to a concert the other day, and they were playing a piece when we went in; and Joe asked me what it was, and I said, 'That's the Fifth Symphony.' And he said, 'Well thank goodness we've missed four of 'em.'[1] He's married, you know – he's married to a lady called Emma, but she's very different from Joe because Joe's a tall thin man – well, he's so thin he has to eat macaroni one at a time – and Emma's fat, you know. Well if Emma gets any fatter she's going to be taller lying down than she is standing up. Joe says a wife's a great comfort – a great comfort in all those troubles that a bachelor never has. He and Emma always think alike about everything, you know – of course, Emma thinks first, but they both think alike at the finish.[2]

All through the middle 1920s there was a fair representation of Variety-type programmes, although usually with names which meant nothing in the world of theatrical Variety. There were often five or six programmes in any one week of this type, though some were from regional stations. Often one or two comedy turns would be inserted into a programme of light music; and some programmes were short, being only fifteen minutes long and consisting of one act, such as John Henry. There were various radio concert parties – 'The Valve Set', 'The Indefinites', and perhaps the most famous, 'The Roosters': and a very few well known names broadcast occasionally – Norah Blaney among them.

Although there had been one or two non-Variety theatrical broadcasts in the early days, in May 1923 a Committee of theatre managers, concert artists, publishers and others was formed which prevented any further relays from theatres until June 1925 when a limited agreement was reached. Since the Variety union, the Variety Artistes' Federation, did not co-operate, there were still no broadcasts from Variety halls with the single exception of a special broadcast from the Variety Artists' Benevolent Fund concert from the Alhambra in May 1926.

By 1927 radio was mounting its own Variety bills – listed in *Radio Times* as 'Variety' – using for the most part their own home-grown artists to make up a bill of four or five acts. These studio performances were given without an audience, and so tended to sound rather 'cold'. There was no regular pattern of Variety broadcasts, so that programmes might turn up on any day (Sundays excepted – the BBC Sunday was very proper) and at almost any time. A procedure called 'diagonalization' was introduced, whereby the same programme would be performed on successive days at different regional stations – these were live performances each time, as recording of broadcasts was not yet practicable.

In 1927 the three principal Variety circuits – Moss, Stoll, and GTC – launched a campaign against the BBC, demanding huge sums in return for the appearance of their artists, and even threatening to apply for permission to run their own broadcasting station (not that that would have been a possibility). Obviously the increased popularity of radio – there were over two million licence-holders by now – had suggested to them that they could do with a slice of the radio cake.

Since the subject of much of the controversy – relays from Variety halls – was the province of the Outside Broadcast Department, the responsibility for negotiations with the theatrical managers lay with its Director, Gerald Cock – described by historian Asa Briggs[3] as 'lively, tough, vigorous and knowledgeable' – who later became the BBC's first Director of Television. He did much to expand the whole area of outside broadcasts – running commentaries on sporting events began in 1927 after the same sort of opposition from sporting interests that was occurring with Variety – and in 1928 he succeeded in persuading George Black of GTC to allow regular fortnightly broadcasts from the Palladium. The first one took place on Monday 22 October 1928, consisting of '20 minutes of Van and Schenk'; the succeeding broadcasts were not regular in the sense of being on the same day of the week, but at approximately fortnightly intervals listeners were able to hear Naughton and Gold, Jackie Coogan, Ella Shields, and the J. Thomas Saxotet. This agreement was followed in 1929 by one with Sir Oswald Stoll for broadcasts from the Alhambra and the Coliseum – again, usually only one act out of the bill.

At the same time studio broadcasts were becoming more organized. Variety bills under the heading *Vaudeville* were broadcast three times a week during 1929, usually with three or four acts. Leading artists included Tommy Handley, Clapham and Dwyer, Gracie Fields, xylophonist Teddy Brown, and the American husband-and-wife team Burns and Allen.

(The use of the term 'vaudeville' raises yet another problem of definition. The name derives from the French, either 'voix de ville' (voices of the streets) or 'Vau de Vire'

(the Valley of the Vire, a location which gave its name to a type of musical entertainment in the fifteenth century) depending upon which authority is referred to; but by the present century it was used for the American equivalent of British music-hall and Variety. It was typical of the BBC to use a French word when an English one would have done perfectly well; in France, just to be awkward, 'vaudeville' was a sort of musical farce, while music-hall translated as 'le music-hall'.)

Among the BBC's new stars was Mabel Constanduros, who started broadcasting in 1925, and who created the imaginary cockney family 'The Bugginses'. This was one of the first radio families to catch the imagination of the listeners, and became extremely popular; radio enabled characters of this sort to be built up in a way that Variety could never allow. The family also appeared on records. In this famous example, 'Mrs Buggins Makes the Christmas Pudding', Mabel Constanduros played all the parts except Father, who was played by Michael Hogan.

FATHER: 'Ere, Emily – you 'aven't forgotten the
              stout, 'ave you?
MOTHER: Stout? Do you want to start baby off
              with a taste for drink? Bad enough
              when it's herridittery, without
              cultivating it.
FATHER (*sniffing*): Cor, it don't smell right to me
              without no stout in it.
MOTHER: Stop sniffing at it like a vacu-um
              cleaner! You're drawing all the
              nutriment out of it! *Alfie!* Take your
              thievin' hooks out of the sugar! – else
              into the coal-cellar you go. And pick up
              that bit of peel off the floor and put it
              back in the basin.
GRANDMA: Father ain't doing your gloves much
              good, Emily.
MOTHER: Father, you 'aven't . . . you 'ave! My
              best gloves! Take 'em off! Half the
              wool's in the pudding now! And what
              are you doing to that suet?
FATHER: Hammering it – what do you think I
              was doing, tickling it?
MOTHER: Hammering the suet! You must have
              gone dippy. Get on and grate it, do.
FATHER: Well what's it got to be grated for,
              anyway?
MOTHER: You don't want it to go into lumps and
              clog up your elementary canal, do you?
GRANDMA: 'Ere – I'm beginning to lose me
              appetite for this pudding.[4]

Although early studio Variety broadcasts had taken place without an audience, it was gradually – though in some quarters reluctantly – accepted that audience reaction was necessary to give the broadcast some life. There were always those listeners who resented the studio audience, and there was a lengthy debate in the correspondence section of *Radio Times* on the subject. There were also accusations that the BBC was faking the audience's appreciation of the show by using pre-recorded laughter (which was – and is – common practice in America); in fact the BBC, as a matter of firm policy (which still holds), never used fake audiences (although the audience's reaction may nowadays be 'improved' in the editing).

Despite some difficulties with GTC over certain artists being banned for broadcasting, the outside broadcasts (OBs) from Variety halls became a regular part of the BBC's output. The technique arose of inserting the outside broadcast – which of course had to fit in with the timing of the theatre concerned – into studio broadcasts of Variety. One problem was that the studio audience, being much smaller than the one in the theatre, sounded rather flat by comparison, which tended to kill the remaining acts for the listener. In the end the OBs were treated as separate programmes from the studio shows. The broadcasts of both types were deliberately not placed at regular times or on regular days, although Stoll and Moss both insisted on the OBs taking place early in the week. One effect they had was to bring Variety artists to a large section of the public who did not frequent Variety theatres; the halls had lost their unsavoury reputation of the last century, but there were still many who either would not or could not go.

In 1929 the Productions Director, R. E. Jeffrey, was succeeded by Val Gielgud (the brother of John Gielgud), who consequently became responsible for Variety programmes as well as the serious drama which was really his main interest. The following year, a major reorganization created for the first time a department specifically for revue and vaudeville. John Watt was brought from the Belfast studio centre to head the revue section, and the vaudeville section – which handled the studio Variety shows – was run by Bertram Fryer, assisted by Denis Freeman and John Sharman. Sharman had worked on the halls and provided a useful professional understanding of Variety.

There was a re-shuffle which affected the listeners more obviously: in March 1930 the transmission pattern was reworked into the Regional and National Programmes. There was no attempt to differentiate in actual style between them – as happened fifteen years later with the Home, Light and Third Programmes – but the National Programme was the same for the entire country, whereas separate regions could break away from the Regional Programme (except in the case of certain programmes, specified by London on a 'must take' basis) to originate their own programmes of more local interest. With new networks, and a newly professional production team, radio Variety moved into a new and different decade.

(*Broadcasting in the 1930s is covered in Chapter 15, p. 126*).

4 'How's your father?'
Sketch comics: One (the 1920s)

FRIEND: Is the muzzle velocity co-incident with the bursting-charge?
TATE (*nonplussed*): Well . . . it isn't really . . . it all depends on the circumference of the
            shrapnel . . . that is . . . *how's your father?*

(*Harry Tate: 'Fortifying the Home'*)[1]

To music-hall audiences of the early 1900s, the term 'sketch' meant any dramatic item, including serious one-act plays. As we have seen, anything of this sort was strictly speaking illegal under the licensing laws, and it was not until 1907 that the position was eased to the extent of allowing items up to half-an-hour in length. With the music halls coming under the Lord Chamberlain in 1912 there was no further bar to the presentation of any sort of 'sketch', but in practice the longer, serious, sort of item gradually disappeared from the bills; the shorter comic sketches which remained are the subject of this chapter and its sequels.

One of the most famous early sketch performers was Fred Karno, who began as a mime comedian in sketches (thus getting round the legal restrictions). By the early 1900s he was more entrepreneur than performer, and had five touring companies, which included Charlie Chaplin among the artists. Karno's name became a byword for broad comedy, and in World War One the troops were referring to themselves as 'Fred Karno's Army'.

His companies were still touring the halls in the 1920s, presenting his famous sketches (which now included dialogue) such as 'Mumming Birds' and 'The Football Match'. The former involves a Variety show being broken up by a drunk and a mischievous boy in the audience; in quick succession they would ruin a (deliberately) bad double-act, a fat soprano's performance, a magician's turn, a dance routine, a monologue and a balancing act; the sketch ended with them on stage in a competition to act a short scene with a 'Gloria Swansneck'. The sketch depended very heavily upon slapstick, and the actual jokes were so spaced out as to make it not worth quoting here; some idea of it can be obtained from Chaplin's 1915 short film *A Night at the Show*, based on this sketch which originally gave Chaplin his break.

'The Football Match' had a rather more complicated plot, involving an attempt to bribe the players to lose the match; there were three scenes, ending with the match

itself. The sketch created the part of Stiffy the goalkeeper, originally played by Harry Weldon, who went on to include the character in his own solo act on the halls.

Here Hobson, the trainer, is being 'assisted' by Stiffy in his examination of the team's sick parade before a practice:

STIFFY: Mr Hobson, may I ask you a question?
HOBSON: What is it?
STIFFY: Do cat burglars have kittens?
HOBSON (*annoyed: to first man*): Now you.
FIRST MAN (*affected voice*): I regret to say I have
                something wrong with my tonsils.
STIFFY: Were you in the Army?
FIRST MAN: Pardon?
STIFFY: Were you in the Army?
FIRST MAN: Yes.
STIFFY: What regiment?
FIRST MAN: Middlesex.
HOBSON: Go and dress. (*To second man*) Well,
                what's the matter with you?
SECOND MAN: I suffer from growing pains.
HOBSON: Get a dose of Ammoniated Tincture of
                Quinine.
STIFFY: Yes. Go and get some animated
                pictures of Queen Anne.
HOBSON (*to third man*): Hullo, your nose is hot.
STIFFY: He wants some sulphur in his water. I
                say, Mr Hobson, can I ask you a
                question?
HOBSON: Well, what is it?
STIFFY: How long is a short circuit?[2]

The sketch continues in much the same vein, with the jokes being rammed into the script any old how, rather than arising from the situation; the football match itself in the last scene is almost entirely comic 'business' (i.e. visual clowning), with very little dialogue.

It was of course unusual for a sketch to tour with a company under the name of its producer rather than its performers. Most sketch comics played in simple situation sketches with their own supporting company – and here it is worth differentiating between a sketch and a double-act, because some sketch artists worked with only one supporting actor. The rule that has been applied in this book is to ask whether it matters who the supporting artist is. If the support is a straight feed part which could be taken on by any suitable performer – and in fact the support often changed as time went on in this sort of sketch – then it counts as a sketch. If the support is part of the character of the sketch – and usually given equal billing – then the act counts as a double-act, and is dealt with separately.

Most sketches were based round a recognizable situation – papering a room, mending a car, an argument with a policeman, and so on – and usually one which would be within the experience of the working-class audience. In many cases the actual text of the sketch would be very thin, with most of the humour being drawn from knockabout gags in the style of the 'kitchen scene' familiar from traditional pantomime. In the case of acts who were very experienced this sort of thing could be quite complex – Karno's football match, at the end of the previously quoted sketch, is a case in point – and some performers of this type of material went on to appear in short silent films, using the same sort of humour.

Where the humour was verbal rather than visual, the situation was often used merely as an excuse for a series of very basic jokes. This sort of thing can sound extremely contrived to a modern ear; but at the time performers such as Albert Burdon – whose various sketches also involved clowning and a range of different situations – were effective and popular. In this example he is up before the Means Test Committee:

CHAIRMAN: Now pay attention – where do you live?
ALBERT: In a house.
CHAIRMAN: In a house.
ALBERT: Aye – a big house.
CHAIRMAN: A big house. Now I've got you – you can afford to live in a big house.
ALBERT: Yes, sir.
CHAIRMAN: What house?
ALBERT: Work-house.
CHAIRMAN: Have you lived there all your life?
ALBERT: Not yet.
CHAIRMAN: Tell me – have you any money in the bank?

ALBERT (laughs): Yes – fifty thousand quid.
CHAIRMAN: Now, come come come – this is no place for joking.
ALBERT: Well, blimey, you started it.
CHAIRMAN: What are you by profession?
ALBERT: I'm a fret-worker.
CHAIRMAN: A fret-worker.
ALBERT: Aye – if there's any work knocking about I fret and fret and fret.
CHAIRMAN: Have you ever done any work?
ALBERT: Yes, once, on the railway.
CHAIRMAN: On the railway. What doing?
ALBERT: You know the man that goes round tapping the wheels with a hammer?
CHAIRMAN: Yes.
ALBERT: Well I helped him to listen.
CHAIRMAN: Are your relatives in business?
ALBERT: Yes – in the iron and steel business.
CHAIRMAN: Oh, indeed.
ALBERT: Yes – me mother irons and me father steals.[3]

The better comedians were drawing the humour out of the situation itself. Charles Austin, who began on the halls in 1896 and toured his sketches featuring 'Parker, PC' until the 1930s, was one who did so, even though his humour is fairly basic. His delivery, in a throaty cockney voice, was rather laboured, but his policeman was a reasonably believable comic character. Here Parker is explaining to Superintendent Hardman and PC Sloman his inadvertent involvement in a robbery.

PARKER: I was standing here, as you might be sitting down there, when all of a sudden I saw four great big fellows – *four* of them, mind you – and one of them had a great big hammer, not one of those little penny ones, a great big one; and another great big handsome fellow something like . . . (*points at Sloman, then Hardman, and finally himself*) me, he was – so I saw them breaking in and I walks up to them and I says . . .
HARDMAN: Yes, and what did you say?
PARKER: I said, 'Now, look here, mates, I don't want to have any row with you, but if a policeman comes along and sees you in there you look like getting locked up.'

HARDMAN:	You idiot! Why didn't you arrest them?
PARKER:	How could I?
HARDMAN:	What do you mean, 'How could I?'
PARKER:	One of them told me it was his father's shop, and do you think I was going to call a man a liar with a great big hammer in his hand? Garn, you must think I'm a mug.
HARDMAN:	Go on, go on.
PARKER:	Well, with that, the big tall handsome chap who I said was something like me, walks up to me and gives me a punch in the stomach, I fell in the gutter, then they walked into the shop, and that's how Nelson lost his eye.
HARDMAN:	Why didn't you follow them in?
PARKER:	Garn! What do you take me for? Supposing I had followed them in and a copper had come along and seen me in there with burglars – he'd very likely have pinched me for it![4]

A sketch comedian who took advantage of what was presumably a glandular deficiency was Wee Georgie Wood. Like Jimmy Clitheroe a few years later, Wood remained small and with an unbroken voice for his whole life. He toured in sketches as a small boy from 1908 to the late 1950s, supported by Dolly Harmer who usually played his mother. His material is difficult to take today – such humour as there is is swamped by a treacly sentimentality – something which Clitheroe, though playing a similar character, managed to avoid. Here Wood plays a boy who is a member of a so-called 'Black Hand' gang.

GEORGIE:	Mother – I have bad news for you.
MOTHER:	Well, what is it?
GEORGIE:	You know Murray Square?
MOTHER:	Yes.
GEORGIE:	You know the Police Station in Murray Square?
MOTHER:	I do.
GEORGIE:	You know that round window that's there?
MOTHER:	Yes.
GEORGIE:	Well, it isn't.
MOTHER:	What's happened to it?
GEORGIE:	Somebody's done it in.
MOTHER:	What – broken it?
GEORGIE:	Yes mother – it's one of the Gang.

	With a brick.
MOTHER:	Which one?
GEORGIE:	Which brick?
MOTHER:	No, which one of the Gang?
GEORGIE:	Oh, I can't tell you that, mother.
MOTHER:	Now come along, sir – tell me instantly!
GEORGIE:	Mother, I can't tell you – we're a Secret Society – we don't give away any of the secrets. That's why we don't have any women in it.[5]

As the sketch progresses Georgie cheeks his mother and gets spanked, which provokes floods of tears – which may have seemed funny in the 1920s but is now merely distasteful – and then has to contend with a visiting policeman who, to his relief, turns out merely to be selling tickets for a Benefit Concert. Georgie is persuaded to show how well he can sing, so that he might take part in the concert, and the sketch ends – as did his other sketches – with his rendition of a sentimental ballad.

An artist who managed a much higher standard of writing and performance was Robb Wilton. His greatest popularity came during World War Two, as a result of his broadcasts, but seen in retrospect he was one of the best comedians of the 1920s. He presented several portraits of incompetent officialdom – police sergeant, fire chief, magistrate, prison governor, and so on – using a gentle Lancashire accent and superb timing, coupled with his characteristic habit of laying his first and second fingers on his cheek in puzzlement. He was usually assisted by his wife, Florence Palmer, as the worried lady who had poisoned several husbands, or whose house was on fire.

Robb Wilton

Wilton's best-known sketch was 'The Fire Chief'. It began, as did most of his sketches, with a monologue.

WILTON: Aye, of course this is a different game to when I first started. Of course, I started when fires first became popular. I started as an ordinary fireman, and now I'm a Chief. Of course, there's not a lot of difference, only now I've got nothing at all to do with fires. Well, when I say 'nothing to do', I mean, if there was like, as we might say, like, a fire today, well I've simply got to ring a bell, and the men spring onto the engine. That's if they're in, you see . . . oh, I know where to put my hands on them when I want them – I've only just come out myself.

He treats the audience to some reminiscences, and is interrupted by a lady in a high state of distress.

WILTON: I don't know, we'll have to get the phone in here – I mean, there must be a lot of fires we never hear about. (*Enter Florence*)
FLORENCE: Are you the Fire Brigade?
WILTON: Not *all* of it – there's some more in the yard.
FLORENCE: Quick, do come along quick, there's a house on fire.
WILTON: A house on fire? Just a moment lady – what's the address?
FLORENCE: Grimshaw Street.
WILTON (*fussing with papers on his desk*): Grimshaw Street – Grimshaw Street . . . now wait a minute, I know it as well as can be, and I can't just place it . . .
FLORENCE: Oh, come along, it's only just round . . .
WILTON: No, no, no – don't tell me, let me try and think of it for myself. Grimshaw Street – oh, isn't that *annoying*, I could walk straight to it, and I can't think of it.
FLORENCE: It's next to Whitely Street.
WILTON: Next to Whitely . . . oh, I know it as well as can be . . . what's the number, lady, what's the number?

FLORENCE: Seventy-eight.
WILTON: Seventy-eight. (*Conversationally*) Turned out nice again today, hasn't it?
FLORENCE: Oh, come along, do please hurry.
WILTON: Now just a moment, lady, there's a form to fill in. (*Searches among the confusion on his desk*) Oh, what the devil have they done with those forms . . . they can leave nothing alone in this place . . . I'll keep those kids out of here altogether in future. . . . Ah, here we are, lady, here we are – now, 'State whether applicant is married or single'. Are you married? . . . or have you heard of anything . . .
FLORENCE: I'm married, but what has that got to do with it?
WILTON: It's got nothing to do with it, but it all has to go down. Married. 'State precise time and place of fire'.
FLORENCE: I've *told* you the place! The time would be . . . the time would be . . . seven-thirty.
WILTON: Seven-thirty – just a minute, we've got to check up on that, because they're very hot on the time lark here . . . Ah – now there's a bloomer to start with. See, seven-thirty. Do you follow what I mean – it's only seven-twenty now. If I'd have put seven-thirty down on that form, we're liable, according to that, to be at the fire ten minutes before it breaks out. That's the very thing we try to avoid.

Eventually the distraught lady manages to persuade him to take some positive action.

WILTON: Excuse me a minute, lady, I'll get on the speaking-tube to Arnold. (*Blows down speaking-tube to operate whistle at far end*) Hullo? Hullo? (*Blows*) Hullo? (*To Florence*) I see Chelsea lost again this week. Hullo? Arnold? Arnold? Oh, what are they doing? . . . would you believe it . . . don't wait now, lady, just slip along and ask them to keep it going a bit, will you?

FLORENCE: Oh, do come along as quickly as ever you can. (*Exits*)

WILTON: We shan't be long now, lady – they ought to be here – I don't know what they're fiddling and messing about . . . I'll sack the whole bunch of them that's what I'll . . . Hullo – hullo – is that you, Arnold? . . . Well where's Arnold? Where *is* he? Oh, good gracious me, never mind about the football sweep. There's more important things in the world than that. Football sweeps, and people's lives at stake. . . . What have *I* drawn? . . . Ah, that's another tanner gone west. Hullo, hullo – is that you, Arnold? . . . Well don't keep going away, there's a fire now in Grimshaw Street and I'm here by myself . . . have you got any petrol? . . . I *know* it's no good for putting fires out, you blithering idiot . . . have you got enough petrol to take you there? . . . What, enough to get there and not to get back? Oh, well, it's no use going if you can't get back. . . . Oh, I see, Arnold, now I understand – so you think you can manage then, eh? . . . Oh, yes, oh aye, it's a pretty big fire . . . should be, by now . . . oh, and I say, Arnold – Arnold – take the dog with you, it'll be a run for him. He hasn't been out lately. Oh, good gracious me, what's the *matter* with the engine, what's the matter with it? . . . Well don't both get *on* it.[6]

The best-known sketch comic of the 1920s, however, was Harry Tate. He had started, like so many others, as a mimic – he used to do as many as forty-two changes of costume in one act, using special clip-on costumes – but after a few years moved into sketches, the first being 'Motoring'. This was followed by 'Golfing', 'Fishing', 'Selling a Car', and others; and he was sufficiently well-respected to perform 'Motoring' and 'Selling a Car' (see page 20) at the 1912 and 1919 Royal Command performances respectively. His son, Ronnie, was with him from a relatively early age – even deputizing for him on occasions – and after Tate's death in 1940 carried on the act as 'Harry Tate Junior' for some years with considerable success. Though inevitably overshadowed by his father, he was an excellent comic in his own right.

Tate toured with a company of six, which varied from time to time. Ronnie Tate remembered some of them.

'The original "son" in the motoring sketch was Tom Tweedly; Dad found him in the Empire Theatre, Liverpool – he had a rather peculiar delivery and face, and he turned out to be a real winner. We had a little fellow called Harry Beasley, who was in the original of Casey's Court [a famous touring sketch act with children]; we had a fellow called Ken, who used to go to school with my father – he used to go on the drink a bit, but he'd got the funniest face you've ever seen – it looked like a violin! – with rather a red nose and a drooping brown moustache.'

Ronnie played all the various parts in the sketches at different times; he can be heard on the 1930 recording of the motoring sketch as the chauffeur and as Tate's friend at the beginning and end of the sketch.

Tate's sketches presented him as a blustering – if basically good-humoured – incompetent, convinced that he was in charge of the situation, but never failing to increase the chaos which surrounded him.

Ronnie Tate: 'Anything that came out new – like the betting tax, so we had a betting sketch – and then we had flying, when Bleriot flew the Channel – we had about fourteen sketches altogether. There was a man called Wal Pink – my father got him a job with de Courville at the London Hippodrome, and he wrote a lot of the revue

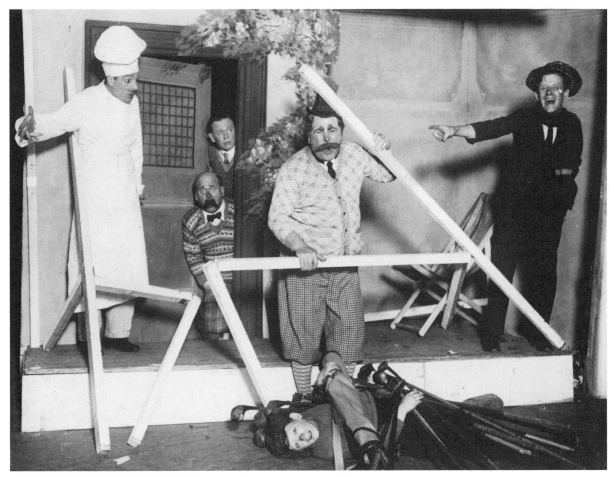

Harry Tate and Company – 'Peacehaven' (*c.* 1925)

material there – he would write a skeleton for Dad; by the time he and Dad had finished with it, there was very little of the original left, but the idea was there. We didn't go round with the same act to all the towns – if we went to Birmingham, we'd do 'Motoring' because they make cars there; if we went to Nottingham, we'd play 'Fishing', and perhaps 'Billiards' in Manchester; and then change it around to keep it fresh.'

'Running an Office' is typical of Tate's approach; inevitably, confusion reigned throughout.

TATE: Any letters?
CLERK: No letters, sir.
TATE: No letters?
CLERK: No, sir.
TATE: Then we must write some. Get some ink in the office – I can't keep writing with chalk,

it's absurd. Take a letter, will you?
CLERK: Where to sir?
TATE: No, no, *write* it!
CLERK: Oh, yes, sir.
TATE: 'Dear Mr Pork and Penson' . . . has he paid his account?
CLERK: No, sir.
TATE: '*Sir* – in answer to yours of the third ult.'
CLERK: 'Ult'? What do you mean by 'ult'?
TATE: *I* don't know – why don't you write shorthand?
CLERK: Yes, sir.
TATE: Then why *don't* you?
CLERK: Well, it takes such a long time.
TATE: Well, put 'With reference to your communication'.
CLERK: 'With reference to your . . . ' how do you

spell 'communication'?

TATE: C - O - M - M - . . . can't you spell 'communication'?

CLERK: No, sir.

TATE: Well, make it 'letter'. Now, what have you got?

CLERK: 'Dear Mr Pork and Penson, has he paid his account?, no sir, Sir, in answer to yours of the third ult, ult? what do you mean by ult? I don't know, don't you write shorthand . . .

TATE: Oh! Oooh – you're writing the conversation down! Fool! Ring him up on the phone – go round and see him – give me that book, will you? Who's been drawing faces in the cash-book? What's this – sealing-wax, £42?

CLERK: Yes, sir.

TATE: Oh yes – that was the registered letter we sent last week. And always put the cash-book *back* in the *drawer*. (*Opens desk drawer*) We must get a bottom in that drawer – everything falls through into the wastebasket. If I want anything I have to go and ask the dustman. (*To Office Boy*) Go and get me a cup of tea, would you? (*To Clerk*) Would you like a cup of tea?

CLERK: Yes, please.

TATE (*to Boy*): Make that two cups of tea. And while you're out, will you call round to the jeweller's and ask him to come and mend the cuckoo-clock – it's lost a cook. Go round to the ironmongers and get my hat ironed, a ball of string, a leg of bread and a cucumber. Got it?

BOY: Yes, sir.

TATE: Well, what is it?

BOY: Go round to the jeweller's, tell him the cuckoo wants a cup of tea, go round to the cucumber and ask him to iron this ball of string and a leg of hat.

TATE: Oh . . . make the best of it. Prepare to leave!

BOY: Oh, dear, dear, dear. (*Exits*)

TATE: Oh, dear, dear, dear? That's a nice thing, everyone walking about, 'oh, dear, dear, dear'. (*Phone rings*) Oh, dear, dear, dear . . . oh? *I'm* saying it now! I don't know what the devil they want to tie this receiver on here at all for. (*Breaks telephone cord*) Hello? Hello? . . . They've gone!

Jolly good job, too.

(*Boy enters with teapot*)

TATE: Ah – a nice cup of tea . . . there's no tea in the pot!

BOY: They wouldn't let you have any tea, sir.

TATE: Why not?

BOY: Not without the money.

TATE: All right – then he won't have the pot back! That's *two* we've got this week![7]

The confusion was not limited to his performances.

Mrs Tate told Norah Blaney, 'You realize Harry's only being himself? At home, everything he does goes wrong! If he takes a photograph and he goes in the dark-room – something explodes!'

Despite the fact that Tate would visit any individual town only once in two or three years, phrases from his sketches went into everyday use. 'How's your father?' became his escape-phrase whenever he was faced with a question he couldn't answer, as in the quotation at the head of this chapter; the expression 'I don't think' (used ironically, as in 'He's a nice chap – I *don't* think') originated in the motoring sketch; they were widely used in ordinary conversation, as was the 'Good-by-ee' which was repeated as the car in the motoring sketch failed to move. This last also inspired the famous song of World War One.

Some of the gags that went into Tate's sketches came from real-life happenings.

Ronnie Tate: 'My father had a lovely car – a Napier, a yellow one, a beautiful thing – and this man came along and struck a match, right across the panel! Of course, my old man nearly went mad – but he suddenly said, "Never mind – that's in the show tonight!" It was one of the best laughs, too.'

By the 1930s Tate found that touring with a company of six was too expensive, and he and Ronnie introduced a new sketch with only the two of them. This grew out of a real incident which happened to Ronnie (who told it with a little appropriate exaggeration).

'I had a car, and I was driving on Salisbury Plain; there was a shocking noise in the engine, so I had to stop. I thought, that's done it – I don't know what to do now. A man comes up with a motorbike and a sidecar – he says, "Are you in trouble?" I said, "Yes, the big end's gone". He said, "Oh, I'll put that right for you, it won't take long." So he opened up the sidecar – he'd got every tool imaginable – he gets underneath, takes the sump off, all oil and nuts and bolts everywhere – he comes up for a breather after about an hour, and looks at his watch . . . he says, "Good God, is that the time? – I've got to go!" – and he went! Leaving me stuck out there, with oil and bolts all over the place – I was there for two days!'

They built the incident into a sketch about a motor-cyclist – it being Tate, the machine sported a propeller – who was supposedly on a rally round the world.

RONNIE: Excuse me, could you tell me the way to Plymouth?

HARRY: Plymouth? I don't know – I've never been abroad. There's a milestone up there.

RONNIE: Well, I can't read.

HARRY: Well there's nothing on it – it ought to just suit you!

RONNIE: Are you going far?

HARRY: Yes – I'm going round the world.

RONNIE: Round the world – on this?

HARRY: Yes. There's six hundred of us left Glasgow a fortnight ago . . . I've just arrived.

RONNIE: It's taken you two weeks to come from Glasgow?

HARRY: Yes . . . I pushed it from Carlisle.

RONNIE: How many cylinders has the engine got?

HARRY: Well, it's two cylinders in one piece . . . or one cylinder in two pieces, I'm not quite sure.

RONNIE (*indicating a number of clocks on the handle-bars*): And what are all these, then?

HARRY: Well, that clock tells you, if you're in India, it's half-past two . . . if you're in Germany it's half-past nine . . . in France, half-past six . . . and of course some places are open all day! That one tells you how much petrol you've got in your tank . . . that one tells you how much money you've got in the bank. It's not working at the moment.

RONNIE (*indicating spring*): What's that for?

HARRY: Well, it doesn't *do* anything – but it's a jolly good idea! Keeps your mind occupied on a long journey.

RONNIE: And what's the propeller for?

HARRY: Oh, that's for flying.

**Harry Tate and Ronnie Tate at the Bristol Hippodrome 1938 –
'Going Round the World'**

RONNIE:	You don't go up in the *air* in this?
HARRY:	Oh, yes.
RONNIE:	How high have you been up in this machine?
HARRY:	Oh, I've been up a good way – up as far as the stratosphere.
RONNIE:	Stratosphere? Have you? Tell me, what's it like up there?
HARRY:	Not bad – the food's different, you know.
RONNIE:	Is it?
HARRY:	You've got to eat tinned food. You see, tinned foods become dangerous at height – they burst at different altitudes.
RONNIE:	Is that so?
HARRY:	Oh yes – that's how I lost my friend, as a matter of fact – he had a tin of peas at 59,000 feet – he got the wind up – I haven't seen him since.
RONNIE:	Hard cheese.
HARRY:	No, you can't eat that.
RONNIE:	Is it cold up there?
HARRY:	Cold? – it's very cold – you know, if you light a match, the flame freezes – you can't blow it out![8]

The sketch then develops along the lines of Ronnie's experience. They toured this for six years, until Tate's death in 1940, after which Ronnie went on working the halls and in pantomime for another twelve years.

Harry Tate was the greatest of all the pre-second-World-War sketch comics, and one of the few artists from before 1914 to be able to maintain his popularity in Variety right through the inter-war period; he was also one of the last sketch artists to make use of a lot of visual business and props; most later sketch comics would rely principally on verbal humour.

(*The subject of sketch comics is resumed in Chapter 12, p. 99.*)

5 18 Charing Cross Road:
The Variety Artistes' Federation, etc: One (1906–1939)

Nowadays the name of the actors' union, Equity, is well known; it also represents members of the Light Entertainment profession. Originally, however, they had their own union – the Variety Artistes' Federation – itself much older than Equity or its predecessor, the Actors' Association.

Like so many of the ideas and organizations designed to help Variety performers, the VAF began with the 'Grand Order of Water Rats'. The Water Rats started as a small social club, taking its name from a trotting pony called 'The Magpie', and afterwards renamed 'The Water Rat', which was given to Jack Lotto in 1899 by Richard Thornton, one of the founders of Moss Empires. Lotto and the cockney comedian Joe Elvin raced it to considerable profit; part of their winnings went to charitable ends.[1]

Even at this early stage there were several organizations which helped music-hall artists. The earliest was The Dramatic, Equestrian and Musical Sick Fund, founded in 1856, followed by The Music Hall Provident Society and Sick Fund in 1867; in the absence of social security these organizations helped performers in need through sickness or personal troubles. Another organization, the Music Hall Benevolent Fund, was founded in 1888. There were also small social clubs similar to the Water Rats such as the Terriers; and the Music Hall Artists Railway Association (which obtained concessions in railway fares – an important point for a profession which depended so much upon travel).

By the early years of this century the Water Rats had progressed from being simply a social club to wider charitable activities within the profession, and many important performers were members. In 1905 several grievances between artists and the managers of the main circuits over contract terms came to a head; as we saw in the Prologue the main point of dispute was that managers were expecting artists to perform matinées, in addition to the normal two evening performances six days a week, without any additional payment. Artists were also being required to undertake long journeys to different theatres without notice, because of last-minute changes. The Water Rats came into the discussion – as an organization rather than individually – and held a meeting with the Music Hall Artists Railway Association and the Terriers. Out of this the Variety Artistes' Federation was born on 18 February 1906, its object being stated as 'To promote the interests of Variety Artistes and to abolish all abuses detrimental to their welfare.'

One of the first moves of the new union was to start a weekly newspaper, *The Performer*, which, for most of its life, shared premises at 18 Charing Cross Road with the union. The paper was both the official organ of the VAF and a journal for the Variety profession (it was on general sale). There were several theatrical papers at the time, but only *The Stage* – then, as now, the principal journal for the theatrical profession – gave any support to the VAF. *The Performer*, which was able to give the VAF's point of view on various matters as well as more general news and information, started on 29 March 1906; but after five years the Registrar of Trade Unions pointed out to the VAF that trading with union funds in this way was in fact illegal, and so *The Performer* became a separately owned concern. It continued to present VAF news and viewpoints, and to give information on the profession in general, until it closed in 1957.

The new union met its first challenge almost immediately, for in early 1907 the disagreements about unpaid matinées grew into full-scale industrial action. Some artists were 'locked-out' from halls controlled by Walter Gibbons, and subsequently twenty-two London theatres were 'blacked' – and indeed picketed – by leading members of the profession, who even gave free performances just outside the affected theatres.

After five weeks of this, the disputants went to arbitration, and although the Arbitrator's Award of 1907, and the subsequent one of 1913, did little to help music-hall artists, they led eventually to the Arbitrator's Award

Contract of 1919 mentioned earlier. As a result of this favourable award the membership of the VAF rose to 5,631 in 1920 (there was a higher number of actual performers, because an act comprising several people would hold only one VAF card), but the number declined thereafter, dropping to 2,690 in 1928 and settling around the 2,000 mark at the end of the 1930s. As there were perhaps 10,000 acts eligible for membership – only a small proportion of them top-liners who were sure of regular employment – it can be seen that there was a good deal of apathy amongst performers.[2]

Shortly after the beginning of the VAF, the other important organization for music-hall artists was formed, with the intention of providing for artists finding themselves in what used to be called 'distressed circumstances' owing to illness or retirement. Called The Variety Artistes' Benevolent Fund, it was founded on 4 December 1907 from an amalgamation of the old Music Hall Benevolent Institution and The Music Hall Home, which ran a retirement home in Gypsy Hill. It was run by a committee limited to music-hall artists, and its benefits were 'for bona fide performers only'. In 1911, after raising a subscription of £2,500, they purchased a large building in Staines Road, Twickenham, called 'Brinsworth House', as a retirement home; the purchase price was £2,400, of which £1,000 was paid in cash. The mortgage for the remaining £1,400 was later paid off by special subscriptions of £2 10s from each of six hundred performers, whose names were inscribed on a tablet which still stands in the entrance hall. When the series of Royal Variety Performances (which has continued to this day, interrupted only by the second World War and the 1956 Suez crisis) began in 1926, the proceeds were devoted largely to the running of Brinsworth.[3]

By the 1920s Variety performers could enjoy a number of benefits as a result of the developments outlined above. *The Performer* was a lively and entertaining paper – a much better read than *The Stage* of the period, which was little more than a list of what was on at various theatres. *The Performer* provided gossip ('so-and-so is doing well this week at the Empire Sheffield' for example – no-one was ever reported as doing badly) as well as hard news, together with comments on various aspects of the business and its history, and numerous small-ads from artists and agents. It also listed, as 'Next Week's Calls', a substantially complete review of the following week's appearances at Variety theatres up and down the country. (Anyone who wished to trace the career of a particular artist in detail could get much information from these listings, but

they would need immense patience and a good magnifying glass.)

The Music Hall Artists Railway Association (MHARA) enabled its members to obtain a reduction of 25 per cent in rail fares for parties of five or more people (this concession was increased to cover parties of three or more in 1927); the Railway Companies attempted to remove the concession altogether in 1920, claiming that fares had risen by only 50 per cent as compared to the cost of living, which had risen by 150 per cent since before 1914 – but after negotiations the concession remained, being finally withdrawn only in 1952. MHARA members could also obtain free medical advice, particularly on ear, nose and throat diseases (whether or not contracted in trains) – a useful concession in the pre-National Health Service days when visits to the doctor had to be paid for.

The VAF itself was active in many ways. Not being a 'closed shop' type of industrial trade union, it could hardly resort to the threat of industrial action, but by negotiations, lobbying of MPs, and encouraging a certain amount of solidarity amongst its members it campaigned for improvements in the lot of performers. In the period immediately following the end of the first World War, the union successfully enforced a ban on 'ex-enemy aliens' being allowed to work in British Variety theatres. This of course arose partly because of the anti-German feeling left over from the War, but had a more practical reason; because of the very low value of the German currency, German acts were prepared to work for starvation wages. This would have presented a danger to British artists' wages – something which in fact affected artists in those continental countries which did not operate a ban. According to *The Performer* these countries found themselves deluged with cut-price German music-hall acts, often of very poor quality. The ban was eventually lifted in April 1924 – largely because, with the German economic scene improving, British artists wanted to be free to work in German cabarets.

Relations between the VAF and the managements seem on the whole to have been good; but those between the VAF and the Actors' Association (the forerunner of Equity) were extremely strained. The AA seems to have been jealous of the VAF, and in April 1924 it persuaded the industrial unions in Barrow-in-Furness to put pressure on the theatrical managements in the town for a 'closed-shop', accepting only AA membership cards in Variety theatres. Behind this was an attempt by the 'Entertainments Federal Council' – consisting of the AA, the Musicians' Union, and the National Association of

Theatrical Employees – to take control of the industry and exclude the VAF. Using the Barrow-in-Furness situation as a lever, the AA was attempting to coerce VAF members into joining the AA as part of an attempt to force the VAF to 'federate' (i.e., be taken over). This row got as far as the Trades Union Congress before the AA climbed down and matters returned to normal; from May 1924 the Barrow-in-Furness theatres accepted both cards.[4]

Probably as a result of this soured relationship, the AA even attempted to block the VAF's pressure for the bill to regulate theatrical employers mentioned in Chapter 1. This bill – the Theatrical Employers Registration Act, 1925 – was intended to stop the all too frequent incidence of artists travelling to a distant town, only to find that the show they were hired for had either been cancelled owing to the disappearance of the manager, or was in a hall which would obviously never take enough money to cover their salaries. Since it was always the artists at the poor end of the profession who fell into this sort of situation, they were liable to be left stranded without money for their fares home, and the VAF had to help out on numerous occasions. With the coming into force of the Act on 1 January 1926 the problem was somewhat reduced, but it was never completely solved.

An even more serious problem was posed by artists being hired to work abroad by bogus managers. The 'White Slave Trade' is often regarded as something of a joke, but there was nothing funny in the plight of girls hired to go abroad, ostensibly as cabaret or music-hall performers, finding that they were then exploited as prostitutes. Their contracts would be deliberately worded so as to offer them no protection, and since they would be unable to afford their fares home their position was extremely unpleasant. All the VAF could do in this matter was to offer to scrutinize contracts, and to advise artists against taking any job which looked suspect.[5]

The VAF offered some practical help in spreading 'cine-variety' – the use of Variety acts to support films – by persuading the London and other councils to relax the rules on safety-curtains (fire-proof proscenium curtains required by law in theatres to protect the audience from a fire occurring on-stage; they were of course not provided in cinemas) provided that the artists used no scenery. Cine-variety presented its own problems, because films were usually changed twice weekly; the VAF stood out against the 'split week' – artists being booked for only half the week, and being changed when the film changed – but advised artists working in this field to change their act for the second half of the week. (This was something that not all artists could readily do.)

In an attempt to alleviate the problems of unemployment in the business, the VAF tried subsidizing Variety bills with a guarantee (i.e., guaranteeing the management a certain profit whatever the takings); but since the artists involved were necessarily all small-time performers, and the public wanted to see stars, the venture lost too much money and had to be abandoned.

Although the welfare of artists in difficulties was the province of the Variety Artistes' Benevolent Fund, the VAF did run one welfare activity – its Death Levy. Whenever the death of a member was announced, each member was required to pay sixpence to the fund. The money thus raised was paid to the family of the deceased – £25 immediately and the balance when the levies were in – to cover funeral and other expenses.

Human nature being what it is, there were many who not only refused to join the VAF, but were actively opposed to it; but for its members it provided a useful protection against the hazards of the profession.

(The post-World-War-Two activities of the VAF are covered in Chapter 26 on page 193).

6 'Oi!'
Double-acts: One (the 1920s and 1930s)

Double-acts – in the sense of two comedians, one of whom usually had the funny lines while the other acted as his stooge – have their origins perhaps further back than any other type of music-hall comedy. Even in the classic Greek and Roman drama of about 300 BC there were often comic servants who argued with their masters; and in Shakespeare's *The Comedy of Errors* a master and servant amuse themselves by putting on a couple of 'extempore' double-act routines.[1] This pattern of a serious or 'straight' man trying to cope with the vagaries of a comic servant set the pattern of the principal type of double-act as it flourished in the first half of this century.

This 'cross-talk' type of double-act – which often took the form of the straight man attempting to perform seriously and being interrupted by the comic – was supplemented by two other principal techniques: the type of act where both performers worked together to the audience, presenting their version of a situation; and, less common, the type where both performers ignored the audience and presented a mini-sketch.

The theoretical legal restrictions mentioned earlier on acts consisting of two or more people talking seem to have been quietly ignored in the days of music-hall since even before the first World War there were a large number of double-acts. Indeed, it is interesting to note that many performers who later became well known as solo acts – Chirgwin, for example – began as double-acts, usually with a brother or sister; this may have been a way of gaining confidence as a performer.

A major source of the style of early double-acts was the American 'Nigger Minstrel' type of show, which was popular in Britain as well as America. Today they are liable to seem racially offensive, their humour consisting as it did of jokes based largely round the slow-witted negro stereotypes which were portrayed by white men. (Later, when blacks themselves presented minstrel shows for white audiences, they wore black make-up and continued the stereotyped style; *real* black American music and humour was a separate tradition in itself.) The humour in

the minstrel shows consisted largely of riddles presented by the performers sitting at each end of the front line of the cast ('Mr Bones' and 'Mr Tambo', so called from the instruments they usually played – 'bones' [as percussion] and tambourine) to the compère, who was usually not in black-face make-up and was often known as 'Mr Interlocutor'. The jokes, at any rate in the early days, were of the 'Why does the chicken cross the road?' variety.

The Irish music-hall comedian Joe O'Gorman, who formed a double-act with Joe Tennyson in 1881, was one of the first performers to expand this primitive style into something more resembling the master-and-servant confrontations of classic drama, thus setting the standard for cross-talk acts up to the present day. Not all double-acts used this technique; the Griffiths Brothers, for example, were more in the tradition of burlesque. Ronnie Tate remembered seeing them (although at the time he saw them they were in fact father and son, the original brother having died):

'They would burlesque anything – there was a man called Jimmy Finney, who used to have a glass tank on the stage full of water; and he and his daughter would go down in the water and play cards. The Griffiths brothers had a very thin tank made, so from the front it looked like the same thing, and they used to supposedly jump into this tank. Then Freddy Griffiths used to light his pipe "underwater"!'

Development from the minstrel-show riddles was also taking place in America, and one of the earliest American double-acts to appear in English music-halls was Sweeney and Ryland. Sweeney, the straight man, was short and plump; Ryland was long and cadaverous. Their humour was rooted in the minstrel shows, but had developed into something nearer modern cross-talk:

SWEENEY: I hear you've lost your dog?
RYLAND: Yes! I've lost my dog.
SWEENEY: What did he die of?
RYLAND: He died of a Tuesday.

SWEENEY:	Yes, but how did he die?
RYLAND:	He died dead.
SWEENEY:	But how did he come to meet his death?
RYLAND:	Didn't go to meet it – it overtook him.
SWEENEY:	But what was the cause of his complaint?
RYLAND:	No complaint. Everybody satisfied.
SWEENEY:	Now look here – your dog's dead.
RYLAND:	Yes! He's dead.
SWEENEY:	Well, what was the cause of his demise?
RYLAND:	That was it.
SWEENEY:	What was it?
RYLAND:	He closed his damn eyes.[2]

One of the top double-acts in the period immediately preceeding World War One was the Poluski Brothers, who continued performing into the early 1920s – Sam, the straight man, died in 1922 and Will in 1924. They com-

The Poluskis

bined several of the techniques mentioned above; they were also knockabout comedians using a good deal of physical comedy. Sam was tall and well-dressed, while Will was short and eccentric. He used to ask Sam questions and then hop round the stage shouting 'He can't do it!'; he also had a routine where he wrestled spectacularly with himself – an idea reworked fifty years later by Graham Chapman of the *Monty Python* team.

The Poluskis' cross-talk was in the classic mould, with Sam struggling to retain his poise against the annoyances presented by Will. They used the 'interrupted act' technique; and also a device afterwards used by many double-acts, where the straight man would be trapped into agreeing with the comic, and then correct himself.

SAM:	Hullo, Bill, how are you?
WILL:	Hullo, how are you, boy?
SAM:	Ah, I'm in the depths of trouble.
WILL:	Why, what's the matter with you?
SAM:	Well didn't you hear?
WILL:	No!
SAM:	Good gracious, you *must* have heard.
WILL:	*Have* I?
SAM:	Didn't you?
WILL:	No!
SAM:	Well you surprise me.
WILL:	Oh, dear!
SAM:	Didn't you hear about the terrible accident?
WILL:	No – did you stand a drink?
SAM:	No I didn't . . . what do you mean, did I stand a drink? I can stand a drink if I wish to!
WILL:	You don't wish to.
SAM:	No! . . . Yes I do! I'm always the first to get *my* hand down.
WILL:	*And* keep it there.
SAM:	Yes . . . *do* I!
WILL:	Yes.
SAM:	But that's neither here or there.
WILL:	Or anywhere
SAM:	No, I . . . *is* it! I want to tell you all about the accident. You know my wife, don't you?
WILL:	The one you introduced me to yesterday?
SAM:	No, not her . . .
WILL:	No, not her . . .
SAM:	Of *course* I mean her!
WILL:	Oh.
SAM:	How many wives do you suppose I've got? I've only got the one wife!

WILL: Oh!

SAM: Oh, it seems to surprise you!

WILL: It do![3]

During the 1920s there was more development of the double-act taking place in America than in Britain, much of it on radio. Billy Jones and Ernest Hare, 'The Happiness Boys' (who took their name from the Happiness Candy Company in whose programme they appeared) developed the type of act where both worked together to the audience; while the minstrel-show black-face act was refined into a more sophisticated form – really more of a sketch upon which the audience eavesdropped – by George Moran and Charles E. Mack, who were popular in American radio and vaudeville in the 1920s. (Moran also later toured in Britain, with a substitute for Mack, who had died.) Though their act still depended to some extent upon negro stereotypes – they were white men working in black-face – the slow, relaxed delivery and the better quality of the humour presented much more sympathetic characters. Here they are discussing a farm that Mack once owned:

MORAN: Well, did you raise any olives?

MACK: We didn't exactly *raise* them – we made them out of green peas. We knew how.

MORAN: You *made* olives?

MACK: We put green peas in vinegar, and when they swell up, they are olives.

MORAN: Well, how did you get the stones in the olives?

MACK: Er . . . what's your idea in bringing that up? And we used to grow pigs . . .

MORAN: Grow your own pigs?

MACK: We used to buy young pigs in August and we used to sell them in April.

MORAN: What did you pay for the pigs in August?

MACK: Er . . . a certain amount.

MORAN: Yes, I know, but how much?

MACK: Four dollars each.

MORAN: And what did you sell them for in April?

MACK: Er . . . four dollars each.

MORAN: You paid four dollars in August and sold them in April for four dollars?

MACK: Yes.

MORAN: Why, you can't make any money that way.

MACK: No, we found that out. And we had a horses . . .

MORAN: Oh, you have eight horses?

MACK: No, not eight horse – *a* horses. A. 'a'. And we found out the white horses eat more than black horses, so we sold all the white horses.

MORAN: The white horses eat more than the black horses?

MACK: Yes, the white ones eat more.

MORAN: Oh, that's silly – why should the white horses eat more than the black horses?

MACK: Oh, I wouldn't be bothered with that. We tried every way to figure it out, and we couldn't figure any reason, unless it was because we had *more* of the white horses.[4]

The sort of repetition featured in that extract, where the straight man would question the statements made by the comic by repeating them and the comic would then repeat them yet again, was common to many double-acts; it was an important comic device and a way of giving a rhythm to the delivery and making it flow better.

The natural successors to Moran and Mack – 'Amos 'n Andy', also played by white men in black-face – moved out of double-acts and into the first radio 'situation comedy', doing a regular short show in which the characters met and reacted to situations and plots, rather than simply talking to each other.

The legacy of riddles left by the old minstrel shows persisted in the tattier double-acts for a long time; it is surprising how often such acts, having started with some sort of discussion or argument, simply degenerate either into riddles, or a question and answer routine intended to let the comic score off the straight man. This routine by the British act Collinson and Dean is typical of many.

COLLINSON: What was the first thing that Henry the
Eighth did when he came to the
throne?
DEAN: Sat on it.
COLLINSON: You're a bright youth, you are. Where
do you live?
DEAN: Up north.
COLLINSON: What town, fathead?
DEAN: Plymouth.
COLLINSON: Plymouth? North? They must have
shifted it. Have you lived there all your
life?
DEAN: Not yet.
COLLINSON: Any big men born there?
DEAN: No, only babies.[5]

When some years later the act changed its comic to
become Collinson and Breen, the humour had become a
little more advanced, relying on devices such as Collinson
attempting to teach Breen a technique – for example
boxing; this at least prevented the act being merely a string
of unrelated jokes.

The sort of double-act which relied upon one-line jokes
and silly riddles, with the comic preventing the straight
man from getting on with a song or a recitation, was
typified by Murray and Mooney. There is a sort of British
'race memory' of the bad double-act with a comic entering
shouting 'I say, I say, I say . . . ' and posing a silly
question, and the straight man, upon finding out the
answer, saying 'I don't wish to know that, kindly leave the
stage'. The 'I say, I say' entry line was used by Lowe and
Webster (although they did not originate it, and there is no
certainty who did).

Murray and Mooney certainly did use the line 'Kindly
leave the stage', or variants of it, and relied on awful jokes
delivered at a fairly high speed. Their real names were
Harry Church and Harry Goodchild, and they began
together as early as 1909. They broke up in 1914 when the
War started, and resumed in 1920, playing revue and
Variety on the smaller circuits. There is a legend that Val
Parnell – then the bookings manager for the General
Theatres Corporation – saw them at a small hall, thought
they were terrible, and booked them at one of his London
halls as a sick joke. They went over so well with the
audience that the following week they were at GTC's
premier theatre, the Palladium.

It may be in part just a good story, but what *is* true is
that in the week beginning on 4 January 1932 they were at
the Metropolitan Edgware Road, their following week

Harry Mooney

being then unbooked (although they did have subsequent
weeks booked at various theatres); by the end of the week
they had a booking to play the following week at the
Palladium. They made several appearances there, and
even played in the 1934 and 1938 Royal Variety
Performances.

MURRAY: Ladies and Gentlemen – a monologue
entitled 'The Stake'.
'There's a job to be done
We must cut out the fun
And stick to our task, one and
all . . . '
MOONEY: Pardon me, what is the title of this
junk?
MURRAY: 'The Stake'.
MOONEY: Have an onion?
MURRAY: What for?
MOONEY: To eat with the steak.
MURRAY: 'The Stake': 'There's a job to be done,
we must cut out the fun . . . '

MOONEY:	What's the difference between a stoat and a weasel?
MURRAY:	I don't know.
MOONEY:	A weasel is weasily distinguished.
MURRAY:	What about the stoat?
MOONEY:	That's stoatally different.
MURRAY:	'The Stake'.
MOONEY:	I know a man who eats nothing but Chinese food.
MURRAY:	Why's that?
MOONEY:	He's a Chinaman.
MURRAY:	'The Stake'.
MOONEY:	Do you know the best way to stop fish-bones from sticking in your throat?
MURRAY:	I do not!
MOONEY:	Eat liver.
MURRAY:	Eat . . . would you kindly keep off the stage, please.[6] 'The Stake'.
MOONEY:	If I had a rabbit in a hutch and I bought another rabbit, how many rabbits would I have?
MURRAY:	Why, two of course.
MOONEY:	No, ten.
MURRAY:	You don't know your arithmetic.
MOONEY:	You don't know my rabbits.[7]

Murray and Mooney eventually split up, and Mooney teamed with Victor King; but the new teaming never had the success of the old. Part of Murray and Mooney's charm was that they never attempted to update their act, but some of those double-acts whose careers went on for long enough adapted to changing tastes. The O'Gorman Brothers – sons of Joe O'Gorman who was mentioned earlier in this chapter – started as a double-act very much in the style of the Poluskis, even to the extent of sounding rather like them. In this 1930 example they were still firmly wedded to the old-fashioned style, even though their delivery was fast.

DAVE:	There are some funny sights to be seen in this world.
JOE:	Yes, I was just looking at you.
DAVE:	And everybody has a double.
JOE:	If he has the money.
DAVE:	Scouring the globe –
JOE:	Cleaning out the goldfish –
DAVE:	Always thirsting for knowledge –
JOE:	And beer –
DAVE:	Travelling this way, then that –
JOE:	Then under the seat –
DAVE:	What do we find, to be sure?
JOE:	Fag-ends and orange-peel.
DAVE:	North, South, East and West.
JOE:	And Midland.
DAVE:	Always on the look-out.
JOE:	For the ticket-collector.
DAVE:	Live and learn.
JOE:	Die and forget it.[8]

Joe and Dave O'Gorman

By the end of the 1930s they had moved to a more modern style, even though it was still on the old-fashioned side.

Being old-fashioned was never necessarily a bar to an act being popular, provided that it was good. Charlie Naughton and Jimmy Gold, who had been in the business from 1908, remained in the old tradition of broad comedy throughout their careers. Their delivery was somewhat ponderous – both had Scots accents – and their material was pretty basic, but they were always a popular act.

Naughton and Gold

JIMMY:	If I asked you to have a drink, what would you say?
CHAS:	Milk and soda.
JIMMY:	So you know about milk?
CHAS:	I wrote three columns in the paper about milk.
JIMMY:	And they published the three columns?
CHAS:	No – they condensed it.
JIMMY:	Do you like milk?
CHAS:	Yes – I like that drunken milk.
JIMMY:	Drunken milk?
CHAS:	The canned stuff. I really drink beer.
JIMMY:	You really drink beer? – why?

CHAS:	Because I'm thirsty.
JIMMY:	Because you're thirsty – then you should drink milk. Milk makes blood.
CHAS:	Oh, I'm not *blood*thirsty. Here – that proves I know something about milk (*hands Jimmy a photo*) – it's a picture of a cow eating grass.
JIMMY:	But there's no grass there.
CHAS:	No – the cow has eaten it.
JIMMY:	Where's the cow?
CHAS:	You don't think the cow is going to stop there after it's eaten the grass?[9]

All the acts mentioned so far made their names in Variety, although some of them did broadcast. However, by the late 1920s radio was making its own stars, and amongst them was one of the best double-acts of the period, Clapham and Dwyer. They began in 1925, working at private functions, and first broadcast in 1926. Because they had to work in a medium which did not allow for repetition of material, they were one of the first double-acts to be able to turn out a large number of routines rather than relying on only one or two.

Bill Dwyer was the straight man, and Charlie Clapham – tall, with a top hat, a monocle and a moustache – was a master of inarticulacy. Their Variety career followed from their radio broadcasts, in which they could develop running jokes which turned up in routine after routine – as, for example, Cissie the Cow, whom Clapham seemed able to drag into any discussion.

DWYER:	Now, do you play golf?
CLAPHAM:	No. But – er – I can't give it up.
DWYER:	Well now, the first important factor in the game . . .
CLAPHAM:	I suppose you've never seen my cow Cissie play golf, have you? . . .
DWYER:	No, I have not, and I don't wish to.
CLAPHAM:	Oh, it's a scream, it is, really. She played a . . . she played one of these well known tenor singers the other day, you know, and – er – it was very good . . . and she beat him, too. He gave her – er – eight moos.
DWYER:	Eight *what?*
CLAPHAM:	Eight moos. You see – every time he took his drive . . . she moo'd, and – er – he being a tenor singer, you see, of course, it upset him, you see . . .

Clapham and Dwyer

because, you know, these tenors do this: 'me-me-me-me . . . hip-bath . . . sponge-bag . . . moo-moo-moo-moo . . .'

DWYER: Yes, well if you don't mind I'll continue.

CLAPHAM: Well, if you don't mind . . . that's all right . . . I'm just trying to help you, that's all.[10]

The most popular and enduring double-act of the inter-war period was of course Flanagan and Allen, whose memory has been kept fresh by shows such as *Underneath the Arches*, which re-enacted the story of their career for a new generation. But Flanagan's real name was Reuben Weinthrop; he always claimed that he used the name of a sergeant he had hated in World War One, but veteran comedian Tommy Trinder (always a veritable store-house of reminiscences about the Variety era) told a BBC interviewer[11] that he thought that the name had been invented by Florrie Forde, an old-time music-hall singer in whose show Flanagan was working (as 'Bud Harlem') in 1924.

He teamed with Chesney Allen – who had worked as a straight actor and as straight man in the double-act Stanford and Allen – and from their debut in Variety in 1931 to Allen's retirement owing to ill-health in 1945 they were the top double-act in the business. One of the things which made them stand out from the others was the on-stage relationship. Most other double-acts had presented the straight man as being totally irritated by the comic's interruptions – a logical enough approach, but one which could become tiresome for the audience. With Flanagan and Allen, there was always a bond of affection to be felt between them. Somehow, no matter how irritated Allen

Flanagan and Allen

seemed by Flanagan's daftnesses, the audience could feel that he still liked the man. This, together with the very high standard of their material, put them well ahead of any other act.

They became known as the 'Oi!' comedians because of one of their favourite devices, which involved Bud Flanagan performing a sort of free-association on what he was trying to say, being corrected by Ches, and then correcting himself with an 'Oi!' which was echoed by the pit orchestra. All this was done very fast.

BUD: I saw all the sights of London. Went to the City, saw Expensive End.
CHES: You saw what?
BUD: Expensive End.
CHES: Expensive End! You saw Cheapside.
BOTH: Cheapside.
BUD: Oi!
BAND: Oi![12]
BUD: I went down to the docks.
CHES: Oh, you saw the ships?
BUD: Yes, I saw all the ships coming into whisky.
CHES: Coming into port.
BUD: Coming into port – oh, a marvellous sight – you ever seen them?
CHES: Never.
BUD: It's avaricious.
CHES: Really?
BUD: See all the labradors at work.
CHES: The what?
BUD: The labradors.
CHES: The labradors – the salvadors!
BUD: The stevedores, you fool – Oi!
BAND: Oi!
BUD: Marvellous sight, see them getting all the sargo off the ships.
CHES: All the what?
BUD: The sargo.
CHES: The sargo – the *cargo!*
BUD: The sargo.
CHES: What are you talking about, 'sargo'?
BUD: What they make the sargo pudding with.
CHES: Sargo . . . *sago!*
BUD: Eh?
CHES: Sago.
BUD: Go!
CHES: No, *sago.*
BUD: Oh, you mean semolina – Oi!
BAND: Oi![13]

Flanagan and Allen

Flanagan's performance – a mixture of shrewdness and innocence, his delivery rapid and slightly slurred but always intelligible – was the act's most obvious asset, but Allen was a superb straight man – sharp-nosed, bright-eyed, dapper, ready to pounce on Flanagan's mistakes but always, one felt, in a tolerant way. They developed some complicated routines – for example the confusion over two whistles, where Bud had one, and Ches had one too . . . 'Two? Why should you have more than me?' – which involved precise timing of speech and business.

The strain of surrealism which ran through so much Variety humour was well represented in their work:

BUD: Nice game, this is – if I could sell my taxi I'd go back to Africa and do what I used to do.
CHES: What's that?
BUD: Dig holes and sell them to the farmers.
CHES: Dig *holes* and sell them to the farmers?
BUD: Yes[14] – The sun pouring down, six, seven hundred degrees in the shade.

CHES: Just a moment – sun pouring down like that
       – you couldn't dig in that heat!

BUD: Never used to – had me overcoat on.

CHES: Just a minute – you couldn't dig in heat like
       that.

BUD: Well, I started at the bottom and dug up.

CHES: Started at the bottom and dug up?

BUD: Yes.

CHES: What did you do for air?

BUD: Eh?

CHES: What did you do for air?

BUD: Well, what am I doing now – look, I'm bald.

CHES: No, no, *air* – air you breathe.

BUD: Oh, *hair* – past tense. I used to dig another
       hole at the side.

CHES: Oh, I see – just a minute, what did you do
       with the dirt?

BUD: Dirt?

CHES: Dirt.

BUD: Have you ever been to Africa?

CHES: No, never.

BUD: Oh, well, I'm all right – there's no dirt out
       there. Now I remember[15] I dug a hole for a
       farmer and he wouldn't have it.

CHES: He wouldn't have the hole?

BUD: He could please himself, it was on appro.,
       but he wouldn't have it.

CHES: Why not?

BUD: I was two feet too far short.

CHES: Two feet too far short? You mean you were
       two feet too deep.

BUD: Well, I wasn't going to waste a good hole like
       that, was I – oh, he's bound to ask a question
       here – so I pulled the hole out of the ground
       . . .

CHES: Just a minute, just a minute . . .

BUD: I thought so, I thought so . . .

BUD: You pulled the *hole* out of the ground?

BUD: I did – don't you believe me?

CHES: I *don't* believe you.

BUD: Call me a liar.

CHES: You're a liar.

BUD: I know, I can prove it. I pulled the hole out
       of the ground, and when I'd got it out the
       farmer wanted it. But I couldn't get it back.

CHES: You couldn't get the hole back?

BUD: No.

CHES: Why?

BUD: I'd bent it.[16]

They always finished their act with a sentimental song, such as 'Home Town', 'Dreaming' or their most famous song 'Underneath the Arches', and these did as much as the humour to build the tremendous affection audiences had for them by the time they split up in 1945. They took the classic cross-talk double-act to its height; but they also became well-known as sketch comics in association with the Crazy Gang, whose story is told as part of the next chapter.

(*The subject of double-acts is resumed in Chapter 17, p. 141.*)

7 Life is crazy
Variety in the 1930s

The economic depression of the 1930s hit harder in America than it did in Britain, because until the stock market crash of 1929 America had been in a boom. Britain, on the other hand, had been in an economic depression throughout the 1920s, so that the decline into the serious situation in the early 1930s, though unpleasant, was at least not sudden. Unemployment had been just over a million at the end of the 1920s; by 1932 it had risen to four million. Taking into account the families of unemployed men, this meant about seven million people dependent upon the unemployment benefit – the 'dole'. The Means Test – basically a method of reducing the already meagre allowance in cases where officials could find the slightest reason – made matters even more miserable for the industrial areas affected.

It was an uneasy decade; in Britain there were hunger marches by unemployed men, and an increasing feeling of division between the working classes and the more comfortably situated middle classes; while abroad the rise of Nazism in Germany was presenting a warning that most people chose to ignore.

They were difficult times for Variety. Despite the relative cheapness of seats, audiences were bound to be reduced when so many people had trouble enough just to live; and the coming in 1929 of the 'all-talking, all-singing, all-dancing' sound films presented a serious threat to the business. Even the leading Moss Empires circuit felt sufficiently threatened for its owners not only to consider following the Stoll circuit and equipping their theatres for sound films, but even going over to the enemy.

Ironically, this was prevented – and thus a reprieve granted to the business of live entertainment – by a film company. As we saw in Chapter 1, the Gaumont-British Film Corporation had gained control of the General Theatres Corporation (the GTC) in 1929. In 1932, with the principal object of preventing Moss Empires from converting to films and thus rivalling their own chain of cinemas, they brought control of Moss and merged it with GTC, thus creating a massive new circuit which was far larger than its rivals. The theatres continued to be listed as being owned by two separate chains – Moss (with thirty-eight theatres and Variety halls including the London Hippodrome), and GTC (with fifteen theatres including the Holborn Empire and the Palladium). The previous managing director of GTC, George Black, was placed in overall charge; Val Parnell (the son of the ventriloquist Fred Russell[1] who was also active in the VAF) was the general manager; and Cissie Williams, who had been a secretary to Charles Gulliver when he ran GTC, was appointed chief booker. In November 1932 they moved into offices in Cranbourn Mansions, adjoining the London Hippodrome (in Cranbourn Street, London WC2) from where Moss theatres have been run ever since.

The principal rivals to the new big circuit were the Stoll circuit – still run by Sir Oswald Stoll – with nine theatres including the London Alhambra and Coliseum; and the Syndicate Halls, also with nine theatres, including the Metropolitan Edgware Road. Other circuits included the Broadhead, the MacNaghten, Fred Collins, and the National Vaudeville Corporation (all largely operating in the north of England); and Howard and Wyndham Ltd, with theatres in Scotland and the North.

The sheer size of the combined Moss-GTC circuit made George Black the most influential man in Variety throughout the 1930s and the war years which followed

George Black

The London Palladium

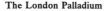
The London Palladium

(he died in 1945). He had started in a small way, running cinemas in the north of England with his brothers Alfred and Edward. Their cinema chain had grown to about forty when George Black was invited by GTC to come to London to run the Palladium, which had been going through a very unsatisfactory (and unprofitable) period. Black's son, Alfred, remembers:

'It was a dead duck – they'd done everything – it had had circuses, it had had revues, it had had films, it had had operettas – but it never had any pattern; and Dad latched onto the idea of modern Variety. Instead of people doing an act for, say, twenty minutes, he gave them twelve minutes, which cut out all the padding and got down to the nitty-gritty.'

The first Variety bill under the new regime started on 3 September 1928, and on 16 May 1932 the Palladium presented its first week of 'continuous Variety', picking up from the cinemas the idea of allowing the audience to come in and leave whenever they liked and still see the whole bill.

Black had an exact feel for show business; he could gauge the appeal of an act to a nicety, and was never afraid to innovate. A popular voice on the radio was Christopher Stone, the first 'disc-jockey' (not that the term was used at that stage) who made his name simply by introducing records.

Alfred Black: 'The cheekiest thing Dad ever did was to put on Christopher Stone at the Palladium – Stone would come on and say, "I'm now going to play you a very nice record, I hope you enjoy it" – and he'd sit there and put a record on, and all the audience sat there like lemons and listened to it!'

The greatest innovation at the Palladium was of course the Crazy Gang, although the popular legend that George Black invented it is something of an over-simplification. The basic idea went back to a touring show called *Young Bloods of Variety*, in which the knockabout and acrobatic comedians Jimmy Nervo (real name Jimmy Holloway) and Teddy Knox had enlivened proceedings by coming on during other performers' acts. This might have been just another one-off idea if the Scottish double-act Naughton and Gold had not had a pantomime contract cancelled in 1931. Their agent bargained with Val Parnell to book them at the Palladium, threatening to obtain them a booking at the Alhambra, run by the rival Stoll Circuit. The problem from Parnell's point of view was that he had already booked two other double-acts – Nervo and Knox, and the husband-and-wife team Billy Caryll and Hilda Mundy. Three double-acts in one bill seemed a bit much;

Nervo and Knox – the wrestling routine (1930)

'Monsewer' Eddie Gray

but Parnell remembered the Nervo and Knox technique of intruding on other people's acts, and suggested that this be revived as a means of getting round the problem. Apparently George Black was dubious about the idea, but thought that it was preferable to letting Naughton and Gold go to a rival circuit.

The show was billed as a 'Crazy Week', and opened with great success on 30 November 1931. Further Crazy Weeks followed, with Flanagan and Allen added; in March 1933 Black mounted the first of seven Crazy Shows, which ran for fourteen weeks. The team was not yet called 'The Crazy Gang' – that billing was not used until 1937 – but the classic line-up was there: Naughton and Gold, Nervo and Knox, Flanagan and Allen, and 'Monsewer' Eddie Gray.

Eddie Gray had started as a straight juggler, gradually introducing comic patter into his act. On a visit to Paris he had started to do his patter in nonsensical French – hence his nick-name, 'Monsewer' – a mixture of cockney English and bent French which, combined with his outrageous curled moustache and a looney sense of humour, made him ideally suited to the Crazy Gang.

> Madames and masseurs – how are you, all right?
> Enjoyin' yourself? I'll soon put a stop to that.
> Now je suis now is goin' to parlez-vous Français,
> and moi's going to do quelque-chose for vous,
> that you 'ave never seen on any stage. As a
> matter of fact I'm going to take this 'ere pack of
> cards, and I'm going to ask Madame, or
> Mainsewer, to extract un card. Not deux, but
> un.[2]

Nervo and Knox were experienced knockabout and acrobatic comedians – their routines included a superb 'slow-motion' wrestling bout. Both were dapper; Teddy Knox sported a neat moustache, while Jimmy Nervo affected a speech impediment: 'Oh, you do shay shertain thingsh in shertain waysh, Sheshil!'

Alfred Black remembers: 'When Dad first started the Crazy Gang they'd have a script conference; Jimmy Nervo couldn't read, and he used to say, "Oh, I've left my glasses behind – Ted, would you read it to me?" He came from circus, and he'd never had a school education.'

Naughton and Gold provided robust, simple humour – seen today, in the films, their jokes seem rather rammed into the material in the way that Fred Karno's used to be. Charlie Naughton – the bald one – got the benefit of most of the Gang's physical comedy; if he didn't get tripped up, slapped, bonked on the head and soaked during a show he thought he was being left out of things.

With Bud Flanagan's complicated word-play and Chesney Allen's educated straight man, it was a strong teaming. In this extract from the sixth Crazy Show in 1934, the team pose questions to Eddie Gray.

CHES: I intend getting married shortly – can you tell me how many Sundays are necessary for the publication of the banns?

EDDIE: Three clear Sundays, young man, the same as for any ordinary execution.

NERVO: What are the worst words in the English language?

EDDIE: Time, gentlemen, please.

KNOX: What is a caterpillar?

EDDIE: A worm with a fur coat on.

NERVO: I've got ten children and I'm out of work. What shall I do?

EDDIE: You've done enough work.

CHES: Where do motor horns come from?

EDDIE: China.

CHES: What part of China?

EDDIE: Hong Kong.

GOLD: If a toe dancer insures her toes and a chorus girl insures her legs, what does a shimmy dancer insure?

BUD: What can I do to cure myself of walking in my sleep?

EDDIE: Take a bicycle to bed with you.

BUD: How can I get rid of some ugly fat?

EDDIE: Send her home to mother.[3]

NAUGHTON: My wife and I have been married seven years, and we've got four children; but we've never lived together since the day we were married, although I've corresponded with her every day.

EDDIE: You have four children and you've never lived with your wife?

NAUGHTON: Yes. (*Eddie turns to go.*)

GOLD: Hi! – where are you going?

EDDIE: I'm going to borrow that pencil.[4]

Havoc reigned in any Crazy Gang show. There were interruptions from the boxes and the audience, intrusions on other acts, and even beyond the show itself the gang caused chaos – they used to spend the time before curtain-up showing members of the audience to the wrong seats.

The Crazy Gang.   *Top*: 'Monsewer' Eddie Gray; *second row, left to right*: Teddy Knox, Charlie Naughton; *middle:* Bud Flanagan; *bottom, left to right:* Jimmy Nervo, Jimmy Gold

They also spent a lot of time playing practical jokes on each other and anyone else within reach, both on- and off-stage. Some of the jokes bordered on the vicious; some were merely harmless, like Eddie Gray's habit of standing by a post-box asking it 'Well how did you get *in* there?', waiting till he had collected a crowd, and then disappearing to 'go for help'. The interruptions in other artists' acts were usually taken in good spirit; but Horace Kenney, a sketch comedian with a gentle and slightly pathetic approach, was rather upset when they did it to him.[5]

With the first of their shows to have a title, *Life Begins at Oxford Circus*, which opened at the Palladium on 4 March 1935, the gang moved into what was really revue rather than Variety, although their broad approach was in the tradition of Variety and music-hall. It was followed by *Round About Regent Street, All Alight at Oxford Circus, O-Kay For Sound, London Rhapsody, These Foolish Things* and *The Little Dog Laughed; Top of the World* was closed by the blitz in the second World War, and the gang split up for a time.

George Black supervised all the shows, which had very high production standards, with expensive scenery and costumes. He exercised a tight control over the comics, whose adherence to the script was always liable to be loose.

Alfred Black: 'He used to let them run for about six weeks, then he'd have a rehearsal to take out the "improvements"; but a lot of the "ad-libs" were rehearsed.'

The 1936 show, *O-Kay For Sound*, was based (loosely) round the idea of the gang making a film. In one scene they discovered that everything in the film magnate's office suggested a film title or a film star.

(Enter a man in a loud suit with a woman dressed in tailor-made.)

BUD: Look! – 'Things to Come!'

KNOX *(mimes fighting)*: Who's this? Who's this?

CHES: I give it up.

KNOX: Conrad 'Fight' [Veidt].
(Enter Naughton who pedals round on an imaginary tricycle)

NAUGHTON: Ding ding! – stop me and buy one!

CHES: Well, who is it?

NAUGHTON: Tom Walls.

NERVO: Here's a missus-piece – master-piece!
(Imitates duck)

KNOX: I've got you – Donald Duck!

NERVO: You're wrong! *(He lays an egg)* Evelyn Laye!
(The hands of the clock on the wall revolve very quickly)

CHES: Look – 'Modern Times'.
(Naughton paces across the stage counting as he walks)

NAUGHTON: ...35...36...37...38...'39 Steps'.
(A ghost is pushed out – Naughton kicks it)

NAUGHTON: 'The Ghost goes West'!
(Naughton walks across stage spraying a Flit fly-spray; Gold walks behind.)

BUD: What picture are you?

GOLD: 'Follow the Flit.' [Follow the Fleet]
(Nervo enters with a typist; stops and kisses her)

BUD: That's not a picture.

KNOX: Yes it is – 'A Little Bit of Fluff'.
(The typist sits on Nervo's knee)

NERVO: Ah! Here's a beautiful picture!

KNOX: What is it?

NERVO: 'After Office Hours.'

BUD *(surprised)*: 'She Married Her Boss.'

NERVO *(bites the end off a rose)*: There you are – 'Chewed a Rose'. [Tudor Rose][6]

The Crazy Gang in 1948

Appropriately enough, in view of the subject-matter, *O-Kay For Sound* became the Crazy Gang's first film, made for Gainsborough Pictures in 1937. Inevitably their particular appeal is muted on film, but the scene quoted above comes over quite well and gives a good idea of their style. The construction of the film is tighter than that of the show, and there are a number of good sequences.

By this time several Variety comedians were making an additional career in films, some of which were very successful. Nowadays the films seem more important, simply because they still exist; but at the time they were secondary to the stage performances of these artists. None of the films had, at that time, the appeal of the glossy products of the Hollywood studios; the atmosphere of British life in the 1930s which the best of them have makes them more valuable now than they seemed then. The Crazy Gang made few concessions to the medium, and in fact many of the routines in their films started life in the stage acts. Most other artists – Will Hay, Gracie Fields and George Formby being the foremost – necessarily became more comic actors than Variety artists in their films, working logically within the confines of the plot.

The success of these films – which did nothing to harm the artists' stage reputation – did not bear out the fears of the Variety profession when talking films first started. The VAF advised its members to have nothing to do with films, motivated principally by a fear that films of Variety acts might be run in direct competition to the live acts. Despite this, many people performed shortened versions of their acts for magazine-type supporting films such as *Pathé Gazette*, which appeared in a new edition each week; in fact these appearances seem to have had no adverse effect on theatrical performances, and today they are an immensely valuable record of many of the best Variety artists. Variety acts were also worked into feature films – as, for example, when the characters in *Those Were The Days* (1934 – a version of Pinero's *The Magistrate*) visited a music hall; or in *Elstree Calling* (1930), a revue format film compèred by comedian Tommy Handley. (This particular film looks very odd because the performers – who included Lily Morris and Will Fyffe – had obviously been told *not* to work directly to the camera, which gives most of their performances a strangely detached appearance.)

The real threat to live Variety came not from these home-grown products but from the products of the Hollywood star system – films made on an enormous budget and with enviable professionalism. To some extent the co-existence between films and Variety continued in the form of cine-variety; but the fact that sound films could present spectacular musical shows made life difficult for live performers in the same field. Imagine the feelings of a dancing act having to follow a Fred Astaire and Ginger Rogers film – and no touring revue could hope to come anywhere near the megalomanic spectaculars of Busby Berkeley.

Cine-variety was the beginning of a major change in the technique of Variety – the use of microphones and amplification (what is now sometimes known as 'sound reinforcement' but was then called 'public address' or PA since it originally derived its methods from outdoor events where large crowds had to be able to hear speeches).

With the appearance in the early 1930s of the huge Odeon cinemas the problems of audibility became severe for acts in cine-variety; the cinemas were much larger than most Variety theatres (except the Coliseum, which had excellent acoustics) and were in any case never designed for unamplified speech. To make matters worse the film soundtracks were fairly loud compared with live speech, and in March 1932 *The Performer* commented that inaudibility was common, and cited the Wintergarten Theatre Berlin – which was being equipped with PA – as an example which cinemas should follow. Gradually PA was installed in these cinemas.

Up to this period microphones had never been used in Variety theatres. Most theatres were of a moderate size, but in any case audiences were used to having to sit still and pay attention in order to hear. Even so artists had to work hard to be heard in the larger theatres. Stanley Holloway, having had his voice properly trained for singing, could make himself heard with no difficulty; but he remembered:

'A lot of laryngitis went on, because people didn't know how to produce the tone without straining.'

Ronnie Tate confirmed this from his own experience.

'We really had to work to get it over. You had to learn to throw it out so that everybody could hear, but you had to shout your guts out to do it. We used to come off wringing wet, after shouting for twenty minutes.'

Almost all Variety comics of the period finished up with a hoarse voice with a cutting edge on it; and throat and chest trouble were common complaints when they became elderly.

Gradually microphones appeared in the Variety theatres. The Palladium had its own system by January 1933; in early 1934 *The Performer* was carrying advertisements for a portable PA system for 'crooners' (who sang quietly close to the microphone in the American style popularized on records), and by 1937 microphones were becoming widespread. Much of the pressure for the use of PA came from American artists, particularly quiet-voiced singers such as the Boswell Sisters, who were developing vocal styles unsuited to projection. With some artists using PA and some not, problems arose.

Stanley Holloway: 'I never used microphones until they put them into the footlights and you couldn't escape it. I never liked them, because when they magnified someone's voice with a microphone, anyone who didn't want the microphone sounded puny and weak by comparison. So if one person had it, they all had to have it.'

Dick Henderson had adapted to the use of microphones when they became common.

His son remembers: 'At the Empire Nottingham, my father was on the bill with Richard Tauber, who spurned the microphone. He was a beautiful singer – but he didn't sound as good as my old man! The audience were disappointed, merely because other singers had been on before and belted it out.'

The northern Broadhead circuit held out for a time against microphones – they displayed a notice in the dressing rooms: 'Real Artists Do Not Need Artificial Aids' – but the spread of PA was inevitable. Wally Thomas – 'Thomé the Young French Violinist' of the early 1920s –

had graduated to straight acting, and went on from there to be manager of the Empire Newport (a Moss theatre leased to Terence Byron Ltd) from 1937 to the outbreak of war in 1939. By this time microphones had been installed in the theatre.

'It was a 1700 seater, a tremendous-sized place; but the acoustics were perfect – there was no need for microphones. Nevertheless a lot of people wouldn't work without them. Albert Whelan [a veteran performer from the old music-hall days] wouldn't use them, but the firm were insistent that he must . . . eventually he did; people were pressured into using microphones so that there was no possibility of their not being heard . . . and to conform with the fashion. I can remember Jack Buchanan[7] actually dancing around with a microphone to his mouth and singing while he danced, which looked ludicrous.'

The quality of theatrical PA was (and is) usually fairly bad – the sound lacking in top, often distorted, and for the most part far too loud (and it was not until the extremely complex system installed at Drury Lane for *A Chorus Line* in 1976 that theatrical PA was ever 'high fidelity').

The use of microphones inevitably altered the styles of performance. Comics were no longer free to move around the stage as they wished, but – at any rate in the earlier days – had to remain tied to the stand microphone at the centre of the stage. It also affected the relationship between the comic and the audience, as Laurence Olivier wrote (in a letter to Peter Honri upon becoming a patron of the Wilton's Music Hall Trust):

'The entertainer or the single act has a *weapon*, you see. No one can shout him down. He's protected by it, almost shielded by it, and the whole spirit of gallantry and courage and temerity that was this medium's great attraction disappeared in front of your eyes.'[8]

On the positive side, the microphone made possible a more intimate sort of comedy, by freeing performers from the necessity of projecting; in particular, artists who had made their names on radio could maintain their style in the theatre. The original dislike of radio on the part of the Variety managements had perforce changed, since they had discovered that the public would pay to come and see radio stars on stage – partly out of a simple desire to find out what they looked like in the flesh. This led to some performances which were not entirely successful – because the artists in question were not suited to a theatre – or plain silly, like the Christopher Stone appearance mentioned earlier; but many artists who had made their names with the BBC went on to successful careers in stage Variety.

This new influx of talent helped to keep the business going, but even so things were becoming increasingly difficult. The Palladium Crazy Shows were a resounding success, but conditions elsewhere were less satisfactory. All through the 1930s Variety was suffering from the economic depression, the competition from cinema (and indeed from radio), and the gradual closure of theatres. Even Stoll's Alhambra Theatre in London's Leicester Square – which in any case had, like the Coliseum, abandoned Variety for musical comedy shows in the early 1930s – closed in October 1936; it was demolished to make way for the Odeon Cinema. (The Coliseum went over to musical comedy with *White Horse Inn* in 1931 and *Casanova* a year later; but as the 1930s went on its presentations met with less and less success, and by the end of the decade it was reduced to running rather uninteresting straight plays.) The Moss-GTC combine had closed over twenty-five theatres by 1939; and cine-variety was almost completely dead, thus removing further opportunities for work.

Things would have gone on getting worse; but Variety was about to receive help from an unexpected quarter. Up until the late 1930s few people had been taking the activities of Adolf Hitler in Germany seriously – comedian John Tilley commented that really the Nazi salute was more of a request than a threat – and even when it became obvious that Hitler was a menace rather than a joke, the all-too-vivid memories of the horrors of the first World War led to attempts on the part of the British Government to avoid a confrontation, no matter what the cost. Only by early 1939 had it become apparent to almost everyone that war was inevitable, sooner or later. Air-raid shelters were hurriedly dug, gas-masks issued, and plans laid for children to be evacuated from the cities; but few people could have guessed that one of the effects of the war would be to revitalize the entertainment industry.

(*Variety during World War Two is covered in Chapter 16, p. 136.*)

8 'Grammatical words to a British tune'
Musical acts

Music was of course an important part of most Variety acts. Even stand-up comedians who did not finish their acts on a straight song would have play-on and play-off music, and would sometimes intersperse the talking with the odd short comic song; and for acrobats and other silent acts the music was an essential part of the atmosphere. This chapter, however, deals with acts which were essentially musical – mostly singers, both of serious and comic songs.

Norah Blaney, whom we met in Chapter 1, worked mostly as a singer of sentimental songs until she left the stage in 1932. On the Variety halls she usually appeared with Gwen Farrar, who provided a sort of comic relief.

Adelaide Hall

Norah Blaney: 'They used to put in the papers, "Beautiful Norah Blaney" – I thought I looked like a brontosaurus, but never mind that – and Gwen was the eccentric. I'd sing one of these awful songs, one of these heartbreaking . . . I was the poor man's Vera Lynn . . . Gwen would fetch her cello, the lights would go down and focus on her, and she'd play an obligato. Beautiful – she played the cello very well. Then she'd get up, put the cello on her shoulder like a sack of coals, and walk off!'

They also appeared in the spectacular revues mounted by André Charlot.

Norah Blaney: 'People said, "Why do you always have Gwen Farrar and Norah Blaney in your shows?" He said, "I have the best of both worlds – Norah fills the stalls with all the young men, and Gwen has all the lesbians in London to see her." '

Most singers, however, managed without such eccentric adornments. The singer Adelaide Hall – famous in jazz circles for her wordless vocal on Duke Ellington's 1926 record of 'Creole Love Call' – came to Paris in the late 1920s with the all-black show *Blackbirds*, and subsequently toured in Britain on the Moss Empires circuit.

'I played all over the place – Scotland and Wales, and everywhere in London; and I was here in 1932 for the Palladium. I toured with a pianist, and used the pit orchestra as well – at that time they were very good – for Moss Empires they had to be good; and a large orchestra, not a small one like they have now. I sang a few swing songs, and did a little tap-dance; and some sentimental songs'.

She made a large number of records for Decca, which helped increase her popularity; and in 1938 she settled permanently in England. Coming to British Variety as a foreigner she always found it very enjoyable to work in – the American vaudeville circuits were more lavishly run but also much less friendly – and she never met any racial prejudice.

Although there were not many black artists in the British Variety field, one of the top acts was black – Layton and Johnstone. They sang popular songs of the time in a relaxed and intimate manner, and made many records and radio appearances as well as touring the halls until the act split up in 1935. Turner Layton – the pianist of the pair – continued as a solo act.

Another 'duets at the piano' act – disc-jockey Christopher Stone used to play their records and compare them to Layton and Johnstone – was Bob and Alf Pearson. Unlike some 'brother' acts they really *were* brothers; Alf, the short one, was born in 1908; Bob, the taller one and the pianist, in 1910. Their career illustrates the hard work that most acts found necessary before they became top artists, for they were no overnight success.

Bob and Alf Pearson in a comedy number

They started in amateur concert parties in their home town, Sunderland, continuing in the same way when the family moved to London when they were teenagers. At one of their performances they were heard by a recording manager for the Vocalian Gramophone Company and invited to make records. The modest success of these led to some radio broadcasts from Savoy Hill and to a few Variety appearances.

Bob Pearson: 'You couldn't jump from being a recording artist to the "number one" circuits. George Black saw us – and of course he was a Sunderland man, and we thought, with us being from Sunderland, it's the "open sesame" into show business . . . he came round to see us, and said, "You've got possibilities; I want you to go round and play the Barnsleys and Crewes – anywhere you can – and get the rough edges knocked off; and I'll come and see you again in maybe eighteen months' time." '

They found it difficult to get bookings at first – as with many artists the catch was that no agent would find them

bookings until he had seen them work; and they couldn't work until an agent had found them bookings. . . As they gradually got work on the smaller circuits they found that, although they were billed in very small type at the theatres, the local record shops would carry a big window display of them as recording stars.

Their early recordings were made for the small labels like Imperial, Broadcast, Piccadilly and Rex; then they went in for, and won, a talent competition for which the prize was a recording contract for Columbia Records. However, as Columbia already had Layton and Johnstone as top artists, they shunted the Pearsons onto one of their subsidiary labels, Regal-Zonophone.

Bob Pearson: 'We went to see the recording manager; and he put a record on of two Americans – and they were singing in thirds all the way through, even when it clashed with the harmonies in the music. He said, "That's the way I want you to sing." So I said, "That's what we call 'Chinese harmony' – we don't sing like that." He said, "That's the way I want you to sing – the people who buy our records are people who eat fish-and-chips, and that's what they sing, and that's what they want to hear." I said, "Well, you can get somebody else . . ." – and that was the finish of our connection with Columbia. We were always putting our foot in it at the beginning of our careers.'

They went to tour with their own road show, mounted in association with a small agent called Sidney Royce.

'He said, "You fix the acts", and then he took a third and we took two-thirds of the profit or loss.'

Alf Pearson: 'We went round the "number two" tours – the MacNaghten circuit, the Broadhead circuit, and any of the small independent theatres. The theatre supplied the orchestra, the staff, the lighting; our touring company supplied the rest of the artists, part of the publicity costs – and then took 55 to 60 per cent of the gross box-office takings for the week. So we'd pay the rest of the company's salaries, then what was left was shared between Sid Royce and ourselves. Some weeks we worked for nothing after we'd paid the digs.'

Eventually George Black saw them again, and gave them a date; this led to another booking the next week.

Bob Pearson: 'He sent a set designer round and built a proper set for us, and presented the act properly. Black came round immediately after first house on the Tuesday night, and we thought he was pulling the act to pieces – "Don't do this, don't do that . . . you want the lights like this . . . and tell your agent to come round and see me tomorrow." And our agent phoned us up and said, "I've got three years' work for you." '

From this they never looked back, and became a very popular act. Bob Pearson describes the typical format:

'We would do a bright opening number – for instance "The King's Horses" – and then we'd do a ballad, such as "Isle of Capri" or "Little Man You've Had a Busy Day". Then we'd do a comedy number – any number of them were written in those days – and then we'd do a standard ballad, like "Until", or "Love's Old Sweet Song". Then we had our own comedy finish – a comparison between Victorian songs like "Come Into the Garden Maud" and the same thing put into swing tempo.'

For years their signature tune was 'You Can't Have Everything', but after World War Two when Frankie Howerd started to sing it, they changed to a specially written one which became more famous than their names: 'We bring you melodies/From out of the sky/My brother and I'.

There were many singing acts, both solo and in various teamings; and also instrumental acts. One of the most notable of these was Herschel Henlere, a remarkable pianist who specialized in musical 'switches' – rapid transitions from one melody to another – and tunes played in various styles. He was an eccentric character, particularly in his apparent inability to bring his act to a close – he persistently over-ran his allocated time, and in the end Moss Empires had to put him on last so that they could at least have the choice of running late or bringing the curtain down on him.

A trend which began only in the late 1920s was that of dance bands appearing on stage. Up to this time – and indeed throughout the 1930s – there were many bands who played specifically for dancing in venues ranging from local dance halls to expensive London restaurants and clubs. During the 1930s many of the top bands, such as Ambrose and his Orchestra, Roy Fox and his Band, and Jack Hylton's Orchestra, appeared in Variety theatres. Their acts sometimes filled the entire second half of the bill, and dance-style arrangements of popular songs were varied with comedy numbers, dance routines, and so on.

Most of the songs featured by musical acts were of course the hit parade tunes of the day; and there was always the danger of the same song appearing too often in different people's acts. In the old-style music-hall, this had been largely avoided because performers would buy the copyright of a song they wanted to feature. As a result, although it might be published, no-one else could perform it in public. If you wanted, for example, to hear 'My Old Man Said Follow the Van', you just had to wait until Marie

Lloyd came round to your theatre. By the 1930s, the so-called 'free song' was more normal – not that it could be performed without payment to the publisher (the payment was however made by the theatre, which was licensed for the use of published numbers) but that anyone could use it. This led to obvious problems.

Bob Pearson: 'Our act was mainly built up on pop songs; if we were on with a band topping the bill we would rush to the notice board – because the bands used to put a list up of the numbers that they were doing – "Will artists please note that Mr Harry Roy will be featuring the following numbers . . ." – and there was the top twenty! And we used to think, "Good! Now what are we going to do? – there's nothing left!" '

Alf Pearson: 'It got to be such a headache that we gradually went off pop songs and built our act on stuff that nobody else was doing, except maybe one or two popular songs, so we weren't dependent upon pop songs for the entire act.'

Competition for numbers was not even restricted to the top artists.

Bob Pearson: 'At Newcastle Empire we were on the bill with Billy Cotton and his band – we saw the list of his numbers, and we had no chance! Nothing left at all – so we went to Billy, who was a very nice fellow, and he said, "You do that one and that one, and I'll take them out." Then the MD – the Musical Director of the pit orchestra – said, "You can't do that number – I'm doing it in the interval, and my drummer's singing the vocal." We went back and saw Billy Cotton – he said, "*I'm* the band here this week" and told the MD, "We don't want any vocals from your drummer – people haven't come in to listen to you. Play 'Light Cavalry' or something." '

So far we have looked at artists who mainly performed 'straight' songs; but of course comic songs were always an important part of music-hall and Variety. In the old-style music-hall they formed a much larger proportion of the comedy performances than they did subsequently – and in that period there was more acknowledgement of the harshness of the real world in the songs – but in the 1920s and 1930s there were still many comic songs being written. The 1920s was the heyday of the nonsense song – for example 'When It's Night-Time in Italy It's Wednesday Over Here' or, perhaps the daftest of them all, 'Do Shrimps Make Good Mothers?' (the answer being, 'Yes, they do').

The king of the nonsense song was Leslie Sarony, who was born in 1897 and entered the business only reluctantly (his sister used to keep on entering him for talent competi-

tions, and he kept on winning them) and went on from juvenile shows – where he did light songs and tap-dancing – to concert party and eventually to appearances on the Variety halls. He began writing his own songs in the 1920s – many of which he recorded, either with dance bands or under his own name – and composed many classics including 'Don't Do That to the Poor Puss Cat' and 'I Lift Up My Finger and I Say "Tweet Tweet" '. He even made a hit by setting limericks – dubious limericks, some of them – but without the last lines. This he presented on record as a 'competition', inviting the listeners to fill in the last line; for example –

> There was a young man of St Paul's
> Who once did a turn on the halls.
> His favourite trick
> Was to stand on a stick –
> La la la-la-la la la-la la la.[1]

Apart from these missing lines, his material was rarely risqué; but there was always someone ready to look for offence.

'I remember when I wrote "Mucking About the Garden" someone was very dubious about "He sits among the cabbage and peas/Watching his onions grow" so instead of putting "Written by Leslie Sarony" I put "Written and composed by Q. Cumber".'

Records were as important as stage appearances in building Sarony's career.

'I had orchestrations done for going on the halls; but when you made a record they were specially arranged. The ordinary pit band arrangement wouldn't be any good on a record; and on recording sessions you'd see people from Hylton's band or Payne's band [playing as 'session men'].

It was quite a different thing from pit bands, and much better, too.'

In the late 1930s he teamed up with Leslie Holmes, who was working as a pianist for a music publishing company, to form 'The Two Leslies'. They indulged in patter of a rather obvious sort, and performed Sarony's songs, complete with dancing from Sarony. All his songs were lively and amusing, with the lyrics sitting well on catchy tunes.

The Two Leslies – Leslie Sarony (*left*) and Leslie Holmes

A much quieter sort of comedy was provided by the team of B. C. Hilliam and Malcolm McEachern – 'Mr Flotsam and Mr Jetsam'. Hilliam, who had worked as an entertainer at the piano in a semi-professional way in England and Canada, teamed with McEachern – already established as a serious singer with a fine bass voice – in 1926. Hilliam composed and accompanied all their numbers, singing them with McEachern. After a couple of try-outs they were launched at the Victoria Palace and became an instant success. They went on to top bills at the major Variety theatres, to make records, and to become popular broadcasters. In a way there is a resemblance between their songs and those of Melville Gideon, the pianist and composer for the concert party *The Co-Optimists* which had included Stanley Holloway – his most famous song was 'I'm In Love With A Girl In A Crinoline Gown' – but where his particular brand of charm has dated badly the records of Flotsam and Jetsam demonstrate a quiet charm and wit, with a natural ease of manner, which shows the reason for their tremendous popularity.

Perhaps the best summing-up of their appeal came in one of their own songs, composed – as was all their material – by Hilliam:

> A professional chap with a face as long as an
>   ordinary window-shutter
> Said, 'Listen and don't tell me I'm wrong –
>   Variety's as dead as butter'.
> Said he, 'These times aren't like the past,
> For they want foreign stuff and they want it fast,
> You must play jazz and you must sing blues
> Or you won't get a job in the new revues.'
> Said he, 'The public taste is wrong
> Nobody wants to hear a decent song –
> And the only chance that a song has got
> Is in being just a little bit "you-know-what"':
>
> > Well, we don't know, and we don't care,
> > We like everybody and we go everywhere
> > And the funny part is that the songs we croon
> > Have grammatical words to a British tune.
> > My word – absurd – of our senses we're
> >   bereft –
> > How dare we – what care we –
> > For there's only a few of us left.[2]

A performer whose songs were rather more than a little bit 'you-know-what' was Douglas Byng. He was born in 1893 and, like so many others, worked his way up in the profession through concert party. He appeared in many of André Charlot's and C. B. Cochran's lavish revues, also appearing in cabaret and Variety. His speciality was to be, if not actually risqué, then something near it. He was never actually 'blue', but managed to give the audiences the thrill of thinking that they were hearing something a little near the knuckle. Most of the jokes were really only in the audiences' minds:

'It was a little bit risqué, but I never said anything unless it was perfectly normal language – I left it to the audience. For example, when I said, as Nell Gwynn: "Oh of course Charles always would have a country dance after dinner – I got sick of putting up the maypole – I said, 'Charles, if you must dance, stick the maypole up yourself . . . and dance round it' " . . . and all the dear old ladies thought the joke was the King dancing round by himself. And I got away with murder with Charlot – for example Boadicea saying "Bronto-bronto-sore-arse to you – which roughly means, let every man hold his peace." '

His style was most suited to cabaret, where there was less control of material than on the Variety halls:

'I was about the first person to do female acts in cabaret – not in full drag like Danny La Rue, I had my collar and tie and coat tails and just put on hats and feather boas – and I found that by being female, it wasn't quite so suggestive as being a male. If you say, as a woman, "Oh! what he did to me!", it's not nearly as indecent as a man saying, "Oh, what I did to her!" '

It is difficult now to recapture the original effect of his songs, because the mildly suggestive humour of his period has been overtaken by the more direct humour of modern times. His songs (which sometimes had a little patter in them) included 'Boadicea', 'Mexican Minnie', 'I'm a Bird', 'I'm a Tree', and this dig at the stars of the silver screen – 'Sex-Appeal Sarah'.

> When I went on the pictures to act,
> I was quite a furore, as they say.
> I appeared first as Carmen, but in fact
> I was much more bizarre than Bizet.
> But the day came for filming the bullfight
> I was just doing one of me stunts –
> When the juvenile lead pinched me casti-o-nets –
> I went all *hors de combat* at once.

But I picked up a picador's spear,
Stabbed him in the bolero and spoilt his career;
 I'm Sex-Appeal Sarah, my body gets barer
 Each time I appear on the screen.
 Oh, I've played such rare pranks with dear
  Douggie Fairbanks
 Really risky – though never obscene.
 I know all the Lupinos – I go to their
  beanos –
 We start off with cocktails and end up with
  Eno's;
 I'm slick Sal, and when I was a gal
 I was constant and clever and clean.
 I was never *de trop* – I was pure as the snow –
 But I drifted, and so – well, you know what I
  mean.[3]

His most popular act in Variety was a one-man version of the traditional British pantomime, in which he impersonated in rapid succession the Fairy Queen, the Demon King, the Heroine, the Dame, the Principal Boy – and the chorus.

'I got sick of doing the pantomime – I'd say, "I really can't go back to the Palace Manchester with the same old thing for the fourth time" – but you see, the thing about English audiences is, they love the things they *know* – so you go somewhere you've been three times, and the fourth time you go better than ever.'

His act as the pantomime was a devastating impression of the traditional format, complete with a Dame ('You know, I don't think my husband was faithful to me – my last child doesn't resemble him a bit') and an audience-sing-along song which (to quote a famous remark by a film

The Western Brothers
(Kenneth and George)
(1947)

censor) '*if* it had a meaning, it was doubtless an objectionable one':

> Who'll come and roll mother's pudding?
> Who'll come and flatten the dough?
> Who'll fold the ends, and straighten the bends –
> You know where good puddings go.
> Daddy is out in Australia,
> Granny has papered the tin;
> So if you're all good, you shall all have some
> pud –
> Now who'll stick the first currant in?[4]

While it was not uncommon for performers to satirize easy targets such as pantomime, political satire was quite unknown in the theatre at the time (and on the whole remained so until *Beyond the Fringe* in the early 1960s). The nearest approach to it was in the act of the Western Brothers (Kenneth and George – actually they were cousins). They sang – or rather drawled – their songs at the piano, smartly dressed in evening dress and monocles. Their jokes were quietly pointed – and if now they seem a little mild, at that time it was considered a little naughty just to mention a politician's name in a Variety act. Inevitably topicality has dulled the edge of the jokes for a modern audience; this excerpt from 'Keeping Up The Old Traditions' gives an idea of their style (the topical references are explained in the notes):

> The latest flats in Tennessee have roses round
> the door –
> Keeping up the old traditions.
> Mr Drage is laying lino down the Polish
> Corridor –
> Keeping up the old traditions.
> When she sees a nudist Lady Oxford always
> grieves –
> She lives beside a colony of Adamses and Eves –
> And she has to eat fig pudding just to send them
> round the leaves –
> Keeping up the old traditions.
>
> In the Commons, Hore-Belisha was looking very
> blue –
> He said, 'I want a knighthood', they said, 'What
> did you do?'
> He simply shouted 'Beacons', and they said 'The
> same to you!'
> Keeping up the old traditions.[5]

Where Byng was sophisticatedly saucy and the Western Brothers were just a little naughty, Ronald Frankau specialized in songs which were genuinely much nearer the knuckle. Although he did make many Variety appearances, he was more at home in cabaret where his audience was less likely to be shocked. This example may seem tame enough now, but for 1937 its uncloaked exhortation to amorality is really rather advanced. (Doing it in private was one thing; but singing about it in public was quite another.)

> Boys may; but girls may not – has been a slogan
> since eternity –
> Unwritten laws have gone to pot, and now in our
> modernity
> The broader view with joy rejects the inequality
> of sex –
> Lady be bad – don't go through life
> Waiting about to be somebody's wife
> Don't forget you may be left on the shelf
> So make a bit of whoopee and enjoy yourself.
> Men prefer a girl who's just a wee bit naughty
> – or they should –
> And if you are, you'll marry just the same,
> that's understood –
> But you'll simply stay at home and help your
> mother if you're good –
> Oh – lady be bad!
>
> 'No, sir' – that's a dead idea – part of woman's
> slavery –
> So eliminate the gossip fear – broad minds will
> praise your bravery.
> And spiteful narrow folk endure – for to the
> pure there's *nothing* pure –
> Lady be bad – don't go through life
> Waiting about to be somebody's wife
> Don't forget you may be left on the shelf
> So make a bit of whoopee and enjoy yourself.
> Fighting for your honour's so old-fashioned –
> why the squall?
> For if you do lose self-control that's nothing to
> appall –
> It's better to have lost and loved, than not to
> lose at all –
> Oh – lady, be bad![6]

Nellie Wallace

Forget all my troubles I can't, though I've
    tried –
There's only one thing left for me, suici-i-ide –
    I don't like my mother's
      Pie-crust
    Eat it? No! – I'd sooner
      Die-fust
    I've tied it round me neck
    And tomorrow I shall be –
    Down at the bottom of
      the deep
        blue
          sea.[7]

What is often not realized about comic songs of this period is that they were not simply sung in a straightforward manner. A good deal of work went into building up little bits of 'business' to go with the song, creating a character study which added a good deal to the actual words. One of the best surviving demonstrations of this can be seen in the film *Elstree Calling*, in which Lily Morris sings two of her songs. She presented a shop-worn spinster, although a more robust one than Nellie Wallace, in 'Why Am I Always The Bridesmaid?', and in others such as 'Only a Working Man' and 'Don't Have Any More, Missus Moore' she presented respectively a tired married woman and the givers of advice to a mother of many children.

Her performance of 'Why Am I Always The Bridesmaid?' in *Elstree Calling* shows the sort of polish that could only be obtained by taking the same act round the halls for years, improving it, tightening it up, and producing a performance where every line has a suitable little visual gag or facial expression; it is one of the funniest pieces of film in existence.

However, the most popular comic artists were those who worked within more traditional bounds. Although the stand-up style was more common by the 1930s, there were a number of popular acts who depended upon comic songs. Nellie Wallace, who was billed as 'The Essence of Eccentricity', worked in the character of a frustrated spinster, dressed in a moth-eaten feather boa, a skimpy hat and a patterned jumper and skirt. She was just as eccentric off-stage – Stanley Holloway remembered her prowling around backstage with a disinfectant spray-gun muttering 'Filthy beasts! Dirty beasts!' – and her songs always had a superb touch of looniness about them.

Tonight I'm alone, broken-hearted
To mother I've murmured 'Good-Byee'
From the home of my youth I've departed
With a tear in my bonny blue eye.

Lily Morris

George Formby

Lily Morris of course was, in this case, merely giving her usual stage performance and ignoring the camera; but some stage artists made fuller use of this different medium. Two of the top performers of comic songs also became top film stars – George Formby and Gracie Fields. Formby – whose father has already been mentioned in Chapter 2 – was the master of the saucy song and the knowing wink; which was a little odd as his stage and film character tended to be the helpless northern 'gowk' who had no idea how to cope with women. This combination of innocence and knowingness – together with the fact that all his songs had an irresistible foot-tapping beat – gave him an appeal which is strong even for a modern audience seeing his films. Songs such as 'When I'm Cleaning Windows' (1936) made him one of Variety's top stars.

Now it's a job that just suits me
A window cleaner you would be
If you can see what I can see
    When I'm cleaning windows.
Honeymooning couples, too –
You should see them bill and coo
You'd be surprised at things they do
    When I'm cleaning windows.
        In my profession I'll work hard, but I'll
            never stop
        I'll climb this blinking ladder till I get right
            to the top.
Pyjamas lying side by side
Ladies' nighties I have spied
I've often seen what goes inside
    When I'm cleaning windows.[8]

The last four lines were responsible for getting the song banned by the BBC – even in the 1950s they were still refusing to broadcast it.

Formby's films – all with much the same plot, made cheaply and quickly, but always entertaining – were tremendously popular. What is interesting to note is that in the early ones he plays his own version of the Tom Foy-type 'Wet Willie' character – totally overborne by his women-folk, helpless, awkward, and only getting on top of the situation in the last reel. In the later films the character has been softened and rounded out – he is more aggressive, talks back to his mother, is more positive with his sweetheart, and generally less of a gowk – presumably to make him more acceptable to southern audiences who had less sympathy for the naïve type of comic.

A comparable softening process took place with Gracie Fields, although where it did Formby's performances no harm, she was never as funny once she had become more dependent on sentimental ballads and gentler humour (although her popularity became higher as a result of the change). She had been in the profession for fifteen years when her appearance in London in 1925 in the revue *Mr Tower of London* made her a star; it was mounted by her then husband Archie Pitt and she had already been touring in it for six years. Variety appearances and gramophone records followed, and films from 1931, and throughout the 1930s she was one of Variety's top stars. In her earlier records and appearances she sang songs – many of them by the excellent writing team of Weston and Lee – based round the idea of working-class life in the north of England, often her native Rochdale. The humour was pawky and almost surreal – as in the song listing all the strange uses to which 'Granny's Little Old Skin Rug' was put, the description of how she rode with 'The Rochdale Hounds' ('Such a lovely thoroughbred with a coal-wagon on the end'), or the saga of Uncle Ebenezer's whiskers, which tickled him to death.

The last-mentioned song was one she included in her act when it was recorded 'live' by the Gramophone Company on 11 October 1933. Nothing of the sort had ever been tried before (although recordings of opera had been made in Covent Garden Opera House) and the uncertainty about the amount of noise the audience would make and the general technical problems led the company to keep

I never cried so much in all mi life

Gracie Fields

Gracie Fields (1937)

the whole procedure strictly secret (although obviously permission had been obtained from Fields). The mobile recording van was disguised as a furniture van and parked in the alley behind the Holborn Empire, and the microphone was carefully hidden from the audience. The result was a resounding success, and after slight editing down was issued on the HMV label.[9]

These recordings are among the most valuable in the history of music-hall and Variety, for they carry the authentic atmosphere of a Variety performance. Fields has the audience under total control; she alternates comic songs – or songs performed in a comic manner, with funny voice-tones and so on – with serious and sentimental ballads beautifully sung in her high, clear voice.

In one of the songs, 'Out In The Cold, Cold Snow', the words and Fields's delivery combine pathos with her robust humour; she is sending up the Victorian hard-luck ballad, but without entirely losing the more serious elements in the characterization.

> It's all through the bloke that I married,
> When he gambled and spent all the dough –
> Then he slung me, oh heck
> By the scruff of the neck
> Out in the cold, cold snow.
>
> He left me with one little offspring.
> Cast your eye on our John Willie Joe . . .
> Does it seem worth a kiss
> To be landed like this?
> Out in the cold, cold snow.
>
>> Out in the cold, cold snow –
>> Out where the cold winds blow –
>> No-one to love me and no-where to go
>> Out in the cold, cold snow.
>
> One dark night I jumped in the river (splash,
>>   splash)
> For to end all my weal and my woe –
> But I just missed the flood
> So I stuck in the mud
> Out in the cold, cold snow.
>
> I don't seek revenge on me husband,
> Cause to blazes I'm sure he will go;
> Then how glad he would be
> To change places with me –
>>   Out in the cold, cold snow.

There was no PA in use in the theatre when the recording was made, and during the quieter songs the silence and concentration of the audience is almost tangible. The pit band, though smaller than the orchestras used on Fields's gramophone records and thus a bit thin-sounding, plays well – and it is most noticeable that they hold their volume down considerably while she is singing, only playing at full volume in the short links between verses, thus giving a far wider dynamic range to the music than is heard in studio performances where there was no danger of the voice being drowned.

At the end of the performance she waits for the audience to demand her 'signature tune', 'Sally', before performing it and then getting the audience to sing it with her. (She comments, 'I bet I'm singing it when I'm seventy' – which turned out to be a conservative estimate, for she sang it in the 1978 Royal Variety Performance at the age of eighty, commenting 'I've been singing a man's song all my life!'.) She then sings 'Stormy Weather' as an encore. Although there have been other live recordings made during Variety performances, several of them very good, no other recording gives so effective an impression of what it was like to sit in the plush seats of the Holborn Empire one evening in 1933 and listen to one of the best-loved artists of the day.

As her career developed she gradually moved away from the pawky humour of her earlier appearances, and went in for a softer, more sentimental approach, with a greater emphasis on the straight songs. Her films – in which she was required to become more of a comic actress, although she also sang in them – were always popular (although their popularity followed the stage appearances rather than the other way about) and the best of them, such as *Sing As We Go* (1934), give a better idea of the atmosphere of the 1930s than most serious films of the time.

After the 1930s comic songs declined in popularity; and although many stand-up comics used comic songs as part of their acts, the wartime and post-war periods produced no new artists of any stature whose acts depended upon comic songs in the manner of Fields and Formby. The way we see them now, as a result of the films, is unbalanced in favour of their character-comic acting; but in their Variety performances they established a rapport with their audiences, by the use of music, which few artists have managed to approach.

9 'We don't book acts with dirty shoes'
Running the business: One (1919–1939)

To the outsider, the world of Variety tended to seem rather free-and-easy; but there was a high degree of organization involved in running it, and for every performer on-stage there were many more behind-the-scenes workers. The principal contact that most artists had with the managerial world was their agent – or agents, because although it was usual for a performer to be represented by the same agent all the time, some artists obtained bookings through a number of different agents. Basically, the agent would arrange the booking with the circuits, agree the fee, and then take a commission (usually 10 per cent) from the artist. Inevitably there were performers who resented losing a tenth of their salary in this way – and indeed some managed perfectly well without agents – but most artists had little business sense and were glad enough for someone else to handle negotiations for them.

Billy Marsh, who later became one of the most respected agents in the business, started as an agent in 1942 having worked as a manager for touring revues. In his view one of the most important functions of an agent, in the days before changes took place in the structure of the business, was in getting unknown acts started.

'You could see somebody that *you* thought had potential, and others didn't; and maybe when you booked them they didn't deliver. But if you had belief that they had got within them something very good – and they needed help, advice and work – then when they *did* develop it was all worth it. But the whole basis of success is completely and utterly in the hands of the public – if the act hasn't got that "feel" for the audience, no manager or agent can do anything about it.'

Another agent, Philip Hindin, started as an assistant in an agent's office in the 1930s and later became an independent agent.

He remembers: 'The big agents – Foster, Charlie Tucker, Reeves and Lamport – were dealing basically only in star acts; and they had the ears of the bookers, and so could sometimes get smaller supporting acts into Variety bills. The smaller agents specialized – for instance, Richards and Marks were probably the finest agency representing speciality acts. They were the only agency you could go to and say, "I've got £35, I've got

such-and-such other acts" – and they would deliver an act that didn't clash with anybody, that could work on the size of stage you had, could do the length of time you wanted, and would be a solid, sound act. The only acts that Moss Empires would book unseen came from Richards and Marks.'

Norman Murray worked for Richards and Marks before, like Hindin and Marsh, becoming an agent in his own right. He defines the function of the speciality acts.

'To enhance the appeal of the programme by the fact of their presentation being different from the attractions that the public had really come to see. For example, if you went to see a star like the xylophonist Teddy Brown, his act might be preceded by the comedy dancers Wilson, Keppel and Betty – who were perhaps the best speciality act in the whole industry – and the point of this was to get the audience in a receptive frame of mind so that Teddy Brown's position would be enhanced. You would sign acts on a "Sole agency" basis because if you were an influential agent – in the sense of being able to telephone Moss Empires and get an immediate hearing – and you saw a new act, and made improvements and suggestions, you didn't create that situation for another agent to come along and take them over.'

Some agents would build up a bill themselves and sell it as a package to the smaller theatres – the big circuits would not buy such 'combinations' but always did their own bookings – often obtaining some of their acts from other, even smaller, agents. In theory agents represented the interests of the artists rather than the managers; but sometimes the distinction would become rather blurred.

Bob Pearson remembers: 'We've been in the office of Sam Richards, of Richards and Marks, when GTC have phoned up and said they wanted an opening act for the next week, but all they'd got left to pay for it was £18. So he gets his list out, and picks someone and rings him: "Fred? . . . You're not working next week? I can get you in on GTC – £16 is the top . . . I know it's not up to your usual money, I know that, but that's all they can afford . . . just a minute . . ." and he puts the phone down for a minute or two, then: "Hullo, Fred – I've managed to get you £18 . . . I knew you would, yes, you'll enjoy the

week." Then he rings back GTC and tells them he's got them an act for £18 – and this act thinks Sam's got him two pounds extra. And Sam would get 10 per cent off the £18; so if he had, say, three acts on that bill, he's getting about £6 a week from them; and he had about sixty acts on his books.'

Some less reputable agents, who mounted their own combination bills and sold them to theatres for a percentage of the takings, might then pay the acts salaries on which they would charge commission, thus cutting the cake at both ends.

Agents who were solely representing individual artists would send in 'vacancy cards' – postcards with the dates of weeks in which the performer was as yet unbooked – to the managers; and artists who were not solely represented would send their own cards round all the agents. In both cases it gave an idea of which acts were available. A trick used by a few acts was to make their card just a little larger than the standard postcard size, so that it would stand out when the cards were stacked together.

The business of organizing bookings, building up bills and dealing with publicity, contracts, and so on, was highly organized. In looking at this subject, we shall be dealing mostly with Moss Empires, as the leading circuit and the one for which the most information is available; but the other major circuits operated in a broadly similar fashion. The bookings manager for the Moss and GTC circuits was Cissie Williams, a shrewd and very tough lady who was highly respected (and not a little feared) in what was a male-dominated business. (Coincidentally, the bookings manager for one of her major rivals – the Syndicate Halls – was a similarly shrewd and tough lady called Florence Leddington.) Cissie Williams was in charge of the day-to-day running of the circuits – Val

Parnell, as General Manager, was more concerned with broader matters of policy and business – and she ruled them with a rod of iron from her appointment in 1932 to her retirement in the 1950s. Not that she was in any way unsympathetic, but she stood no nonsense from anybody and was rigidly fair-minded – refusing, for example, to have lunch with performers (which might have led to accusations of favouritism).

Ted Gollop was her assistant for many years, and took over from her when she retired.

'She and Val Parnell were the key figures in the business. She used to love her work – she had no other interests. We used to start in the office at ten in the morning, and during the day we'd plan out which theatres we were going to in the evening to see various acts. We'd be written to by agents, to say they'd got an act appearing somewhere; so we might go to see an act at Finsbury Park, go over to the Metropolitan Edgware Road and see an act there, then belt up to Kilburn Empire – we'd do three or four acts a night. I seldom got home before eleven or half-past.'

They would take in theatres belonging to other circuits as well, in order to assess the potential of newer acts.

'We were issued with a badge with a number on it by the Agents' Association, so that we could go into a theatre without wasting time buying tickets; and we wouldn't mention any names, because if anybody knew we were in, the word was round the back before we even sat down – "Moss Empires are in tonight" – and it would scare all the little acts stiff. Of course we'd just go in, see the one act, and come out without waiting for anything else.'

After seeing acts in this way, Cissie Williams might then book them into one or two of the provincial halls to see how they did; on the basis of reports from the local managers she might then continue to book them and eventually bring them into London. She was extremely adept at assessing an act's potential; and she was also very exacting in her judgements. Norman Murray once took her to see a two-girl dancing act he represented.

'I was a young man – it was a great privilege to be allowed to take her. We saw them – and you never asked her what she thought, she'd tell you when she was ready – and she said, "Well, Norman – very good, those girls – very pretty girls – can't use them." I, in my innocent manner, said, "Miss Williams – if you think they're pretty and they're good, why can't you use them?" She said, "They had dirty shoes, Norman. We don't book acts with dirty shoes." She could have told me to get their shoes cleaned; but her standard was such that they shouldn't have had dirty shoes in the first place.'

Once an act had been accepted for the Moss circuit, there was a regular routine involved in arranging their bookings. Brenda Thomas worked for Moss Empires as a secretary and assistant in the contracts, bookings and publicity departments; she joined in 1949, but at that time the technique was unchanged from the 1930s.

'If Miss Williams was booking an act, the first thing she would do would be to look in the records to see what theatres they had worked before. Every week, the manager of each theatre sent in a report on every artist there; and whatever the manager said was written on record cards we kept for each artist. We had cabinets full of cards, so when she was booking Variety there was a continual run of cards going in to her. We also did what we called "oppositions" every week; *The Stage* would tell us what was on at all the opposition theatres. So if an artist played an opposition theatre in, say, Nottingham, then that was entered in the card in red; so that when Miss Williams looked at the card she knew they had been there within the last three months, and so it wouldn't be a good idea to book them there. So in that way she could prevent artists re-appearing too often, and keep them moving around the circuit.'

Acts were not only kept away from towns they had appeared in recently, but from any Moss theatre within about twenty miles – on the assumption that people living *between* towns might travel up to ten miles in either direction to go to a Variety theatre.

Once the decision had been taken where to book an act, a contract had to be issued. Louis Benjamin – who became managing director of Moss Empires in 1970 – began as an office-boy in the contracts department in 1937 (demonstrating that people really *could* start as an office-boy and work their way to the top in the Variety business).

'Contracts department was a very large department in those days, servicing about thirty-six theatres on a twice-nightly basis with up to twelve acts a bill; so you can imagine how many contracts went out per week. Part of my job was to take the contracts round to the agents – who were all in the same square mile as our office – by hand, for speed and economy; and pick up the confirmations of the ones that had been delivered the day before. That happened twice a day, there were so many. It was one contract for each act for each week – maybe several weeks for a touring show, but for individual artists normally a one-week contract.'

Even if an artist had been booked for several years ahead – as could happen with the top performers – the contracts were issued on a weekly basis. Brenda Thomas also spent a fair amount of time ferrying contracts around central London.

'In those days all contracts had to be stamped at Bush House, so every week I went galloping off there with a stack of contracts; and the manager of the theatre had to have a copy of that contract before the artist went on the stage.'

(The practice of contracts having to be stamped by the Inland Revenue was later replaced by a tax collected by the use of ordinary postage stamps, over which the contractor signed.) The contracts themselves were standard forms – the 1919 Arbitrator's Award Contract; managements were prohibited by law from making any alterations to them.

The selection of acts, and the order in which they were placed, was extremely important; obviously no-one would place, for example, four piano acts or five stand-up comics on the same bill (at least, not in the 1930s; in the 1950s strange things of this sort did sometimes happen). The running order for a typical Variety bill had become a fairly standard form by the 1930s. It was usual to begin with a dancing act – usually two girls doing a simple tap-dance; there were any number of that sort of act – who would be on for only about three minutes. The second item, or 'spot', would usually be a stand-up comic – hence the often used term, 'second-spot comic'. He would usually play in front of a 'front-cloth' – a painted scene on a back-drop only a few feet back from the stage front – hence the other widely-used term, 'front-cloth comic'. In some theatres this cloth carried advertisements for local businesses, and the comedian was expected to walk about on the stage as he talked, in order not to obscure any one advertisement all the time.

The second-spot comic had a difficult task, partly

Next Week's Calls · ·

GENERAL THEATRES CORPORATION, LTD.

BIRMINGHAM, Hippodrome (R. 12).—Aileen Stanley, Teddy Brown, Shaw and Weston, Carr Bros. and Betty, Gaston Palmer, Dennis Boys and Rita, Gaudsmith Bros., Bennett and Williams.

BRIGHTON, Hippodrome (R. 11).—Jack Payne and His Band, Jack Payne's Radio Party, Leslie Sarony and Leslie Holmes, Jimmy James and Co., Janet Joye, Donald Stuart, Garland Wilson, Courtnay, Peggy and Sylvia, Two Shamvas.

HOLBORN, Empire (R. 11). — Nervo and Knox, Leon and Lucette, Peter Fannan, Toni Raglan, Billy Caryll and Hilda Mundy, Don Alfonso, Four Casting Pearls, Eddy Gray, Three Ehtor Girls, Jack Edge.

LONDON, Palladium (R. 11).—Second Edition of " Life Begins at Oxford Circus " (Mats. Wed. and Thurs. at 2.30).

PENGE, Empire (R. 12).—Julian Wylie's "Scrap Book of 1935 " (cast includes George Lacy, Doris Bransgrove, and Daisy Elliston).

PORTSMOUTH, Hippodrome (R. 12).—Will Mahoney in Radio New York, with Evie Hayes, Joe Griffin, Bob Garr, Omar, Ernest Shannon, Twelve Tiller Girls, The Six Greene Bros., Lennox and Loranna.

SOUTHAMPTON, Hippodrome (R. 12).—Company as booked.

WOLVERHAMPTON, Hippodrome (R. 12). — Nat Gonella and his Georgians, Lucan and McShane, Chick Farr and George Hughes, Tessie O'Shea, Victor Moreton, The Carson Sisters, etc., etc.

MOSS TOUR

BIRMINGHAM, Empire (R. 11) (low pitch). — Kitty Masters, Val Rosing and his Radio Rhythm Rascals, Windsor and Wilton, Claude Lester, The Jovers, The Juvelys, etc.

BIRMINGHAM, Theatre Royal (R. 11) (low pitch). Gladys Cooper and Raymond Massey in " The Shining Hour " (cast includes Adrianne Allen) (Mats. Thurs. and Sat. at 2.30).

BLACKPOOL, Opera House (R. 11) (low pitch).— " Hullo, Prosperity ! "

BRADFORD, Alhambra (R. 12.15) (low pitch).—Francis Laidler's " Red Riding Hood " (once nightly at 7) (Mats. Wed. and Sat. at 2).

EDINBURGH, Empire (R. 11) (low pitch).—Billy Cotton and his Band, Bower and Rutherford, Helen Mitchell and Dad, Bob and Alf Pearson, George Dormonde, Four Herzogs, Ju-Lio-San, Art Frank.

FINSBURY PARK, Empire (R. 11.30) (low pitch).—Tom Arnold presents The Houston Sisters in " More Dam Things " (cast includes Sara Preece, Alec Dane, Percy Val, Shirley Brent, Gloria Day, Fox and Evans, The Two Marconis, Rosalind Wade's Radiolympia Girls, Jack Daly).

GATESHEAD, Empire (R. 1) (low pitch).—Company as booked.

GLASGOW, Empire (R. 11). (low pitch).—Jack Taylor presents " King Folly " (cast includes Billy Bennett, Anton Dolin, Velda and Vann, Armand Band, Toni Stanella with Mexano's Accordion Band, Forty Mannequins, Darmora Can-Can Dancers, Pamela Foster).

GLASGOW, Alhambra (R. 11) (low pitch).—(For two weeks.) Lee Ephraim's Company in " The Gay Deceivers " (Mats. : Wed. and Saturday at 2.)

HULL, Palace (R. 11) (low pitch).—Roy Fox presents Peter Fielding with his Band, Du Roy Sisters, George Betton, Ted Ray, Five Cleveres, Murray and Mooney, etc., etc.

LEEDS, Empire (R. 11) (low pitch).—Ernie Lotinga and Company in " Up She Goes ! "

LEEDS, Theatre Royal (R. 11) (low pitch). — J. B. Priestley's " Eden End " (Mat. Tues. at 2.30).

LIVERPOOL, Empire (R. 11) (low pitch). — Georgia Players present Lew Leslie's " Blackbirds," with Valaida, and Company (2nd week) (Mats. Mon., Wed. and Sat. at 2.30).

LONDON, Hippodrome (R. 11) (low pitch).—Jack Waller presents " Yes, Madam ? " (cast includes Bobby Howes, Binnie Hale, Vera Pearce, Wylie Watson, Bertha Belmore, Billy Leonard) (Mats. Thurs. and Sat. at 2.30).

MANCHESTER, Palace (R. 11) (low pitch). — Tom Arnold's " Jubilee Revue " (cast includes Max Miller) (2nd week).

NEWCASTLE, Empire (R. 11) (low pitch).—" This Year of Carnival " (cast includes George Doonan and Lalla Dodd).

NEW CROSS, Empire (R. 11.30) (low pitch).—Les Allen and his Melody Four, Phyllis Robins, Bob Lloyd and Betty, The Dakotas, Billy Russell, Alma Victoria, Scott Sanders, Carvey and Mac, etc.

NOTTINGHAM, Empire (R. 12) (low pitch).—Hughie Green and his B.B.C. Gang, Jack Hart and his Broadcasting Band, Tamara, Herbert and Hatton, Paul Remos and his Toy Boys, Clarkson Rose, Olsen and Louise.

NOTTINGHAM, Theatre Royal (R. 12) (low pitch).— " Someone at the Door " (cast incudes Henry Kendall and Nancy O'Neill) (Mats. Wed. and Sat. at 2).

SHEFFIELD, Empire (R. 11) (low pitch).—" La Revue D'Amour " (Nat Mills and Bobbie).

SOUTHSEA, King's (R. 11) (low pitch). — " Sporting Love " (Mat. Thurs. at 2.30).

STRATFORD, Empire (R. 11.30) (low pitch). — Teddy Joyce and his Band, Georgie Wood and Co., Togo, Carvey and Mac, Nord and Jeanne, Karina with Vadio and Hertz, Chevalier Bros., Billy Russell.

SUNDERLAND, Empire (R. 11) (low pitch). — Archie Pitt, Ltd., present " Mr. Tower of London."

SWANSEA, Empire (R. 12) (low pitch).—Sandy Powell's Album, including The Harmonica Band, Sandy Powell, etc.

SYNDICATE HALLS

BRIXTON, Empress (R. 3).—Lily Morris, Naughton and Gold, Clayton and Bates, Bemand's Pigeons, Anderson and Allan, Sam Rayne, Peter Cotes, Welsh Miners' Quartette, The Gomez Hardy Trio.

METROPOLITAN (R. 3). — Will Fyffe, Talbot O'Farrell, Iris Whyte and Partner, Capt. Ricks, Ten English Roses, Welsh Miners' Quartette, Five Canadian Wonders, Ella Retford.

CHELSEA, Palace (R. 3.45).—Mrs. Jack Hylton and her Boys and Company.

SOUTH LONDON, Palace (R. 3).—Three Stars, Bula and Arnold, Syd Vernon, Nouvelle Sisters, Susie Ward, Seymour and Wills, Douglas Four, Arthur Worsley, Harry Taft, Nixon Grey, etc.

WALTHAMSTOW, Palace (R. 3.30).—" Beauties of the Night."

STOLL TOUR

CHISWICK, Empire (R. 11).—Ella Shields, Max and Harry Nesbitt, G. H. Elliott, Three Rhythm Sisters, Jackson Three, Sherkot, Stewart and Olive, Lena Brown, Reco and May, Empire Girls.

HACKNEY, Empire (R. 11).—James Shirvell presents " The Desert Song."

LONDON, Alhambra—Jack Buchanan in " The Flying Trapeze," Erik Charell Production, with June Clyde, Ivy St. Helier, Fred Emney.

LONDON, Coliseum—Andre Charlot's Musical Play, " Dancing City," with Lea Seidl, France Forester, Leslie Laurier.

MANCHESTER, New Hippodrome (Ardwick Green) (R. 11).—Gene Dennis, Mackey Twins, Vine, More and Nevard, Jack Stocks, Johnny Regan, Jean Florian, Dudley Dale and his Gang, Two Hoffmans, Betty and Pamela, Dezso Retter.

SHEPHERD'S BUSH, Empire (R. 11). — Layton and Johnstone, Three Astons, Shaw and Kennedy, Four White Flashes, Five Marywards, Joe Boganny, Max Wall, Ford and Chris.

---

because he had only seven or eight minutes as a rule – hardly time to register properly – and because the audience would still be settling down. Leslie Sarony had a lot of experience in this rôle.

'When I was in The Two Leslies, we were usually top of the bill; but when I was doing my own solo act I was usually on second, and I used to get so fed up with it; and I said to Val Parnell one day, "Why do you always put me on second?" He said, "You're booked as second act, and that's where you'll be – it's one of the most important acts on the bill." It wasn't until I ran my own show that I realized it was – it sets the pace for the whole show.'

After the second-spot comic there would usually be an acrobatic act, or a juggler, or a high-wire act. They would be on for perhaps five minutes. They would be followed by a comedian – someone like Dick Henderson, perhaps – who would play for about twelve minutes. Then the last act before the interval would be a 'feature act' – perhaps an acrobat or 'adagio' act (a cross between acrobatics and ballet) who had worked their act into a consistent theme, or who used props or scenery. They would do perhaps ten or twelve minutes.

Then would come the interval – eight or ten minutes – and the rush for the bar (most important). The first act after the interval would usually be the dancing act again, doing another three minutes to the distraction of people making their way *back* from the bar. They would be followed by a small speciality act – perhaps a paper-tearer (who would tear up a folded newspaper and pray that he came up with a pretty pattern at the end). This sort of act would be able to sustain only about five minutes.

The next act would depend upon what sort of act was top of the bill. It might well be another comic – perhaps a sketch act – but not if the top of the bill was also a comic act; if that was the case then this act might be a straight musical act. Sometimes this placing would be another appearance by the comic from the fourth spot in the first half, if it was an act who could come up with a sufficiently differentiated routine from their first appearance; but, at any rate in the 1930s, this was less usual.

Then came the star's act; the 'top of the bill'. Their normal length would be about twenty minutes – it was only in the 1950s that star acts began doing forty minutes or even the entire second half – except where the top of the bill was a band, who would be able to offer sufficient variety in their act to sustain a much longer placing (in which case there would be fewer supporting acts, of course). The Gracie Fields 'live' recording mentioned in the last chapter runs for some twenty-seven minutes; this might have been a longer timing allowed for an exceptional artist, but since the recordings have evidently been edited, it is possible that they combine items from different first and second house performances. Certainly twenty minutes was the usual maximum.

Oddly, to modern eyes, the star turn did not close the performance; there was always a small-time speciality act as a 'closer' – usually an acrobat or a juggler (obviously not a juggler if one had been on earlier). This was a thankless position to be in, because no-one was paying much attention to them; their main function was to prevent the inevitable early leavers in the audience making their rush for the exits during the star's act. There is an old joke in the business about the Chinese acrobat who has lost his

music; when asked by the conductor what tunes he normally has, he whistles three bars of 'Entry of the Gladiators' and then goes straight into the National Anthem.

The timing allowed for each act had to be rigidly adhered to. If a comic had been allocated eight minutes, he was expected to *do* eight minutes – not seven, and most certainly not nine. This sort of tight timing is not as difficult to achieve as it sounds – broadcasters do it as a matter of course, often to the second – but outsiders do not normally associate it with theatrical Variety. There was a very good reason for it: if every act over-ran by two minutes during first house, that would take up the whole of the break between first and second houses and keep the audience for the second house waiting. Similarly, if the second house over-ran, the audience would start leaving to catch its last buses and trains. Some theatres had coloured lights placed in the footlights – where the performer could see them but the audience couldn't – which would flash to warn him that he was coming to the end of his time.

The order of the acts having been decided upon, programmes and posters had to be printed. The programmes listed the acts, giving them numbers; many theatres had boards or lights at the side of the stage which would display the number, so that the audience was always clear who they were seeing. Even if the running order was changed – the manager could alter the order if he saw fit, but not after 12 p.m. on the Tuesday – the number matched that on the programme so that the identification of the artist was clear.

Brenda Thomas spent some time in Moss Empires' publicity department, dealing with posters.

'Every week we had posters and box-office cards drawn out; often they didn't get to the printer until the Tuesday – they were printed and sent out by the Thursday for the following week. The only advertising was by box-office cards – a 15 by 10 inches card hung up in shops and so on; leaflets; and double crown (20 by 30 inches) and quad crown (30 by 40 inches) posters which were posted round the towns – bill posting was very cheap. The local newspapers might have two lines in the classified ads the week before, and a couple of display ads during the week. We showed slides in the theatres; we had a vast number of slides – I should think we had a slide for every artist that ever appeared on Moss Empires – and they were shown in the intervals to advertise what was coming the next week.'

The posters had a traditional format (although as time went on it altered slightly and became more simplified). The star was placed in large letters at the top: 'top of the bill'. Confusingly, 'bottom of the bill' was not the smallest act, but the second most important; they were placed, in slightly smaller letters, at the bottom of the poster. The remaining acts were placed in between, in letters ranging from small to minute. The smallest billings were known as the 'wines and spirits' because they were in type no larger than the advertising for the bar, which was placed at the extreme bottom of the poster. Positions on the bill were jealously regarded – particularly as the best dressing-rooms went with the best positions. As time went on, the technique of giving more than one act star billing arose; the top of the poster would display two acts, one on the left and one on the right: 'first top' and 'second top'. The same technique led to 'first bottom' and 'second bottom' – and even these distinctions sometimes caused arguments from performers who felt they deserved a better placing.

All poster billings included what was known as the artist's 'bill matter', this being a short phrase intended to give some idea of their act. Nellie Wallace was billed as 'The Essence of Eccentricity', George Robey as 'The Prime Minister of Mirth', Stanley Holloway as 'Old Sam', and so on. This information had to be in to the office before posters could be printed, but as a back-up Moss Empires kept a large book with all the bill matters filed. If all else failed the office could make something up – old-time star Vesta Tilley's brother worked in the Moss publicity office, and, for example, any animal act for which he couldn't find the bill matter automatically became 'The Acme of Animal Training'.

Normally, of course, performers (or their agents) made up their own bill matter. Frequently they made up their names as well – Harry Tate's real name was Ronald Hutchinson, Gracie Fields's was Grace Stansfield, George Robey's was George Wade, and the comedian Vernon Watson made a joke out of his stage name – 'Nosmo King'. In this book the stage name has normally been used in preference to the 'real' name; and many artists disdain the use of the term 'real name', preferring to say 'family name', feeling – with some reason – that the stage name is just as real. What mattered, both with the name and the bill matter, was that they should stand out well on a poster.

With the week's show organized, advertised, and under way, it fell to the theatre managers to keep everything running smoothly. Louis Benjamin had graduated from being an office-boy to being a trainee assistant manager at the age of sixteen (very young for the job, but the second World War had just started and many managers were being called up into the forces). He acted as a relief at theatres such as the Penge Empire, the New Cross Empire and the Finsbury Park Empire.

'It was a very full day – one started in the morning by banking the money from the night before; and every week you had "special pay", which is overtime – the staff had their basic salary plus overtime for rehearsals and so on; you had to prepare the salary list, by hand, look after the petty cash, and actually pay the staff (in cash) on the Friday. These were just the morning chores. For the evening work, you had to have a dinner-jacket and a black tie – that and the laundry for it came out of your own £4 a week and no expenses. You got the first house in – standing on the front taking care of queries – then maybe you had a short break up to the interval, when you stood around in the bar (not drinking); there was the changeover – getting a 2,000-seater house out and in again in twenty minutes; same thing in the second house interval; taking the box-office sheets and making up the returns for head office; going round the bars collecting the cash; checking the sales of programmes, chocolates, ice-creams and so on; and then seeing the house out, dealing with any complaints. If you were through by 11.15 p.m. you were pretty efficient. You had time off from about 1 p.m. to 4.30 p.m. to change; a pretty good day, from about nine-thirty in the morning, and never home before midnight, six days a week, I loved it – I was young, I had a lot of energy.'

The manager of the theatre had absolute control; he was in full authority over the artists and the staff. This could also mean his being held responsible if anything went wrong. Sam Harbour was general manager of the Coliseum for forty years – and another manager who started at the bottom; he was a page-boy at the Trocadero restaurant when he happened to be the person who answered the phone and took a message from Sir Oswald Stoll, who wanted the manager to send round someone he thought suitable for a job in the Alhambra box-office. Harbour nipped round there smartly and got the job; he eventually became manager at the Alhambra before going on to the Coliseum.

He once found himself in court explaining why Max Miller – a stand-up comic with a reputation for being risqué – had gone somewhat too far with one of his jokes. (This was not unusual.) Harbour was able to convince them that Miller had put this joke into the act without Harbour's knowledge; but he was fairly lucky to get away with it (although at the worst he would only have been fined) because ultimately the manager took responsibility for everything that happened in his theatre.

The manager's duties also included writing reports on each act every week – reports which were filed at head office and formed the basis of the bookers' assessment of the act – and liaising with the representatives of head office who came round periodically to see that the theatre was kept in good repair. He also had charge of the theatre staff – in an average Variety theatre this could be as many as sixty or seventy, some of them perhaps part-time, including the orchestra who usually numbered about fifteen. Few artists brought their own Musical Directors (MDs) so the local MD had to be able to cope with anything.

Performers were paid, usually in cash, by the manager on the Friday. The salaries – which were of course arranged by head office, not locally – were fairly standardized for any particular type of act. In order to be able to make sense of both the salaries and seat prices of the time it is necessary to take the value of money into account.

Philip Hindin: 'In the 1930s, £3 a week was a very good salary – a clerk would get £2 10s [£2.50 in decimal coinage]; I was getting 17/6d [87½p] when I started – eventually I went up to 25s [£1.25] and I ran a car on that! – a six-horsepower Peugeot. Petrol was 10½d a gallon. A box of matches was a halfpenny; in 1939 I bought a brand-new Ford motor-car for £100; and a Rover – the poor man's Rolls-Royce – would cost you £600.'

Prices, on the whole, stayed fairly stable throughout the later 1920s and the 1930s, only rising noticeably when the war started.

These details are intended to throw performers' salaries into some sort of relief. The lowest level of salary for performers on Moss Empires would be about £12 for, say, a solo juggling act. Set against the details outlined above, this sounds a fair amount of money; but there were no additional expenses paid – the £12 had to cover props, costumes, lodgings, agent's fees, photos or other publicity expenses – and travel, which could come expensive if engagements were at opposite ends of the country. (The payment might be increased if the act had to get to Scotland from the south of England; but otherwise their travel costs were their own affair.)

Fees went up as the acts were bigger or better known – although there was little negotiation; a £25 act was a £25 act and that was the end of it – until the stars were being paid perhaps £200 a week. Of course, in all cases it must be remembered that any week that an act didn't work, it didn't get paid – which in some cases would cut the average wage down a fair amount. The very much higher fees that a small handful of stars could command – the

£1,000 or so level – arose not from a normal salary but from their being on 'a percentage' – a proportion of the profits; this was not normal until the second World War, when the whole business underwent an upheaval.

Even the seemingly high fees around £200 have to be considered in relation to the sometimes very high costs of running an act – expensive costumes, perhaps a couple of stage sets, a dresser and possibly an assistant or two, not to mention agent's commission and (always a terrible bugbear) income tax (paid half-yearly in arrears, to make matters more difficult – by the time it was due it had like enough been spent).

Naturally, whenever times were difficult – which was most of the time – fees came under pressure from the management. In the early 1920s various managements operated a 'mutual agreement' on salaries (a polite term for price-fixing)[1] and in 1931 the top circuits announced that they were actually cutting salaries above £20 by 15 per cent upwards, rising to a 50 per cent cut in salaries over £175.[2]

Seat prices remained fairly stable through the 1930s – there was always public resistance to increases, and when Moss Empires put the price of back stalls in the Finsbury Park Empire up from 1/6d to 1/9d they had empty seats for months. Typical seat prices would be from 6d in the 'gods' to 2/6d in the stalls and circle; seats in the posh boxes near the side of the stage would be 5s. The most popular seats would be around 1/6d to 1/9d – comparable with a suburban cinema. Obviously in poorer areas prices would be lower; while the Coliseum prices ranged (in the late 1920s) from 1s in the balcony, through 2 to 3 shillings in the grand tier, to 2s and 7/6d in the 'fauteuils' – stalls, in plain English.

To the managements' great annoyance, Entertainment Tax was payable on tickets; in 1931 this was raised to an average of 20 per cent of the price before tax; ½d on 2½d seats, 1d on seats up to 5d, 1½d on seats up to 7d, and so on. Already hard hit by the depression, the Variety industry felt the increase – which was necessarily passed on to the customers – as just another nail in the coffin.

The 1/9d, or whatever it was, bought more than just entertainment; all the bigger theatres were impressive in the extreme. Many Moss Empires were designed by Frank Matcham – who also designed the Coliseum – and they had a strong family resemblance, tending to superfluous towers on the outside and a good deal of Edwardian ornate plasterwork, plush seats and red carpets on the inside. The general atmosphere was one of impressive comfort – and indeed all the better-run theatres (and cinemas) were

**The Metropolitan Edgware Road
as it existed in 1903**

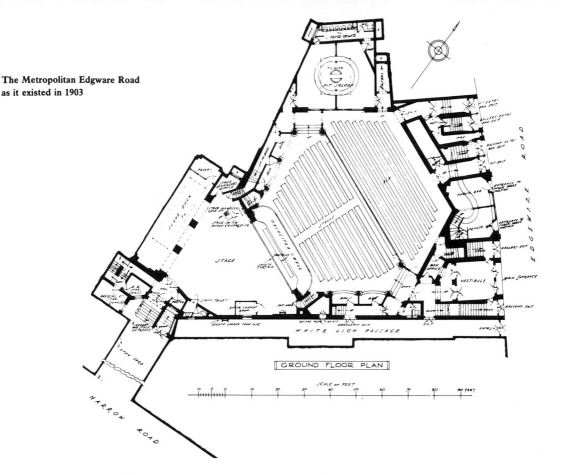

GROUND FLOOR PLAN

SCALE OF FEET

more comfortable and, in the winter, warmer than many people's homes. The actual sizes of the theatres varied; there were still a few of the old Victorian halls in use, with their deep and narrow auditoria, but one of the smaller of the more regular halls was the Holborn Empire. Its stage width was just over 30 feet, and the maximum depth of the auditorium from the proscenium was about 80 feet; this size made it easier for artists to obtain a rapport with the audience. The Metropolitan Edgware Road was slightly smaller (the stage was actually triangular, because the theatre was squeezed into an awkward site at the corner of Edgware and Harrow Roads).

At the other extreme was the Coliseum, with a stage width of over 80 feet, and a throw of over 115 feet from the stage to the back of the very wide balcony. It originally seated 2,200 – 47 less than Drury Lane – but in later years Sam Harbour persuaded the council to allow him to install a further 158 seats, thus making it the largest theatre in London in all respects. Most Moss theatres were between the Coliseum and the Holborn Empire in size, but most of the theatres run by the smaller circuits – the 'number twos' – were more intimate, and often a bit tatty.

At the head of all this activity in Moss Empires were Val Parnell and George Black. Black concerned himself

directly with the running of the Palladium; and both were responsible for the overall running of the circuit, including decisions about whether broadcasts should be allowed from theatres and other general policy matters. Parnell remained a shadowy figure until the death of Black in 1945 placed him in overall control, and changing times led him to make changes in the handling of the circuit in general and the Palladium in particular.

The structure of the business as described in this chapter – the agents, bookers, managers and so on – remained substantially unchanged even by the second World War (apart from an increase in 'combination' bills and shows mounted by agents and performers); but major changes would take place in the 1950s. The man who was to play a significant part in these changes was in the late 1930s an unimportant agent in partnership with Joe Collins; prior to that he had been a small dancing act whose only merit was that he danced the Charleston on top of a narrow table. The attraction was not that he danced it quite well, but that he could do it without falling off. His name was Lew Grade.

(*The subject of running the business is resumed in Chapter 25, p. 190.*)

10 'Too lazy to learn a comic song'
Acrobats: One (straight acrobatic and adagio acts)

There is an apocryphal story in the business which has been told about many comedians. On this occasion it is being told about Robb Wilton. Wilton was once standing with a friend on the side of the stage, watching a Japanese acrobatic troupe. They leapt off and on each other's shoulders; they sprang on and off chairs balanced on the tops of poles; they leapt and spun dangerously in mid-air. After some time watching this, Wilton turned to his friend. 'Look at that,' he observed sadly. 'All that, just because the buggers are too lazy to learn a comic song.'

This chapter, and a later one, is about that sort of act; acrobatic or what used to be called 'Risley acts' after Professor Risley, an acrobat of the previous century. Depending on the definition used, these acts could be classed as speciality acts; but for the purpose of this book non-acrobatic speciality acts have been dealt with in separate chapters. Of course, trying to provide adequate descriptions of a whole string of different acrobatic acts would be an exercise doomed to failure from the start – and a long list of names of acts belongs in an encyclopaedia, not here – so this chapter and its successor will deal with only a handful of acts, using them as the basis for an examination of some of the techniques.

Acrobats, as a style of act, had their origination in the different world of circus; and although there was no regular exchange of artists between the two media, many Variety acrobats had originally come either directly from circus, or from circus families. It has generally been assumed that, to be an acrobat, one has to be born into it – if not from the point of view of heredity, then because of the necessity of starting at an extremely early age. Certainly the majority of acrobats started this way.

Marée Authie, who as an adult worked in Variety as a dancer and contortionist, was the daughter of a con- certina-player and comedian called Tom Taylor; she began travelling round the halls with him as a baby, and by the time she was of school age was picking up acrobatic techniques:

'When I was about ten my parents wanted me to go to boarding school, and I didn't want to go; so they just travelled me around. I went to a different school every week; and learnt acrobatics, ballet and music from various acts that were on the bills. My back was loosened up by performers – I was always in the chorus-girls' dressing- room, and it would be "Come on, limber up, Marée" – and Jean Kent's mother was a ballerina, and Jean [who was later a film star] was travelled around; and we used to go down in the morning and her mother would teach us. So I learnt from everybody.'

Marée Authie, although trained from childhood, was not actually born into an acrobatic family. Rikki McCor- mick and his wife 'Copper' both came from such families. He had done a bit of everything by the time he married her in 1954; his family goes back hundreds of years as artists in circus, boxing, Variety, touring drama, acrobatics – and was reputed to have been jesters at the court of James I. After they married they did a cycling and tightrope act under various stage names, eventually settling on 'Del Oro' (and their son Richard carries on the tradition and the stage name with a tap-dancing, juggling and uni- cycling act).

Copper McCormick's father had been in the business as a gymnast and hand balancer from 1901; her mother had been in a juvenile troupe, and when they married they formed an acrobatic act:

'He was billed as "Buster Bandon, the Dandy Randy Daring Acrobat" . . . "randy" didn't mean then what it means now.[1] . . . and then, with my brother and me, we became "The Four Bandons". That caused a lot of prob- lems because we used to fix work by telegram, and bookers kept thinking we were a band. So we changed it to "The Four Astounderz" – it was going to be billed as "The A to Z of Acrobatics" but that sounded corny. We did the sort of aerial work you could do on a stage – a low-set trapeze and rings, and acrobatics and adagio work.' (Adagio work consists of acrobatic routines performed in a balletic style.)

Trapeze work in particular could normally only be seen in a circus, so the novelty of presenting even a scaled-down version of it on an ordinary stage made the Four Astounderz a popular act until it eventually broke up when Copper was hospitalized for TB during the second World War.

Many artists in this field came originally from circus:

Bob Konyot was born in 1915 into a European circus family, making his first appearance in the ring at the age of five. He came to England when he was seventeen with a springboard act, and worked mostly in this country from then on. As with so many acts, they started in the least important theatres – 'the number threes':

'You start in a little revue in the "number threes", and they give you eight minutes; if you do well, you spread yourself up to thirteen minutes. When you get up to the "number two" circuits, they cut you down again to eight minutes; so naturally you leave out the worst part of your act. When you go up to the "number ones", the same thing happens – so that's how you improve your act; you spread yourself, and then you were trimmed like a rosebush. So after you have done all this, and been in a few good shows, you had a good act.'

The first act he was with had seven men; then later two more were added, and afterwards Konyot took round his own act, again with nine men.

'We used to work from one springboard to another one, rather than doing tricks, because it was more showy; we flew from one side of the stage to the other, and so it was more exciting for the audience than seeing people turn a double somersault, or a treble . . . it means nothing unless the audience get excited about it – will you get on the springboard, or will you miss? You could only do this with people who had been together five or ten years, and today people don't stay together that long.'

Rikki McCormick ('Del Oro')

Rikki and 'Copper' McCormick ('Del Oro')

Half of the attraction of most acrobatic acts was that they looked dangerous; but the more sensible acts took few chances.

Konyot: 'We didn't have any accidents, because we didn't do anything amateurish. If someone somersaulted up to me on a two-man-high, or on a perch, it was always perfect; but there were a couple of men at the bottom to catch him *if* he missed. It's the same in adagio acts – you don't see cricketers missing a little ball, so a big person you cannot possibly miss! Of course, there are people who go up on a high wire, and in my book they're not performers, because if they did the same thing on a stage nobody would applaud – the only good thing about it is that they go up there, and that's an idiotic thing to do. The audience just come to watch you fall down! – like the Wallendas, they had a lot of accidents. It's like the stunt riders who jump a motor-bike over a lot of cars – they're idiots. Unless they know exactly what they're doing – there was a man called Gadbin, who used to jump from the top of the circus tent into a kind of chute, which broke his fall, and then he'd jump up and do a somersault. Many people did it after him, and many of them got killed; but Gadbin died in his bed – he was a professional.'

Konyot does not agree with the popular idea that acrobats have to be born into it.

'Many people started when they were in their twenties. If you are physically fit, you can pick up a lot of it – if you want to do it, and you have a good teacher – an acrobatic troupe can take a complete amateur with them in his twenties, and, being with good people, after only eighteen months he can come back a good acrobat. A lot of rubbish is talked about it being in the blood.'

Even by the late 1930s, audiences were beginning to be blasé about straightforward acrobatic acts, so Konyot based his act round comedy, having, for example, a man who did none of the stunts, but took all the bows. All the better acts either used comedy, or worked their performance round a central theme so that the tricks blended into a more interesting whole than simply being a collection of separate stunts in the circus tradition.

One of the absolutely top acrobatic acts – and one of the very few speciality/acrobatic acts ever to top a bill – was The Ganjou Brothers and Juanita. Technically they were an adagio act, which was the sort of act that originally consisted simply of a man and a woman, or more usually two men and a woman, doing leaps, throws and catches, and similar acrobatic tricks, in a balletic manner – the accent being on grace rather than speed. The Ganjous were the first act in Britain to use three men and a woman, thus being able to use two men to throw and one to catch, so that the girl could be thrown much higher in dizzying spins and curves.

The story of the family – the men were genuinely brothers, though Juanita was a stage name – is an involved one; if anyone wanted a romantic adventure story from the

The Ganjou Brothers and Juanita

world of Variety, this is it. The family name was originally Ganjoulevitch; the three sons, Serge, George and Bob (Bogdan) were born in Poland – their father was Russian and their mother Polish.

Serge Ganjou: 'When the first War started in 1914 we had to emigrate from Poland to Russia, first to Moscow and then the Ukraine. Then George and Bob went to south Russia after the revolution in 1917. Bob went to Turkey, and then to New York – he worked at all kinds of things; in a biscuit factory, a garage. . . . He had friends in the Russian Ballet over there. Some of the men weren't strong enough to lift the women dancers up, and Bob was very strong, and so he started working with them as an adagio dancer. [In old-fashioned ballet, the male dancer was merely a partner for the ballerina and was not expected to do the sort of spectacular dancing which is now normal.] He'd had no training as a dancer – none of us had.

'George went from the Ukraine to join the Polish Army; then he came back to Poland as a musician – flute and piccolo – he worked in a symphony orchestra in Warsaw, from where he went to Canada and the USA; he played in a symphony orchestra in America. I was a singer in Warsaw – I specialized in Russian gypsy songs with a guitar. The family had come back to Poland in 1922 – I

The Ganjou Brothers and Juanita

knew George was all right, because he'd been in Warsaw, but we didn't know what had happened to Bob since he went to Turkey.'

Bob had started doing a traditional adagio act with the Russian ballerina Natasha Natova, and one other man. When she got married, her husband had to be put into the act; and so, almost accidentally, was formed the very first adagio act with three men throwing one woman about. They were a sensation when they came to New York with the act, and were later copied by a number of other acts. They appeared in one of the earliest sound films, MGM's spectacular *Hollywood Revue of 1929* (billed simply as Natasha Natova and Company); the film still exists, and so the act can still be seen.

Shortly afterwards, Bob left Natova and started up a similar act with George and a Danish acrobat. They were billed for a short time as 'Pantus, Coatus and Vestus', then changing the name to 'Ganjou Brothers and Juanita'. They came to England in 1933, and Serge replaced the

Dane; in the same year they appeared in the Royal Variety Performance, together with two singers. They were billed as 'A Romance In Porcelain', and were dressed in the style of Dresden china figures. They toured the top circuits for many years, as well as working abroad, although in 1934 they had to find another Juanita in a hurry – the original girl, who had come with them from America, met an English boy in Blackpool and left the act to marry him. Her replacement was Joy Marlowe, who had been at the Italian Conti Stage School; after only a week or two's rehearsal the act was on tour again.

A generous excerpt from their act appears in the film *Variety Jubilee*, made by a small British company in 1943. At the back of the stage is a much enlarged version of an ornate clock; through an oval aperture beneath the face can be seen the pendulum, on which Joy Marlowe is posing as it swings. She then comes out of the clock, and the team begin their routine; after some simple dance movements they begin the complicated and dangerous-

KINGSTON EMPIRE
6.30   Twice Nightly   8.50
Monday, Nov. 14th, 1938, and during week

A few of the latest Gramophone Records

Olly Aston and his Empire Melody Masters — "Blue Devils"

1	ANNETTE & DURNO, Unicyclists De-Luxe.
2	WINNIE COLLINS & CHARLES BROOKS, Caught in a Storm.
3	SIX YUK CHING, Chinese Wonders.
4	FIELDS & ROSSINI, A Kouple of Komics.
5	SCOTT & WHALEY, The Original B.B.C. Corner-Men of the Kentucky Minstrels.
6	INTERVAL.—Stanley-Watson presents OLLY ASTON & HIS EMPIRE MELODY MASTERS. "Temptation Swing"

Continued on Next Page

looking acrobatic routines, and Joy Marlowe smiles bravely as two of the men spin her round or throw her, spinning rapidly, into the air for the remaining man to catch. She poses while the three men hold her aloft; two of the men hold her by a wrist and ankle each and swing her in an arc which increases to a full circle; then one man at a time, holding her by one wrist and ankle, spins round, passing her in mid-air to another man who continues the arc from her other side.

All this is performed elegantly and fitted in closely with the music – in this case 'The Blue Danube'. This was always an important feature in their act.

Serge Ganjou: 'We were the first act to do adagio work like a ballet, where every movement was done to the music. It was very very hard, and many times we would take our own Musical Director because it was so difficult for an ordinary MD – he had to know our movements and tempos. We were known in an American Variety paper as the most imitated act in show business, because later on even jugglers and speciality acts copied us and tried to work with music.'

The act usually began with music played by George and Serge, although this is omitted from the film mentioned above (they can be seen to be holding a flute and mandolin respectively at the beginning of the act, while a short dance is performed in front of the clock by the chorus girls).

As with all acrobatic acts, constant practice was necessary to keep the throws polished or to add new routines.

Serge Ganjou: 'We rehearsed by swinging her and running towards Bob, who was catching; then small throws, then bigger and bigger, until we were throwing her twenty-two feet up.'

Not surprisingly, Joy Marlowe was nervous before going on-stage.

'You're nervous every performance, because something can go wrong so quickly; it was a hard act mentally and physically.'

Serge Ganjou was also nervous: 'Every good artist is nervous before he starts the act – or he should be nervous. I was always nervous before I started moving on the stage, then I calmed down. If you miss a trick, you cover up somehow, and forget about it – because you've got so many tricks to make before you finish the act. After we've finished the act, on the way back to the dressing-room, *then* we'd start arguing why we messed up a trick!'

Joy Marlowe married Serge Ganjou, and the act went on – often touring abroad – until 1957. Bob went on to be dance director for a troupe of girls, George to be an agent, and Serge to run a Polish restaurant in Kensington and a small electronics factory; he also played an active part on the VAF committee. No other acrobatic act ever matched them in popularity, with the possible exception of Gaston and Andrée, a one-man-one-woman adagio act who – like the Ganjous – achieved the rare distinction for an adagio act of topping bills.

Acrobatic acts in general continued to be an important part of Variety bills; but as early as 1924 *The Performer* commented that legal restrictions on the use of children on-stage were preventing early training and causing a decline in the number of acrobatic performers.[2] As time went on the old-fashioned large troupes disappeared, to be replaced by smaller acts who, to retain the interest of the audience, increasingly had to find 'gimmicks' which would make their act different in some way from the others.

(*The subject of acrobats is resumed in Chapter 23, p. 182.*)

11 An Ass?
Variety and the law

We have already seen how the Music Hall Strike of 1907 led first to the 1913 Arbitrator's Award, which was not obligatory, and then the 1919 Award Contract, which was; not only did it provide better protection for performers, but managements were obliged to use it, and not allowed to make alterations in it.

The Award set out a standard form of contract into which only the fee and details of the place and type of act might be written. The artist(s) would be engaged for one week for 'the number of performances usually played at the theatre (such number not to exceed twelve)'; all extra performances were to be paid at one-twelfth the agreed fee. (Marée Authie's husband was once appearing at a theatre run by a committee consisting of local mineworkers; they said they couldn't afford the one-twelfth for a matinée, and would he accept one-sixth?) In the case of a troupe, or a company such as a sketch act, the leading artist agreed to furnish the manager with names and nationalities of his colleagues (if so required), and not to vary or substitute performers.

The management were allowed to transfer artists to another theatre at short notice, but with the consent of the artists (such consent 'not to be unreasonably withheld'), and provided they paid all actual expenses involved plus an extra 5 per cent of the salary if the transfer involved a journey of more than thirty miles. This sort of situation could arise if an act at another theatre had become ill, for example.

The matter of 'barring clauses', which had been a major source of discontent in earlier times, was properly defined; they were designed to prevent an artist appearing at an opposition theatre too close – both in time and distance – to the performance in question. By signing the contract the artists agreed not to perform, or to give consent to the giving of any 'colourable imitation' by others of his performance (including 'moving pictures or cinematograph shows') within the time or distance specified. The distances were: in the West End of London – 1 mile; for suburban theatres in the Metropolitan Police District – 2 miles; and for theatres in the provinces – 3 miles. (These restrictions were placed on the *artists*; we have already seen that Moss Empires would not book artists to theatres closer than 20 miles for several months.) The times specified in the contract were: in the West End – 16 weeks; in the Metropolitan Police District – 32 weeks; in the provinces – 40 weeks. These time bars operated for the period *prior* to the engagement; in the case of the provinces artists also agreed not to appear within the following two weeks.

These restrictions were not as onerous as they look on paper, since there were still plenty of theatres outside the specified distance; and it was in any case in the artist's own interest not to appear too often and cause his welcome to go stale. (There were also some minor variations permitted in special cases, such as low-paid artists.)

The artist also agreed to comply with local regulations – such as fireproofing of scenery and props – not to be vulgar (in word or gesture), to ensure that his act was not dangerous to the public, and to arrive at the theatre on time and sober. Provision was made for situations such as illness, unexpected closure of the theatre, and so on.

These provisions may sound as if they were entirely designed to protect the management, rather than the artist – although the requirements were quite reasonable – but the agreements on extra performances and transfers in particular were much more favourable than in the 1913 Award.[1] Extra protection was provided for young persons under sixteen. Under the Children's Dangerous Performances Act, 1879[2] it was illegal for children to take part in any public performance or exhibition which was 'dangerous to life and limb' (which would seem to rule out appearances by young acrobats, though not their training – it all depends on the definition of 'dangerous').

Much tighter restrictions on the employment of children in general – theatrical appearances included – came with the Education Act of 1921.[3] No boy under fourteen or girl under sixteen might appear between 9 p.m. and 6 a.m.; indeed for anyone under fourteen the hours were *8 p.m.* to 6 a.m. No children under twelve might appear at any time, this being an absolute prohibition; and for those above twelve a licence was required, which would be granted only if the local authorities were satisfied as to the child's welfare and health. Furthermore, no child under sixteen might even be *trained* as an acrobat, contortionist or circus performer unless the courts were thoroughly satisfied as to the fitness of the child, and that proper provision had been made to secure its 'health and kind treatment'.

Marée Authie made her first stage appearances at the age of twelve.

'If you went on the stage in England you had to have a licence – which was a very complicated business – but in Scotland you didn't need a licence, so we went up there and I started in the act. Then when I was fourteen we went into a circus in Ireland [where British law did not hold anyway] and then into the proper theatres in England.'

Copper McCormick was taken to Scotland by her family for the same reason.

'You didn't need a licence, but you still had to pass a health examination and an educational one in some of the Scottish towns; and I went to school each week and took these exams.'

Florence Desmond – then still unknown Florence Dawson – was working in England before she was fourteen and so had to be licensed.

'Every week before I opened I used to have to go before a Magistrate's Court . . . "Do you get plenty of food, my dear? – what about your education?" . . . I told them I went to school in the mornings – I had no schooling at all! And Noël Coward had exactly the same life.'

Marée Authie was not allowed to get away with this sort of thing in Scotland.

'There was no playing hookey – you weren't neglected just because you were only there for a week – they were very hot on it, looking at what I'd done and perhaps saying "She ought to be further on than this". And I had to be out of the theatre by nine – if there was a child act on in Variety, the second half had to be timed so they were not just off the stage, but out of the theatre by nine.'

By the 1920s nearly every aspect of the Variety world was legally controlled. As we have seen, theatrical managers and animal trainers had to be licensed; and agents operating within the London area (as most of them did) had to be registered under the London County Council (General Powers) Act of 1921.[4] Theatrical premises themselves were licensed, under the provision of the 1843 Theatres Act. In London, they were licensed by the Lord Chamberlain (the LCC also imposing a number of safety rules, such as number of exits, size of gangways and so on); outside London they were licensed by the local councils.[5] To complicate matters further, those places where the sovereign 'Occasionally resided' were licensable by the Lord Chamberlain during the residence of the monarch – a hangover from the Lord Chamberlain's original function of protecting the monarch (and, where necessary, God) from impertinent on-stage references.

These licensing regulations were under the practical control of the local Watch Committees – a descendant of the local policing bodies of medieval times – run by the local council; magistrates granted the licences on a yearly basis, but the responsibility for keeping an eye on the theatres and making sure that they complied with the regulations lay with the Watch Committees.

This was where the fun really started. The regulations just described were intended to control the physical condition – and hence the safety – of the theatres. Theatrical fires had been all too common in previous times; and with the coming of cinemas (whose films were on a highly inflammable base of cellulose nitrate until 1945) strict fire regulations were (very properly) enforced. However, no self-respecting Watch Committee could be expected to leave matters at that. From the earliest days of the cinema, Watch Committees started prohibiting certain classes of film, and generally censoring the medium – something they probably had no actual *legal* right to do; and in the theatre they maintained a strict – often ludicrously strict – control over the subject-matter on show.

Birmingham was notorious – it was known in the Variety business as 'the holy city'. Members of the Watch Committee would often turn up to performances and be ready to pounce on even the mildest innuendo. On one occasion before the first World War, or so the legend goes, a visiting ballet company upset the Watch Committee because the ladies exhibited a little too much bare leg. They were ordered to wear tights. Some weeks later George Robey appeared at the same theatre, performing with accompaniment from an on-stage piano. It took the audience some time to realize that the legs of the piano were decently covered – with Aston Villa football socks. Robey was summonsed for contempt of council and fined.

That was an extreme case, but there was a lot of often very silly interference with performers' material. Jokes which are so mild that nowadays it is very difficult to see what all the fuss was about were censored, and the regular appearances of Watch Committee members in the audience boxes were much resented by Variety comedians. The silliest point about the whole thing was that there was *already* a theatrical censor – who was strict enough by any reasonable standards – the Lord Chamberlain's Office.

Any play, or any performance coming within the definition of a 'stage play' – and this included solo acts if they were included in a revue for which an overall licence was required – had to be submitted for reading (together with a fee for two guineas [£2.10]) before it could be performed in public; and any deletions or alterations required by the Lord Chamberlain's representatives had to be rigidly adhered to.

Even tiny deviations were strictly speaking illegal (although it was usually only alterations which were thought to be vulgar, obscene or dubious that resulted in prosecution). Under the original terms of the 1843 Act the licence of any theatre where such an offence was committed was automatically cancelled, but this unreasonably harsh ruling was relaxed in 1925[6] to permit magistrates to impose a fine (on the theatre), or to suspend the licence for a period. The prosecutions would be brought, in the provinces, by the Watch Committee; and it was not uncommon for managers and performers to be in trouble because a comedian had surreptitiously re-instated a line which had been deleted from his act.

The whole matter of theatrical censorship provoked row after row in the first twenty years of this century (although matters quietened down with the appointment in 1922 of Lord Cromer, who seemed to be able to handle the theatrical profession with more tact than his predecessor); but the battles were fought entirely in the field of serious drama, and so are not considered in this book. (Neither are the battles of the 1950s which eventually led to the abolition of censorship in 1968. For a detailed account of the story, see *Banned!*, written, shortly before the abolition, by Richard Findlater.[7]) In the field of Variety performers merely did their best to comply with the regulations, or to evade them without being noticed.

Since all scripts submitted for a licence were filed (and later transferred to the British Library Manuscript Collection) it is possible to examine a number of Variety acts (the collection has been the source for some of the extracts in this book) and also to see what sort of jokes caused the censor to wield his blue pencil (it really *was* blue). Solo comics were not required to be licensed, unless they were part of a revue, but double and sketch acts, and entire shows, were. Looking at the reasons for complaint nowadays, it is difficult to assess them in the light of the period. The husband-and-wife double-act Nat Mills and Bobbie brought a query (it is not clear whether it was actually deleted) with: 'But you know what we men are – we're born hunters' – 'Yes, and you're none too careful what you do with your bows and arrows'. A reference in a monologue by northern comedian Frank Randle to 'Barney's Bull'[8] was allowed before the second World War, but banned after it. A moment in a sketch by cockney comedian Leon Cortez where a small boy whispers in his father's ear and is told 'It's over there' was cut. 'Damn' and 'bloody' were cut as a matter of course.

More understandable – although it must have scuppered the entire sketch – was a cut in a sketch in the 1943 edition of Clarkson Rose's show *Twinkle*. A character called Eddie, who is drunk, is lent a (brightly coloured) pair of pyjamas by Rose ('Clarkie'), so that he can put them on over his dress suit, and when he goes to bed his wife will wake up and see them and think he has been there for some time. He enters the bedroom, wearing the pyjamas over his suit; and the censor deleted the final line:

WIFE: Good heavens, Clarkie, haven't you gone home yet? – Eddie will be home any moment.

The Crazy Gang, of course, had more trouble than most. Often their scripts would simply say 'business' to cover a far from innocent piece of visual clowning; when asked what that was supposed to mean George Black would try to waffle round it. They didn't get away with this verbal gag:

'BESSIE' (NURSE):   That reminds me, you want your castor oil.
'WILLIE' (IN BED):   When I've had my castor oil, can I get up?
'BESSIE':   Will you be strong enough to get up?
VOICE FROM BOX: He won't be strong enough to stay in bed.[9]

Many of the objections raised look so pathetic today that one is tempted to wonder what the point of the whole exercise was; but there were always the tattier comedians who would slip in smutty (and usually unfunny) jokes given half a chance.

Ted Gollop thinks that on the whole it was a good thing because Variety was meant for a family audience (and children were much more sheltered then) and smut would only bring it into disrepute. (The effects of censorship on serious drama are not part of this discussion.) Variety performers just accepted it, usually without rancour; and in fact the Actors' Association actually opposed attempts to remove censorship, because they were afraid that if local authorities were given sole control (which would have been the alternative – as it has been since 1968[10]) actors would find themselves in a much more precarious position.

In theory, once a script had been passed by the censor, it was safe to perform it anywhere; and anyone doing so was safe from prosecution under the obscenity laws. In practice, although Watch Committees could not prosecute a performance without warning, they frequently required cuts and changes in scripts already approved by the Lord Chamberlain; failure to comply with these *would* lead to prosecution and fines. Although, from the point of view of the managers and performers, it was a safer situation than allowing the local authorities to take over the Lord Chamberlain's function completely, it was still a confusing situation for everyone caught in it. A query to the Lord Chamberlain's office in 1925 about the right of Watch Committees to censor scripts which he had already passed brought the answer that 'the local licensing authorities undoubtedly have the power to impose conditions when granting stage play licences to *buildings* within their jurisdiction' and therefore could refuse to renew if there had been 'impropriety'; they admitted that this produced an anomaly without offering any solution.[11]

In fact neither the Local Government Act of 1888 nor the 1843 Theatres Act gave local authorities specific powers to censor scripts; the only remotely applicable comment is in section 9 of the Theatres Act, which says that 'The said justices of the peace . . . shall make suitable rules for ensuring order and decency at the several theatres licensed by them' and to regulate the times at which they might open; 'in case of any riot or breach of the said rules' the theatre could be closed. It is strongly arguable that 'order and decency' was intended to refer to the behaviour of the *audience*, leaving the *performance* to the jurisdiction of the Lord Chamberlain; but since Watch Committees could easily prevent renewal of the licence to use the building as a theatre, their right to censor became established. (It was a nonsense that was never resolved, particularly in the case of cinema films where local authorities continued to over-rule the official censor even in recent times.[12])

However, it is agreeable to be able to record one occasion when the Lord Chamberlain's office must have been asleep; the following gag by Leon Cortez – part of a sequence of stand-up jokes within his 1939 show *'Appy 'Arf 'Our* – was passed without demur:

Met a nice girl this morning, she'd been out shopping with her arms all full of parcels. What struck me most was the way she was dressed all in the latest fashion – tightly cut jacket – striped skirt, with a hip pocket just like us men.

Crossing the road she dropped her handkerchief. I picked it up and said, 'Excuse me, madam, you've dropped your handkerchief'. She said, 'It's very nice of you to pick it up – I've got my arms full of parcels – would you mind putting it in my pocket?'

I put it in her pocket, and I've never felt such an ass in all my life.[13]

12 'Our 'Erbert's fell in the river'
Sketch comics: Two (the 1930s)

As we saw in Chapter 4, there was already in the 1920s a move away from comedy sketches consisting merely of one-line gags towards better-constructed sketches making more use of character observation. This trend continued during the 1930s; but even so there were plenty of old-fashioned comics around. Ernie Lotinga was a sketch comic who maintained much the same sort of humour in his acts right through to the 1950s. Apart from his Variety appearances – where he was normally only a supporting act – he also wrote several full-length comedy plays. They are rather mechanically constructed, and the sketches for which he was better known are similarly written, using any excuse for a gag in the same manner as Fred Karno.

Usually Lotinga played a character called 'Jimmy Josser' who would appear in all the familiar situations – in the police, in the army, on a farm, and so on. In this example, however – which dates from the early 1930s – his character is called Drinkwater; thus allowing a string of puns on the name: Pinkwater, Stinkwater, Bathwater . . . He is supposedly running a matrimonial agency; one of his clients is an attractive French lady called LaBlanc.

LABLANC: Monsieur la Drink-Water?
LOTINGA: No, I never touch it – I only drink whisky. Now, what's your name, madman . . . madam.
LABLANC: I am Madame LaBlanc.
LOTINGA: You've had some what?
LABLANC: I am Madame LaBlanc.
LOTINGA: You've had some ham and blancmange?
LABLANC: No, no, no – my name it is Madame LaBlanc.
LOTINGA: Of course, how silly of me – I'll put that down. How do you do, Mrs Blancmange? How's your little sister Jelly, I mean Nellie? Sit down and mind you don't wobble off. Now what can I do for you?
LABLANC: Oh, Monsieur – I have something on my mind – I can not sit still.
LOTINGA: You've got something on your mind and you can't sit still? Something on

your *mind* and you can't sit still?
LABLANC: Oui, oui, Monsieur.
LOTINGA: Are you sure it's on your mind? Oh, I should stand if I were you, lady.[1]

Lotinga was still performing similar material in the 1950s, which can have done nothing to increase Variety's life expectancy.

There were plenty of small-time artists offering material no better than that but the better quality artists were using character observation to build their sketches. Horace Kenney presented a mournful old cockney who had an exaggerated idea of his own abilities. In 'A Music Hall Trial Turn' he offered a new act – the Fearless Fireman and Happy Laughing Cobbler Song – to a theatre manager who could not believe anyone could be so awful. In 'The Stagehand's Impromptu' his highest ambition was to be the man who swept up the orange peel in the stalls (so that

Horace Kenney – 'The Trial Turn'

he could make a fortune selling it to the marmalade manufacturers). In 'Almost A Film Star' he attempted to sell his personality to a film producer:

PRODUCER: What kind of parts have you played?

KENNEY: I've played all kinds, sir.

PRODUCER: *All* kinds?

KENNEY: Yes, sir, all kinds.

PRODUCER: Have you ever played leads?

KENNEY: Leeds, Sheffield, Manchester . . .

PRODUCER: No, I mean leading parts.

KENNEY: Yes, sir, I've played leading parts.

PRODUCER: Well, who are you – what's your name?

KENNEY: My card, sir. (*Hands producer a card*) The name's in the middle.

PRODUCER: I can see that. What's this? – 'Horace Kenney, Comedian and Turf Adviser'? In other words you're a racing tipster as well?

KENNEY: Well, I do a bit of that in the summer-time, sir.

PRODUCER: In the summer-time!

KENNEY: Yes, sir. In the winter I go back on the stage again and . . . make the people laugh.

PRODUCER: After making them cry all through the summer, I suppose.[2] You say you've played leading parts?

KENNEY: Yes, sir.

PRODUCER: What in?

KENNEY: I played in *The Face at the Window*.

PRODUCER: *The Face at the Window*?

KENNEY: Yes, sir.

PRODUCER: And what did you play in that?

KENNEY: The face.

PRODUCER: The face?

KENNEY: Yes, sir. I had to show me face at the window four times, and go, 'Oooh, ooh, ooooh, ooooooh'.

PRODUCER: Oooh, ooh, ooh?

KENNEY: Yes, sir. And every time I showed my face, somebody committed a murder.

PRODUCER: After seeing your face. I can well understand it. Now, what other 'leading parts' have you played?

KENNEY: A camel.

PRODUCER: A *camel*?

KENNEY: Yes, sir – I played a camel in *The Sons of the Desert*.

PRODUCER: A *camel*?

KENNEY: Well – I played the head and front legs of the camel, sir.

PRODUCER: Do you call that a *leading* part?

KENNEY: Well, it was the leading part of the camel.[3]

It is the continual repetition as much as the actual jokes that make Kenney's material look old-fashioned today; but audiences were prepared to take their humour more slowly then, and half the attraction of the act was Kenney's characterization as the doleful old cockney.

This sort of character-building was important to many acts. Claude Dampier, for example, built a convincing slow-witted and literal-minded character – aided by his looks; his teeth seemed to be three sizes too large. He was normally partnered by his wife, Billie Carlyle, whom he

Claude Dampier

had met in Australia while touring in 1926; perhaps they should be regarded as a double-act, but she was a straightforward – though effective – stooge to him, rather than indulging in cross-talk; she had her own charm, but Dampier could still work well without her, or with another performer. She did, however, help to write his material, and in that respect brought her own perception to the act.

Dampier made great use of an imaginary character, 'Mrs Gibson', who was invented by accident. On the Australian tour during which he met Billie Carlyle, Dampier one evening (30 August 1926) forgot which sketch he was supposed to be in. While trying to remember what cue to give Billie for her entrance, he pretended to spot a friend, Mrs Gibson, in the audience, and improvised patter on the 'How are you, haven't seen you for years' line while he tried to remember what he was supposed to be doing; then making a joke of it because she turned out not to be 'Mrs Gibson' after all. It went down well, and became a regular feature of the act; when they came to Britain in 1927 to tour in Variety he always included some patter about Mrs Gibson's doings.

A similar inclusion in a broadcast got him into trouble with the BBC on one occasion: he said that Mrs Gibson was in bed ill, and the doctor had put her on a diet of nuts and orange juice; he was rushing away because he had 'promised to squeeze Mrs Gibson's oranges'. This phrase upset some BBC official and Dampier was banned from broadcasting for three months[4] (thus demonstrating Ronald Frankau's dictum that 'to the pure there's *nothing* pure').

This extract from a broadcast illustrates something of his relationship with the off-stage Mrs Gibson:

BILLIE: Claude, is there any necessity for you to carry that large suitcase with you wherever you go?

CLAUDE: This? Oh, I always carry this wherever I go.

BILLIE: Why?

CLAUDE: Good gracious – I always do – you don't know what's in it, I'll bet.

BILLIE: I'm afraid I don't – what is there?

CLAUDE: You wait till I show you – you'll be surprised when you see it . . . there you are. Have a look at that – what would you think that was?

BILLIE: Well, it looks like a very ordinary umbrella to me.

CLAUDE: No, no, don't jump at conclusions – have a good look at it.

BILLIE: I don't know – if it isn't an umbrella, what is it?

CLAUDE: It's a present from Mrs Gibson!

BILLIE: Yes, but why carry an umbrella in a case – it isn't raining anyway.

CLAUDE: Oh, I know – but Mrs Gibson made me promise that I'd always carry it, in case.

BILLIE: But she didn't mean to carry *in* a case!

CLAUDE: Well that's what she said – always carry it in case.

BILLIE: No, she means in case it rains!

CLAUDE: No . . . what! . . . Oh, good gracious – I never thought of that – and I bought the case specially for it![5]

Just as it was as much Mrs Gibson as his characteristic delivery and appearance that made Claude Dampier popular, it was an off-stage lady who made Sandy Powell famous – his mother. In real life his mother, Lily Powell, was a music-hall entertainer in a small way, and Sandy worked with her on the halls in his early days; he was born in 1900 and by 1912 was doing solo comedy as well. It was twenty years later, in a radio broadcast, that he found his catchphrase. He was doing a sketch in which he was supposed to be reporting from the north pole against a background of noisy weather and poor reception. The line 'Can you hear me, Mother?' had been written into the script, arising from the background noises; but Powell dropped his script and had to improvise while he picked it up. He used the phrase several times in this improvisation, and then forgot about it; at his next theatrical appearance he found that he had inadvertently created a popular catch-phrase which audiences expected to hear, so he included it in his act from then on.

In the 1920s Powell was working the halls only as a small act, doing stand-up comedy and sketches. He had begun in comedy, as did so many people, by doing impressions.

'I used to do Harry Lauder, Harry Weldon, Jack Pleasants, the original George Formby; and the man running this little show said, "Who do you like best? You've got to plan your style on somebody." I said, "Harry Weldon", who was a big star in those days ["Stiffy the Goalkeeper" in the Fred Karno football match sketch]; and that's how I started, doing an impression of Weldon.'

It was gramophone records, rather than stage

appearances, that made him famous even before his catch-phrase was invented.

'I think there's more luck in show business than in any other profession in the world. I was working the London Palladium [in May 1929] as quite a small act; and the recording people asked me to go and make a record. I went to the studio, and I said, "I don't sing – what am I going to do?" I didn't think about sketches and talking – so they said, "Well, what are you doing at the Palladium?" I said, "A little comedy sketch called 'The Lost Policeman' ", and they said, "We'll try that and see how it works." So I did it; it was exactly word for word as I was doing it on the stage.'

Sandy Powell and 'Little Peggy' – 'The Lost Policeman'

The sketch was issued – without any special publicity – on cheap eight-inch 'Broadcast' records. Powell was offered a flat fee of £60, with the record company retaining the rights, or a session fee of £30 plus a royalty of 1½d per record. He took the chance on the royalty; and the record sold nearly half a million copies.

He was assisted on the record by 'Little Percy', a small boy, and it provides a useful preservation of his complete stage act. Like Robb Wilton, he poked fun at the official mind's love of taking down particulars – as well as its incompetence – but his sketch is slightly unusual in that Percy, although theoretically the stooge, gets most of the laugh lines.

SANDY: Oh, what a life, what a life to be a policeman. You know, I've been on my beat all day, I haven't had one case yet, not one case. Hullo, here's a little boy coming along – I wonder what he wants. Hullo, son – what's the matter?

PERCY: Can you tell me where I can find a policeman, please?

SANDY: I beg your pardon?

PERCY: Can you tell me where I can find a policeman, please?

SANDY: What do you think I am, a sea-lion or something? Why – what do you want a policeman for?

PERCY: Our 'Erbert's fell in the river.

SANDY: Your 'Erbert's fell in the river? Oh, I *am* sorry, really I am. Your 'Erbert's fell in the river, eh. Oh, it *is* a shame – has he – er – has he been in the river very long?

PERCY: Oh no, just now.

SANDY: Just now? Oh, well, that isn't so bad, then. He'll get used to it when he's been in a bit, you know. Has he ever been in a river before?

PERCY: No.

SANDY: Oh, well, it'll be a change for him, then. Can your 'Erbert swim?

PERCY: No.

SANDY: Oh, well now's his chance to learn, then. Well I'll take a few particulars down if you don't mind . . .

PERCY: But what about our 'Erbert?

SANDY: It's all right, now – I'm doing my best. I'm going to take it all down. I'm going to get my book out – 'the above have arrived' – oh, that's the wrong one. Ah, this is the one . . .

PERCY: What about our 'Erbert?

SANDY: All right, now give me a fair chance, now, give me a fair chance. Now your 'Erbert's in the river, isn't he?

PERCY: Yes.

SANDY: That is one boy in one river. Now, what is your name, please?

PERCY: It's not *me* that's in the river, it's our 'Erbert.

SANDY: I know all about that – I want to know who *you* are. I know where your 'Erbert is – he's in the river. I want to know your name. And anything you say will be taken down and used in your favour against you. Now, what is your name, please?

PERCY: Percy.

SANDY: Percy. And where were you born?

PERCY: London.

SANDY: Born in London – what part?

PERCY: All of me.

SANDY: Another one like that and you'll be where your 'Erbert is. And do you live in London?

PERCY: Yes.

SANDY: Yes, well how long have you lived in London?

PERCY: Fifteen years.

SANDY: Fifteen years. How old are you?

PERCY: Twelve.

SANDY: And we don't want any sarcasm at all. And have you lived in London all your life?

PERCY: Not yet.

SANDY: You're just about my size, you are, you know. Now – have you got a mother and father at all?

PERCY: What about our 'Erbert?

SANDY: I know, I know where he is – he's in the river, isn't he?

PERCY: Yes.

SANDY: Well, it's all right – I can't do two things at once. Have you got a mother and father?

PERCY: I've got a father, but I haven't got a mother.

SANDY: You haven't got a mother?

PERCY: No.

SANDY: Have you never had a mother?

PERCY: No.

SANDY: I must put that down. Now, you've got a father, haven't you?

PERCY: Yes.

SANDY: Does your father work?

PERCY: Yes.

SANDY: Shame. Well – how long has your father been in his present position?

PERCY: Three months.

SANDY: Three months? And what is he doing?

PERCY: Six months.[6]

The tremendous popularity of 'The Lost Policeman' led to a whole succession of records on the Broadcast and Rex labels. The sketches were mostly specially written for the records, rather than being based on stage work, and presented him as all manner of things – a goalkeeper, a farmer, a gangster, a boxer – even a nudist. Altogether he recorded eighty-one double-sided sketches, many of which sold extremely well.

'When they play one of my old records, to me they're so corny! They were good fifty years ago . . . and a lot of today's comics still do gags that I did fifty years ago on those records! I remember, I was working at the Holborn Empire, and I said to the recording people, "Why don't we try it with an audience? Let me record on the stage." You'd have thought I was going to destroy the world!'

It is a pity they did not listen to him – he made the suggestion to them in the late 1920s, and they might have beaten the Gracie Fields recording to be the first live

Variety record. Even so, it was the records that made his name.

'I used my stage work to advertise the records, rather than the other way round.'

By 1930, although still not a big star, he had done so much work in Variety that Val Parnell was refusing to book him, claiming that he was 'worn out'.

'I couldn't get any work – and the records were doing well – so I put on a little show, very cheaply, with two or three of my pals; I put them all on a percentage. We called it "Sandy Powell's Road Show", and that was my jump into the big money and big success. That ran for ten years.'

The show's success was an irritant to many other producers. Their shows, with spectacular sets and a huge cast, were flopping, while 'Sandy Powell's Road Show', with only a handful of performers and two backdrops, was doing good business.

'George Black came up when we were at the Empire Newcastle; it was a full house and the show went well, and after first house he came round to see me in my dressing-room. I said, "I hope you were satisfied with the show, Mr Black." He said, "I didn't see it. I think I should spoil it – I should make a lot of suggestions; it'd cost you a lot of money – you'll have a troupe of girls and be paying hundreds of pounds a week for star supporting acts – so I've no intention of seeing it. You keep sending me the box-office returns, and we'll all be happy."'

Powell continued working, in his own shows and then later in summer season, until his death in 1982. His most popular act was his spoof ventriloquist turn.

'I was running my own little show, and I had a ventriloquist who was supposed to be very good. He was *terrible*. then I sacked him and got another one – he was worse, if anything. So I thought, how can I get my own back on these fellows! So I bought a doll and just put it in the show as a gag to amuse myself. It developed into my living, really, for twenty years. Wherever I go, people say "Oh, you must do the vent."'

The ventriloquist sketch was a classic skit; Powell, dressed as a Chelsea Pensioner, obviously had no ability whatsoever to talk without moving his lips, and was interrupted by a lady – usually played by his wife, Kay.

SANDY: Now, tell me, my little man – how are you this evening? (*Clamps his jaw shut under his moustache and produces unintelligible spluttering noises. He promptly chokes*) . . . I shall be all right in a minute. He says he's very well. (*To doll*) So you're very well, are you? (*More unintelligible noises*) Tell me – have you any brothers and sisters? (*More noises*)

(*Enter Kay*)

KAY: Here – I say – I saw your lips move then!

SANDY: You mind your own business.

KAY: Well I did, I was only standing here . . .

SANDY: My own flesh and blood! Now don't interfere, please. Every man to his own trade. I'm talking to my little friend. (*To doll*) Now tell me, sonny, was your father a soldier? . . . 'Oh, no . . . he was . . . (*splutter*)'

KAY: No, I don't eat meat either.

SANDY: 'And when he joined the army . . . (*splutter*)' . . .

KAY: I said, I don't eat meat either.

SANDY: Meat?

KAY: No.

SANDY: We're not talking about meat? We're talking about his father!

KAY: I know; well, he says his father was a vegetarian.

SANDY: No, no, what he said . . . (*gestures emphatically with his right hand, forgetting that it is inside the dummy*) I was here, I can prove it . . . (*the dummy's head has come away from the body, still gripped in Sandy's hand*) Oh, I beg your pardon . . . (*puts dummy back together*) I think I've given the game away . . . No, he said his father was a *Presbyterian*.

KAY: Oh, did he?

SANDY: I'm nearer to him than you are, you see.

KAY: Well, what's the difference between a vegetarian and a Presbyterian?

SANDY: Well, a vegetarian of course, they don't eat meat; and his father, a Presbyterian, that's his *belief*.

KAY: Oh, I see – and what are you?

SANDY (*proudly*): I'm a ventriloquist.

KAY: That's *your* belief.[7]

In these two chapters on sketch comics we have seen the technique of sketch writing moving away from single gags to sketches based much more on character, with the gags integrated into the overall idea of the sketch. With Will Hay, we meet for the first time sketches with a complex construction, within which gags recur or are referred back to. In terms of writing technique, Hay's sketches are the forerunners of the more sophisticated sketches of the 1960s onwards.

Unusually among Variety performers, Hay was well (though self-) educated. He was born in 1888, and although a bright student, left school before taking his examinations because of a family move in search of work. He taught himself French, German and Italian, and became a well-respected amateur astronomer.

He began in the entertainment world as a stand-up comic at smoking concerts, and eventually decided to make a career in the music-halls. He performed various types of comic act, but it was in 1909 when he first appeared as a comic schoolmaster in a rhyming monologue called 'Bend Down' – in which he used a joke familiar from his later acts, about the boy who thinks that Noah's wife was Joan of Arc. He found that he got a better audience reaction from that than from his other material, and built the idea into a sketch with a schoolmaster and one boy. He performed this, together with various other sketches, in one of Fred Karno's touring troupes, where he gained invaluable experience in comic timing. One of the earliest versions of this act was licensed by the Lord Chamberlain's office in December 1916. The official who approved the sketch commented in his report on the fact that the boy received frequent canings during the course of it, which might have given cause for complaint on the grounds that it represented cruel behaviour on stage; but since it was evident that the boy took no harm from the canings, which were comically ineffectual, the sketch itself could be licensed as harmless. Hay brandished a cane in most of his later sketches; today's audiences might not find the joke so acceptable, but the audiences of the period simply saw it as another dig at the traditional schoolmaster figure.

The 1916 sketch is well-enough written – though not as complex in construction as the later ones – and Hay was able to misuse his own knowledge to create the beginning of his famous incompetent schoolmaster.

HAY: I want to know why you're late.
BOY: I was having an argument with a boy from the other school.

HAY: And who gave you permission to hold arguments when you ought to be in here?
BOY: Please, sir, I couldn't help it.
HAY: Couldn't help it? Who couldn't?
BOY: Me!
HAY: 'Me?' Why on earth don't you speak the King's English? Here have I wasted all this time teaching you grammar, and you say 'me'. It's not 'me' at all. It's 'I' – 'I couldn't help it'. You couldn't say 'Me couldn't help it', could you? It's only me when it's in the objective. Well, go on, you couldn't help it, and why?
BOY: Because he said something very nasty about you.
HAY: Said something nasty about me? Oh! – all right – I'll tell his headmaster about him. I'm not going to have boys from that tuppenny-ha'penny school saying things about me. And what did you do?
BOY: Oh, I stuck up for you, of course.
HAY: That's right, always stick up for your headmaster. Never mind what anybody says about me, always stick up for me. And what was it he said that was very nasty?
BOY: He said you weren't fit to associate with pigs.
HAY: He said what?
BOY: He said you weren't fit to associate with pigs.
HAY: He said that? And you stuck up for me. What did you say?
BOY: I said you were.[8]

This sketch shows Hay's technique of getting the maximum mileage out of a simple gag; he said himself that his sketches consisted of only two or three actual jokes, and the rest was padding – but Hay's 'padding' was vastly better than many people's best material.

In the early 1920s, Hay expanded the basic construction of the sketches by including an old man, usually called 'Harbottle', as another pupil. Apart from the fact that three characters allowed for more flexibility in the writing, it also expanded the range of comedy available; the boy was smarter than the schoolmaster, but both of them were smarter than the old man; this enabled Hay to be in the

middle, both scoring and being scored off. Harbottle and the boy were played by various performers over the years; originally by Bert and Cyril Platt, Hay's nephews, with Harbottle later being played by an ex-concert party comedian called Charlie Harvey after Bert Platt walked out following a disagreement. (Hay was not easy to get on

with, being a perfectionist, as well as jealous of his position as the comic.)

The fairly well-known gramophone records of 'Will Hay and his Scholars', made in 1929 and 1933, do not give a satisfactory impression of his performance on stage. In the absence of an audience, the humour is rather dead and lacks pace. The sketches on the three double-sided records are not exactly as performed on-stage, but consist of sections of the various stage sketches reworked for the records. To make matters worse, on the last two sides, recorded in 1933, Hay arranged for the boy to be played by his current girlfriend, with disastrous results.

A much clearer idea of Hay's style can be gained by watching the best of his films, even though these use sections of the stage act only incidentally. His later films, made for Ealing Studios, are less suited to his style than the best of the films he made in the 1930s for the less well-known Gainsborough studios. Of these, *Oh, Mr Porter* (1937), *Convict 99* (1938), *Old Bones of the River* (1939) and *Ask a Policeman* (1939) are excellent; *Oh, Mr Porter* is one of the finest comedy films ever made. Much of its success is due to his supporting players – Graham Moffatt as the boy Albert, and Moore Marriott as the old fool Harbottle. Their timing and interaction, together with a superbly written script by Marriott Edgar and Val Guest, show Hay at his best – bumptious, ignorant, argumentative and incompetent.

Graham Moffatt and Moore Marriott were the ideal incarnations of the standard Hay sidekicks, although they did not perform with him on stage.[9] The stage act was rewritten several times, always along the same lines, but incorporating new material in order to keep it fresh on return engagements. By the time Hay gave up stage work in the late 1930s to concentrate on films the act had been refined to a complicated and excellent piece of writing, of which the 1938 version quoted below is typical. As Hay was topping bills, the act lasted for about twenty minutes, and in it he developed the technique of referring back to earlier jokes.

It is the first day at Hay's school; two pupils arrive – the boy and the old man (whose name, for once, is not Harbottle). It emerges that the old man has come to school because he has lost his job as a wheel-tapper on the railway. This leads to immediate confusion because Hay thinks the old man has said that he 'taps the wheels with Emma' and it takes a few moments to extricate 'hammer' from the absent aspirate. It becomes apparent that the old man has never had any idea *why* he taps the wheels – this leads to a discussion as to whether it's to see if they're *round* or to see if they're *sound*, because the old man is not only stupid but deaf.

Hay then attempts to enter the names in the school register, and the confusion escalates immediately:

Will Hay with Charles Hawtrey, John Clark and Billy Nicholls in 'The Will Hay Programme' (1944)

HAY (*to boy*):	I'll have your name first.
BOY:	Wye.
HAY:	Why? There's no particular reason why, simply that you came in first. You see, it doesn't matter to me whether I have your name first or his, only I'm expecting a bit of bother with him, so I thought I'd settle yours. Well, come on, what is it?
BOY:	Wye.
HAY:	Well, when you open a school one of the first things that you do, after the school is built and the mortgage arranged, is to buy a register, and in it you enter the names of the boys.
BOY:	Yes.
HAY:	Well, I've bought this, and I'm going to use it. Well come on, what is it?
BOY:	Wye.
HAY:	Because I want to put it in the book.
BOY:	Well, put it in the book.
HAY:	I will, when I know it.
BOY:	But you *do* know it!
HAY:	No I don't!
BOY:	Well you ought to.
HAY:	Why?
BOY:	Yes.

HAY (*to Old Man*): Have you got your hammer with you?

BOY: Don't you understand – my *name* is Wye.

HAY: Oh, your *name* is Wye – I thought you were being inquisitive. (*To Old Man*) His name's Wye.

OLD MAN: Why?

HAY: To see if they're sound.

Hay then mis-hears the boy's Christian names – Arthur Court – as "Alf a Quart"; once this has been sorted out the 'Why?' joke re-emerges in reverse:

HAY: Arthur Court Wye.

BOY: Because those are my names.

HAY: Yes, that's what I've got, Arthur Court Wye.

BOY: Because I was christened that.

HAY: I *know* you were. Shut up – I know what I'm doing. Arthur – Court – W-Y-E. Where do you live?

BOY: Streatham.

HAY: That's S.E.

BOY: 16.

HAY: I know, I know a girl . . . there's a girls' school round there somewhere. (*To Old Man*) And what do they call you?

OLD MAN: Eh?

HAY: What do they call you?

OLD MAN: Barmy.

HAY: Yes, and you look it, but I can't put 'barmy' in the book. I want your proper name.

OLD MAN: Oh, me proper name.

HAY: Yes.

OLD MAN: Reginald Clarence D'Arcy.

HAY: Joe what?

OLD MAN: No, Reginald Clarence D'Arcy.

HAY: Reginald Clarence D'Arcy. And you worked on the railway with a name like that.

OLD MAN: Yes.

HAY: D'Arcy – that's an old French name.

OLD MAN: Yes.

HAY: Came over with the Conqueror.

OLD MAN: Yes.

HAY: Were you seasick?

OLD MAN: No.

HAY: Well, where do you live?

OLD MAN: Eh?

HAY: I said, where do you live?

OLD MAN: Ware.

HAY: Yes.

OLD MAN: Yes.

HAY: No, I said, where do you live?

OLD MAN: Ware.

HAY: Yes.

OLD MAN: Yes.

HAY: He's as deaf as a post. I said, *where do you live*?

OLD MAN: Ware.

HAY: Yes.

OLD MAN: Yes.

HAY: You see what tapping wheels does.

OLD MAN (*getting annoyed*): Don't you know Ware?

HAY: If I knew where, I wouldn't ask, would I?[10]

Hay added yet another dimension to the style of his material in his wartime radio series *Diary of a Schoolmaster* (co-written with Max Kester, Alex Hayes and Rex Diamond), with the addition of a younger pupil (re-using the name D'Arcy) who was extremely bright and could be counted upon to reduce Hay to confused silence with his erudition. The other boy and the old fool – now called Beckett – were still there, and the confusion arising out of the simplest matter continued the tradition of the stage acts. In one show, total chaos arose from a discussion of the old brain-teaser about the man who has a boat, a hyena, a goat and some cabbages, and who can only take two at a time in his boat when needing to cross a river. ('Please, sir,' asked Beckett helpfully, 'why don't they go round by the bridge?')

Hay suffered a stroke in 1946 which ended his performing career; he died in 1949. His son went round the Variety halls with the act, as Will Hay Junior – in this case Graham Moffat and Moore Marriott did appear on stage, but even so the act was never as successful as the original had been.

Hay's films remain classics which, at their best, are unrivalled by later more apparently polished efforts;[11] his stage performances placed him in the very forefront of Variety comedians.

(The subject of sketch comics is resumed in Chapter 27, p. 196.)

13 'A nice little act'
Speciality acts: One (dancers and animals)

The function of speciality acts has already been defined for us by Norman Murray (see page 82), as basically to provide contrasting support to the stars on a bill. Defining the actual kinds of acts that would be classed as speciality acts is more difficult: 'anything involving props' is one definition, but this would exclude hypnotists or costume-dancers. Straight dance acts would normally be excluded from the definition (although this chapter will consider several which were built round gimmicks or a theme, and thus might qualify); acrobats (who are dealt with separately in this book) *would* perhaps be classed as speciality, depending upon who is doing the classifying. Other branches of the category include jugglers, magicians and ventriloquists; these are dealt with in a later chapter on speciality acts.

One thing, however, *is* consistent; ask anyone who used to work in the business about a particular speciality act, and the chances are that they will immediately describe them as 'a nice little act'. Speciality acts were, of course, not top-liners – they could entertain the audience effectively while it waited for the star attraction to appear; but they could not themselves pull audiences into theatres.

Apart from the straight dancers – such as the two-girl tap-dancing acts who often opened bills – there were many dancing acts who found that they achieved greater success by being different in some way. One of the older ones was The Eight Lancashire Lads, a northern clog-dancing troupe who in their earlier days had included the young Charlie Chaplin. Johnny Cooper (family name Johnny Lawson) was with them in 1928 and again in 1932, and remembers the novel opening to the act.

'The curtain would rise exposing a cinema screen hung from the flies so that the bottom of the screen was about 18 inches from the stage. Immediately behind the screen, we did a clog dance wearing gold clogs and black tights. Behind us was a black drop which made our legs invisible so that it would appear as though only the clogs were dancing. While this was going on, slides of the original "Eight Lancashire Lads" were shown on the screen.'[1]

After his first stint with the team, he joined another dancer called Bill Burke to form an act which they called 'Burke-and-Head' (having started at the Argyle Theatre, Birkenhead).

'It was a comedy dancing act; we did dance routines on

Johnny Cooper (Lawson) in the dancing act 'Averard and Lawson'

everyday happenings – we were a couple of bill-posters, or a couple of firemen. No talking, just dancing. In the fireman routine, we used to get the stagehands to shout "Fire!" and ring a bell off-stage – at one place they were really going to town, and we thought, "Marvellous" . . . of course, there was a real fire. Everything went – and we had to go back to the hotel in our firemen's costumes.'

Cooper subsequently toured with two girls as 'The Johnny Lawson Trio', mostly playing Moss Empires.

'I had my own scenery, including a house that used to light up with ultra-violet light.'

Most dancers worked to arrangements of the popular dance-tempo hits of the day (which were all fairly similar in construction – the number of bars in a chorus and so on). Johnny Cooper's experience of the mechanics of setting up a routine would be typical of many.

'All the big publishers – Francis Day and Hunter, Campbell Connelly, Lawrence Wright – were all in Denmark Street [off London's Charing Cross Road] – "Tin Pan Alley". You could walk into any one of them, as a pro, and ask for "professional copies". These were the piano copies. So you got a whole bunch of copies, free. Most of these publishers also employed a pianist, who would run through the copy for you; so you'd pick out what you wanted. You'd go into rehearsal with a pianist – either you'd have to pay him, or it might be somebody you knew – and you start setting the act. You'd mark on the copy – one bit might take two-and-a-half choruses, or whatever – and then you'd have to have it orchestrated. There were several people who could do that for you; and finally you got yourself a set of band books – the parts for, say, eight or ten instruments – a few more for Moss Empires.'

Artists often used to gather to talk in the Express Dairy tea-rooms at 18 Charing Cross Road (under the offices of *The Performer* and the VAF – it is now a pub called 'The Cockney') and male dancing acts sometimes used to rehearse in the gents downstairs – it was cheaper than hiring rehearsal rooms.

People sometimes got into dancing for unexpected reasons. Jack Marks had started his working life in the 1920s as a boy apprentice selling motorcycles. An accident left him with a limp which was diagnosed as psychological, and he was advised to take up dancing as a means of overcoming it.

'This was when Lew Grade was doing Charleston dancing; I started doing this, and I won a competition – the prize was a week's work with Sam Mayo, the London comic. He kept me on – he offered me £6 a week, which in 1927 in Cardiff, where I came from, was a princely sum.'

Marks learnt to tap-dance, and then worked in various jobs – including appearing as a 'Russian' dancer in *Casanova* at the London Coliseum. He worked with a girl dancer as 'Jack and Jill', and with his sister as 'Marks and Marks' until the second World War started.

Each act had to work out its own routines, which – for the most part – other acts would not copy both from professional ethics and managerial discouragement. Things were quite otherwise in America, as Jack Marks discovered when he became friendly with a black American dancer called Sammy Van.

'He was saying how vicious it was in America – they might have five dancing acts on a bill, all following each other – all watching each other like mad to see what they were doing, so there was fierce competition. Now, in my act I used to do one solo – in between doubles with the girl – and I'd done the same routine for about a year. Sammy and I were on the same bill, working at both the Brixton Empress and the Holborn Empire each evening – at Brixton he was on before me, and at Holborn I was in front of him. So one night, we'd been at Holborn and we were going to Brixton in a coach – and he said, "This is what happens in the States"; and at Brixton he went on, and did all my routine! All my tricks, all my steps – I was standing on the side; I said "You bastard – what have you done?" – he said, "That's what happens!" – so I had to go on and improvise something! After about three nights of this, I went on at Holborn and managed to do *his* act – so he had to do mine there, which was a "number one" theatre. This was an aspect of show business which had never struck me, because we never had that fierce competition over here.'

Another dancer who started with the Eight Lancashire Lads, and who later became better known as a sketch comedian, was Nat Jackley – the son of the famous comedian and pantomime dame George Jackley. When he left the Lancashire Lads in 1925, Nat went round the cine-variety theatres with his sister Joy. His description of their routine – a typical 'nice little act' – shows the ingenuity and effort which many artists put into their work in order to make their acts stand out from the others:

'Joy was a very good pianist; we did concerted numbers, and a pal of mine used to come on and do [spoken] gags with me; and then I'd do my clog-dance on a steel table. Then we had an eight-step staircase which was formed into a xylophone, and we used to do our tap-dancing and play tunes on the xylophone.' After his sister became ill, he moved on into verbal comedy (see Chapter 27).

Because each act would put together the sort of material that suited them, they were all individual. Since the performing time was usually fairly short, the act could be essentially quite simple – but by the same token it had to make its impact in a short time. Harry and Marjorie Ristori (bill matter: 'Punch, Personality and Pep!') had both toured with their parents' acts – Harry doing comedy adagio work in 'drag', Marjorie playing in sketches, although she had also learnt to dance. After they married, they built up an act based on comedy and music, as Marjorie remembers:

'Harry played the violin, and danced with it; I learnt adagio dancing from Harry, and we made up the act – he played the violin and I played the banjulele and danced with it, so that we both finished up dancing and playing. And I did a comedy number because I had double-jointed arms – they turned inside-out – I can't do it now! And he would do a dance, with pirouettes. I was very lucky to be part of a team that could play on the continent, because with my father we couldn't' (because he was a talking act).

Many speciality acts, being non-verbal, were able to tour Europe and South America – an advantage denied to most comedians. The USA, being English-speaking (after a fashion), did provide opportunities, although conditions were very different and a change of style was often necessary, as Marjorie Ristori discovered.

'We went on the Radio-Keith-Orpheum circuit – and by nine o'clock in the evening we'd done six shows! We were a quick-fire act, but when we went over there we were told we weren't quick enough. When we came back we opened at the Holborn Empire, and Cissie Williams came round and said, "*What* have you done to your act? You've no repose – you've killed it. Now, whatever the Americans have told you to do – go back!" And we had to slow ourselves down to the English audiences.'

The top comedy dancing act of Wilson, Keppel and Betty came originally from America, but it is doubtful whether they bothered to adapt their style for British audiences – they were always very popular and still look hilarious today on film. Jack Wilson was born in Liverpool and Joe Keppel in Ireland, but both started their careers in America, forming the trio with the original 'Betty', Betty Knox, in 1910. The original Betty's daughter, also called Betty, succeeded her when they came to Britain for a few weeks in 1932 and stayed permanently; *her* daughter Patsy Knox took over in 1941, and there were subsequent other 'Betty's.

The act consisted of eccentric dancing in pseudo-Arabian style by the two men, who were usually dressed in something resembling long nightshirts and fezzes; Betty's main function was to look pretty and be admired by the other two as they carried her in on a litter or danced

Wilson, Keppel and Betty

around her. Wilson and Keppel's dancing – often on a thin layer of sand to give the shuffling noise – was done in perfect unison with a single-mindedness that made the already comic movements look even more hilarious. One of their routines, 'Cleopatra's Nightmare', for which they wore shorter smocks, produced a complaint from no less a person than Dr Goebbels when they performed it in 1936 at the Wintergarten Berlin – he said that their bare legs were 'bad for the morals of the Nazi Youth' and suggested that they wear long trousers.

British audiences, being less prudish, enjoyed their act right up to their retirement in 1963.

The divisions of performers into speciality acts, or dancing acts, or comedians, can be misleading; many acts blurred over the dividing lines. Horace Mashford, who before the war toured in a comedy dancing act with his wife Edna, worked within a wider range than many performers.

Mashford's early work included seashore Pierrot troupes, summer seasons and concert party, and working for a while with Fred Karno (hard work but useful experience). A séance he attended in his younger days (the ouija board apparently told him he would make a living as a performer, but he was silly enough to ask it whether he would ever be a big star and it said 'No') seems to have pre-decided him that he would never be more than a supporting artist but the routines which he and his wife toured in the late 1930s, as 'Horace and Edna', were well put together and might have developed into something better-known but for Edna's death in 1940. The act was principally dancing, with a good deal of comedy thrown in, as Mashford remembers.

'We did all sorts of things – we had a crinoline act, a golliwog act, a Scottish dance – we got every detail of the costumes right – a military one, Dutch one. . . . We'd open with a single item each, and then do a double in evening dress – a love duet; and we'd introduce patter. We had six or seven strong patter routines; and we did a hunting act – I'd been a bugler in the scouts, so I used to open up with the posthorn gallop. As the applause for that started, there'd be a big crash off, and shouts . . . and Edna would come on, and saying [pointing between her legs] "There should be a horse under there!" '

They then did fairly basic patter about hunting before building into a dance routine. The weakness of this kind of material was that their patter could never hope to compete with the best comedians; but the variety of costumes and dance routines gave them a different sort of appeal in which the quality of the jokes was more or less incidental.

Horace and Edna Mashford in the 1930s

Like many small-time artists, Horace and Edna also performed in working-men's clubs – the descendants of the old music hall where, since the audience were club members and thus not 'the public', the performances were not subject to the censorship regulations surrounding Variety theatres (see also Chapters 26 and 29).

Horace Mashford: 'We found that what the club audience laughed at, the Variety audience didn't; but the Variety audiences laughed at things that the club audiences never laughed at. So we had to do two versions . . . the audiences were much the same, but it must have been the different environment – the clubs had their own types of artists which were entirely different to the Variety theatres. And a lot of the club audiences had had a few drinks.'

Artists performing in clubs could also get away with broader material, because of the lack of censorship – indeed it was to some extent expected of them.

After Edna's death in 1940, Horace Mashford went on to work on radio and in Variety as a 'light comedian' – another confusing definition, for a light comedian is not a funny man; he sings jolly songs like 'Put Me Among The Girls'. Mashford modelled his style on the Edwardian light comedian Whit Cunliffe – the originator of 'Who Were You With Last Night?' – who retired from the business before Mashford entered it. As Mashford's ouija board had foretold, he never became a star but he continued to work in the business and made a reasonable living at it.

As with Horace and Edna, attention to the quality of costumes was important to many acts. Chris Wortman worked for many years as a black-face act, starting in minstrel shows in the early 1920s. He went on to do solo costume work in black-face – this sort of act was then known as a 'coon act', the word 'coon' not at that time being considered a deliberate insult. The most famous exponent of this sort of act was G. H. Elliott, 'The Chocolate-Coloured Coon', who was in effect a sort of dark light comedian.

Wortman remembers: 'I always had Elliott rammed down my throat until I devised an act doing characters – I did a mammy, and an old man, and a comedy character. I went round the halls for years; I was usually second turn, and I started off singing off-stage "Is It True What They Say About Dixie?" – with the advent of Phyllis Dixey [the famous nude posing artist] I had to cut that out! Then I did an introduction, and in four bars of music I changed from a G. H. Elliott type of dandy coon into a fat mammy, with padded clothes – changing behind a screen. Then I did "Curly-Headed Baby" and "Mighty Lak' a Rose". Then I changed and did a comedy number, with an eccentric dance including sixteen Russian elevations – jumping splits; then in eight bars of music I changed into a doddering old man, singing "That's Why Darkies Were Born", doing a bit of a dance.'

Black-face performances of this type were popular in their day, and – since there were very few black people living in Britain at the time – were not felt to be offensive (though what visiting blacks might have thought of them is not recorded). The *Black and White Minstrel Show* on television which was very popular in the late 1960s and the early 1970s was not accurately in the old tradition. Chris Wortman objected to its whole style, particularly the make-up.

'They were made up like pandas – great big white eyes; in our day the lips were *pink*, and the eyes just lined with white. I used the old burnt cork [which was used to make a paste, not just dabbed straight on]; but G. H. Elliott never used burnt cork in his life – it was a chocolate-coloured make up, and the secret died with him.'

(Of course modern make-ups can reproduce most colours; the point about the burnt cork, and other devices of the time, was that it was a good solid black.)

Chris Wortman retired from the business for many years, returning to it only about 1970. To today's more sophisticated audience, his sort of act – in its original form – would seem rather too simple and old-fashioned; but, unlike modern performers, since Wortman would be seen only at very wide intervals in any one town, he could polish the act and take great care with the costumes so that its appeal, though simple, was effective.

Few speciality acts of the type discussed so far in this chapter ever made films, and even had they done so it would be difficult to assess their appeal for the audiences of the day. Modern audiences, used to glossy television productions which can afford the best and which thrive on slickness, would probably find little appeal in the simpler pleasures of Horace and Edna or Harry and Marjorie Ristori were they to see them in the theatre today; and in any case their acts were specifically designed to work in the context of surrounding, different, acts on a bill.

As for the dancers, their appeal was often more in the novelty of each particular act than in the actual technique of their dancing. Straight dancing acts inevitably suffered the most as Hollywood films began to dominate the entertainment industry in the 1930s; Fred Astaire, Ginger Rogers, and later Gene Kelly, Anne Miller and Eleanor Powell provided dazzling displays of technique, aided by weeks of rehearsal and the ability to keep on filming until a perfect 'take' was achieved. There were only ever a handful of such talents, but their films could appear all over the country in a short time. Ordinary dancing acts could never hope to match that sort of standard of performance; but they had one important advantage – they were *real*, not shadows; they were *there*, and could establish a relationship with their audience. The occasional stage dancing act which did find its way onto film often looks far less attractive now than it would have done then, since in an unfamiliar medium the dancers compete at a disadvantage with those who were masters of it. (Wilson, Keppel and Betty were a glorious exception – on film or off it their appeal was unmistakable; but they were in the very top bracket of speciality acts.)

If one is dealing in exact definitions, animal acts would not really come under the heading of speciality acts; but for the purposes of this book they will be included here. As with acrobats, there is little point in describing a large number of routines which basically consist of animals doing tricks. There were some odd acts – Koringa and her crocodiles, performing doves, performing geese – even performing pigs! Wally Thomas, when he was manager of the Empire Newport, had a little difficulty with a performing elephant that put its feet through the stage floor (thus closing the theatre for a week while a new stage was fitted). Harry Harbour (the son of Sam Harbour, the manager of the Coliseum) was manager of the Chiswick Empire in the fifties when the Roberts Brothers Circus appeared there.

'The local council was red-hot on animals, and they came in one day; there was an enormous mangy lion, and the RSPCA and the council asked me, "Where does the lion exercise?" Well, *I* didn't know where it exercised, so I told them that they put the ring up in the mornings and exercised it there. They said, "Right, we'll be in tomorrow morning to see the lion exercise." So I told Mr Roberts – and he said, "Don't be so daft – if I exercise the lion this morning it won't do anything tonight – it's too old". I said, "We've got to do it, otherwise we've got no lion act". So the council people came in and saw the lion exercised, round and round – they were happy. That evening we announced "The most ferocious lion in captivity" – it wouldn't budge. Eventually somebody went into the cage and dragged it out into the centre of the ring – it just lay there and we had to drop the curtain on it.'

Of course the most common type of animal act was the dog act, since dogs are relatively easy to train and control. One of the best of all these was Duncan's Collies – and also the longest running; the act itself ran for almost eighty years. Vic Duncan took it over from his father in 1927,

having been appearing in it since he was about five; the act originally started when his father, who had one dog which could do fifty-two tricks, did a charity performance for the widows and orphans of the Tay Bridge Disaster in 1879. Vic Duncan's appearances in the act were as part of a 'fire brigade' scene.

'There was a building which was supposed to be on fire, and a dog came on on a fire ladder and went up to rescue the "baby" – then the dog came down with the baby [a doll] and fell "exhausted" on the stage, and I came down in a night-shirt, picked up the baby and ran off the stage with it. That's the earliest recollection I have of going on the stage.'

Vic Duncan ran the act from 1927 until he retired in the late 1950s, touring abroad as well as in Britain.

'When we came back we'd play a circus, because of the quarantine laws – we were able to work while the dogs were in quarantine, provided the Ministry of Agriculture had passed the place where the dogs were going to be housed.'

He had a special trailer which was acceptable for quarantine purposes, so that he could move the dogs about while they were still quarantined. Once the quarantine period had expired, of course, he could take them anywhere, and would then work in the Variety theatres – many theatres had good facilities for housing animals, and dogs would stay there during the week; Duncan employed two people as staff and someone would always stay with the dogs.

Duncan's Collies

'It was a hard life, but I enjoyed it – I'd have breakfast about half-past eight and be down at the theatre about nine o'clock; we'd have a rehearsal, for about an hour, and then the dogs had to be combed; we'd go back to the digs for lunch, and have the afternoon off; then be back at the theatre about five o'clock. Then we'd be there until about half-past ten or eleven at night – day after day. I used to look forward to Sunday.'

The act was complicated, justifying the bill matter 'Canine Actors'.

'When the curtain went up, there were six dogs in line, standing, then in twos, then all six. Then they would do skipping, with one then two ropes. Then we did our chair trick – the dog would jump from the ground onto the back of a [kitchen-type] chair, and go into a balance on his hind

Vic Duncan
rehearsing the
chair-back trick

legs on the back of the chair – which was really a remarkable trick. None of our tricks was ever copied – they were too damned hard. Then we'd go into the motor-car scene; the car would come onto the stage, with a dog "driving" and a passenger; circle the stage, and stop; then there was a crash and a big explosion, the driver fell under the car, and the passenger went to a telephone and barked for help. I came on; one dog "died" in my arms – this used to get a big round of applause – and – I revived the other with "whisky".'

The scene finished with the appearance of an ambulance, complete with a widow for the dead dog. Obviously the hardest work took place away from the audience.

'You can train a dog to do a certain thing, but when you get him on the stage it's a totally different matter. You've got to get him used to the stage, so you keep him in the wings at first, then you get him sitting on the stage, and get him used to it.'

A trick such as the jump to the back of a chair took immense patience in training a dog.

'You've got to get a good hind-leg dog – it takes about a month to teach a dog to walk on its hind legs. It would probably take another three months to get him on the back of that chair. You don't teach a dog to *walk* on his hind legs, you teach him to *balance* – when he falls forward he puts his paws on your chest, and you move backwards, and eventually he's walking. For the chair trick, I had a wide board a short way off the ground, and the dog would jump onto that and go into his balance quite easily. Then I brought the board up gradually until it was the height of the back of the chair. Then the board was in sections, and I took a third away, and then another third; and then there was a smaller board, also in three parts; and I stood the chair up against the board until the dog could jump onto it. The great thing was to make sure the dog didn't fall. If he fell and hurt himself you were back to where you started. All the dogs were trained to do everything, so that it didn't matter if one dog fell out – we used to carry ten dogs, and each one could do all the tricks.'

Things rarely went wrong during performances – but if Duncan tried to have a dress rehearsal, the dogs would detect that there was no audience and play him up.

Duncan always took good care of his dogs, but of course the RSPCA kept a tight watch on all animal acts. Duncan had a friend who worked for the RSPCA, and whenever his friend wanted an afternoon off, Duncan would phone the RSPCA with a complaint against himself. The friend would be sent off to investigate, would go nowhere near Duncan, and return to report that there was no cause for complaint. The life seems to have done the dogs no harm.

'I've had dogs live to nearly eighteen; they used to retire themselves at about ten – you could see when they were getting too old, but they could always sit on the stage and look pretty. When I retired, all the dogs retired too, and I kept them all going – I had a paddock for them.'

Duncan's Collies often topped the bill in small provincial theatres, and were a consistently good middle-of-the-bill supporting act in the bigger theatres; as with other animal acts and speciality acts in general they helped to give Variety its particular appeal.

(*The subject of speciality acts is resumed in Chapter 22, p. 175.*)

14 'It's the way I tells 'em, lady'
Stand-up comics: Two (the 1930s)

We saw in Chapter 2 how the general style of stand-up comics altered during the 1920s, moving away from purely character comedy into patter, with the jokes linked into a loose framework. During the 1930s, the trend continued, with the move being towards strings of unrelated jokes which depended upon their own quality and the skill of the performer to keep the audience involved, rather than any overall structure. It is a little odd that sketch comedy was moving in exactly the opposite direction – away from gags rammed uneasily into some sort of framework and towards the carefully constructed comedy of character performers such as Will Hay.

The trend was an overall one, of course, not a strictly observable chronological one. Older performers inevitably hung on to their own style; and there were newer performers who worked in a manner which more or less ignored the trend. Oliver Wakefield (bill matter: 'The Voice of Inexperience') presented patter – which did not contain gags in the usual sense – in the character of an upper-class silly ass, smartly dressed and chattering in a vague way about a subject which seemed to recede even as he approached it. His material was much more cleverly written than that of most Variety comics, using a sort of stream-of-consciousness technique in which allusions came and went almost before the audience could latch on to them.

> H-h-hello, everybody . . . I'm terribly pleased you could all . . . hear this . . . and as I look into your simple faces . . . I – I feel . . . simply . . . and, and how many of you – can look into my . . . with a cast in your . . . and throw stones in your neighbours? Because as men and women, we must have *feelings*. Didn't Shakespeare say, very aptly, in – Om . . . Hamlet . . . Twelve . . . Summer-Night's . . . Pinch Me . . . do I not bleed? Stick a pin in me and – and there's no knowing what'll . . . and that of course is a very rough idea of inflation. And I – I'd like, if I may, to take you back . . . to dear old . . . to show you the *glamour* of your hysterical past.[1]

> I – I should like you to cast your minds . . . back to the persp . . . er, respiration period. Everyone was gasping . . . er, grasping . . . there . . . because Cromwell and his band of Iron Head . . . Round si . . . Back si- . . . from the wars . . . of the Roses. He came. Laying the country waste . . . Tooting . . . er, looting . . . and, and pillaging . . . as he went . . . from pillage – to pillage. Collecting arms . . . legs . . . and anything he could lay . . . his hands on.[2]

Most comedians stuck firmly to the traditional subjects – wives, families, mothers-in-law – presenting the domestic life that their audiences were familiar with, although not always in as sour a way as, for example, Dick Henderson.

Not everyone worked in the straightforward monologue style. The child impersonator Harry Hemsley – whose voices were so well characterized that he sometimes played straight parts as children on gramophone records, being easier to direct than the real thing – would simply sit on the stage and use a newspaper to cover his lip movements as he carried on a conversation with his imaginary family of

children – including the baby, Horace, whose remarks were always unintelligible and had to be translated by his sister Winnie. Because the voices were so convincing he was also very effective on radio, and his sketches were unusual for their period in being based on quiet observation rather than actual one-line gags; in fact the characters were more important than the humour.

JOHNNY: Daddy – do you know Freddy Dunn?
HEMSLEY: Yes, I know Freddy.
JOHNNY: He got the *measles*.
HEMSLEY: I'm sorry to hear that.
JOHNNY: He has to stay in bed all day!
HEMSLEY: That's the right place for him.
JOHNNY: His mother reads to him, he doesn't go to school, he has grapes and all nice things to eat, and toys to play with – he has a fine time.
HEMSLEY: Well, what about it?
JOHNNY: When can I have the measles?
HEMSLEY: Never, I hope.
WINNIE: Da-ddy.
HEMSLEY: Hello – is that you, Winnie?
WINNIE: I don't feel very well.
HEMSLEY: Oh? – what have you been eating?
WINNIE: Nothin', Daddy, I eat nothin' all day.
JOHNNY: Ask her if she drank anything, Daddy.
HEMSLEY: Did you drink anything, Winnie?
WINNIE: Yes . . . I drink a glass of water.
JOHNNY: Ask her if there was anything in it, Daddy.
JOHNNY: Was there anything in it, Winnie?
WINNIE: No, Daddy, there was nothin' in it.
HEMSLEY: Johnny, what made you want me to ask Winnie just now was there anything in it?
JOHNNY: Well, Daddy, I had a frog in a glass of water yesterday, and it's gone.
HEMSLEY: Oh, good gracious me!
JOHNNY: 's all right, Daddy, I got another.[3]

Many stand-up comics also worked in sketches – indeed the problem with categorizing people, in the manner which is necessary in this book to give it some sort of structure, is that it tends to give the impression that everybody stuck firmly to one particular field. Tommy Handley – whose greatest fame came with his radio series *ITMA* during World War Two (see Chapter 18) – was basically a stand-up comedian in the 1930s; but he had also

worked in concert party, and his biggest pre-*ITMA* success was with a musical sketch called 'The Disorderly Room' in which army disciplinary proceedings were conducted in the form of new words to popular songs. (This sketch was written by Eric Blore, the obsequious butler in Hollywood films such as *Top Hat*.) 'The Disorderly Room' was almost too successful, for its popularity led Handley to travel it round the halls for rather too long than was good for him or it.

As a stand-up comic he was rather old-fashioned, relying heavily on odd-sounding combinations of words as opposed to puns – although he did of course also use the more common types of gags. There was a touch of surrealism about his work – partly arising from his Liverpudlian origins, for Liverpool comics have a background style of their own.

> Well, folks, it's nice to be back here in this part of the world again, and to see all the old familiar faces full of anticipation and extra strong peppermints. I'm staying in a lovely hotel here – or rather it's a pub. It's called 'The Announcers' Annexe'. A pound a week all in, find your own food, and sleep next door. The waiters don't go around the tables – the tables go round the waiters. We have three meals a day – soup for breakfast; for lunch, soup; and no soup for dinner. The hotel motto is 'Short sheets make the beds seem longer.' I've got a lovely room, overlooking nothing. From my window I can see Oxshott, Bagshot, Bullford, Hookham, Cookham and Farnham. (Of course if you don't know the places, you don't know the gag.) Anyway, the manager's a charming man – clean-shaven, blue eyes, and a black-handled penknife. He used to work in a shirt factory, but business was so-so . . . so he left. Then he got a job as an articled clerk in a laundry. He used to count the articles as they came in. One day, however, they found they were short of a pair of step-ins, so he stepped out. He's a mothball addict – swallows two mothballs, dives into the wardrobe, and eats his overcoat.[4]

But the general trend was away from this sort of material, and towards jokes as such. George Bolton was a stand-up and revue comic – never a big name, but another of the small reliable acts upon whom Variety depended so much. He began in a juvenile troupe in 1909, at the age of fourteen, and worked in concert party and revue for many years – experience he found invaluable, because of the wide range of abilities needed for revue. In 1936 he went on a tour of Australia with a revue.

'In every revue I was in, the last ten minutes before the finish I always went on before the frontcloth and did an act – I always registered as an individual in that one spot, having been on all evening in the sketches. When I came back from Australia, I went up to see my agent, and he said, "I don't want you to go back into revue, I want you to concentrate on your music-hall act. I've booked you at the Metropolitan Edgware Road next week – no billing, but you've got fourteen minutes. I'll get some people in to see you". I opened on the Monday; and by Saturday I'd got thirty-five weeks' work booked – and from then I never looked back, because having been away in Australia I was a new face with a new act.'

Although he did do routines dressed as a parson, or as a Salvation Army officer, Bolton worked principally in an ordinary suit, instead of relying on some eccentricity of dress to get the first laugh (as with Robey's eyebrows, Henderson's hat, or Billy Bennett's complete *équipage*). He was billed as 'The New Gagster', and relied on quick-fire jokes:

> A Scotsman bought a chemist's shop – he
> stopped up all night to watch the vanishing
> cream. He was too mean to go on his holiday, he
> stopped at home and let his mind wander.
> Another Scotsman walked ten miles to a football
> match and when he got there he was too tired to
> climb the fence.

Bolton estimated that he got through about half-an-hour's worth of material in his fourteen minutes, because of the speed of his delivery. This sort of style precluded any joke with a long build-up, but domestic relations were a target for him just as with most comedians:

> A man buried his wife on a very windy day – he
> left the cemetery and went straight home, and as
> he was walking through the door a slate blew off
> the roof and hit him on the top of the head – he
> looked up and said, 'Blimey – are you up there
> already?'[5]

Although he was never a suggestive comedian, Bolton found the local Watch Committees keeping a close eye on his material. He had little trouble with them, although he remembers that if he did a joke hinting at homosexuality he was not allowed to do the limp wrist movements.

One of the problems with this sort of comedy style was that the gags were easily pinched – no-one could use Robey's material, for example, and expect to be able to make it work (unless he was deliberately imitating Robey for laughs); but the sort of gags quoted above could be told by anybody. The same stories could turn up in various people's acts (some of them still do, even today on television); and many gags had their origins in gag books – something whose existence was not exactly advertised to the public by the comedians. One such was *Ten Thousand Jokes, Toasts and Stories,* edited by Lewis and Fay Copland, and published by Doubleday and Co, New York, in 1939 – a massive compendium of jokes on every conceivable subject. Other – mostly later – books were compiled by Robert Orben (the best-known name in the market after World War Two) and Peter Cagney. There were many books of this type, listing thousands and thousands of jokes, often arranged by subject; any aspiring comic could build an act by compiling jokes from the books in some sort of order – although of course actually *telling* them convincingly was another matter.

In a way, doing a routine on a Variety stage which consisted simply of jokes without much of a linking theme took more skill and nerve than doing the older kind of routine – after all, the comedian was only as good as his last joke. In order to keep the audience's attention a faster delivery became normal, and most comics of this type developed a relationship with the audience which was closer than that built up by the character comics – who, though they needed laughs, could use the character almost as a shield if necessary.

Ted Ray, who became one of George Black's mainstays at the Palladium before the war as a supporting comic, was one of the earliest stand-up comics to wear an ordinary suit and tell unlinked gags – he was doing this several years before George Bolton, although unlike Bolton he used a linking joke to tie the act together – his violin-playing. (He could play quite well, in fact, but obviously he was working for laughs, not musical appreciation.)

Ray's family name was George Olden, and he started in the business as a violinist, working first with a pianist as 'Wardle and Olden' and then solo as 'Nedlo the Gypsy Violinist'. He adopted the name Ted Ray from 1930, and in the following few years became well known as a patter comic (although his greatest fame came in the post-war years). He was more relaxed in his delivery than most comics – a style he had perhaps developed as a result of

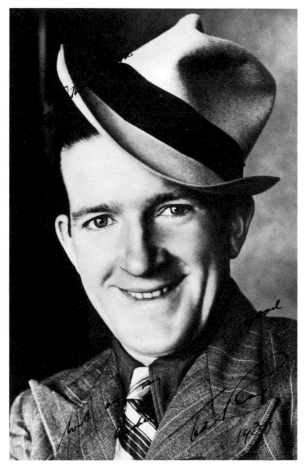

Ted Ray

watching visiting American comics – although he combined this with a high speed of performance. This may seem a contradiction in terms, but where most other comics of the period were more obviously outgoing, Ray was able to present a natural friendliness even while he buttonholed the audience and force-fed it rapid gags hung on the loosest possible framework:

> Talking about food – I went into a restaurant the other day. The waiter walked across and I recognized him as a comedian I used to work with years ago. I said, 'Well – you've certainly come down in the world, working in a dump like this.' He said 'Yes, but I don't *eat* here.' Well, he brought me a salad and I called him back – I said, 'Just a moment – do you know I've found a button in my salad?' He said 'Yes – I suppose it must have come off while the salad was dressing.'
>
> I finished the meal, and the waiter said, 'Well, how did you like it?' I said, 'Well, it wasn't bad really – all except the sweet, and that was terrible.' He said, 'What did you have – the apple fritter or the jam roll?' I said, 'I don't know, but it tasted like glue.' He said, 'It was the jam roll – the apple fritter tastes like putty.'[6]

Where Ted Ray charmed the audience, Tommy Trinder practically insulted it – his approach was based on aggression, although it was skilfully controlled to fall short of the point where the audience could have taken offence. He began in the juvenile show *Casey's Court* and then went on to gain experience in various concert parties, moving into Variety as a stand-up comic in 1931. He worked as a second-spot comic, taking advantage of the fact that latecomers would still be walking in and settling down during his act ('Good evening, sir – you're late – trouble with the bike? Good evening, madam – don't bother with the programme – my name's Trinder'). Because most theatres used a frontcloth depicting a street scene for their second-spot comics, he adopted a soft – almost deformed – hat, which became his trademark.

In 1933 he was seen by George Black and offered two years' work on Moss Empires, with better placing; later Black featured him in some of the Palladium's spectacular shows. Adopting the catchphrase 'Trinder's the name – you lucky people!', Trinder built his style into a unique mixture of aggression and charm, almost browbeating the audience into sympathy with him. Indeed in the preliminaries to one Royal Variety Performance – before the royal party had arrived – he roundly abused the audience for not laughing enough at the previous year's show, and threatened to set the Crazy Gang on them if they didn't do better this time. He was only half joking – the audience at a Royal Variety Performance has always been a terribly difficult one for the performers, as it is abnormally 'refained' and is reluctant to let itself go – and it tends to keep looking at the royal box to see whether the royal family is laughing before reacting itself.

Trinder managed to temper the apparent aggression of his style with a good deal of charm – there was always something appealing about his long thin face and prominent chin, and the smile which almost seemed to bisect it – so that his attacks on the audience were never upsetting. As he became more popular, and moved to the top of the

Tommy Trinder

bill, he had to abandon his jokes about late arrivals (though anyone who popped out to the toilets would be met on their return with remarks like 'a nice time to buy fish-and-chips'). During the war he would draw attention to any uniformed officer who arrived during his act: 'We can't have officers arriving late, sir – makes the place look like a camp concert', adding, after a slight pause, 'No, you can't put me on a charge – I'm a civilian!'

Like Will Hay, Gracie Fields and George Formby, Tommy Trinder made a separate career for himself in films – usually, for a Variety performer, in straight rôles in films such as *The Foreman Went To France* and *The Bells Go Down*; and in *Champagne Charlie* (1944) he starred with Stanley Holloway in an affectionate if romanticized story of the Victorian music-hall.

Where Tommy Trinder was moderately aggressive, Billy Russell positively harangued his audience. There were distinct shades of Billy Bennett in his approach, but Russell was resolutely a caricature of an old-fashioned working man. His character was originally based on Bruce Bairnsfather's cartoon character from *Punch* – Old Bill, who was the originator in World War One of the famous phrase 'If you knows of a better 'ole, go to it.' Russell created an elderly gravel-voiced navvy, complete with clay pipe and scruffy clothing. His bill matter was 'On Behalf of the Working Classes', and, like Billy Bennett, he appeared almost to be making an election address.

> The last bloke to get any consideration in this world is the working man – look at 'em in parliament, what do they do for the working man? *What do they do?* Promise him everything, give him nothing, and before he gets it they take it off him. Not only here but all over the world – it's the same even in Russia. Russia! – and they brag of their freedom! They're interfering with the working man's innocent amusements! Taking all the kings and queens out of the packs of playing cards. Now if you want to go nap, you've got to have four town councillors and a sanitary inspector!

Russell's portrait of married life was firmly in the tradition of the older comics – with marriage a 'sentence' and the wife some sort of a monster.

> My old woman's all right in her place – she ain't there yet – but I will say this for her, she's one

Billy Russell

in a million. One in a million. If you saw her you'd think she was won in a raffle – you never saw anything like it. And what a boiling piece – what a size! What a figure! She's like a venetian blind with the cord broke. It's remarkable how far the human skin will stretch without bursting.[7] To see her with the nose-bag on, it's an education – her stomach's got no memory! She sat down today, she had a beefsteak, if it had been any bigger she could have milked it! Worrying about her figure – *four hours* yesterday up at the beauty specialists. I don't think she got served. Keeps going up there having her face lifted – she's had her face lifted so many times, her skin's that tight, every time she sits down her mouth flies open.[8] Always finds something to worry about – she's been worrying about these air-raid precautions. She wasn't satisfied – she went up to the Town Hall, the bloke give her a gas mask, she put it on, it's an improvement.[9]

Russell's gag construction owed something to Dick Henderson – although he did tell longer, separate jokes, they still fitted within the character framework. In the late 1930s, however, this framework was less usual; and the comedian who more than anyone else typified the separate-gag-type stand-up comic style of the period was Max Miller – bill matter 'The Cheekie Chappie'.

Unlike the people we have met so far, Miller was able to break away from the relatively safe type of joke, and to get away with gags which until then had been more the province of the travelling salesman than the Variety comedian. It is a considerable tribute to his skill in selecting and creating jokes that his once risqué material can still get a laugh today – some of it is still used by comedians – but at the time only Miller could get away with it. Anyone else would have found that he had tipped over the edge into what then would have been considered dirt; but Miller used to make the audience do half the work. 'It's the way I tells 'em, lady' he would say to some female member of the audience who had been incautious enough to laugh louder than the rest; and it was true enough, for he had a unique combination of self-confidence and charm which enabled him to be saucy where a more aggressive comedian would have seemed lewd.

He dressed in outrageous brightly coloured clothes which helped to take the sting out of his suggestiveness; and he developed to a fine art the technique of not quite saying the closing word of a gag, but breaking off to shout. ''Ere. I'll tell you what I'll do', or just ''Ere!'

Max Miller at the Holborn Empire (1940)

> I started courting a smashing fan-dancer
> To marry her, that was my plan
> Now it's all off with the smashing fan-dancer
> She fell down and damaged her fan- . . . 'Ere![10]

The world of Miller's jokes was a little different from most other comics; where they presented characters who were helpless faced with any woman, Miller showed his audiences a world of happy sexuality – conquests made with a self-confidence which would have been distasteful in anyone who did not have his energetic charm. No other comic of the time could have got away with bouncing on to

the stage, singing his first song, and then commenting, 'I'm ready for bed . . . anybody?' He softened the effect of his double meanings by insisting that it was all in the audience's mind – there always *was* a straightforward meaning to his jokes, and he would upbraid the audience for picking the wrong one.

> . . . The other night a loving couple courting
> close to me –
> She was just turned twenty-one, he was
> eighty-three:

The rain came down, they'd got no gamp
They both sat down, the grass was damp
He couldn't get up – he'd got the cramp –
Passing the time away!

(*spoken*) I know exactly, I know exactly what
you're saying to yourselves . . . you're wrong! I
know what you're saying! Ooh, you *wicked* lot!
You're the kind of people who get me a bad
name![11]

He used the stage to its full extent (not being, at any rate
before the war, obliged to use a microphone and thus stay
in one place all the time) – peering off to see if the stage
manager was away so that he could tell dirtier jokes
('More? . . . Worse?'); he would offer the audience jokes
from two books – the white book (clean jokes) and the blue
book (risqué jokes), creating a sense of conspiracy
between himself and the audience – the feeling that they
were getting away with something a little bit naughty. He
danced a little, and sang to his guitar – tuning it with
reference to the conductor ('That's down, is it? That one's
down? . . . must be the cold weather').

It is fortunate that Miller is so well represented on
gramophone records. His studio recordings – mostly of
songs – do not give a very helpful idea of his style; but
there are recordings of five stage routines plus two special
wartime performances for the troops and some war workers. These latter are technically poor and not generally as
successful as the others; but the theatre recordings give an
excellent idea of his command of the audience.

The earliest, recorded at first and second houses at the
Holborn Empire on 7 October 1938, bear comparison
with the 1933 Gracie Fields recording in their preservation
of the atmosphere of the occasion; they do not appear to
have been edited, and the warmth of Miller's relationship
with the audience is apparent. (Of course, being at the top
of the bill he is dealing with an audience which is already
well warmed up.) He is not using Public Address equipment, so that there is a direct bond between him and the
audience. Other theatre recordings were made in 1939 and
1942; and in 1957 one complete performance (it is not
stated which house it was) was recorded at the
Metropolitan Edgware Road – here he is obviously using
PA, and although the record is perhaps the most successful of all the ones he made, it is noticeable that to an extent
he can bludgeon the audience into helpless laughter
whereas at the Holborn Empire he gets his results by
coaxing them – the difference is not extreme, but is

sufficient to illustrate Laurence Olivier's comment,
quoted earlier (page 69) about the microphone being a
weapon.

The pace and rhythm of Miller's delivery is most
important – he worked quite fast, but skilful use of
repetitions and asides give the material a much greater
impetus than if it were simply delivered straight; written
down, many of the repetitions simply seem redundant,
but in performance they help to make the gag something
which Miller shares with the audience rather than something he hands them on a plate – he makes them work for
it.

Timing of laughs, of course, is of paramount importance, as for any comic: too soon with the next line and it
will be smothered (keep that sort of thing up and the
audience will be afraid to let go in case it misses something); too late, and the laugh will have died down and
momentum be lost. By building on each laugh just before
it is finished, so that the audience never got the chance to
calm down, Miller would reduce them to the state where
they would laugh at anything he said, funny or not.

The construction of the act in its various versions –
usually a song, some gags, a monologue or two, a 'half exit'
while he went off to get his guitar, and then a further
song interspersed with further – perhaps longer – gags,
and a final song – make the recordings seem to go much
faster than the twenty minutes or so which is their usual
length.

On one of the records he departed from his usual style to
do a short sketch with Jean Carr – a mistake, because as
soon as he had to share the stage with someone else his
technique worked against him. He was similarly unsuccessful in films, although he made a number of low-budget
starring vehicles; he needed the live audience to work to.
Only when he could put ideas directly into an audience's
head could he achieve the rapport with them that made
him one of the top stars of the 1930s.

I've got my own studios at Brighton, and a
woman came to my house on Monday morning –
she said, 'Max I want you to paint a snake on
my knee.' I went dead white, honest I did. No,
well I'm not strong, I'm not strong. So, listen –
I jumped out of bed, see . . . no, listen a minute
. . . so I started to paint the snake just above her
knee, that's where I started. But I had to chuck
it – she smacked me in the face – I didn't know
a snake was so long – how long's an ordinary
snake?[12]

I've been a bit of a bad lad in my time – and I remember many years ago my brother and I, he was two years younger than me, we went out together and after two or three weeks I said, 'Johnny – I've got a confession to make' – he said, 'Well go in and tell your father.' I went into the drawing-room to see me dad – he was sitting in a deck-chair – I said, 'Dad – I've got a confession to make.' He said, 'What is it, son?' and I didn't like to tell him. He said, 'Tell me – who was it?' I wouldn't tell him. He said, 'Was it Mrs Brown?' I said, 'No, no' – he said, 'Was it Mrs Mitchell?' – I said, 'No', I wouldn't crack on, you see – He said, 'Was it Mrs Smith?' – I said, 'No' – he said, 'Get out of the room', he was disgusted with me. I walked out of the room, and my brother said, 'How did you get on – did he forgive you?' I said, 'No – but he gave me three very good addresses.'[13]

Listen, listen . . . are you listening? Father and son, father and son – the boy would be about eight or nine – he might be nine or ten, we don't know – who cares, anyway? Eight or nine – his father took him round a cattle-show on a Saturday afternoon when the farmers are buying the bulls and the cows – mostly bulls – when all of a sudden, the little boy saw a farmer go up to a bull. And the farmer started feeling the bull – all along the back, he was feeling it, all down and all round . . . feeling him all over . . . and the little boy said, 'Daddy – what's he doing?' and his father told him – his father said, 'He's feeling it to see if there's any meat on it – if there's any meat on it he's going to buy it.' The boy said, 'Thanks very much, Father, for telling me.' Two or three weeks later the boy went in to see his father – his father was having breakfast – his father said, 'What do you want?' – the boy said, 'I think the butler wants to buy the cook.'[14]

Max Miller raised pure gag-telling to its highest level; although his cockiness was never popular with northern audiences so that he was effectively limited to the southern half of England, he was one of the highest-paid performers in Variety in the late 1930s and during the war years. Although many comics modelled themselves to some extent on him, no-one ever matched his particular success; for though he was never *really* blue he seemed to make the dirty joke respectable. With him the pure gag style of stand-up comedy reached its peak, and the better solo comedians of the post-war era tended to move away from pure jokes and back into a character framework for their gags.

(*The subject of stand-up comics is resumed in Chapter 20, p. 161.*)

ax Miller

15 'They get in for nothing and laugh at us'
Broadcasting in the 1930s

By September 1930 there were 3,195,553 holders of receiving licences, which the BBC estimated represented about 12 million listeners. The number increased at what for the BBC must have been a satisfying speed; throughout the 1930s, as the transmitters improved and the programmes became more varied, the number of listeners increased until by 1939 there were 9 million licence-holders.

In some ways it was a 'Golden Age of Wireless' – the title used by Asa Briggs for his history of broadcasting in this period – but from the point of view of Variety broadcasts it was rather less than golden. The number of vaudeville or Variety programmes dropped sharply in 1929, and throughout the early 1930s there were usually only two or three such programmes a week. The programmes, usually billed simply as *Vaudeville* or, from early 1933, as *Variety*, ran an hour, and were no more than collections of acts by various artists. With the easing of the difficult situation between the BBC and the Variety managements a wider range of popular artists could broadcast – although there were periodic bans on individual artists imposed, rather erratically, by the theatrical managements.

Vaudeville bills in the early 1930s included appearances by Leslie Sarony, Florence Desmond, Teddy Brown, Wee Georgie Wood, Harry Tate and even ventriloquists such as Arthur Prince. There was no real pattern to the placing of the programmes; they were usually in the mid-evening at half-past seven or eight o'clock, and although not placed on adjacent days might be on any days of the week (except Sunday, of course).

It is perhaps fanciful to deduce the attitude of the BBC hierarchy from the scheduling of programmes; but the relative paucity of Variety programmes leads one to suspect that the BBC regarded them as something which had to be put up with to provide a little entertainment, but that the time would be much better spent on something more worthy. (The BBC was very high-minded at that time.)

There were frictions within the BBC about Variety; the various Regions always felt that they were too much subordinated to London, and North Region rebelled against a diet of London-based Variety and produced more home-grown programmes than was expected of it. London took little interest in the special need of regional audiences, and the Productions Director, Val Gielgud, embarked on something of a feud with the North Regional Director, E. W. Liveing. In September 1931 Gielgud wrote complaining that North Region had originated *all* its Variety programmes itself in the course of one particular week, instead of taking London's offerings. Liveing, who had earlier criticized London's Variety output as 'repetitive, jejune and boring' and had rejected London's objections to dialect comics, wrote to the Director of Programmes in London.

'The type of cockney humour as exemplified by Mabel Constanduros and the Buggins family is as much execrated by the artisan, lower middle, and working classes in the north as it is appreciated by the same classes in the south. Again, Americanized vaudeville in general frequently comes in for criticism in the north.'[1]

What weakened his case as the argument progressed was that northern Variety programmes of the period tended to be of much poorer quality than those mounted in London; but North Region in particular maintained its efforts to provide Variety programmes suited to the particular tastes of its audience, with varying degrees of success.

Studio broadcasts were in a majority in the early 1930s, but outside broadcasts from Variety theatres continued to form an important part of the output. The practice of inserting one act from an outside broadcast into a studio show was discontinued, but excerpts of about 45 minutes were taken from the bills at various theatres. Since the artists at the theatre in question were not necessarily chosen for their broadcasting suitability, this led to some odd transmissions. Until the matter of arranging timing was sorted out, the transmission would be of whatever acts happened to be on during the scheduled period; in one particularly silly example the OB from the Grand Theatre Doncaster on 11 November 1934 included not only Florrie Forde – whose popular chorus songs were highly suitable – but jugglers and a paper-tearing act! As time went on the choice of acts and the timing of the OB improved to avoid this sort of nonsense.

It was through Outside Broadcasts of Variety that Michael Standing – who in later years was to be the Head of Radio Variety – first came into contact with Variety Department. He joined the BBC in 1935 – achieving the unusual distinction of being hired as redundant, since the job in Talks Department he had been accepted for disappeared before he took up his appointment. After brief spells in Talks and in Drama, he joined Outside Broadcast Department. This gave him experience of working with Variety programmes.

Michael Standing (1945)

'Before the war the staff of the BBC was comparatively small – in the neighbourhood of 3,000 nationwide – and so you became acquainted much more easily with the activities of other Departments than happened in subsequent years; and the OB Department serviced, and sometimes actively participated in, OB contributions to Variety programmes.'

The slightly free-and-easy atmosphere – which disappeared in later years when the BBC became a massive bureaucratic machine – extended to the planning of programmes. The plans for a particular week would simply indicate a few times left blank for Variety Department, marked 'Variety to fill'; it was left entirely up to Variety Department how they filled it. Their main restriction was of course the cost; in January 1933 the budget of £120 per hour-long studio Variety programme was increased to £150 (with a reserve fund for the occasional expensive star) – which even so was hardly big money compared with the amount being spent in the theatres. (Studio broadcasts of course only involved the artists for one evening, unless the show were given a live repeat; but any performer appearing in an evening broadcast would of course not be able to appear in a provincial Variety theatre that evening – nor in a London theatre if the broadcast were inconveniently timed – and this would prevent him from appearing for the whole week. This consideration was a major factor in the increase in fees as time went on, although broadcasting fees were never particularly high.)

Although Variety Department were responsible only to themselves for the construction of their programmes, they were held responsible by all and sundry if anything in the programme was thought to be offensive. One of the problems lay in the fact that comedians were unable to use jokes which were perfectly acceptable in the Variety theatres; the Controller (Programmes) wrote in a memo to various Departmental Heads in 1937: 'Doubtful jokes, which might conceivably pass muster in a music hall, are not fit material for a broadcast service which goes direct into individual homes'[2] – it was the fact of jokes being heard at home, by anyone listening (including those who would not normally go to Variety halls), that necessitated the BBC's extra caution.

This caution rather undermined the *Radio Times*'s assertion in December 1932 that the series of broadcasts entitled *Music Hall* (a studio Variety programme which had been broadcast at intervals since March 1932) 'aims to capture the "free-and-easy atmosphere" of the halls'. However, despite the restrictions on material, *Music Hall*'s producer John Sharman managed to convey something of the feeling of a theatrical performance, by the careful choice of artists, and the use of a good band and a fairly large audience. Under another internal reorganization of 1933 (the BBC was rather fond of reorganizing itself) Sharman was in charge of all Variety and vaudeville programmes for Britain (his colleague M. C. Webster dealt with programmes for the Empire Service's overseas broadcasts) under the departmental control of Eric Maschwitz, head of the new Variety Department (created to allow Val Gielgud to concentrate on radio drama). Revue and concert-party programmes were produced by John Watt and Harry S. Pepper.

Music Hall was the 'flagship' Variety programme of the mid-1930s. It was usually broadcast on Saturdays, though not on a regular basis; in the later 1930s it alternated for a time with *Palace of Varieties*, a broadly similar programme but with more accent on audience-sing-along type of acts. *Music Hall*'s attempts to create the 'free-and-easy atmosphere' of the halls led Sharman to include a dancing troupe, called the 'Dancing Daughters', to open the programmes; but tap-dancing on radio had a limited appeal and the idea was dropped by mid-1935.

The complete edition of *Music Hall* of Saturday 14 November 1936 is preserved in the BBC Sound Archives, and it provides a fascinating glimpse of the style of the programme – it is in fact the earliest existing recording of a complete British Variety programme. The performers – who are announced merely by their names, with no attempt by the announcer to act as compère – are Arthur Askey (then a little-known stand-up comic); the musical comedy team Les Allen and Kitty Masters; another rather broader musical comedy team, Rupert Hazell and his wife Elsie Day; a rather poor stand-up comic called Leslie Hatton; Billy Cotton and his band (whose slick and well-drilled playing makes the resident BBC Variety Orchestra sound rather ragged); and Will Hay and his Scholars.

Hay performs a shortened version of one of his stage sketches from a few years earlier, running some eleven minutes; since by 1936 he was doing a different version on stage he could afford to use this one on air. The usual boy and stupid old man spend the sketch arguing about their examination results. 'You marked mine all wrong' says the old man; 'Yours?' says Hay, '– I didn't even bother to look at yours' – which is not surprising since a typical answer in the old man's paper is 'A martyr is a pile of wood with a man on top'.

Music Hall regularly brought top acts to listeners, including Harry Tate, Lily Morris, The Two Leslies, Flanagan and Allen and many others; and the BBC also created its own stars who then appeared on the Variety halls.

One such was Gillie Potter, who specialized in a sort of clipped facetiousness, and always thought – with some justification – that he was better working solo without an audience (something with which the BBC disagreed). Beginning 'Good evening, England, this is Gillie Potter

speaking to you in English', he would talk for some ten or fifteen minutes. One of his themes was the latest news from the imaginary village of Hogsnorton, which he peopled with characters such as Canon Fodder, General Sir Stimulant Maudlin-Tite, and Lord Marshmallow ('His Lordship played bridge with his guests until he had won back the cost of their keep') to create one of radio's first imaginary communities. He would also talk about his experiences of the world in general, as in this early monologue which predates the invention of Hogsnorton and is more in the style of his stage appearances.

Good evening, ladies and gentlemen. I've just returned from America. I don't know whether you've ever been to America – I went out first class, and came back on an American boat. I know a great deal about America – my third wife was an American. The other two were no good, either. And yet one always learns something from these Americans – there was an American on the boat who told me something I did not know before – do you know that you and I, we human beings, are actually taller in the morning than we are at night? I didn't know that. I know I'm always short at the end of the week.[3] When we returned our friends looked us over, and suggested a holiday. They said, 'Why don't you go to the seaside?' I said, 'No thank you – I hate the sea. I loathe the sea. If I go anywhere at all,

I want to go somewhere where you can't even see the sea.' They said, 'You should go to Southend.' So I bought a hymnbook to find where Southend was, and went down by train.[4] We went on what they call the sea-front, and watched them ploughing. There was some talk about going down to the sea itself, but the man who knew the way was ill.[5]

One of Potter's frequent complaints to the BBC did have some basis – broadcasts from live performances were paid for by the BBC to the management of the theatre concerned; the management were supposed to pass some of the fee on to the artists involved, but some managements were lax about doing this; only after pressure was applied by the VAF was the situation improved, and by the late 1930s proper separate contracts were being issued for broadcasts from stage performances. The relationship between the BBC and the theatrical managements – and George Black in particular – had its ups and downs throughout the 1930s, but by 1938 things had settled somewhat.

In January 1938 George Black told the *Daily Mail*: 'Formerly we had to deal at Broadcasting House with what I might term the cuff-and-collar brigade – young men with little or no knowledge of the stage, but who considered themselves qualified to teach us our business whenever a theatre broadcast or a microphone turn by a stage artiste was being considered. But now there is a set of very nice fellows there, who do understand something of the business, and who realize that when theatrical entertainment is going over the air it should be handled by experts. Accordingly my attitude has undergone a change, and I shall now give every facility to Broadcasting House to bring radio audiences and our own public closer together.'[6]

It is possible that part of this change of heart on Black's part was encouraged by the fact that audiences were by now beginning to go to Variety halls in order to see stars whom they had only heard on the radio – the desire to see what the performers looked like provided a useful boost for theatrical Variety, which was just beginning to see radio as an advantage. The new agreement with Black led immediately to a fortnightly series of broadcasts from the Holborn Empire, starting on 2 February 1938 – *Radio Times* announced that 'the management will co-operate to ensure the most suitable broadcast material' (no more paper-tearers).

Eventually the divisions between broadcasting per-

formers and stage performers disappeared; but in the earlier days each found it a little difficult to adjust to the other medium. Dick Henderson, though completely at home on stage, found broadcasting difficult, as his son remembers.

'Dad was brought up in a school where you have your twelve or sixteen minutes which was dynamite, and you'd honed it, and it was perfect. But stick a script in his hand, and try to make that funny . . . that's why the early radio days produced stars from good readers, not funny men . . . his nerve went when you put a script in his hand, even though he was a better performer than the guy alongside him. He finished up doing his stage material because he was so frightened – but how many broadcasts can you do? But when these broadcasters were topping a bill, Dad would go on halfway through the second half and just do his act – there was no way they could follow him!'

Though stage Variety was complementary with rather than competition for radio, the BBC had direct competition from the new commercial stations on the continent. They filled a public need because the BBC's Sunday programmes were carefully planned to be devoid of any frivolity. While the BBC offered nothing more unseemly than light music, Radio Luxembourg and Radio Normandie, which had been operating since the early 1930s, provided dance music, record programmes and shows featuring Variety artists such as Gracie Fields and George Formby.

Charles Maxwell, later a BBC producer, worked as a presenter for Radio Luxembourg in the late 1930s. His job was to link the records and programmes sent over from England; he later came back to England to produce programmes.

'These were recorded and sent out by boat and train to Luxembourg; we did a long series with Gracie Fields, recorded at the Scala Theatre with an audience. And we did a series with George Formby, recorded without an audience in a studio in Bond Street.'

The programmes were sponsored, and thus carried advertisements. The BBC was of course flatly forbidden to take advertisements by the terms of its Charter, and had – with some justification – a horror of the typical American radio station, with its constant interruptions for advertising and a free-for-all lack of control. This distaste for the commercial aspect of broadcasting led the BBC to be reluctant to consider any of the other American techniques of comedy shows.

Much of the actual writing in these early American programmes now sounds very poor (if no worse than the patter of Variety artists such as Leslie Hatton) but the experimentation with formats and the use of radio as a medium in itself left the BBC far behind. In other fields – drama, music, and in particular the new format of radio features – the BBC tried some bold experiments and often produced exciting results; but Variety Department was content to go on with studio Variety shows and Outside Broadcasts from theatres.

There were occasional attempts to ring the changes, with revues which had a particular theme, for example; but it was not until *Monday Night At Seven* (which began in 1937 as *Monday At Seven*) that the first signs of a real willingness to experiment appeared. *Monday Night At Seven* was really a magazine rather than a Variety show – although it did have appearances by Variety artists. There was no audience, which led to the humour being of a rather quieter nature; one of the most successful examples of the programme's humour was the teaming of Ronald Frankau and Tommy Handley as 'Mr Murgatroyd and Mr Winterbottom' – their use of puns was almost stream-of-consciousness:

Band Waggon – **Richard Murdoch (*left*) and Arthur Askey (1938)**

HANDLEY:	Mr Murgatroyd, I'm very interested to know why you're sighing.
FRANKAU:	Ah, you're keen on sigh-cology?
HANDLEY:	Only downhill.
FRANKAU:	Give me a break.
HANDLEY:	Oh, yes, we must have one of those.
FRANKAU:	By psychology I mean the study of human nature. Take hypo-chondriacs.
HANDLEY:	Well how do they develop?
FRANKAU:	They sham-pain.
HANDLEY:	Now you're talking of fizzy-ology. But as a matter of fact, I know my fellow men pretty well.
FRANKAU:	I met a man the other day you couldn't have understood.
HANDLEY:	Why?
FRANKAU:	He was a Czechoslovakian.
HANDLEY:	Serbia right. I didn't mean I understood foreigners – neither Swedes Nor-wegians.
FRANKAU:	Argentine to pull my leg?[7]

But the most important step forward in BBC Variety came on Wednesday 5 January 1938 with the first edition of *Band Waggon*. For the first time, a Variety programme was placed on a regular day, at a more-or-less regular time, and with a regular comedian – Arthur Askey. It was in the idea of the 'resident comedian' – much play was made in *Radio Times* of this new expression – that the real novelty lay. The scripts were written by Vernon Harris, who had worked in the theatre but was new to writing for radio.

'I said, "I cannot write gags – I can write a sketch with a beginning, a middle and an end; but it's got to be a little play." '

Because Askey was the 'resident comedian', someone suggested that this should be taken literally; the idea caught on immediately – many listeners were convinced that there really *was* a flat in Broadcasting House – and running gags involving Askey's pets – Lewis the goat and the pigeons Basil and Lucy – and his fiancée Nausea Bagwash (who never appeared) were built into the sketches. The audience response was tremendous and *Band Waggon* rapidly became one of the BBC's most popular programmes.

In each programme Askey and Murdoch would do an opening sketch as from the studio itself, a sketch from the flat, 'Chestnut Corner', with some even older old jokes, a solo spot each, and another sketch in which Murdoch would usually be attempting to teach Askey how to do something, with varying degrees of success. For the first time in BBC Variety, the regular structure of the programme allowed for catchphrases – such as Askey's 'Ay Thang Yew' and Murdoch's 'You silly little man' – and running gags (such as the one involving the top BBC announcer Stuart Hibberd, to whom they often spoke – he was alleged to live in the flat below – but who never answered them).

Vernon Harris's comment on hearing recordings of *Band Waggon*[8] after a lapse of many years was that he had forgotten how ingenuous they were; and this sums it up exactly. Askey and Murdoch deliver their lines expertly, and favourite old jokes are used neatly in the basic framework of the sketches. The ingenuousness is part of the charm of the programme, and it was the characters created by the two performers that made the programme such a success – and made Askey a star.

A favourite technique was for Murdoch to be attempting to teach Askey to do something – in this example (based on an Askey and Murdoch concert-party sketch), to be a waiter – by first demonstrating it himself and then getting Askey to have a go.

ASKEY: I'm the waiter this time, and you're the man what comes in and has something to eat.

MURDOCH: That's right, yes.

ASKEY: You'll be lucky.

MURDOCH: Now, this is me coming in.

ASKEY: You amaze me.

MURDOCH: Good morning.

ASKEY: Good gracious! . . . that's witty, isn't it!

MURDOCH: Do you serve lobsters?

ASKEY: We serve anybody, sir . . . you see? I knew the answer to that one, didn't I?

MURDOCH: Well I want something to eat.

ASKEY: On a plate or in a nosebag?

MURDOCH: I'm so hungry I could eat a horse.

ASKEY: We've only got the d'oeuvres.

MURDOCH: Well, have you any soup?

ASKEY: Soup? – here, wait a minute, you can't rush me like that – we've got to come to some arrangement first. Do you want the 10/6d luncheon or the half-crown special?

MURDOCH: The half-crown special will do.

ASKEY: Right you are – it's the same thing, only I've got to take these flowers off the table.

MURDOCH: Well, have you any soup?

ASKEY: Have we any soup? Now let me see – I'll have to ring up the head office and enquire (*phone lifted*) Hello! Give me Welbeck 4468 . . . Yes, 6844 . . . Hello, is that Museum 00013? Oh, put me through to the catering department, will you? . . . Oh, is that you, Charlie? Look here, have we any soup? Yes . . . yes . . . yes . . . yes . . . yes . . . yes . . . yes . . . yes . . . (*phone down*) No. Would you like some porridge?

MURDOCH: *No*, I don't want any porridge – I want some soup.

ASKEY: Would you like noodle, poodle or cock-a-doodle?

MURDOCH: Well what's the difference?

ASKEY: There is none.

MURDOCH: What, no difference?

ASKEY: No, no soup. Would you like some tripe?

MURDOCH: Yes, I'd like some tripe.

ASKEY: Right – George,[9] switch on the wireless, would you? (He's an old friend.) (*Indicating the audience*) They get in for nothing and laugh at us.[10]

Another milestone in British broadcasting for *Band Waggon* was in the use of a writer in the employment of the BBC – a common enough practice in America, but previously the performers had always provided their own material (even if they did not always write it themselves). The script was a team effort, with Askey and Murdoch adding gags to Harris's framework; but no on-air credit was given for the script.

Vernon Harris: 'I never got a credit – it was the policy of the BBC that they wanted the public to believe that Arthur and Dickie made it up on the spot! – it was as ingenuous as that – so they would *not* give me a credit.' Writers were to be increasingly important in the development of radio comedy; as radio comedy eventually moved away from theatrical imitations into pure radio techniques, the provision of a weekly script became a major part of the effort involved in putting on a show.

Band Waggon was a turning point in British broadcast Variety, and as such is one of the most important of all programmes in this genre; its good humour and charm make it agreeable listening even after so many years. There were two direct spin-offs from the show: a film, made in 1939, and a theatrical version which toured the Variety circuits with some success – the first of many spin-offs from radio shows to do so.

Variety Department, well pleased with the success of *Band Waggon*, started to experiment with other personality shows. A new fortnightly series, starring Tommy Handley and called *It's That Man Again*, began on 12 July 1939; it was in a semi-magazine format, influenced by *Band Waggon* and *Monday Night At Seven* and it was not until the war began that it took on its more familiar format (see Chapter 18).

Meanwhile a whole new medium was establishing itself – television. Following the early 30-line experiments by John Logie Baird, regular broadcasts started in November 1936, with the Baird 240-line system being used in alternate weeks with the EMI high-definition system. The EMI system, which used 405 lines, won the contest and was used from February 1937; it established a transmission standard which was not superseded until 1964. The number of viewers was relatively tiny – there were around 20,000 to 25,000 sets in use by August 1939 – and so as far as Variety is concerned the importance of television lay more in its future potential than in what it achieved at the time.

Pat Hillyard, who had worked as a theatrical director and producer before he joined the BBC in 1938, was the Deputy Head of television productions for a short period before the outbreak of war put a stop to television transmissions.

'In the early days of television we did a lot of revue sketches – people like Nelson Keys used to come up, and we did little intimate shows; we used to take the Dorchester Follies, for instance. And we had dance bands every week – Roy Fox and Jack Jackson and so on – and also straight Variety bills.'

The hours of television were limited to only three or four a night, and there was perhaps one Variety programme a week – usually consisting of a handful of small-time speciality or dance acts. A very few bigger names did appear – including Tommy Trinder and Sandy Powell – but on the whole television impinged very little on the world of Variety. Indeed many people confidently predic-

ted that it was a novelty in which audiences would quickly lose interest – the BBC hierarchy, being entirely concerned with radio, showed very little interest in television and could not see that it had any future. It certainly had no *immediate* future, for the imminence of war caused television transmissions to come to an abrupt end on 1 September 1939 – partly because the BBC wanted to be able to concentrate its resources (and money) on radio, but largely because the frequencies would be needed for the still highly secret radar system.

Meanwhile, in the last few months of peace the BBC's radio Variety output had increased from the two-hours-a-week of the early 1930s to include several personality-based shows which took their lead from *Band Waggon*. In the very last week of peace, from Sunday 27 August 1939, listeners could hear Flotsam and Jetsam for fifteen minutes, forty minutes of *Dance Cabaret* (with music and Variety turns), *It's That Man Again*, a *Variety Half-Hour* from 'Radiolympia' (a trade fair, open to the public, at Olympia exhibition hall) and *Theatres of Variety* from the Bristol Hippodrome. On the Saturday listeners were promised an hour of *Up With The Curtain* with Tommy Trinder and *The 'Appy 'Arf 'Our* with Leon Cortez; but Saturday's programmes were mostly replaced with gramophone records as the BBC, in anticipation of the declaration of war, decentralized its departments. Variety Department packed its suitcases and descended upon Bristol, leaving Broadcasting House half empty and surrounded by sandbags.

On Sunday 3 September 1939, the Prime Minister Neville Chamberlain announced over the radio that Britain was now at war with Germany. All aspects of life immediately became different – Variety artists being affected no less than anybody else. In those first few days of the war – even though it was the 'phoney war' in which Britain was involved in no immediate hostilities – the managements, performers and broadcasters for whom Variety was a way of life as well as a livelihood looked with some apprehension at the days ahead and wondered how Variety would fare in wartime conditions.

(Broadcasting in wartime is covered in Chapter 18, p. 151.)

A week in Variety

In Chapter 9 we examined the regular weekly routine followed by the Variety managements as they organized the business. In this Interlude we will look at the week-by-week pattern of life in Variety from the point of view of the performers. It was a way of life which changed very little from the 1920s to the mid-1950s (apart from the wartime difficulties of transport, food rationing and so on), so the sort of routine described might have taken place in any single week in the period.

As Vic Duncan has commented, it was a hard life in many ways – six days a week working and the seventh travelling – and despite the relatively high pay compared with that of people in ordinary occupations, it is obvious that money was not the principal motivation – people who worked in Variety did so because they very much wanted to; it was a way of life which fascinated them and absorbed all their interest. For them there was no ordinary home life; no suburban Sundays, regular hours or steady jobs; but most of them seem to have loved every minute of it.

The week's routine began on Sunday afternoon when each act arrived at the town of that week's booking, usually by train. Prop baskets and luggage would be delivered to the theatre, and the first job for the performers would be to find 'digs' for the week. Digs were rarely booked in advance; in most cases performers would obtain a list of landladies specializing in theatrical lettings from the theatre, and go round until they found suitable lodgings. The landladies were used to the needs of performers – a late dinner after the show, a late breakfast (few performers crawled out of bed before nine o'clock in the morning), lunch, and a snack before the performance. On the whole performers and landladies got on well, but there were always exceptions – most performers can tell horror stories of appalling cooking, damp sheets and dirty rooms. One hears less from the landladies' point of view about performers being difficult or disappearing without paying, but it did happen.

George Robey had his own method of dealing with nosey landladies – he left a tin in his rooms which was empty apart from a recently caught live fly. If the fly had disappeared when he returned, the landlady was likely to receive a lecture on the evils of snooping.

The actual work began on Monday morning with rehearsals – 'band call'. Each act would go through the music they required with the orchestra, making sure that the conductor knew the cues, etc. There was a tradition that each act, as they arrived in the morning, would put their band parts down on the stage, the first one there putting his music at the front centre, and then the others along the stage; each act was then dealt with in the order in which they had put their music down, regardless of who was the star.

The band had to be able to cope with anything that was given to them, more or less on sight – with varying degrees of success. The bands in the best theatres were generally very good, but in smaller theatres difficulties could arise. Roy Castle, who came into the business in the 1950s, developed an act which included him imitating various instruments; in each case the band would then follow him with the real thing.

'The Musicians' Union insisted that if there were, say, eleven men in the orchestra, three must be locally employed – and in this band one of these was the drummer. I used to build up a whole orchestration, and I started out with the drummer – I'd just imitate the "hi-hat" cymbal; but he couldn't play it, he'd got a really old-fashioned drum-kit. All he could do was bash the bass drum. We tried it again, and he still didn't get it right, so I went down into the pit and showed him; he looked at me and said, "All right, I'll have a go" . . . so I sang it to him again from the stage – and he still got it wrong. I was getting a little bit fed up, and I said, "No, that's not it – I don't *want* the bass drum" – and he looked me straight in the eye and said, "Listen mate, I'm delivering milk at five o'clock in the morning." There's no answer to that!'

Harry Secombe (who was knighted many years later – a rare honour for a Variety comic, and one shared only by George Robey and Scots comic Harry Lauder) also started his career in the tattier theatres in the post-war period.

He remembers: 'If the musicians knew where you were playing next week they'd write little messages on your music – "Love to the missus; Jack" – one trombonist to another! In the end you couldn't see for marks. They couldn't all read music, either – the worst player in the band was always the shop steward. And you'd have orchestrations and go to the theatre on the Monday . . . "*Flute?* we don't have a bloody flute!" and he'd throw your parts back at you! Just trombone, trumpet, sax . . . it used to sound awful sometimes. Especially if it had been scored for violins.'

Fortunately these examples were fairly extreme, and in the 'number ones' the orchestras usually were of a high degree of competence.

Then came the first house on Monday evening – the most difficult test for the performers. The audience would usually be fairly small – many of them theatrical landladies and their families in on free passes. If attendance was really poor, the manager would sometimes give away tickets – often to unemployed men hanging around the town; this technique at least ensured a moderate-sized audience for the first performance, and was known as 'papering the house' (free tickets being referred to as 'paper'). This performance placed more strain on the performer than any other, as Alf Pearson remembers.

'You'd got only ten or fifteen minutes to establish yourself with the audience – to make them like you, because if they didn't like you they didn't applaud or laugh. If you didn't make a success of those fifteen minutes, you had a miserable week. And if you had a few bad weeks, it would go round like jungle drums – "He's dying the death, that fellow, don't book him" . . . '

Bob Pearson adds: 'Every theatre's different – when you're thrown in on the Monday night first house it's entirely different to the last week – the audience is entirely different, the band's different, the stage is different – you've got to adapt and put yourself across as though you've been working in that theatre for weeks.'

An act which went really badly on the Monday could be paid off by the manager – he had to pay them for the week even if he cancelled the rest of their appearances so it was not done without a good reason; in some towns the news that an act had failed badly would be all round the town within hours, so that that act was doomed for the rest of the week.

Second house would probably be easier than first – and indeed second house audiences throughout the week might well be easier to play to than first house audiences (the recordings of Max Miller at the Holborn Empire in 1938 show that he altered his act considerably for second house). Wally Thomas explains the probable reason for this.

'You got a more robust audience in for the second house – and perhaps they'd all had a few drinks by then – where

your first house audience was probably people who had got to get to work in the morning.'

Audiences might get a bit *too* robust sometimes, and start heckling performers – though fortunately this was relatively rare. Experienced comics learnt to deal with this problem; Will Hay, faced with a group of rowdy students, silenced them by saying firmly, 'Now then – only one fool at a time, and I'm talking'.

Not everyone managed so well; Bob Pearson remembers: 'This was in Scotland, and it was the fellow's own fault – it was Scott Saunders, and he wasn't doing too well – probably the audience had seen it so many times that they knew it. He started to blow raspberries at the audience, and they blew raspberries back . . . in the end he had to go off, he got the "bird". And we were the next act. That's a frightening experience . . . and our act then was twelve minutes – I think we did it in four minutes and got off quickly.'

Artists working in London might be booked to perform at two theatres each evening – a procedure known as 'doubling' or 'turns', which had its origin in Victorian music-hall where artists might play as many as five theatres in one night. Artists playing two theatres – and thus four performances each night – would be paid less than double their usual fee – a £50 act would perhaps get £80 – so the management saved money, while the artists still earned a lot more than usual. (Because of the shortage of work, the VAF permitted this practice only in London; it was forbidden anywhere else under their Rule 40 – it was in any case less practicable in the provinces.)

The timings of their appearances would be arranged to permit them to be on early at the first theatre, travel to the second theatre and appear late in the first half; stay there and appear early in the second house, and then get back to the first theatre in time to make their final appearance. Acts which relied on props or scenery had to have two sets to avoid trying to move them about.

Ronnie Tate remembered: 'Setting up on Monday morning at two theatres was murder.'

Doubling could take place between theatres several miles apart – there was, for example, no difficulty in travelling between Poplar and Hackney, or even Shepherds Bush and Holborn, in the time available. (It would be quite impossible now owing to the tremendous increase in traffic. Bob and Alf Pearson once even came to central London for a radio broadcast between houses in Reading!) One of the secrets in doubling was to *hire* a car for the week, rather than using one's own – thus removing the problem of finding a parking space.

With the hurdles of the Monday's performance over, everyone could settle into the routine for the rest of the week – perhaps rehearse in the mornings, play golf or go to a cinema (usually on a free pass) in the afternoon; and then be in the theatre all evening. Because of the enclosed nature of the business most artists had little interest in anything outside it and would simply pass the time until the evening.

Inevitably one of the dangers of a life-style like this was over-indulgence in alcohol, and it is if anything surprising that so few performers succumbed to it.

George Bolton: 'There's always a bar in a theatre, and people would come round and say, "I'll see you in the bar after the show" – well, after I'd done two shows, I didn't want to go up in the bar and meet a lot of people that I didn't know – but of course a lot of people got lonely when they were on tour.'

Drinking with members of the audience in the bar had other dangers, as Harry Harbour points out.

'The theatre should be an illusion – the performers were an illusion; but then they used to go in bars and mix with people, so the illusion was no longer there. When I was made manager of Chiswick Empire I felt very strongly that artists should stay on their side of the curtain, and I decided to keep the pass door [between the auditorium and backstage] locked – if the artists wanted a drink they could send out and have what they wanted – but I thought it was wrong for the artists to go in the bar and mix with the public; they were no longer magic – if you bought them a pint of bitter, you were on the same level as they were.'

Apart from this sort of social drinking, there were occasional cases of actual alcoholism. One comedian, Claude Lester, was well known in the business as an alcoholic, and one week the manager of the theatre he was working in decided to put a stop to it; he searched the dressing-room thoroughly, locked the window, left Lester there cold sober and locked the door on him. When the manager came back to let Lester out for his appearance, he found that Lester had created a locked-room mystery all of his own – for despite the precautions he was hopelessly drunk. He had bribed the call-boy to go out and fetch a bottle of whisky and a straw, to place the straw through the keyhole of the door and hold the bottle while Lester sucked himself into oblivion.

After second house on Saturday the performers would leave the theatre for the last time in that visit – and would be expected to tip the staff – a little for the band, a little for the stagehands, and so on; the actual amount depending on their place on the bill. The VAF tried in the early 1920s to get an agreement abolishing tipping, but they never quite succeeded; it was of course 'entirely voluntary', but any artist omitting to place a few shillings in the right palms might find on a return visit that a stage weight was 'accidentally' and noisily dropped off-stage at a crucial point in his act.

Then on Sunday came the business of travelling to the next engagement (assuming the artist was lucky enough to have one). At some time during the week artists who were members of the Music Hall Artists Railway Association would call on the local representative and get a signed card which would enable them to get a discount on their train tickets. (The representative was often the landlord of the nearest pub, so that the cost of having a drink there had to be entered into the calculations.) Bob and Alf Pearson remember that someone from the local railway office used to come round to the theatre early in the week and advise on the best route and arrange the details of the baggage (which could take two porters to move in the case of, say, an acrobatic act).

Sunday travel on the railways was better than it is now, but it could still take most of the day if the journey was halfway across the country. For some unfathomable reason to do with the construction of timetables, almost any journey (at least those to or from the north) seemed to involve changing at Crewe – a dismal station at the best of times. With so many performers congregating there, it became almost a social occasion and a chance to exchange gossip – hence Ted Ray's description of Crewe station on a Sunday morning – 'Actors and fish'.

And then, upon arrival at the destination on Sunday afternoon, the whole week's routine would start all over again; and for forty years this was the life-style of most of those in the Variety profession.

16 'All dark and no petrol'
Variety in World War Two

Do you like these black nights, ducky – do you like 'em, lady? No, no, they're nice, ain't they – I don't care how dark it is, I don't care – I like it! All dark and no petrol! I don't want any petrol – I didn't ask for any. I don't – I used to take 'em out in the country – any doorway, now – 'Ere!

(Max Miller, November 1939)[1]

Only a matter of minutes after Neville Chamberlain's radio announcement of the declaration of war on 3 September 1939, a BBC announcer was reading out the first wartime regulations. Among them was one which seemed to spell doom for the Variety profession – all theatres, cinemas, sports grounds and other places where the public might congregate in large numbers were immediately closed until further notice. This decision was taken because of the worrying possibility of a crowded theatre being hit by a bomb – although, in a touching act of faith, churches were excepted from the ban. The move brought immediate protests against the government's lack of foresight – George Bernard Shaw, for example, wrote to *The Times* pointing out that in the previous War there had been some 80,000 soldiers on leave every night looking for amusement, which the theatres had done much to provide.

Common sense prevailed, and from 16 September theatres were allowed to reopen, provided that they were closed by 10 p.m. each evening. They did not all reopen at once, but over the next few months the theatrical and Variety business worked its way into a boom period – as did the cinema. The atmosphere in which they operated was vastly different from that of only a short period earlier; petrol was rationed (and its use for pleasure banned), food was rationed, consumer goods were in short supply and a total blackout was in force – after dark all premises had to make sure that not a ray of light escaped.

Air-raid precautions had been well rehearsed since 1938, and on hearing the sirens the large numbers of people would make their way to the air-raid shelters and underground stations. The practice was established in theatres whereby the show was stopped in the event of an air-raid warning and the audience offered the chance to leave – few did, as a rule – those remaining being entertained until the all-clear sounded. Despite the nagging fear of a bomb hitting a crowded theatre and killing large numbers of people, it never happened; a number of theatres were destroyed – the Holborn Empire among them – but all were empty at the time.

In the early stages of the war no-one was too sure of the future.

Billy Marsh: 'The managements did not know what to offer the artists in the way of salaries; so they suggested to their agents that they work on a percentage [of the takings]. And then one or two agents said, "If you're putting them on a percentage, I'll take a percentage for the rest of the show." So the theatre managements were then getting a visiting company, which the agents had put together, to put on Variety bills – without them having to take the responsibility. In point of fact the business flourished, and it gave the agents who had stars the power to say, "Our star wants to put the bill in". This wasn't completely unique, because prior to the war Gracie Fields used to put her own shows in' (as did Sandy Powell and Ernie Lotinga but in the smaller theatres).

As a result of this change – for even Moss Empires was now accepting package shows – the war brought the heyday of small-time revues; although many of these were in fact only a more-or-less standard type of Variety bill which happened to have a title and be toured as a package. A few of them revived the old presentation device of the compère to introduce the acts, harking back to the chairman of Victorian music-halls; perhaps they were inspired to do so by the presentation of BBC Variety programmes, which had much improved since the simple announcements of the mid-1930s. (These touring revues should not be confused with the relatively new format of 'intimate revue', which emerged in the London theatre in the 1940s; shows such as the *Sweet and Low* series and *Sky High* were much more intelligent in style and belonged to a different theatrical area, which later became associated with the Cambridge Footlights and similar revues.)

The tremendous boom in entertainment generally might have been predicted; unemployment had suddenly disappeared, as people either joined the forces or went to work in aircraft and munitions factories (in both cases either voluntarily or compulsorily through the draft) and relatively good wages were being paid. On the other hand, there was little to spend money on – luxuries more or less disappeared from the market, house purchase became impossible, and necessities were rationed and price-controlled; so suddenly vast numbers of people, with money to spend and a need to forget for a few hours the dismal and nerve-racking life they were leading, flooded into the theatres and cinemas.

In the case of one particularly shrewd manager it was not only the entertainment which brought people into his theatres, as Alf Pearson remembers:

'Horace Collins had about five theatres in Scotland as well as an agency and a wardrobe business; at the beginning of the war – nobody knows how it happened – he bought a bonded warehouse, and had its contents transferred into two dressing-rooms in the Theatre Royal Edinburgh – they were stacked from floor to ceiling with bottles of Scotch. So throughout the war, *his* theatres had got whisky to sell in the bar. Now in the Edinburgh Empire, in the bar, if you were lucky you'd get a bottle of beer [whisky was not rationed, it was simply unobtainable]; but the Scots like their whisky, and they could get it in the Theatre Royal bar – so it was packed!'

If the war was in some ways a gift to the Variety business in general and Horace Collins in particular, it was also a gift to the comedians – suddenly they had a whole new range of subjects to make jokes on. Nellie Wallace commented of her latest beau, 'He's in the air force. Aren't they wonderful? Aren't they marvellous? But they're beggars for bringing things down!'[2]

Billy Russell put the working man's view of domestic conditions:

> In the house we're living in now, we've got the wife's sister come to stay with us – she's brought her four kids – they've evacuated on us; and then there's our sixteen . . . We don't know where to put them all – running about – the wife gets worried these dark nights, kids running about – she feeds them on onions so she can find 'em in the dark. Well, you know how it is yourself, us grown-ups groping about in these blackouts – you never know where you get to. I found myself in me own house two nights last week! We've got one of those RIP chaps round our way – he's a damned nuisance! With his blacking out, blacking out – we've hardly got

any clothes on the bed. Me and the missus in bed, shivering – we have to work up a heated argument.[3]

The most enduringly famous comment came from Robb Wilton and was aimed at the Home Guard, the civilian volunteers, rejected by the draft boards for the services on grounds of age or health, who trained (with inadequate equipment) against a possible German invasion.

> The day war broke out, my Missus looked at me, and she said, 'What *good* are you?' . . .

So he joined the Home Guard:

> The first day I got my Home Guard uniform . . . I'm getting the trousers next year . . . but the first day I got . . . I went home, and I slipped upstairs, and I put it on. And I came down, into the kitchen, and the Missus looked at me, and she said, 'What *are* you supposed to be?' I said, 'Supposed to be . . . ' I said, 'I'm one of the Home Guard.' She said, 'One of the Home . . . ' She said, 'What are the *others* like?' And then, the Missus said, she said, 'Well, what do you *do* in the Home Guard?' I said, 'I've got to stop Hitler's army landing.' She said, 'What, *you*?' I said, 'No, there's Harry Bates, and Charlie Evans . . . ' – I said, 'There's seven or eight of us altogether.' I said, 'We're in a group.' I said, 'We're on guard in a little hut behind the Dog and Pullet.' She said, 'Now, what's the good of being on guard in a little hut behind the Dog and Pull . . . ' – she said, 'I suppose that was *your* idea.' I said, 'Aye – and that Charlie Evans wants to claim it as his!'[4]

Apart from the shows put on for the public in Variety theatres, there was a whole sub-culture of entertainment for the armed forces. Basil Dean – a film and theatrical produce and director – had foreseen the need for entertainment for the troops, and, remembering the disorganized arrangements of World War One, formed an organization for bringing professional artists to the troops at their stations both at home and abroad. Dean was a very difficult man – Michael Standing, who had dealings with him on many occasions (the BBC broadcast a number of Dean's shows, and there was considerable rivalry between the organizations) remembered him.

'A terrible chap – he was able, but his narkiness cost him the honour that might have been due to him after the war.'

Nevertheless, few men could have achieved the results that Dean did under the difficult conditions he had to face.

The organization was called the Entertainments National Service Association – ENSA; Tommy Trinder promptly dubbed it 'Every Night Something Awful' which was unkind but had a ring of truth, for many of the acts recruited were very poor. There were other, rival organizations; and the forces themselves organized entertainments in the form of touring revues such as the Army's 'Stars in Battledress' and the RAF 'Gang Shows', drawn not from civilian entertainers but from amateur and occasionally professional performers in the services themselves.

The standard of these shows was very variable – often very bad – but it gave performing experience to a new generation of people who were to form the backbone of the Variety profession after the war – Tony Hancock, Peter Sellers, Robert Moreton, Dick Emery, Spike Milligan and Harry Secombe.

However much fun all this may have been for the amateur performers, many acrobatic and speciality acts were finding the war a lot less amusing; most circuses had closed at the outbreak of war, and quite a few Variety performers had enlisted in the early weeks of the war when it looked as if their business might collapse; this left them trapped with no chance to keep in practice.

Rikki McCormick comments sourly: 'The *real* performers and pros were flying aeroplanes and transporting munitions and all the rest of it, and they got left out of it [ENSA etc]; and then all the others, who wanted to get away from carrying a gun got stuck into the Gang Shows, and they weren't performers at all. Then when the war finished the pros came back, and started to try to polish their acts up, but the Gang Show performers were already there . . . and nowadays *they're* all on television and the real performers are out. Many of them never recovered from the war.'

This statement has an exaggeration born of bitterness; but there *is* a certain amount of truth in it.

As the war progressed, professional artists were sent by ENSA to the Middle and Far East, and often performed under appalling conditions. The story of ENSA and the forces shows – and the other organizations such as those which brought serious drama to the troops – is complicated; and the present book is not really concerned with the details, since its brief is Variety for the *public*. The

detailed story is well told in Richard Fawkes's book *Fighting For A Laugh*.[5] There were, of course, large numbers of servicemen on leave – or on station waiting to go abroad – in Britain at various times, and so any Variety audience would contain a fair proportion of uniformed men and women.

The need to keep off-duty troops entertained led to a slackening in the tight controls over what might be presented on stage. The most interesting aspect of this was the phenomenon of nude shows, which – although there had been a very little of this sort of thing before the war – suddenly flourished on the British Variety circuits from the beginning of 1940. Under the Lord Chamberlain's regulations, nude posing by women was initially permitted only if the tableau presented was intended to be, for example, a copy of a famous picture or had 'artistic' merit of some sort. That idea was the first thing to go, at any rate in its strict application; even so, the acts were still supposed to be tasteful, and prospective posers had to submit photographs of their intended presentation to the Lord Chamberlain's Office. (The attitudes suggested by their rulings make it doubtful whether the officials saw this as a perk of the job.) Any movement by the nude performers was most strictly forbidden; as was any direct view of the pubis, which was usually covered with sticking-plaster (the removal of which must have occasioned much discomfort in the cause of art).

The Windmill Theatre in London's Soho had already been presenting this sort of show, and there had been very occasional touring acts involving discreet nudity; but in early 1940 the smaller circuits suddenly flowered with revues which featured a few nudes. The titles suggested a riot of abandoned unadornment – *Naughty Girls of 1940*, *Fig Leaves*, *Strip Strip Hooray*, *Eve Takes a Bow* and *Bare Idea* were all presented in the first few months of 1940 – but the nudity would really have seemed very tame to modern eyes; the attraction lay in the fact that opportunities for men to see a naked female figure in films or newspapers then were virtually non-existent. The most famous nude act of the period, Phyllis Dixey, sang and recited as well as posing; she later ran her own show with a troupe of girls who presented artistic tableaux. She thought she was presenting art to the masses; but no doubt what they really came for was an unaccustomed glimpse of 'tits and bums'.

Watch Committees would probably have made more fuss if the whole thing had not been classed as a necessary wartime expedient; but nevertheless there was some concern and in April 1940 a conference of managers and

Phyllis Dixey

cockney singing comic and originator of songs such as *Boiled Beef and Carrots* and *Any Old Iron*, which he used to sing with tremendous energy at a breathtaking speed. Bob Konyot was on the bill with him at the Shepherds Bush Empire early in the war.

'Gracie Fields was supposed to get £500 a week – she was the highest paid star; our springboard act was getting around £75 a week; and some of these old timers like Harry Champion were lucky if they could pick up £40. I went down to see his act; they played his signature tune – and no Harry Champion. They played it a second time – no Harry Champion. They played it a third time – still no Harry Champion; the boss of the show said, "All these old-timers do that, to create an atmosphere before they go on." And it was true that Harry Champion went on that stage – and *Whoomph!* – you know, that man couldn't sing, that man couldn't dance, he looked like a cabbie and he danced like Donald Duck . . . he couldn't do nothing; but he had the audience in the palm of his hand, and they loved him every minute of his act. He didn't do anything, but he was one of the greatest performers I've ever seen.'

There may have been plenty of work to go round – even for old stars who were past it – but conditions were not easy. Clothes were rationed – although there were special

Harry Champion

controlling authorities discussed the subject and decided to continue to allow nude posing, while banning 'suggestive dancing' or striptease.[6] In December 1940 the nude show *This Is The Show* was passed by most Watch Committees but the *title* was banned in York – it was not so much the title they objected to as the method of billing, which heavily featured the initial letters.

Nude shows continued throughout the war, but they were not yet a major part of Variety – and indeed did not appear on the major circuits; it was only in the post-war years that nude shows began to be an important factor in the business.

In the wartime scramble to keep the theatres booked each week – no easy matter with many acts called up or abroad – a number of old-time stars were persuaded out of retirement. Many of them were now too slow in their approach to compete with the slick methods of the 1940s – particularly when the Americans entered the war in 1942 and the British audiences became more familiar with their artists – but one exception was Harry Champion, the great

concessions for theatrical costumes. Railway baggage was restricted to 100 lb, which caused severe problems for acts with props or scenery to travel. Entertainment tax was doubled in April 1942, with the inevitable result that seat prices rose. In 1944 theatres were prohibited from using electricity or fuel for heating from mid-April to the end of October. The VAF attempted to get an increased soap ration for artists (because of the need to wash after removing make-up) but this was rejected. Make-up itself was in short supply, although arrangements were made with the agreement of the Board of Trade for VAF members to be able to purchase it on presentation of their membership cards. This last concession may have had something to do with the much-increased membership level of the VAF, which rose from about 2,000 just before the war to more than 5,500 in 1944.

Despite these problems, and the competition from the cinema (British films in particular were in a boom of their own) the Variety theatres continued to provide entertainment up and down the country. The Moss/GTC and Stoll circuits continued to dominate the business, both in quality and quantity (despite the death of Sir Oswald Stoll in January 1942; he was succeeded as managing director by Prince Littler); but the Variety boom was good news for the smaller circuits as well as the Syndicate Halls, Fred Collins, Bernard Delfont (Lew Grade's brother), Howard and Wyndham, and the Butterworth circuit, all of which ran Variety and small touring revues with reasonable success.

In central London the destruction of the Holborn Empire in September 1940 left the Palladium and the Victoria Palace as the only Variety theatres – and even they presented glossy revues for most of the time rather than true Variety. (The Coliseum had long since abandoned Variety bills; the London Pavilion had become a cinema, and the Alhambra had of course been demolished in 1936.) The Crazy Gang's last Palladium show, *The Little Dog Laughed*, was to have been followed by *Top Of The World* (with the Crazy Gang minus Naughton and Gold but plus Tommy Trinder) but the show was closed after only four days because of the blitz in 1940 and the Palladium stayed shut for a year. It reopened with *Applesauce* – transferred from the Holborn Empire and starring Max Miller – and continued with several more long-running shows, plus a few weeks of pure Variety. The last wartime show, *Happy and Glorious*, starred Tommy Trinder, and despite being delayed by the buzz-bombs in the summer of 1944 eventually opened to great success.

It was also George Black's last show; he died on 4 March 1945. With his death the world of Variety lost its shrewdest producer; a man who never stinted on quality and built his shows on the framework of his experience in Variety. He was succeeded by his right-hand man, Val Parnell, under whose management the Palladium in particular was to go in quite a different direction.

The war in Europe ended on 8 May 1945; for the first time in nearly six years the lights went on in front of the Variety theatres. The wartime boom created a momentum which carried over well into the post-war period; but the pre-war world had gone for ever and as the momentum subsided the changes in the outside world were reflected in the enclosed world of Variety.

(*The post-war boom in Variety is covered in Chapter 19, p. 156.*)

17 'Let's get *on* with it'
Double-acts: Two (the 1930s and 1940s)

As we saw in Chapter 6, by the end of the 1930s Flanagan and Allen had brought the pure cross-talk double-act to its peak. Few teams could hope to match their appeal, and most later double-acts worked within a character framework, building the gags into a narrative routine or setting them within strong character situations.

Jimmy Jewel and Ben Warriss – who were cousins – formed their double-act in 1934; their style was somewhere between pure cross-talk and character. By the end of the 1930s they had established themselves as second

Jimmy Jewel (*right*) and Ben Warriss

only to Flanagan and Allen in that range of humour. Jewel, who had toured for years with his father's family road-show in the north of England, presented himself as a speeded-up version of the northern 'gowk', while Warriss was slick and smart. The character building was less subtle than with Flanagan and Allen – where Allen, the classic straight man was obviously smarter than Flanagan, but even so Flanagan was no fool. Jewel was always the idiot and Warriss, as the straight man, usually came out on top. Like some stand-up comics of the 1930s, they abandoned eccentric clothing for smart suits. Warriss, in particular, was a very natty dresser on-stage.

Alfred Black remembers: 'Whenever we had a script conference for the summer shows in Blackpool – which used to run for twenty-odd weeks – Ben's first comment was always, "I'll have a new suit made for that". His first interest was what he was going to look like.'

Their style was sufficiently different from Flanagan and Allen for them to appear on the same bill on occasions. Although they did indulge in quick gags, they also relied on longer routines in which individual gags were subordinated to the overall situation. In this example Jewel has only just discovered that Warriss has entered him in a boxing match to challenge the then champion Joe Louis, and Warriss is attempting to sell Jewel the idea by dramatizing the proposed match.

WARRISS: Now there's more excitement – it is . . . yes, it is! It's Battling Jimmy Jewel, the Brookwood Basher! And he's walking into the . . . he's walking . . . they're *carrying* him into the ring! And Jewel's down! One – two – three – four . . .

JEWEL: Wait a minute!

WARRISS: What's the matter?

JEWEL: The fight hasn't started yet!

WARRISS: I'm sorry – I was carried away.

JEWEL: They'll be carrying *me* away in a minute!

WARRISS: Never mind – and there goes the bell

for the first round. Now they're in the centre of the ring – they're sparring round for an opening – they're both sparring round for an opening – and – Jewel's found one!

JEWEL: I have?

WARRISS: They've just put you back in the ring. And now Jewel lands a left to the jaw . . . and Jewel hits him with a left to the body . . . and Jewel lands a right uppercut . . . Jewel's giving him everything he's got.

JEWEL: I'm terrific!

WARRISS: Yes, and Jewel's down! Listen to the crowd roar!

JEWEL: To hell with the crowd – how did I get down there?

WARRISS: Never mind, my friend – now Jewel's up, Jewel's down, Jewel's up, Jewel's down, Jewel's up . . .

JEWEL: Wait a minute! – what do you think I am, a yo-yo?

WARRISS: Wait a minute – and now Louis lands a hard left to the body, with a left – right – left – right – left – right . . .

JEWEL: Squad . . . halt! Left . . . turn! May I have this waltz?

WARRISS: Don't be silly, Jimmy – can't you hear the crowd roaring? They want blood, they want blood!

JEWEL: Tell them to apply to the Red Cross.

WARRISS: Never mind . . . go on, Jimmy boy, keep punching there, give him the old one-three, give him the old one-three . . .

JEWEL: What happens to two?

WARRISS: You get that.[1]

The retirement of Chesney Allen in 1945 left Jewel and Warriss as the foremost cross-talk act in the business, and although their style became dated as time went on, their radio series *Up The Pole* – in which they got themselves into awkward situations rather than simply relying upon the relationship between them – kept them popular, and even after it finished they were able to continue as a cross-talk act as late as 1967.

But there were many double-acts who relied much more heavily upon character-building, such as the husband-and-wife team of Arthur Lucan and Kitty McShane.

Lucan – one of the very few Irish character comics to make top billing in Britain – appeared as a diminutive, aggressive Irish washerwoman, with Kitty as her daughter – originally called Kathleen, while Lucan's character was called simply Mother. After establishing the act in Ireland, they came to England in 1919, with a family row sketch called 'Come Over' in which the naïvety of the writing must have been compensated for by the enthusiasm of their characterizations, since they met with considerable success.

MOTHER: So you have a sweetheart?

KATHLEEN: Yes, Mother.

MOTHER: Was that the boy I saw you with on the corner?

KATHLEEN: Yes, Mother.

MOTHER: Well, tell me everything that passed between the two of you.

KATHLEEN: Oh, Mother – not *everything*?

MOTHER: Well, as much as you can without making me blush.

KATHLEEN: We were talking about getting married.

MOTHER: Come over. (*Business of walking across the stage dragging Kathleen with her*). Well, what about it?

KATHLEEN: Peter says we should be married on the 1st of March.

MOTHER: Yes, dear, on the 1st of April – is there anything else?

KATHLEEN: Yes, lots.

MOTHER: Come over. (*Business*) What is it?

KATHLEEN: Oh, Mother, I'm ashamed.

MOTHER: Now, you needn't be afraid.

KATHLEEN: Well, he wanted to kiss me.

MOTHER: Come over. (*Business*) And did he kiss you?

KATHLEEN: Yes, and I liked it, and I kissed him back.

MOTHER: Come over. (*Business*) Where did he kiss you?

KATHLEEN: Between the Post Office and the Railway Station.[2]

As time went on Lucan improved the quality of his writing – although it remained old-fashioned, with heavy use of word-play – and developed the characterization. The characters were renamed Old Mother Riley and her daughter Kitty, and became very popular on the Variety circuits and in low-budget films.

'Old Mother Riley' (Arthur Lucan) and Kitty McShane

These films give a good idea of their style; Kitty, as the foil to Lucan and often the romantic lead, is all saccharine and ham, but Old Mother Riley is a magnificent creation, aggressive, leaping about and arguing, wheedling, coaxing . . . ready to confront anyone at any time. Faced with a bemedalled General, she demands 'Why aren't you in front of your cinema?'

Lucan and Kitty's married life was turbulent, and sometimes the rows off-stage matched those on; perhaps it gave an extra edge to the characterizations as Lucan played the possessive mother and Kitty the lively daughter, as in this 1941 stage routine.

KITTY: Hello Mother. (*To audience*) Hello, boys!

RILEY: Did you hear that! She's been all round the army, all round the navy and air force, and the first thing she says when she gets here is 'Hello boys'! How dare you be so familiar?

KITTY: That's not being familiar, saying 'Hello' to the boys.

RILEY: *I* think it's familiar. You don't know them, do you?

KITTY: No, but I will before the night's out.

RILEY (*outraged*): Oh, did you hear that, Mrs Girochie? S.O.S.! Me daughter's at it again! Oh, give me patience, give me a crowbar, give me a gun to play with, I've got a 'Target for Tonight'. Let me see you talking to a boy tonight and I won't be responsible for my actions.

KITTY: Why do you object to me speaking to my boy friends?

RILEY:	I don't object to you speaking to your boy friends. It's what you're speaking *about* to them that worries me.
KITTY:	Don't let that worry you. I only speak about the same things that you spoke about when you were courting.
RILEY:	Oh, you ought to be ashamed of yourself! How did you know? Were you listening? I mean, who told you? I deny it![3]

There were quite a number of acts who, like Lucan and McShane, were husband-and-wife; it was quite natural that a couple, working and thus meeting in the context of the business, should both build up an act together and marry. This is exactly how Nan Kenway and Douglas Young became both a marriage and an act. They built up an act consisting of short sketches in various characters, and also capitalized on Nan Kenway's training as a pianist. She always included a piano item – usually the scherzo from the Concerto Symphonique by Litolff; indeed she was largely responsible for its considerable popularity.

She remembers: 'I've never lived it down – you'd think I'd never played anything else! I played Tchaikovsky, and Grieg – and the extrordinary part about it is . . . I've always maintained that if you do a thing sufficiently well, and you are sincere about it, you really can make people listen.'

Because they established themselves on radio, they were able to indulge in running characters and catchphrases, but they were at their most successful in their own radio series, *Very Tasty, Very Sweet.*

Despite their success on the halls, Nan Kenway never really felt that they were Variety comedians:

'Real Variety comedians could cope with semi-hostile audiences; they could reach out and grab them. We were pitchforked into Variety as a result of having success on radio – we couldn't adapt, we were too sophisticated. We never really enjoyed working in Variety.'

Part of the reason why they fitted a little uneasily into the world of Variety was that they never established readily identifiable characters. Their style of doing sketches with different characters worked better on radio; in Variety audiences needed a definite single character – like Old Mother Riley, or Will Hay's schoolmaster – to latch on to.

The American comedy team of George Burns and Gracie Allen were an instant success when they visited Britain in the early 1930s, precisely because of the strength of their characterizations as the long-suffering husband and the scatterbrained wife. They had worked for some years in the tough world of American vaudeville, but had never broadcast until they made an appearance in a BBC programme while appearing in Variety; this went over so well that Burns, realizing that vaudeville's days were numbered, transferred their career to American radio with tremendous success.

Gracie's total absence of any apparent desire to be funny was an important part of their style; indeed any joke cracked by Burns – normally the straight man – was usually received by her with a pause, then, 'I don't get it'. Her logic was unassailable:

GEORGE:	I keep my money in a bank, and I get 6 per cent on it.
GRACIE:	Oh, I get 12 per cent on my money.
GEORGE:	How do you do that?
GRACIE:	I keep it in two banks.[4]

Gracie's command of the English (or American) language was somewhat bent at the corners:

GEORGE:	You're absolutely brilliant. I'm beginning to think that you are a wizard.
GRACIE:	I'm a wizard?
GEORGE:	Yes. You know what a wizard is?
GRACIE:	Yes, a snowstorm.
GEORGE:	Well, if that's a snowstorm, what's a blizzard?
GRACIE:	A blizzard is the inside of a chicken. Anybody knows that.
GEORGE:	Then if that's a blizzard, what's a lizard?
GRACIE:	A lizard is a man that's smart – a genius.
GEORGE:	Did something happen to you when you were a baby?
GRACIE:	When I was born, I was so surprised I couldn't talk for a year and a half.[5]

A major part of the humour was in George Burns' frustration in attempting to deal with Gracie – who, though apparently stupid, could somehow always win an argument. A similar characterization was developed by the English act Nat Mills and Bobbie – who were actually described at one time as 'The English Burns and Allen', although they did not model their style directly upon the Americans.

Nat Mills was born in 1900, and like so many other artists began his career in juvenile troupes and went on to concert party. He was working in cabaret in 1923 when he met a girl called Bobbie MacCauley and suggested that they put together an act. They worked out a patter routine based on Bobbie taking figurative sayings literally (such as 'putting all your eggs in one basket' – 'what basket?'); they were both dancers, so they also included a dance routine. Work was difficult to find at first, although early on they did a tour of South Africa.

Nat Mills remembers: 'We played eight weeks, and we were so good over there we stayed for sixteen. We were an absolute riot. We came back, starving – couldn't get any work at all. That was when I married Bobbie; and we struggled to get work until 1927.'

At last they were booked to replace an act that had fallen out of a show mounted by the singer-comedian Talbot O'Farrell.

'We were third turn, and I'm not exaggerating – we absolutely stopped the bill. And sitting in the audience was Florence Leddington, who booked the Syndicate Halls.'

They went on to the Metropolitan Edgware Road, and from there were booked by Val Parnell for the Holborn Empire. From there they never looked back, and toured on the Moss circuit. They also toured extensively in America, with great success (except that they managed to lose most of their money in the Wall Street crash).

Throughout the 1930s they continued to tour in Variety and revues. They had built the act into a very funny routine, with Bobbie as a scatterbrain and Nat getting exasperated with her. He had injured his right arm severely when he was a child, with the result that the hand was bent back at the wrist and the whole arm was useless and kept shaking; he hid this by wearing loose-fitting long-sleeved clothing, so that the shaking arm appeared to be part of his exasperation.

They came late in their careers to radio, which increased their popularity. Early in the war they went over to France to do a concert-party broadcast entertaining the troops.

Nat Mills: 'When we came back, John Sharman offered us a broadcast; and during that we did one of our best routines, which was a burlesque of *Romeo and Juliet*; and overnight BBC work flocked in. That's when "Let's get *on* with it", which was our stock phrase, became nationwide.'

NAT:	'Juliet – I have come to ask thee for thy hand.'
BOBBIE:	'Verily, verily, thou shalt have thy pound of flesh.'
NAT:	That's not it! That's in *The Merchant of Venice*.
BOBBIE:	What's in *The Merchant of Venice*?
NAT:	The pound of flesh.
BOBBIE:	They must have served him over his ration.
NAT:	It's nothing to do with rations. Get *on* with it!
BOBBIE:	'Whither art thou going to take me, Romeo?'
NAT:	'To a land many miles distant. What sayest thou, Juliet?'
BOBBIE:	'My kingdom for a horse – my kingdom for a horse!'
NAT:	Juliet never said that – King Richard said that when he was stuck for a mount.
BOBBIE:	What amount was he stuck for!
NAT:	No amount – it was a lift he wanted.
BOBBIE:	If he wanted a lift, why did he ask for a horse?
NAT:	I have no idea – let me get *on* with it![6]

'Let's get *on* with it' – said in a drawn-out whining voice – became a very popular catchphrase; even Churchill used it on one occasion. Nat's whining voice and hilarious facial expressions were a major part of the act's appeal, but he gives full credit to Bobbie for her part:

'What a performer . . . we were just like brother and sister, we matched so well – the timing was sensational. We used to do a silly little gag and get yells of laughter with that daft face of hers looking at the audience. We were the first ones to revive the song "There's a Hole In My Bucket" – we were a riot with that; and the long wait between each verse – I just used to look at her as much as to say, "I can't get on with this woman at all".'

As well as the cross-talk, they did sketches, dancing and songs – Nat Mills wrote a number of songs, including 'Nice People', which Flanagan and Allen made famous. Even on radio they were able to capitalize on the visual appeal of the act:

'Listeners used to say, "What are they laughing at?" because it was the expressions on our faces that the studio audience used to laugh at; that's why we became such a big draw, because people were inquisitive to see what the

Nat Mills and
Bobbie (1928)

audience had been laughing at!' So they amended their act less for radio than did many others, getting the maximum value out of fairly simple material.

NAT (*with* BOBBIE *following a few words behind*):
Ladies and Gentlemen, we've been asked to come here tonight to tell you how we're getting on with our garden.

NAT: We both can't talk at once, can we?

BOBBIE: No.

NAT: They won't understand us, will they?

BOBBIE: No.

NAT: Well, let me tell them. I will do the talking.

BOBBIE: You see – you don't want me to talk.

NAT: Yes, I want you to talk, but not now.

BOBBIE: If not now, when?

NAT: When I stop.

BOBBIE: When are you going to stop?

NAT: After I've started.

BOBBIE: When are you going to start?

NAT: Listen – you can talk, but at the right time.

BOBBIE: Well, who's talking now?

NAT: Me.

BOBBIE: Oh no – *I'm* 'me'.

NAT: No – I'm 'me'.

BOBBIE: Then who am I?

NAT: You're 'you'.

BOBBIE: I can't be you – I must be me!

NAT: You're only 'me' to you! I'm 'me' to me and I'm 'you' to you.

BOBBIE: What relation does that make me to Aunt Polly?

NAT: Aunt Polly my foot!

BOBBIE: Oh – I've got two.

NAT: Two *what*?

BOBBIE: Two feet. Give me one more and I'll have a yard.

NAT: You've got hold of the wrong end of the stick.

BOBBIE: What stick?

NAT: When I say, 'You've got hold of the wrong end of the stick', I don't mean there *is* a stick, I mean there *isn't* a stick!

BOBBIE: You're talking through your hat.

NAT: *What* hat?

BOBBIE: When I say 'You're talking through

your hat', I don't mean there is a hat, I mean there *isn't* a hat!

NAT: Oh, let's – get – *on* – with – it . . . and *stop arguing*.[7]

The act ended when Bobbie died in 1955; Nat Mills tried to continue with other actresses, but Bobbie's style was so individual that he was unable to make the routines work, and so he retired from the stage.

Nat Mills and Bobbie presented grotesque characters – as did most of the comedians mentioned so far in this book. The need to project in order to be heard clearly, and the robust humour preferred by the audiences, tended to encourage performers to develop exaggerated characterizations. Of those we have mentioned so far, only Mabel Constanduros built her characterizations upon something approaching real types. But as the 1930s progressed the beginnings of a more naturalistic form of humour could be seen in one or two acts.

The most important of these was Elsie and Doris Waters, with their famous cockney characters 'Gert and Daisy'. They started as a purely musical act; their father was very keen on music, and each of the six children in the family had to learn a musical instrument. From playing in charity concerts, Elsie and Doris found themselves playing at friends' houses. Elsie would play the violin, and Doris – always the more ebullient one – told funny stories and played the piano; they were encouraged to get into concert party, where they gained a good deal of useful experience. From there they went on to do Masonic dinners and other private functions, although not as yet Variety.

Elsie Waters remembers: 'We didn't do any Gert and Daisy, or anything like that – I played the violin and hardly spoke on stage, except in sketches in concert party. We'd had good training at the Guildhall School of Music – and we'd both had elocution lessons, so there was some background to it. And then we did a bit of broadcasting – people always thought we broadcast an awful lot, but we never did; there was plenty of other work for us. I did my violin, Doris would do her bits and then we'd do very light duets.'

A concert they gave at a church hall led to their first experience of Variety; the parson who ran the hall contacted Reeves and Lamport – important Variety agents – and suggested that they give the girls a trial booking.

Elsie Waters: 'I don't know why they booked us, I'm sure . . . They put us on first turn – at the Alhambra! Imagine it! All we could hear was people coming into their seats – and in those days there was a paper called *The Sunday Referee*, which all the artists used to put their advertisements in; so I put an advert in saying, "*Elsie and Doris Waters, all last week, first turn, three times daily at the London Alhambra – thereby disproving the old saying 'You can only die once'* " . . . that got us more publicity than anything in this world!'

This experience discouraged them from trying any more Variety appearances for a time; they continued with the private functions and concerts, and started making gramophone records in 1929, sticking to lightweight songs which were quietly amusing. They created Gert and Daisy quite accidentally.

'We'd done one side of a record and we had to do another side – we'd been sitting up half the night worrying about what we were going to do; so we said, "Let's do a talking record for a change." What could we talk about? Well, people always like weddings – so Doris sat down and wrote a little tune, and I put the words to it; and we wrote a few gags. We said, "What shall we call them?" Doris said, "I'll call you Gert because I like saying it" – and I called her Daisy because there was always a Daisy in a group of cockney women.'

So in September 1930 Gert and Daisy were born in the Parlophone recording studio.

DAISY:	It reminds me of my brother's wedding. He got married last week.
GERT:	What, 'Arry?
DAISY:	Yes.
GERT:	No!
DAISY:	Yes!
GERT:	*No!*
DAISY:	Don't say 'No' when I'm telling you 'Yes'!
GERT:	How did he come to meet her?
DAISY:	Oh, he didn't – she overtook him.
GERT:	Is she nice?
DAISY:	No. I don't like her much – first time she come in the place she upset a cup of tea all over our clean tablecloth – and we hadn't even read it.[8]

The voices on the record are not quite those which became so familiar – the speech is slower and almost a little slurred; and the quality of the writing improved later to be less reliant on obvious gags; but the record made an immediate impact.

Elsie Waters: 'The recording manager phoned up ten days later and said, "You've struck oil!" – and we said "Oh, good" and went on doing our usual material – because we hadn't got any Gert and Daisy routines. And about three weeks later we were doing three places in one evening – one at the Holborn restaurant, one at the Savoy, and one at Frascati's – and at each place they said, "Do the cockney women". We said, "We don't do cockney women – it must be someone else", and at the last place we asked a chap about it – and Christopher Stone had played our record on the wireless . . . and we went on an improvised something. After that it was the tail wagging the dog – it all got to be Gert and Daisy in the end.'

Gert and Daisy's accent is not the very rough street-trader cockney which is all that most actors learn to do; but it is completely realistic. Elsie and Doris Waters did not naturally speak with that sort of accent.

'I don't think we were *quite* acting, because we were born in Bromley-by-Bow in the East End of London, and we not only knew how they spoke but how they thought.'

The difference between the old music-hall-grotesque characters and this naturalism was most effective.

'They were on the music halls, belting it out, and we were just doing it quietly over the radio; and from there we were always able to project our voices – we worked at the Coliseum and the Palladium without a microphone, so you can tell how hard we worked on our voices, because they were very small to begin with. I always say that cockneys don't shout unless they're selling something – they just say what they think in a nice quiet way.'

From the mid-1930s they toured on Moss Empires, first in ordinary Variety and then taking their own show round because they didn't want to keep on doing second turn.

**Elsie and Doris
Waters**

They did various characterizations – a smartly dressed number, a spoken routine as a couple of barmaids or usherettes, a song or two and a violin solo from Elsie; usually finishing with Gert and Daisy. On radio they usually restricted themselves to Gert and Daisy.

There was no particular attempt to divide the characters into comic and 'straight person', but in practice Daisy tended to be the one with the more gags; Doris was the more outgoing of the two, and Daisy was married to the slightly disreputable Bert (whom we heard about but never met) while Gert was engaged to Wally and was the quieter of the two. The humour became more rooted in observation than in cross-talk type gags, most of it arising from the everyday lives of the characters.

DAISY: Oh – Bert's had his summons.

GERT: No.

DAISY: Yes. The usual copper brought it.

GERT: Did he?

DAISY: He was quite nice about it – read out all the important parts – you know, where it tells you what you can land up in if you're not careful.

GERT: Here, Dais – didn't the coppers call once before?

DAISY: Call once? Don't be silly – they come round the house so often the neighbours thought we took in policemen as lodgers.

GERT: What's his summons for?

DAISY: He don't know! – and he was afraid to ask in case it was for something else! Gert, I've just thought of something.

GERT: What?

DAISY: Perhaps it's the car that's got him into trouble. You know, motoring offence.

GERT: Dais, I thought you'd given up the car and gone back to the tandem – I saw Bert this morning with his cycling clips on.

DAISY: Oh, no, he has to wear them – you see he's broken his braces.

GERT: Well, perhaps he was speeding, Dais – hasn't he got a speedometer?

DAISY: Well, he has, but he doesn't bother to look at it. He goes more by signs and indications – you know, speed signs.

GERT: Oh, yes.

DAISY: You see, like, when he does ten miles an hour the mudguards rattle; when he does twenty the windows rattle; when he does thirty his teeth rattle.

GERT: Here, Dais, when the coppers stop him, don't he offer any resistance?

DAISY: Oh, well, he does, Gert, but never more than a couple of bob.[9]

They wrote their own material, never relying on risqué jokes; however they did once run into a little trouble with a gag – inevitably this was with Birmingham's very strict Watch Committee.

Elsie Waters: 'The gag was, "How's Bert? – "He's got lumbago" – "Has he had it before?" – "No, he always gets it behind". The manager said, "You must take it out" – we said, "We did it last week at the Command Performance before King George and Queen Mary, and they didn't complain" – so we never heard any more about that; they told us afterwards that they were so worried that they gave the lady from the Watch Committee a lot to drink so that she didn't know what she was looking at and said everything was all right!'

In wartime they became even more popular; they did a series for the BBC called *Kitchen Front* in which they built acts round Ministry of Food information on how to make the best of available foodstuffs, thus sugaring the propaganda with their own humour. In their ordinary appearances they helped to make the difficulties of the time – husbands away in the army and so on – less unhappy by sharing their characters' experiences with the audience; Bert's adventures as retailed by Daisy helped those left at home to face their own predicaments with more humour.

The natural comedy of Elsie and Doris Waters pointed the way of later comedians, such as Tony Hancock, who rooted their humour in observation of reality. They, and Jewel and Warriss, remained in the forefront of Variety acts throughout the 1950s; but strangely there were no further major double-acts in the period up to the virtual end of Variety around 1960.

There was one more step to come in the development of the double-act from the minstrels and their riddles, through the stupid comic and smart straight man of Flanagan and Allen and Jewel and Warriss, but it was to come from an act who were of little importance until the 1970s. In the late 1940s they were a very poor and unoriginal cross-talk act in their early twenties; their names were Morecambe and Wise, and their contributions to the double-act as a comedy style will be covered in the final Interlude (p. 220).

18 'From somewhere in Britain'
Broadcasting in wartime

The early days of the war were dismal ones for radio listeners; with its staff packed off to various provincial towns and not yet ready to provide much programme material, the BBC had to rely heavily upon news bulletins, gramophone records, and organ recitals by Sandy MacPherson. There was only one network – the BBC wanted to provide an alternative programme but at first was prevented by the Air Ministry.

The BBC's original plans had allowed for a considerable reduction in the amount of Variety, but as time went on it was realized that programmes of this type would be essential to maintain morale, and by early in 1940 there was a very considerable increase in the number of Variety programmes – including, for the first time, Sunday placings. (Reith had left the BBC in 1938, and the exigencies of wartime finished the idea of the 'BBC Sunday' for good.)

Variety Department moved to Bristol, with John Watt in charge and Pat Hillyard, transferred from Television with its closedown, as his assistant. Vernon Harris also went to Bristol.

'We'd hired a little "rep." company – Tommy Handley, Michael North, Fred Yule, and a few girls – and I got Max Kester to write a couple of songs, and I wrote a couple of sketches. In the end I got a show together. One of the things was that John Watt said, "You can now say what you like about Hitler" [previously protected from acid comments on-air as a Head of State] so Max Kester wrote a song for Tommy Handley – "Who Is This Man Who Looks Like Charlie Chaplin?".'

As these early difficulties were overcome and Variety Department began to expand its output, considerable thought was given to the rôle of Variety in the new situation. John Watt wrote a memorandum setting out the aims of his Department (one of a number of such documents prepared by the various Departments for the Home Service Control Board).

He commented: 'It would be very difficult, and possibly ineffective, to say to us "We want to propagand [sic] antipacifism"; and if we manufacture a piece of synthetic entertainment to this end, the result would probably smell so much of propaganda that everyone would fight shy of it

Pat Hillyard (*left*) and John Watt (1948)

. . . I think the only method is . . . to bear the tendency to be aimed at in mind, and to allow the existing piece of entertainment to veer in that direction.'[1]

Early in 1940 the BBC began preparations for another service, originally intended for the British Expeditionary Force in France, for whom boredom was becoming a severe problem in the phoney war. The Air Ministry approved a wavelength for this, and the 'Forces Programme' began on 18 February. Many servicemen still stationed in Britain also listened to the Forces Programme, which took on a lighter character as a contrast to the Home Service.

The whole style of presentation changed. Whereas before the war there had been very little in the way of a weekly pattern, programmes were now broadcast at regular times and days; this began because of the difficulty many people had in obtaining the *Radio Times*.

In order to avoid monotony, Variety bills were disguised in a number of ways. Shows purporting to come from air-raid shelters, factories, a town hall or other locales were constructed round Variety performers – some 'resident', some making guest appearances.

There were also many broadcasts of camp concerts, ENSA shows and similar troop entertainments. Shows such as *Gunner Smith Entertains*, *Private Smith Entertains*, and *Artists in Uniform* presented performances by servicemen (both amateurs and professional performers who had been called up), while *ENSA Half-Hour* allowed listeners to eavesdrop on ENSA shows for troops stationed in Britain. Michael Standing, now Director of Outside Broadcasts, was involved closely with these as the facilities and production were the responsibility of OB Department.

'We used to do a lot of ENSA broadcasting – which was not too hot; it was really the Variety and theatrical profession at large being recruited by ENSA, some of which were very good – but generally speaking from the broadcasting point of view the ENSA offerings did not attract very enthusiastic audiences. ENSA was anxious to put itself forward as the fount and origin of all forces entertainment, and the BBC regarded itself as a far more important element in this . . . and probably both were rather wrong.'

By the summer of 1940 Bristol had turned out not to be the quietest place from which to broadcast (it was after all a sea port and was fairly heavily bombed) and in 1941 the Department moved to Bangor. By late 1942 the BBC was able to move many of its staff back to London.

The sorts of programmes which could come from Bangor were those relying on a resident company; the most famous of these was *It's That Man Again* – later shortened to *ITMA*. With the demise of *Band Waggon* in December 1939 when Richard Murdoch was called up, *ITMA* became the most popular of the BBC's wartime comedy shows.

Being built round one performer, the show owed something to the American radio personality series in format, though not in the style of the writing. Ted Kavanagh explained his approach in his 1949 biography of Tommy Handley.

'My own idea of radio-writing was an obvious one – it was to use sound for all it was worth, the sound of different voices and accents, the use of catchphrases, the impact of funny sounds in words, of grotesque effects to give atmosphere – every device to create the illusion of rather crazy or inverted reality.'[2]

The catchphrases were particularly effective, and listeners who were otherwise quite staid would go around saying 'This is Funf speaking', 'Can I do you now, sir?', 'Don't forget the Diver', 'After you, Claude – no, after *you*, Cecil' and so on.

The construction of the show established a format imitated by many later radio comedy series. There was a narrative of sorts, in which Handley would usually be up to something nefarious; the half-hour would be broken up by two musical items – a song, and a special orchestral arrangement of a well-known tune.

This sample is reasonably typical, as Handley copes with one of a string of interruptions while trying to solve the problem of a hotel full of animals. His charlady, Mrs Mopp, was played by Dorothy Summers.

ITMA – **Tommy Handley with Dorothy Summers (***left***) and Jean Capra (1944)**

MRS MOPP:	Can I do you now, sir?
HANDLEY:	Well, if it isn't Figurehead Fanny, the winch with the Plymouth hose.
MRS MOPP:	I haven't been called that for years, sir.
HANDLEY:	I'll bet you've been over a few decks in your time?
MRS MOPP:	Oh, yes, sir – I came home in convoy last night.

HANDLEY: I saw you – followed by a flotilla of he-boats. Any luck?

MRS MOPP: Oh, yes, sir – it was a successful engagement.

HANDLEY: You reached port safely?

MRS MOPP: Yes sir – and stout as well.

HANDLEY: Well I must introduce you to the Colonel – he drinks like a tin fish.

MRS MOPP: I've met him, sir – saucy old rascal. Trying to come the old soldier with *me*!

HANDLEY: Well don't tell me he wanted to blanco your bonnet.

MRS MOPP: Would you do something for me, sir?

HANDLEY: Certainly, Mrs Mopp – what is it?

MRS MOPP: Would you take the elephant out of my room, sir? I never know which end he's speaking from.

HANDLEY: Well, listen, Mrs Mopp – you throw a bun at him, and if it bounces back, it's the other end.

MRS MOPP: Oh, thank you, sir. T.T.F.N.[3]

HANDLEY: S.U.T.S.A.S.I.T.S.

MRS MOPP: What's that?

HANDLEY: Shut up the shutters and sit in the shop! (*Door closes*) You have just heard Flanagan and camel doing a running dromedary.[4]

The speed and the catchphrases would have been nothing, however, without Handley himself. He illustrated perfectly Dickie Henderson's comment about radio performers being good readers – Handley had the essential ability to get the best out of every line in a new script every week; he was less effective on stage, where he seemed almost diffident. The show was immensely popular and became a tremendous morale-booster.

One of *ITMA*'s rivals in popularity was *Garrison Theatre*, which started early in the war. It purported to come from a real Garrison Theatre, where the artists entertained the troops stationed there, but in fact it usually came from a studio. The audience certainly sounded as if they were entirely servicemen. (Forces audiences were always far more lively than ordinary ones – they had after all got in either for free or very cheaply, and were often disposed to enter in the fun as much as possible. This could prove exhausting for the artists. Theatrical audiences, on the other hand, had paid their admission fee and were more critical and reserved.)

Garrison Theatre included several Variety acts in each show, but a good deal of the programme (which usually ran an hour) was taken up with the activities of Jack Warner (who was really Jack Waters – a brother of Elsie and Doris Waters). Warner was not really a Variety artist – he had done a number of different things, but in the end settled as a straight actor; he appeared in innumerable wartime and post-war films as a solid dependable type, and later became famous as P.C. Dixon in the TV series *Dixon of Dock Green*.

His characterization in *Garrison Theatre* was a long way from solid dependable P.C. Dixon, as he arrived noisily on his bicycle each week ('Mind my bike, mind my bike') and set about cheeking the Sergeant-Major who kept order in the 'theatre' (a real one – R.S.M. Filtness). That aspect of the show was of course pure wish-fulfilment for the uniformed audience. Warner also attempted to carry on a romance with the cigarette girl, Joan Winters, whom he always addressed as 'little gel'. These in-jokes all sound rather odd now, but at the time they went down extremely well with the audience.

Warner always read out a letter from his 'brother Sid' at some stage in the proceedings, and it was from these that he earned his nick-name Jack 'Blue-Pencil' Warner:

Here we go with another letter from my brother: 'My dear Jack, It's all very well to talk but what's the good of talking, how are you Jack, all right I 'ope.' Silly start anyway. 'Well as the old lady said when she got caught on a runaway roundabout for two hours, things seem to be moving a bit. And as the same old lady said when she 'ad a machine-gun fitted to 'er bath-chair, we're ready for anything whatever may befall, as they say. I been 'elping Marie and 'er

Garrison Theatre – **Jack Warner with Joan Winters (1940)**

old Grandad do a bit of gardening. Talk about
Dig For Victory, he can't dig for nuts. And all
he does is to walk round treading on the rake
and you know what 'appens when the . . . blue-
pencil 'andle flies up and knocks him for six or
more it depends how 'ard you tread.'[5]

Jack Warner also made a feature of some recitations
with piano accompaniment about strange jobs which his
family had held, beginning in the first one with his own
function as a 'Bunger-up of Rat-'Oles' (which was sufficiently popular to justify his making a gramophone record
of it). In this later monologue he introduced another
'Necessary Occupation':

You've heard about my family that's got some
    funny jobs –
I mean jobs that must be done right on the spot.
Well, take my Uncle Oswald, now he does a bit
    of gardening –
I'll tell you just what kind of job he's got:
    He's a bloke what shaves off gooseberries with
        a penknife.
    He's a gooseberry-shaver-off, see what I mean?
    He holds them in his left hand, and he shaves

them with his right hand
Until like grapes they're nice and smooth and
    clean.
But now and then his hand is rather shaky
Then he pricks them, and the juice goes in his
    eye;
Still, all the time there's gooseberries, there'll
    be shavers-off-of-gooseberries –
And he don't know why he does it – nor do
    I![6]

A theatrical version of *Garrison Theatre*, with Jack
Warner, toured the Variety circuits; there were also stage
versions of *ITMA*, *Band Waggon*, and another popular
programme, *Happidrome*. This last was built round the
broad northern humour of Harry Korris (as Mr Lovejoy),
Cecil Frederick (as Mr Ramsbottom) and Robbie Vincent
(as Enoch). Like *Garrison Theatre* it also included
appearances by different Variety artists each week. Their
signature tune 'We Three' became well known, and the
humour, though unsophisticated, had a wide appeal.

LOVEJOY: Ah, yes, I remember when I was out
                in India, in the 99th.
RAMSBOTTOM: Oh, yes, the jolly old 99th.

LOVEJOY:	Aye, we only wanted one for game.
RAMSBOTTOM:	Tell me, Guv'nor, did you get a commission?
LOVEJOY:	No, no, just wages.
RAMSBOTTOM:	Enoch tells me that he was in the Sergeants' Mess.
LOVEJOY:	Don't believe him – he *was* the Sergeants' Mess. Of course I found my great trouble out there was getting down from the elephant's back.
RAMSBOTTOM:	Oh, no, no – you're wrong there, Guv'nor – you don't get down from an elephant's back – you get down from a swan.
LOVEJOY:	Swansdown . . . I'll tell him . . .
ENOCH:	Let me tell *you* . . . my sister went to India and came back a princess.
LOVEJOY:	Oh, that's nothing – my sister went to Egypt and came back a mummy.[7]

For those with more sophisticated tastes there were programmes like *Very Tasty, Very Sweet,* and the off-beat series *Danger, Men at Work.* Each of the services had its own comedy team: for the navy, Eric Barker in *Merry-Go-Round* (which became *Waterlogged Spa* after the war); for the RAF, Richard Murdoch and Kenneth Horne also appeared in *Merry-Go-Round* in sketches which led to the post-war *Much Binding in the Marsh*; while Charlie Chester, detailed by his superior officer (he was then an army sergeant) to write 'a hit show', helped to create the broad humour of *Stand Easy.*

In the meantime there were many more-or-less straight Variety programmes – *Music Hall, Top of the Bill, Saturday Spotlight, The Stuff To Give The Troops* and so on. Being a Variety producer was no sinecure; there was a whole new range of forbidden topics. Banned subjects supposedly included the Home Guard, sergeants, colonels, drink, fire guards, the black market, and 'derogatory references to Spam'.

In 1943 Tommy Trinder was furious when the BBC cut one of his gags on the grounds that it might lower morale: 'A man was walking down Whitehall and asked a passer-by, "Which side is the War Office on?" – he answered, "Ours, I hope."'[8]

As well as the straight Variety shows, there were many which were more of a cross between a magazine programme and a Variety bill; they would be aimed at a specific audience, and would include informative sections as well as one or two Variety acts. One of the earliest was *Ack-Ack, Beer Beer,* which was aimed at anti-aircraft gun personnel; others were *Under Your Tin Hat* for the Civil Defence, *Make and Mend* for the Royal Navy, and *Shipmates Ashore* for the Merchant Navy.

With the entry of America into the war in 1942 listeners had the opportunity to hear more American acts and programmes – shows such as *The Jack Benny Show* and *The Charlie McCarthy Show* were broadcast (from recordings flown over) by the BBC, partly for the benefit of the thousands of American troops stationed in Britain. British listeners had already had a taste of the American-style personality show with *Hi, Gang!,* starring Bebe Daniels and Ben Lyon – an American husband-and-wife team whom Pat Hillyard had teamed with the comedian Vic Oliver to produce a show which had something of the American style about it. British audiences were gradually acclimatized to the recordings of the genuine American article, and the developing taste for American stars was to have an important effect on Variety after the war.

In February 1944 the Forces Programme was replaced by the General Forces Programme – in effect the General Overseas Service (which itself had grown out of the pre-war Empire Service) under another name.

With the end of the war in Europe in May 1945 there was a further reorganization of networks. The General Forces Programme was replaced for British listeners in July 1945 by the Light Programme, which presented a lighter alternative to the Home Service. (The GFP continued on short-waves, and became the General Overseas Service – which continues today as the World Service – in 1947).

Broadcasting had made an incalculable contribution to the war effort, particularly in maintaining morale; and Variety programmes had established themselves as a major and essential part of broadcasting. It was the following decade, rather than the 1930s, which was the 'Golden Age of Broadcasting' as far as Variety Department was concerned.

(*Broadcasting from 1945 to 1960 is covered in Chapter 28, p. 208.*)

19 Americans and nudes
The post-war boom, 1945–1952

Between VE Day on 8 May 1945 and the end of the war with Japan on 15 August 1945 Britain had begun the readjustment to peace with a general election in which the Labour Party came into power with a large majority. The unusual social conditions of the time, with the 'all-pull-together' attitudes of wartime still a habit, enabled the setting up of the Welfare State and the National Health Service; but the continuing shortages of food and fuel became increasingly unpopular with the public. Difficult economic conditions, caused by having to fight a war, made it necessary for the country to concentrate on production of all luxuries for export rather than the home market.

In the years immediately following the end of the war, a continuing shortage of consumer goods caused the boom in Variety and other entertainments to continue, since, as during the war, there was little else for people to spend money on. It was several years before all the servicemen were demobilized, so although there was no more fear of air-raids, the general atmosphere of a country in uniform continued in Variety, giving way only gradually to a normal peace-time routine.

One of the most noticeable changes in Variety was in the number of new performers coming into the business from the armed forces. People who had developed a taste for performing while in the Gang Shows and similar outfits began to make their way – often slowly and with difficulty – into the world of Variety. In many cases they started by touring with complete forces shows before going solo.

Inevitably there were tensions between these new performers and the older 'pros'; we have already had Rikki McCormick's comments on that subject, and Harry Secombe gives the ex-servicemen's view.

'All the ex-servicemen had a kind of camaraderie that didn't exist between the old-time pros [most older Variety performers would challenge that statement] who were more jealous of each other than we were. I found we were resented – we were called "NAAFI comics" by some of the old pros, but it didn't last long because so many of them disappeared. There were all sorts of new ideas coming in, because the young pros had gone into the forces; and those that stayed behind – it was survival of the weakest, because the fittest went into the army! And we resented them because they were earning good money. The new people who came out of the services were more educated – Jimmy Edwards, Frank Muir, Denis Norden – they brought a fresh approach to the whole thing. University people used to go into the straight theatre – people like Jack Hulbert – Variety comics had been working-class, essentially; mostly it was the sly humour of the streets or broad knockabout domestic comedy. I think we did bring something different to it.'

Other changes were less obvious. With the death of George Black in 1945, Val Parnell took over the running of Moss Empires and GTC. In 1946 the two circuits were rationalized, so that GTC took over all Moss's cinemas, while Moss Empires took over all GTC's theatres. Thus GTC disappeared as a Variety circuit, while Moss became the largest circuit with about twenty-four theatres includ-

Val Parnell

ing the Palladium. The Stoll circuit, with twelve theatres, was their main rival, while other circuits included the Butterworth and Syndicate theatres, and a number of smaller circuits run by agencies such as Nat Tennens, Fred Collins, Nat Day, and Mannie Jay.

Lew Grade, who had started in the agency business with Joe Collins, ran a couple of theatres with his brother Leslie, while building up an agency that eventually represented most of the top stars. His older brother, Bernard Delfont (the surname had been chosen to avoid competing with Lew Grade in their performing days – Delfont was also a dancer) ran several theatres including, for a time, the London Casino (which went over to Cinerama in 1954, then became a cinema, and was later renamed the Prince Edward when *Evita* began its long run there). Delfont attempted to turn the Casino into a rival to the Palladium, but without success; Val Parnell was making changes in the Palladium's style which gave it an appeal which Delfont could not match – and Delfont was also squeezed out by the high salaries Parnell was prepared to pay his top acts.

The Palladium had continued with the sort of spectacular revue which George Black had started; but in 1948 Parnell began to change to Variety bills featuring American artists. The first was Mickey Rooney, who started on 5 January 1948, with a supporting bill of British acts. He had been booked for four weeks; but although he was an experienced and energetic performer he was unable to suit his act to British audiences and was so unsuccessful that during his last week he pleaded illness and cancelled his last few performances.

Rooney's failure resulted in poor advance bookings for Parnell's next American star, Danny Kaye, who opened at the top of the bill on 2 February. Kaye was nervous, understandably enough, before going on, and, after he had been introduced by Ted Ray, had to be pushed to get him started on the walk from the side of the stage. Reaching the microphone, he said 'I'm shaking like a leaf, honestly'. There was immediate applause, and Kaye never looked back. His success was immediate and extraordinary; the critics raved and the Palladium was booked solidly for the six-week run with tickets changing hands for inflated prices on the black market.

Unlike previous tops-of-the-bill in ordinary Variety, who normally played only twenty minutes or so, Kaye was on for forty-five minutes (which he sometimes over-ran) – this began the trend towards performers, particularly Americans, playing the entire second half of a bill. Kaye also had the band on the stage behind him instead of in the

Danny Kaye

pit – common enough since, but in 1948 this was almost revolutionary. Some idea of his style – which included widely varied songs and patter ranging from the sentimental to the manic – can be obtained from his songs and comedy routines in films such as *Up In Arms, Knock On Wood* and *The Court Jester*; his approach and material was so individual, and depended so much upon his own spring-tensioned personality, that no quotation from his act could give any idea of his tremendous appeal.

Following Kaye's success a string of American artists came to the Palladium – they included Martha Raye, Carmen Miranda, Tony Martin, Duke Ellington, Edgar Bergen, Harpo and Chico Marx, Jack Benny, The Andrews Sisters, Dinah Shore, Betty Hutton and Ella Fitzgerald. The newspapers complained that British acts were being pushed out and not given a fair chance, but Parnell pointed out that he could not fill the theatre for several weeks at a time with a British act at the top of the bill.

Even though Parnell was paying high fees by British standards, American artists could have earned more money by staying in America, if money had been the only consideration.

Philip Hindin: 'The Palladium was the mecca; that's why the American acts came over to play at less money than they had been getting in America. They didn't need to come to London – Frank Sinatra, for example, had been playing the RKO theatre in New York – a 5,000 seater, doing three shows a day; how can you take that sort of money at the Palladium with two shows a day? The Palladium had that stamp of quality – plus the fact that the record companies could capitalize on the fact that their star was at the Palladium – plus the fact that most stars want to be international anyway.'

One of the American artists who appeared at the Palladium, Jimmy Durante, had a catchphrase, 'Everybody's trying to get in on the act'; and this was certainly true once the success of Parnell's policy became apparent. Lew and Leslie Grade came to an agreement with the General Artists Corporation of America, thus becoming international agents; they represented many of the American performers while they were in Britain. Leslie Grade was one of the shrewdest people in the business, but even he could misjudge a situation, as Harry Harbour, who was by this time bookings manager for the Stoll circuit, remembers.

'At the Bristol Hippodrome we used to run an eight-week season of Variety in the summer – the rest of the time was taken up with operas, Gilbert and Sullivan, and various shows. Leslie Grade came to me and said, "I have a great attraction for you, for the Bristol Hippodrome – could you hold the date open for me?" The Grades used to put most of the Variety bills in at Bristol, which always played to capacity business. I said "Yes", but it got very near the date and I was worried in case we turned up without an attraction. So I phoned him up, and he said, "Just give me three more days and I will give you the biggest attraction you have ever had – provided you are prepared to double your prices, have the band on stage, and I want a guarantee." [The Grades would take a percentage of the gross, but a guarantee meant that the theatre would agree to pay them a certain minimum whatever happened.] And it turned out to be Frank Sinatra, playing the only date outside London that he had ever done. Great excitement was generated, we doubled our prices, everything was marvellous . . . and the outcome of it was that we lost £8,000 on the week, we played to less money than we had the week before with Billy Cotton, and the Grades even gave us back our guarantee, they were so shattered by the result!'

American artists may have been popular in London, but the provinces were not yet ready for them.

However, Harbour managed to find an attraction of his own:

'We decided to try putting our own shows in – we had twelve theatres, so it was a worthwhile tour – and I was looking through our returns for the previous year, and I noticed that there were three dates which had played way above average business. Each one had a different top of the bill, and there was only one person on all three bills – Benny Hill.'

So Harbour booked Hill for twelve weeks and built a bill round him. There was some haggling about Hill's salary – Harbour offered £100, then, after some haggling, £125, and in the end Hill decided to go for a percentage.

'We broke every record – Benny Hill walked out with over £500 a week; we had to put extra matinées in . . . and that was really the start of Benny Hill!'

Shortly after this, in 1952, Hill began appearing in his own TV shows, and became a major TV star.

Meanwhile life continued much as before for the ordinary Variety performers; the post-war boom reached its peak somewhere about 1948–9 and from then on there was a slow decline, although it was not particularly severe at first. At the bottom of the business life was extremely tatty (although it always had been); Harry Secombe's novel *Twice Brightly*[1] paints a fictionalized but barely exaggerated picture of a week in Variety at a dilapidated theatre in a tired town; and this was precisely how many of the NAAFI comedians were working their way into the business. There were perhaps more touring revues than previously, but many of them were really only Variety bills given a title. The changes in presentation brought about by the American stars made life less attractive for the supporting artists.

Jack Marks remembers: 'Before the war, there was a much friendlier, warmer atmosphere – it brought in a family audience, and a much friendlier, happy type of audience. But after the war, the type of performer altered – they became more brash; and the American stars demanded big salaries and went on for three-quarters of an hour. I did a tour with Johnny Ray, who was a big success, but he brought in almost entirely youngsters and did the entire second half. There was no sort of nice atmosphere – the people who came to see the star didn't give a damn about the supporting act. Before the war, even if you were only the opening act you were given a reception, and you felt that you were part of the show – after the war you were just a warmer-upper.'

Life was getting harder off-stage as well. The Music Hall Artists Railway Association was closed down in 1952 and the concessions on tickets withdrawn. The new Welfare State regulations proved somewhat unfair for

Variety artists; under the National Insurance Act of 1948 performers who were either soloists or partners in a Variety act, or who appeared in productions on a percentage rather than a salary, were held to be self-employed. This meant that not only were they ineligible for unemployment benefit when not working, but also that they still had to continue stamping their National Insurance cards.

Cine-variety was almost completely dead – the Empire Leicester Square presented Variety acts and films during 1950 and 1951, but its example was not followed by anywhere else. Television was still very much secondary to radio, but there were already fears that it might present a serious threat to live theatre. (These same fears had been voiced when radio was new, but in this case they turned out to have more foundation.)

Inevitably, bookers of smaller theatres turned more and more to nude shows. These had been running in the tattier places throughout the war; now they began to appear on the 'number two' circuits. Phyllis Dixey – who did at least present an act with some sort of artistic merit – was popular in the late 1940s but by the time she left the stage in 1956 her style, which she had refused to change, was too old-fashioned to interest audiences. Another well-known nude artist was Christabel Leighton-Porter, the model for the strip (in both senses of the word) cartoon 'Jane' drawn by Norman Petts for the *Daily Mirror*.

'Jane' was always being surprised in the bath by servicemen, or losing most of her clothes and having to flee from embarrassing situations clad only in her bra and frilly panties – in later days even without them. On stage, 'Jane' appeared on a bill with other girls and a couple of Variety acts; she posed nude, danced (lightly clad), and sang (very badly).

One theatre in London had specialized entirely in nude shows – the Windmill; it presented a continuous show alternating something approximating end-of-pier concert party with tastefully posed nudes; the programme reminded patrons that 'artificial aids to vision are not allowed'. Many budding young comics got their start at the Windmill – Tony Hancock, Harry Worth and Dick Emery among them. The comics had to get used to customers leaping over the seats from the row behind in order to get closer as other people left the front rows – at least it taught them to 'die' gracefully.

Vivian Van Damm, who ran the Windmill, used to boast 'We never closed' (immediately corrupted to 'We never clothed' by comedians); in fact the theatre had closed for a week when all the theatres closed at the outbreak of war, but he did keep it open throughout the blitz.

The man who more than anyone else became associated with nude shows in Britain started presenting them in 1952: Paul Raymond. He began in the business as a drummer in small-time dance bands; then worked in summer season and third-rate Variety in the late 1940s as a mind-reading act – the sort where a girl assistant walks round the audience holding up odd items borrowed from them (pens, watches, and so on), and the performer on the stage, who is blindfolded, tells what they are by 'telepathy'.

Raymond started booking his own Variety bills, putting himself at the top of the bill and getting the supporting acts for a low (or no) guarantee and a percentage.

He remembers: 'I was at the Queens Park Hippodrome in Manchester – the manager had said he would book the show if I would put in some nudes. The two dancers we had on the bill agreed to take off their bras for an extra ten shillings a week each; they did a single posing act each in the first half, and a double posing act in the second half. So the show, which had been called *Vaudeville Express*, overnight became *Festival of Nudes*. We took twice or three times what we'd been taking in normal circumstances – I decided therefore that it wasn't that *I* had suddenly become a draw . . . '

He gave up the mindreading act (although it could be said that he has been reading the public's mind ever since) and produced straight Variety for a time. Then in 1952 he presented the first of his nude shows, featuring 'Jane'.

'I had her under contract from Lew and Leslie Grade, who took commission the whole time, from 1952 to 1958; and the contract said that provided she didn't have four weeks not working in any one year she was with me for life; and she never had more than four weeks out in any year. She would play two weeks in a town, she would go back two or three times – and every time she went back she played to more money than she had in the first place.'

In the period from 1953 to the end of the 1950s nude shows became a more and more important part of the business – much to the disgust of many people in it – and that period and the importance of nude shows is dealt with in a later chapter. The decline in Variety became more rapid as the 1950s progressed, partly – possibly largely – because of the increased popularity of television. In 1949 there were only 126,000 television licences; in 1952 there were $1\frac{1}{2}$ million – nearly double the number of the previous year, an increase partly caused by anticipation of the Coronation in 1953.

The number of television licences continued to increase spectacularly, reaching $4\frac{1}{2}$ million in 1955 and over 10 million by 1960; and from 1953 onwards television became a very real threat to Variety. For the remainder of the 1950s – at the end of which time it was effectively dead – the story of Variety is one of decline.

(*The decline of Variety 1953–1960 is covered in Chapter 29, p. 215.*)

20 'I'm proper poorly'
Stand-up comics: Three (the 1940s and 1950s)

In the period following the war there was no one stand-up comic who stood above the rest in the way that Max Miller had done in the 1930s (although Miller continued well into the 1950s); and there was a move away from the pure gag type of approach exemplified by Miller and Ted Ray. Once again comics tended to hang their gags on a characterization, or found some unusual aspect of performance to make themselves stand out. Not all comics did this – there were still a number who carried on the smart suit and pure gag tradition, but they tended to operate under the difficulty that they had little individuality, and indeed there was a danger of them all telling the same gags. The best comics, however, brought something special to their performances.

Jeanne de Casalis (1949)

A performer who worked in the traditional character-comic format – though with less exaggeration than most – was Jeanne de Casalis; her character 'Mrs Feather' originated in a pre-war revue sketch, but reached her main popularity during and just after the war in Variety and broadcasts. Mrs Feather was a scatterbrained upper-middle-class lady who was usually overheard as she struggled to make herself clear on the telephone.

> Hello? Hello, hello – Exchange? Supervision? Operations? Aberrations? Hello – hello . . . who is that? Engineers? You again? Well, nothing's gone wrong, Engineers – I say, who . . . what's gone wrong? Why are you tinkling my bell every two minutes? Two hours ago you told me I was in working order – I've been as dead as mutton ever since. I mean to say, this . . . this sort of thing can't go on, you know. First you put me right, then you put me out of order again – what's the idea? Here I am, trying to pluck a duck in the pantry – down up to my eyes, feathers in my hat . . . my hair – and every two minutes I have to rush in here because my bell's being tickled. I mean to say, you're tickling it to death, you're . . . you're testing the line? Well, stop testing it – it's not worth testing, give it up now. Throw it away, there's no hope for it, it's been an invalid for years. And another thing, why – why is that man of yours still up the pole outside my bathroom window? What's that? . . . But he must have been there all night – isn't he ever coming down? Doesn't he want to eat? Hasn't he got a mother? It's all very well, you know, but I haven't been able to have a bath for two days! Mr Feather doesn't like it at all.[1]

Mrs Feather, being 'upper-middle-class' was the sort of person who in that period would have had a charwoman; and the sort of charwoman she might well have attracted was portrayed by Suzette Tarri – a whining cockney woman more interested in talk than work, and more interested in men than either.

The comparison between those two acts is interesting – the contrast between Mrs Feather, whose style is reminiscent of the smart revues in which the character started, and Suzette Tarri's bawdy music-hall approach.

As had always been the case, there were some post-war performers who began as impressionists – although less than in the old music-hall days (partly because the NAAFI comics had gained their first experience away from the professional stage, and had found some sort of style of their own by the time they got into Variety). Peter Sellers began as an excellent impressionist; he found his greatest fame not in Variety but as a character supporting comic in radio, and then later in films, where his uncanny ability to create a totally convincing character was his greatest strength. (Oddly enough, one of his greatest performances was as an elderly and failed music-hall comedian of the old school, in the under-rated film *The Optimists of Nine Elms*.)

Peter Cavanagh, 'The Voice of Them All', became famous on radio – some of his impressions were very good, some only moderately so – but there were otherwise few impressionists in the Florence Desmond tradition. Victor Seaforth (family name: Seyforth) began as a child per-former in clubs, singing Flanagan-and-Allen-type songs in a tramp costume. At the age of sixteen he ran away to sea; he was in the RNVR during the war, but was invalided out in 1943; entering a Carroll Levis talent competition he found that at that time the main essential for winning such competitions was to be in uniform – the audience always tended to favour servicemen.

He worked with Harry Morris and Frank Cowley in their road-show *The Squire's Party* for two years, which gave him invaluable stage experience in sketches; then he set up as an impressionist.

He remembers: 'There was a newsreel in the cinemas called *The March of Time*, and I based my act on this, introducing various film stars . . . but I didn't have any laughs in it, and I found it rather hard to get work. My bill matter was "The Man of 100 Voices" – and Billy Marsh used to have a joke with my billing sometimes – "The Man of 99 Voices", or "The Man of 101 Voices". Then my second wife [acrobat Suma Lamonte] made me change my style – she said "You should relax more – you want to get a bit of humour in the act" – and slowly but surely, I completely changed; I became a comedian first and an impressionist second.'

Only yesterday my friend Mrs Jenkinson said to me, 'Now, Suzie, your face looks as if it could do with a change – why don't you go out and forget yourself?' So I went into the park and tried to – but a policeman gave me such a look, you know, that I blushed right down to me corn pads and went home. But I always say, if ever I fall for a pair of trousers, they'll have to have a crease down the middle. Of course, you know, a sailor would be different, wouldn't it? . . . or a Gordon Highlander. Of course, you know, I've had some experiences at sea – now there was that time when me and Mrs Jenkinson went to America on the 'Queen Mary' . . . well, we didn't exactly go to America, we went to Southampton to see her daughter Florrie off. The Captain showed Mrs Jenkinson and me all over the ship . . . all over . . . well, excepting one or two little places, of course . . . (all right, all right, I heard you) . . . well, then the Captain introduced us to a friend of his – a stoker – such a nice man, he was . . . with his shirt off and a map of the continent of America tattooed on his chest. Well I'd just managed to trace Florrie's journey down to California when the foghorn sounded.[2]

Harry Secombe, on the other hand, was a comedian first, second and third – although he had a fine singing voice, it was only in later years that he made the singing an equal part of his appeal. On the Variety halls in the period following his demobilization he presented a turn based on shaving (wet-shaving – electric razors were far less commonplace then), which was basically the act he had built up while in the army concert party.

Harry Secombe (1959)

'The shaving act was born in a tent in Italy – I was desperate to think of something to do; you had to do something each week or you got booted back into action again, and I didn't fancy that – it was cold out there! – I started off by mucking about in the tent as I shaved – everyone fell about laughing, so I thought, "I've got something here", and I went up on the hill behind the camp and wrote it down . . . I did a small boy shaving with his father's razor, and then a man shaving in a bucket of ice-cold water at four o'clock in the morning with a blunt blade, and a man who got embarrassed when people watched him shaving. I finished up by drinking the shaving water – which wasn't very good for my heartburn.

And my hair was constantly tacky with the soap – I used to come out in bubbles when it rained.'

He appeared at the Windmill, like so many others, and then toured in Variety with considerable success – except at Bolton.

'I was taken off the bill! It was a packed theatre – Ben Jenkins and his Singing Miners were on, and Norman Vaughan was on the bill – and the audience were hysterical with laughter at the act before me, which was very "Joey-Joey" [knockabout and falls] with false noses and funny walks. Then I came on, shaving – "I've only just arrived, I haven't had a chance to shave; but as I'm shaving I'll show you how other people shave" . . . so they sat back and waited for me to finish shaving, thinking that when I'd done it I'd carry on with the act. I got faster and faster in my delivery, because panic was building up . . . lynch-mob murmuring started . . . and afterwards the manager said, "You're not shaving in my bloody time – here's your money"! He had to give me all my money – but I couldn't really take it because the agent who had booked the bill had to find another act for the week – I just kept a fiver . . . and then I had to pay my digs for the whole week, so I had about a quid left. I went home on the milk train to Swansea. And the following week I was on at Oldham – and by this time it had got around, so everybody was in the wings waiting for the fiasco – and they were a marvellous audience.'

Secombe normally worked as a second-spot comic in those days:

'You *had* to get the audience's attention . . . whereas a comic is paid to get laughs, the audience is not beholden to give up its laughter . . . you went out to face the enemy in some cases. They came to see the top of the bill, and you had to be sat through. Someone said to me at Oldham, "Nearly had me laughing when you were on, you know" – that was a compliment!'

Another NAAFI comic with a highly individual style, Frankie Howerd, developed a natural tendency to stammer into a major part of his act. He began on stage in 1946 after his demobilization – before the war he had tried to begin a stage career but with no success – doing a stand-up routine, assisted by a silent stooge in the shape of his pianist, 'Madame Blanchie Moore':

Well, now I'm going to be accompanied for this particular performance on the piano-forte by Madame Blanchie Moore. Madame Blanchie Moore, known to me as 'Flossie' . . . known to Southend as 'Dockyard Dora'. Now, er . . .

don't laugh – poor old soul . . . Now, er . . . funny woman . . . no don't . . . don't laugh – it might be one of your own.[3]

However it was radio rather than stage which gave him his first fame; he was engaged as resident comedian for one of the BBC's top Variety programmes, *Variety Bandbox*, and after only a short time was topping bills at Variety theatres. His appeal was not so much in the strength of his basic material, but in his delivery – utilizing the nervous stammer, and breaking off to address or admonish the audience. He was (and still is) the master of a lugubrious form of high camp which enabled him to make the most of every line.

Frankie Howerd

Today I'm going to tell you what happened to me in the Sahara desert. In the Sahara-ha-ra de-*sert*![4] And – ooh, no . . . it was hot! Ooh, it was real hot! Even the Sphinx had sunglasses on. No . . . because you see, like a fool, I wanted to rest me feet . . . so I sat down on a little hummock. And did that hummock *hum*! No . . . well . . .

you see . . . I'd just settled back, on this hummock, and it *moved*! And before you could say 'Attenborough' . . . not that you'd want to, mind you, but still . . . I was up in the air! I was on the top of a *camel*! (*Falsetto voice*) I was a-*mazed*! (*Normal voice*) I was way up in the air! But mind you . . . mind you, high though I was, high though I was, the camel beat me. What a pong! – Ooh! Ooh, and it knew, you know – ooh, it *knew*! No, I could tell that by the look on its face, oh, no . . . then without warning . . . without warning, it set off like a thing possessed! It was so sudden I slipped down between its humps – I couldn't move! I was wedged! Then just as suddenly as it started, it stopped . . . I didn't, mind you . . . it did – *I* didn't . . . straight over its head! I landed right in the middle of a . . . of a dune. A dune. Mind you, considering I was off in May it was very good going! And, er . . . yes . . . so, er . . . mind you . . . 'ere . . . the camel just turned round and set off home – left me . . . ooh, callous *it*! There I was – stranded! Stranded in the middle of the pi-ti-less de-*sert*! I wasn't alone . . . no . . . I wasn't alone for long though . . . because you see, in the distance, I saw three riders coming towards me. Bedouins. Yes, Bedouins. No . . . they're called that, you know, 'cos if they have to decide . . . if they have to decide between work and sleep, the Bed-wins! Yes . . . yes . . . good, you know, good . . . the boy has it! As they got nearer . . . no, give in now . . . as they . . . no, please, now . . . now, control please, control . . . now please, *control* . . . con-ever-so-*trol*! . . . [5]

The last section of that extract is a reworking of George Robey's technique of apparently trying to *prevent* the audience from laughing – which makes them laugh all the more, of course.

With the decline of Variety, Howerd went through a period when he found work difficult to get, but he bounced back in the 1960s with his appearance at *The Establishment*, the satirical nightclub founded by Peter Cook, and as the star of the musical *A Funny Thing Happened On The Way To The Forum*. This, and the spin-off TV series *Up Pompeii*, provided excellent vehicles for his lugubrious and bawdy style; but perhaps the best demonstration of his particular abilities came when he performed the song made famous by Frank Sinatra – 'My

Way' – keeping the words intact, but performing them in such a way that 'I did it my way' suggested all *sorts* of meanings.

Many of the peculiar stories told by stand-up comics, as with the one above, were told as if they were a first-person experience (not that any attempt was made to make them believable). Beryl Reid – since better known as a serious actress, particularly in *The Killing of Sister George* – sent up the first-person idea in her Variety act, in which she appeared as the Birmingham girl 'Marlene' (pronounced 'Mar-leen') and worked with a strong Birmingham accent reminiscent of a tightly-stretched rubber band with adenoids. Here she tells a typical stand-up comic routine, but keeps undermining it.

> Well now, I start off by saying my mother's not very well. (She's all right, see, but I have to say that because it's part of the joke.) This morning she swallowed an egg, whole. Now she's afraid to move in case she breaks it, and she's afraid to sit still in case she hatches it. You couldn't help laughing at that, now, could you?
>
> Now I like say 'any road up', like, a sign that I'm going to say another joke. Any road up – you know I said my mother's not very well – it's making her very irritable, 'coz just before I came here she hit me on the head with an oak leaf. The one out of the centre of the dining-room table. Didn't 'arf 'urt my 'ead. (I like rub my head, see – acting, like she hit me. She never touch me – nice woman, my mother.)
>
> Now I'm going to say it again . . . any road up, my boy friend took me down to Devon last

year. (I never been there, see – Birmingham, I come from. I never been abroad till I came here on the coach.) He'd never been to Devon before. (It's a lot of lies – he lives there.)[6]

'Marlene' was a character used to relay the jokes, just as Frankie Howerd created a character which he used to get the most mileage out of his material. Many comics were working within a tighter character-framework, in the style of the older music-hall comics. (Jeanne de Casalis of course worked within a character framework but she did not address the audience directly – rather, she performed a one-person sketch on which they eavesdropped; much more a revue than Variety technique.)

Cardew Robinson, who had done a little stage work before going into the RAF, where he appeared in their Gang Show, created 'Cardew the Cad, the Bad Boy of St Fanny's', building his act entirely round the delinquent schoolboy's experiences. Because of his height, the school uniform, cap and scarf looked funnier than it would have done on most people, so in this way too his act was a link with the music-hall comics who could get a laugh before they uttered a word.

He remembers: 'After the war I toured in the commercial production of the Gang Show; then I went into Variety as Cardew the Cad, and into radio – I got my own series, *Variety Fanfare*, where I did a different episode about the school every week; my character was in the children's comic *Radio Fun* for seven years, and from that they did a movie called *Fun at St Fanny's*. I went on doing the character in Variety for about ten years, but ultimately I realized that Variety was going the way of the steam engine, so I stopped doing Cardew the Cad – but the press has never let me forget it. I still occasionally do it in pantomime.'

His material was naïve but well delivered – of course in those departed days the sort of antics he described were obviously comic fantasy; nowadays he would be competing with reports in the Sunday newspapers. In this radio monologue he looked back over a year well spent:

> In 1951 the cadet corps was put under the supervision of a Regular Army sergeant. So Chomondley Minor, who had no idea of cooking, was put in the kitchen; Fatty Gilbert, who can't drive, was put in charge of transport; and I was put in the Intelligence Corps. At the end of the Christmas Term we had our Speech Day, and all the parents turned up. My father didn't have far

to come – he's a member of the Sixth Form. The Head read out the exam results before the assembly: boys passing scholarship exams – nil; boys passing University exams – nil – after extra time. He announced that the redecorations were proceeding smoothly; the Ministry had given permission for the construction of a very smart cocktail bar in the school – he was hoping in due course to receive permission to put a roof over the classrooms. Amenities had been improved – since the boys had returned to the school from their annual visit to France, several books had been added to the school library.[7]

Many comedians working in a character format made the obvious choice of using a strong accent to strengthen their character. Leon Cortez, who had appeared in his own touring show before the war as a cockney comedian, made a feature in his post-war stand-up work not only of his accent, but of brief summaries of the plots of Shakespeare's plays. In this example he presented a dissertation on the Scottish play.

> Now, when Macbeth gets 'ome, 'e tells 'is missus all about this, and she bein' a bit of a cunnin' old commando, already sees 'erself with a crown for a titfer, and knowin' the King was comin' to stay for the weekend, decides to do 'im.
> Well, King Duncan and 'is sons Malcolm and Donalbain arrive, and bein' a bit tired the old cock goes straight for kip, and no sooner 'as 'e dropped off to sleep than Mrs Mac, just like the cat, crept up to 'is cot, copped 'is clock, coughed and crept out again. 'Ain't yer done 'im?' sez Macbeth. 'No' she sez – ''is clock reminded me of my father. You 'ave a bash.' 'What?' sez Macbeth – 'Don't you think *I* 'ad a father?' 'Now take this dagger and cut off 'is future' – which 'e does, and so becomes King.
> Now Macbeth, thinking Banquo might know too much, invites 'im to a dinner party, but 'as 'im done on the way and excuses 'is absence by tellin' the guests as 'ow Banquo's bein' demobbed that day and per'aps can't find a sporran ter fit 'im.[8]

In contrast to Cortez's traditional cockney character, Arthur English portrayed a type which was very common at that period – the 'spiv', who dressed very flashily and usually dealt in black market goods or luxuries 'off the back of a lorry'. Like many others, he gained a lot of experience in the army, where English began as an elegantly-dressed comic but progressed to the spiv character with the addition of an outrageous 'kipper' tie. After the war ended he appeared at the Windmill – which he describes as 'Variety for a very selected audience – they didn't really come to see *you*'. Because, as a solo act, he was not subject to the Lord Chamberlain's censorship, he was able to ad-lib a good deal.

'I had a framework, and I had a set lot of gags, but it was basically very elastic . . . part of the act was to get mixed up, and I've actually forgotten where I was and told the same joke twice in the one appearance! I learnt to be irresponsible, and not to control myself – the hardest part was when I took the call at the end and did all the business of being out of breath.'

He was basically a clean comic, but because his style was raucous Watch Committees were liable to pick on him:

'I had a nudist colony routine – could be a bit saucy, but it was nice – one gag went; "I love this house, overlooking a nudist colony – disgusting! *And* dangerous – I fell out of the window three times. The third time I fell right in the middle of them – wallop! Sounded like a jelly-tester . . . what are you laughing for? There's no such thing as a jelly-tester." And at Dudley they made me take it out!'

His routine was basically stand-up gags – some of them old favourites – mostly told in first-person and in character, although, as he says, in a very loose framework. In some of them one can detect the authentic ring of post-war London, the shortages, and the spivs:

> I'm walking down the street the other day, there's an old lady walking in front of me, she comes a tumble, ace-king-queen-jack on the deck, I'm behind, I want to help her, see – I give her the one-two-three-four, open her handbag, give her a bit of fresh air – she opened her eyes, she said, 'Where am I? Where am I?' – I said 'Map of London, lady – half-a-crown'. And this fellow come up to me – don't keep scratching, I've just swept up – this fellow comes up to me, he said, 'Listen, do you want to join the spiv's union?' I said, 'Spiv's union – what are you talking about?' – he said, 'Half-a-crown a week, after the first three weeks you come into full benefit.' I said, 'Full benefit?' – he said, 'Yes, you go down the Labour Exchange, they offer you a job, we fight your case for you.' . . .

I keep thinking I've left the tap running in the dressing-room . . . I'm flogging . . . I'm flogging . . . Shut up when I'm talking! Anybody'd think I was a comic or something – I'm flogging the stuff on the barrow, you see, down the Whitehall, there – and a lady come up, she said, 'How much are your lemons?' – I said, 'Seven a bob' – so I gave her a load – she come back, she said, 'Here, how much did you say they was?' I said, 'Seven a bob' – she said, 'You only gave me five' – I said, 'I know – two of yours was bad – threw them away, I'm not going to swindle you!'[9]

At the climax of the act he would talk faster and faster until he was totally unintelligible, ending by shouting 'Start the music – open the cage!' As well as touring in Variety he appeared in touring versions of the later Crazy Gang shows (which toured with only one or two members of the gang, the others being replaced by performers who were willing to tour). Since the demise of Variety he has become well known as a straight actor.

English's cockney accent was not genuine, as he was born in Aldershot. Someone who might have had an authentic accent but who deliberately avoided it was the Jewish comedian, Issy Bonn. Although his patter was much slicker, and consisted of gags rather than the old-fashioned character narrative, his material had distinct links with Julian Rose, the Jewish comedian of an earlier generation. Bonn worked with an accent that was mid-Atlantic rather than obviously London Jewish; his gags, however, were firmly in the Jewish tradition, and he also became famous for his rendering of the sentimental ballad 'My Yiddisher Momma'. Here he relates the adventures of his friends the Finkelfeffers:

Issy Bonn

They got a boy, Sammy – what a boy! Last week in school the teacher said, 'Come here, I'll try you out in' . . . er . . . arith . . . math . . . adding up things, you know? The teacher said, 'If one pair trousers costs ten shillings, how much would you pay for ten pair?' – Sammy said, 'Ten pair, ten shilling a pair – four pound ten.' The teacher said, 'You're wrong, it's five pounds.' He said, 'No, no – four pound ten, it's my best offer – take it or leave it.'

They got a general store and a restaurant – they sell everything. Fellow came in for a pair of shoes – after he fitted the customer he said, 'They cost fifteen shillings' – the customer said, 'I'm sorry, I've only got ten shillings – will you trust me to come back tomorrow with the other five shillings?' – Finkelfeffer said, 'Sure, I'll wrap them up for you'. And the man went outside – I said, 'Do you know him?' – he said, 'No' – I said, 'You're crazy – why do you trust a fellow that . . . he won't come back with the five shillings' – Finkelfeffer said, 'Yes, he's bound to come back – I wrapped him up two shoes for the left foot.'

You know, his nephew was very ill – they rushed him to the hospital and they operated on him just in time. Two days later he would have got better without it.[10]

Reg Dixon

But the most frequently used comic accent was that of the north of England – specifically Yorkshire or Lancashire. The tradition of northern comedy continued unabated. Albert Modley, on his way to London, is somewhat smarter than Tom Foy half a century earlier, but the idea of the northerner visiting the big city was, as then, a useful comic format.

> I must tell you how I got here. I went to the booking office window and said, 'I want a return, please.' He said, 'Where to?' I said, 'Back here'. He said, 'I *know* that, but where are you going to?' I said, 'London'. He said, 'King's Cross?' I said, 'Is he?' He said, 'Here's your ticket', so I gave him t'brass. The porter said, 'This way to London, sir', and he took hold of my arm and opened t'carriage door. So I gave him a threepenny bit. He said, 'What's this?' So I said, 'Heads', and won it back again.[11]

The north of England itself, of course, is not one homogeneous lump – even if some Londoners do consider that it begins at Watford. Harry Secombe found that his reception varied from town to town.

'Halifax was like playing the West End of London, a very quick audience. Bradford Alhambra was very hard work – same act, different audience. Newcastle Empire was a good place to work, a very with-it audience.'

It was generally said that northern comedy did not travel – at any rate not south of Birmingham. James Casey, for many years a writer and producer of radio comedy for the BBC's North Region, and the son of the splendid northern sketch comic Jimmy James, puts this into perspective.

'If comedy is parochial it doesn't travel from anywhere – and southern comedy doesn't travel; Max Miller was never big in the north – nobody was bigger than Miller in show business, and yet he didn't mean anything at the Sunderland Empire. If he played it, he'd get by, that's all. Today it's changing, because television is flattening everything out; but I think there's a basic difference in concept of comedy because the traditional northern comic gets great sympathy. The southern comics didn't get sympathy – they were smart, they would basically tell you how they topped somebody. He did this, and I said . . . and topped him. The northern comedian would tell you how he was made a fool of. It's a slower kind of humour – not in the sense of being less witty, but in the sense of not "attacking". The northern comic would tend to build a situation,

rather than going in for the one-liner. And northern accents are basically funnier – when most people want to be funny in ordinary conversation, they will adopt a northern voice. And northerners go broader north, not realizing that they're northern anyway.'

Northern audiences prefer the warmth of northern comedy to the hustling attitude of southern comics.

'If you walk out and tell them how smart you are, they immediately sit back and say, "Go on, then – let's see how clever you are".'

Sympathetic northern comedy was the style adopted by Reg Dixon (not to be confused with Reginald Dixon the organist) who was in fact born in Coventry, but used a gentle northern accent in his act. His entrance into the business was standard enough – a little professional work before the war, then an RAF Gang Show (in which he toured with Peter Sellers, David Lodge, Tony Hancock, Graham Stark, Dick Emery and Cardew Robinson) and then in the post-war period front-cloth comic appearances in Variety and radio appearances in shows like *Variety Bandbox*. Part of his first fame stemmed from his theme song, which he wrote himself, 'Confidentially'.

'I used to open with a few bars of "Confidentially", and finish with a few bars of it. This programme was at a peak time every Sunday night, and I got literally hundreds and hundreds of letters asking, "How does the middle part go?" I made a record of it for Decca – and I sold hundreds and thousands of sheet-music copies and records, and it became a number one hit. I went round all the Moss Empires then as top of the bill.'

His catchphrase, 'proper poorly', arose by accident.

'I was playing the Palace Theatre Manchester; and I'd got a boil inside my nose, and it was terribly painful. I walked on the stage one night, and in the middle of my act, I looked at the audience, and I said: "To look at me, you wouldn't think I was in pain, would you?" And there was a big laugh. "I don't feel well." Another big laugh. "I feel poorly." Another big laugh. "I feel proper poorly." Another big laugh. "Have you ever had a boil . . . have you ever had a boil up your nose? Oh, it's terrible. I can hear it, ticking." All this was getting very big laughs – and I came off, and thought that's a very good theme, and something I can alter every week in my act.'

Part of the joke was in the delivery – 'proper' was pitched quite high compared with the rest of the sentence – and 'I've been proper poorly' became a widely-known catchphrase. This radio monologue is typical of his style:

But you know – to look at me, you wouldn't think that I was lonely, would you? You wouldn't think that nobody loved me. But it's true. It's true – to look at me, you would say, 'There is someone that should have lots of love, oodles of cuddle, a bottle of medicine and some fresh air'. I'm not getting anything. Penelope's left me. She said to me last week, 'How much money have you got in your moneybox? I'm going to Monte Carlo.' I said, 'Couldn't I come – I'd like to see the fast cars.' She says, 'You can go to Brighton next year with the old crocks. Now then, how much money have you got?' I says, 'Fifteen pounds, four-and-threepence ha'penny, two buttons and the end of your nail-file. I don't know how that got there.' She says, 'That's just enough – you can keep the buttons.' I says, 'But you can't do that, Petal. I've been saving that up for my old age.' She says, 'You're too optimistic. How long do you think you're going to live, anyway?' I said, 'I hope to reach three score and ten.' She says, 'If you do I shall lose money. I shall have paid out more for you on the Health Scheme than what I'm getting back on the insurance.' I said, 'That isn't very kind – I haven't been to the doctor for three days.' She says, 'Well, it's about time you went. The fowl were going very well on those pills that you had for your constitution.'[12]

As with many performers, once Dixon was known on radio, audiences came to see him in Variety.

'One of the biggest laughs I got was when I walked out on the stage – I'm six feet tall and sixteen stone – so I used to say, "You didn't think I was like this, did you? You thought I was about this size, didn't you?" – they expected to see a small man. Of course that only happened on my first appearances.'

As Dixon pointed out, stand-up comics could work better on radio or in the theatre than in television.

'They're not obstructed by batteries of cameras and monitors which of course are very distracting to the audience in a television studio. If you did radio, there would just be one microphone, so the audience would hardly know you were on the air.'

As television became the dominant medium, so it became more difficult for stand-up comics to maintain the sort of relationship with the audience upon which their acts depended. There have continued to be stand-up comics on television, but as a medium it is more suited to sketches and comedy-dramas.

Northern comedy has tended to be diluted by the smoothing-out of regional differences caused by television; but there are two particular comics who still work in sharply differentiated styles which have distinct links with the old northern humour of Variety; they are Ken Dodd and Les Dawson, and they will be examined in the final Interlude (p. 220).

21 Couthy comedy
Variety in Scotland (from the 1920s to the 1950s)

Harry Lauder

The major Variety circuits extended into Scotland, and there were also many theatres run by smaller and local circuits; so Variety had its place in popular entertainment north of the border just as everywhere else. At the peak of the business in the 1920s there were twenty-four theatres in Glasgow, fourteen in Edinburgh, ten in Dundee and many others round the country. Variety acts would tour in Scotland as part of their normal work; but most of them approached the Glasgow Empire with some trepidation. Singing acts were probably safe enough, but comedians could get a very unfriendly reception – particularly on Friday and Saturday nights when the percentage of alcohol in the audience's bloodstream was higher.

One of the problems, at least before the war, was that Scottish audiences found English accents difficult to understand – this was before radio had made so-called 'standard English' so widely known; an English accent was as unintelligible to a Glaswegian as a thick Scottish accent was to a Londoner. The audiences did not warm to bright self-confident English comics, and was quite capable of heckling or throwing things. (When Morecambe and Wise played there for about the third time they walked off to dead silence – 'Aye, lads,' said the stage doorkeeper – 'they're beginning to like you'.)

Scottish comics coming south would be met with similar lack of understanding (if less obvious disapproval). Although a few small-time Scottish acts played in Variety in England, the first performer to become really popular was Harry Lauder, who took the trouble to temper his approach to suit the English. Even more than the only other main Scottish comic of the pre-war period, Will Fyffe, Lauder presented 'couthy' (cosy) comedy; indeed the comedy part of his material sounds very thin indeed today on his records, particularly as he persists in laughing at his own jokes. He was, however, immensely popular – partly because his songs were set to lively dance rhythms, and were jaunty and easily remembered. The character Lauder portrayed was the classic Scots caricature – cranky and rather odd-looking; he also made a point of fostering an undeserved reputation for meanness off-stage.

Will Fyffe worked in something more like the usual English format, mixing songs and patter. His most famous

Will Fyffe (in the film *The Brothers*)

song was of course 'I Belong To Glasgow', but he did a number of character studies such as 'I'm Ninety-Four Today' (the old man who is getting married not for love but for spite – to cut his sons out of his will), 'Daft Sandy' and 'The Railway Guard'.

Few other comics managed to appeal to English audiences; Jimmy Logan, the son of the Scottish dancing act Jack Short and May Dalziel, did manage to make the difficult transition, but only after many years working in summer season shows, which were a much more important rival to Variety in Scotland than they were in England. He played these at a number of theatres, beginning in Rothesay; in each season he would play at the same theatre for many weeks, usually to an audience which came regularly. He describes the demands this made upon the artists.

'In these seaside summer shows, the comedian might play for fifteen weeks, changing the programme every week, with the same company. When I appeared at Rothesay – I was seventeen – we had twice nightly; Monday, Tuesday, Wednesday, was programme number one; Thursday, Friday, Saturday was programme number two; and on Friday night there was a midnight matinée, for which you were supposed to do a fresh programme. Then fresh programmes the next week – and you spent most of your time when you weren't on stage trying to write material for the following week's programme. These shows developed comedians who were known personally to the whole community – and indeed the whole company became part and parcel of the life of the local community.'

This approach was quite different from the Variety comics' technique of doing twenty minutes of top-flight material – which was all he had – to a different audience every night. When Logan was asked to appear at the London Palladium in 1953 he found difficulty in adapting his material.

'I had dozens of acts – within a season, they were all very strong, because the people knew you, and after the third programme they'd say, "Och, he's selling onions this week" or whatever; that's different from an audience that's only going to see you once. The timing is different, the attack is different. I have a marvellous two weeks at the Palladium – there is nothing to compare with appearing on-stage at the Palladium – but what I normally do, appearing in a theatre where they know you personally, is quite different from appearing in a theatre where they don't know who you are and they're waiting for you to be marvellous.'

The Scottish summer-season shows, having resident comics and a regular audience, enjoyed a similar advantage to modern television situation comedy in that the comedians could build up familiar characters and rely upon the cumulative effect of putting these characters into situations rather than having strong gags in the acts. The characters would be familiar types, and would be in situations which the audiences could recognize and identify with. Of course, the sheer pressure of providing this much material meant that much of it was semi-improvised.

Jimmy Logan: 'I've seen us so desperate that we were actually rehearsing a sketch while the audience were coming in – and saying, for instance, "Look, I'm ill in bed, and you want me to come out and have a drink".'

This sort of improvising and hurried writing produced material which would hardly stand up for today's sophisticated audiences; but in the context of the summer seasons they provided a simple humour which was well suited to

Harry Gordon

the situation. The biggest joke was that all this was in fact highly illegal; everyone just assumed that the Lord Chamberlain's writ did not run in Scotland – there were no Watch Committees, local government being differently structured – and so all these shows went ahead without a licence. (Only in the last few years of theatrical censorship, when someone in Howard and Wyndham's applied for a licence for one of their shows, did the Lord Chamberlain's office realize what had been going on. English touring revues and straight plays would already have been licensed before reaching Scotland, of course.) In fact this absence of censorship did not lead to immediate licentiousness, as Jimmy Logan explains.

'The audiences themselves would censor the show. If somebody came on and was foul-mouthed, the audience just wouldn't turn up.'

Scottish audiences had different tastes in comedy from English ones.

'In Scotland – death: great subject for humour; in England – blank. In Scotland, you don't make jokes about the minister; in England they like to make jokes about the vicar.'

The summer-season type of show was taken up and improved on by Howard and Wyndham's Theatres, who presented a summer season show called *Half-Past Eight* in Glasgow, during what had up to then been an off-period, in 1933 and subsequent years. The original show starred Billy Caryll and Hilda Mundy, and later editions starred Scottish comic Dave Willis, who specialized in physical clowning as well as character comedy. *Half-Past Eight* and its various imitators were highly successful, and continued well into the 1950s – Jimmy Logan was in the show for ten years, and remembers it for its high production values and spectacle.

There were a number of popular Scots comics, including Jack Radcliffe, Tommy Morgan and Harry Gordon, but they made little impression in England because of the difficulties of dialect and style. Harry Gordon created an imaginary village of Inversnecky, and portrayed various members of the community in different monologues and songs. To some extent this was a created community like Gillie Potter's later Hogsnorton, but where Potter told stories set within the village, Gordon simply did stand-up routines which were separate in themselves, but linked by having the characters living in Inversnecky. His basic format was that of Leno and Robey – a song, some patter, and a few more bars of the song, creating a character study. As the 'Inversnecky Postie' he simply built the character out of a string of postman jokes:

You know, even when I was a laddie I used to
play at Posties. I rushed in one day and cried,
'Hey Mother, I've just delivered a real letter to
every hoose in the street.' She said, 'That's a
smart boy – but where did ye get the real
letters?' I said, 'Oh, I found them in the dresser,
a' tied up wi' pink ribbon.'[1]

In 'The Inversnecky Fireman' he carried on a phone call
with the sufferer of a conflagration – he was obviously a
Scottish relative of Robb Wilton's fireman.

Oh, but we canna' come the day, though – no,
no, this is oor half-holiday, the day, ye see . . .
aye, . . . eh? . . . oh, no, no, the horses are awa'
– we dinna ken what time they'll be back at . . .
it's a pity ye did not ring up yesterday; we might
have arranged something, ye see . . . ye could na
keep it going until the morning, could ye?[2] Is
there a lot of smoke? Much? . . . oh . . . ye have
na' got a drop of petrol lying round aboot, have
ye? Then we could come roond an' see ye in the
morrow's morning, just after breakfast time –
aye, mebbe in time for a fly cup, one never
knows. Well well, then we'll see you the morrow
– oh, I hope it disnae' rain – no, that would spile
it, wouldn't it?'[3]

Harry Gordon played the Palladium in 1929, but with
no success. Many years later, according to Jimmy Logan,
a television director seriously considered doing a show
with the comic Tommy Morgan, but subtitling it because
his accent was so thick. Variety continued side-by-side
with these long-running shows, but the top Scottish
comics got used to being able to star for years in the same
theatres – and for good money – so there was little
incentive for them to tour.

As the 1950s came to an end, theatres began to close in
Scotland, just as in England, and both Variety and
resident shows declined and eventually disappeared. The
BBC's Scottish Region mounted its own radio Variety
programmes – although Logan feels that many Scots
comics were intimidated by the BBC's pompousness, at
least in the earlier days – but gradually even this disappeared. Scots humour has not died completely – Jimmy
Logan and others are still popular entertainers on both
sides of the border, and Billy Connolly has demonstrated
that it is possible for a Scots comic to make no concessions
whatever to Sassenachs and still be a roaring success. In its
heyday, the Scottish Variety and summer-season scene
had an individuality all its own, which gave it a quite
separate character from the more widely-known world of
Variety in England.

22 Magic and 'a gottle of geer'
Speciality acts: Two (magicians and ventriloquists)

In the wide range of different types of acts which can be classed as 'speciality', magicians and illusionists rank among the most spectacular and complicated. Although there were many magicians who would do about eight minutes as a second turn on a Variety bill, the names which have tended to be remembered are those of the presenters of big illusions – Houdini, Maskelyne and Devant, Dante, Selbit, and Kalanag. Most of the time, however, these performers ran their own shows rather than touring in Variety.

Maskelyne – one of the most famous names in magic – continued for three generations. The first, John Nevil Maskelyne, was born in 1839, and presented shows with his partner David Devant. Maskelyne died in 1917, and Devant retired in 1919; Nevil Maskelyne succeeded his father, and his son Jasper worked in his own shows and in Variety until 1949. For many years the Maskelynes presented their own shows at St George's Hall, until it was taken over by the BBC in 1933.

The other well remembered name in magic was Harry Houdini, an American who specialized in spectacular escapes; he toured America, Britain and Europe as well as appearing in films. Selbit originated the best-known of all illusions – sawing a woman in half – in 1921; Golden improved on this by using a buzz-saw, and also did complicated illusions with flags, people walking through panes of glass, and so on. Dante – another American, Harry Hansen – toured for some years in Britain with his show *Sim Bala Bim*; and Levante – an Australian, Leslie George Cole – toured in the 1930s with feats such as escaping from a sack and a metal trunk. Apart from Dante, Kalanag was one of the few illusionists to tour Britain with his own show in the post-war period.

The more complex illusions presented by these artists were hardly suitable for Variety; they were complicated to set up, and they often took too long to perform to allow their use in the twenty minutes which was the normal maximum in a Variety bill. Houdini in particular would spin out his escapes, being searched by committees from the audience who also examined his props, and then sometimes keeping the audience waiting for half-an-hour while he 'made his escape' (having in reality taken only

David Devant

seconds to do it and spending the remaining time out of sight reading a newspaper – this heightened the tension, particularly in escapes where he seemed to be in danger of drowning or asphyxiation). As well as escapes, Houdini also presented more ordinary illusions, and was also able to simulate many effects presented by so-called 'mediums' at seances.

A typical Houdini escape was from a large metal box whose lid was secured by bolts, pushed through from the inside, with the nuts screwed onto the outside by members of the audience and then further secured by split pins pushed through a transverse hole in the bolt. Houdini simply substituted special bolts after the normal ones had been examined, pushing them through from the inside (where he was out of sight); they had heads which unscrewed so that it was a simple matter for him to remove them and push them out (the box being hidden by a screen during this). The really skilled part consisted of getting the original bolts back into the box and lid from the *outside*, but with the heads inside. The orchestra played an essential part in all this by providing music loud enough to cover the sound of the fake bolts falling on the stage as he pushed them out.

In normal Variety bills the magic was of a simpler and less time-consuming nature, and mostly performed by less well-known artists. Harold Taylor, who has made a study of magic as well as having been a performer since the war, thinks that no one magician has ever topped a Variety bill; those who were big enough names to do so usually presented their own shows. Taylor himself started during the war when he was in the RAF, and did some Variety work in the following years.

He remembers: 'They used to call me Harold "Three Tricks" Taylor. I had a flow of inane patter – carefully rehearsed ad-libs; and I don't like magic with boxes – I'd do a trick getting one handkerchief in between two others which were knotted together, and the band would go "Ta-ra!" – and if I was lucky four people would clap. Then I'd cut a bit of rope up and keep joining it back together; and I finished up with a trick where I put some cigarette papers on a black fan, tossed them up in the air and they formed the shape of an egg – and then I would take the egg and crack it into a tumbler! And that was it – just those three tricks, with the patter.' Even before Variety started its decline in the 1950s Taylor had moved into private entertainments – a field worked by many magicians to the present day; he also acts as an adviser on magic (for example on the film *Dragonslayer*).

Another Variety magician who began in the services during the war, but who preferred illusions to Harold Taylor's more sleight-of-hand type of tricks, was Pat Hatton, who worked with his wife as 'Pat Hatton and Peggy' (and later as 'Pat Hatton and Gloria' – he changed the name of the act to match that of his wife, not vice versa).

He remembers: 'I thought up an idea with an Eastern snake-basket, where I got two men up from the audience, dressed them in beards and turbans and got them to do a cod Eastern dance. Then we pretended to charm snakes out of the basket – which was Gloria with long black gloves on, waving her arms out of the basket. Then she would get out and dance round the men and kiss them – leaving lipstick on their faces; and then she would get back into the basket and I'd thrust ten swords through it – take them out, and demonstrate that she had vanished. This was all a vehicle for comedy, and that's the important thing – if you can get comedy into any speciality act it's a great help.'

With the decline in Variety he moved into cabaret and cruises – where he had to be able to put together anything up to ten shows, changing twice a week.

Illusions were the mainstay of one of the most influential magicians of the post-war period, Robert Harbin (a South African whose family name was Ned Williams). He was never able to realize his dream of having his own touring show, but he worked extensively in Variety and had his own regular television show for several years in the 1950s. He was famous for illusions such as the 'Production Box', which, though apparently empty, brought forth a large number of assorted objects including a stack of water-filled fish-bowls; and his 'Zig-Zag Lady' illusion, in which the centre third of a vertical cabinet containing a girl is slid sideways by almost its entire width, is still seen in magic shows. His work paved the way for the present-day popularity of performers such as Paul Daniels.

With the increasing sophistication of audiences, comedy became an important factor in many magicians' acts. The most famous comedy-magician of the post-war period was Tommy Cooper, whose tricks – which inevitably went wrong – were punctuated with optimistic predictions of success ('Just like that!') and maniacal laughter; he developed his style to include eccentric jokes and visual routines, but the magic remained a central part of his act.

Johnny Cooper – no relation – whom we met earlier as a dancer, had changed his act to magic after the war, although he kept some dancing in as part of it, together with some comedy. As with many others, he has had to branch away from Variety in its decline, into cabaret and children's parties. In cabaret he worked as a drunk, with the act titled 'Sleightly Inebriated' – the tricks seemed to mystify him as much as the audience. Cabaret presents its own problems.

'In a theatre you have a front audience – a lot of the old tricks, if you stood at the side you would see how they were done. In cabaret, where you've got the audience all round you, the tricks have got to be angle-proof; you've got to do tricks where nothing shows from the back – no back-palming or anything like that.'

In his other main field – children's parties – he has found that (unlike Pat Hatton on cruises) he does not have to change his act – children appreciate seeing the same tricks again and again.

Johnny Cooper

Comedy and characterization were important to most speciality acts. The more successful jugglers, for example, got away from the traditional balls or Indian clubs to work in individual styles. Rebler used to predict disaster – which never struck – as he worked; Stetson juggled with top hats; Gaston Palmer used to make a mess of everything he attempted.

Bob Konyot worked with Palmer and remembers: 'He once showed me – in his dressing-room – that he could juggle well; he said, "You see, I'm a good juggler, but nobody would pay me for this. What I do on stage, messing around, that's what they pay for." He used to carry his entire act in a small attaché case, and he said to

me, "You don't want to bother with all these springboards . . . I just walk in and I walk out!" '

The disadvantage, of course, of doing a juggling act was the regular practice needed to keep the tricks polished – usually done in the digs (over the bed – less far to bend down to pick up anything you drop, and quieter too). There were other types of speciality acts which lent themselves to comedy – one good example was the trick cyclist Slim Ryder, whose long skinny body looked hilarious on unicycles or tiny bicycles only about eighteen inches high.

Audience participation was always popular in the few types of acts which were suitable, such as magic – members of the audience always enjoyed seeing other members of the audience making fools of themselves. For a short time in the early 1950s there was a spate of hypnotists, who took audience participation even further by getting members of the audience on-stage, hypnotizing them, and getting them to act the fool in some way. Peter Casson ran a one-man show in 1949 using this idea; and several others appeared on Variety bills.

The idea was short-lived (although it has surfaced occasionally since, most recently on American television) because of the suspicions of mental harm being done to the participants. In March 1952 damages of £1,132 were awarded against the hypnotist Ralph Salter to a young lady described as a 'shop-girl' who was alleged to have suffered eighteen months of acute depression after being hypnotized by him on-stage in December 1948;[1] within the next year a number of local authorities had banned displays of hypnotism and this type of act quietly died out.

There was a small sub-category of speciality acts consisting of *imitators* – not impressionists, but people who imitated the sounds of trains, motor cars, indeed almost anything. Of those who imitated birdsong, the most lastingly famous is of course Percy Edwards; he did tour on the halls for a time, but has also become something of a personality in his own right. He was not restricted to birds – he could do many other animals with equal skill – and built up a considerable sideline in radio, providing animal effects which were predictable and reliable without being obviously pre-recorded. His most famous character part was as the dog Psyche in the 1950s radio comedy series *A Life Of Bliss* – he provided natural-sounding reactions which would have been impossible to obtain to order from a real animal.

A type of speciality act which usually disguised itself as a double-act was ventriloquism. The technique of appearing to make the performer's voice come from somewhere else goes back to the Greek and Roman priests who used it to provide the pronouncements of their oracles; and it was used by many people through the succeeding centuries for purposes of amusement or deception (although practitioners of the art in the Middle Ages were liable to find themselves being burnt for witchcraft).

It was not until around 1750 that ventriloquists began to use doll figures as the apparent source of the voice, but throughout the early music-hall period performers such as Walter Cole, Frank Mordaunt and Frederic Maccabe appeared, often with groups of life-sized dolls. The credit for inventing the single small doll, usually perched on the ventriloquist's knee, belongs to Fred Russell (also well known in the business for his work for the VAF) who first presented his dummy 'Coster Joe' in 1896 and set the format for ventriloquism which has survived with little variation to the present day.

Coram and 'Jerry Fisher'

Fred Russell and 'Coster Joe' (1905)

One of Russell's successors, Coram (Thomas Whittaker) developed the idea further by enabling his doll to walk, smoke, and even spit. Like so many dummies of the period, Coram's 'Jerry Fisher' was uniformed – in this case in an army rank junior to his operator. Coram and Jerry Fisher worked the halls from the first World War until Coram's death in 1937; their material, though basic, set the pattern for many later acts.

CORAM:	Is this the Colonel's bulldog you've got there?
JERRY:	Yes, sir.
CORAM:	He does not look very happy, does he?
JERRY:	No, sir. He is very miserable because I won't let him have his own way. He says he wants to go to the Sergeant-Major's funeral.
CORAM:	The bulldog says he wants to go?
JERRY:	Yes, sir.
CORAM:	But the Sergeant-Major is not dead.
JERRY:	I told him that, but he wants to go just the same.[2]

Coram's rival, Arthur Prince, worked in a similar style except that his dummy 'Jim' was a naval junior rank. Existing film of his act shows that, though he was well thought of in his time, his technique was very poor compared with more modern ventriloquists such as Ray Alan and Shari Lewis. Prince used a cigar to help to hide his lip movements – which were still somewhat apparent to the camera, although in a theatre they would have been less noticeable – and he tended to be rather rigid during the dummy's lines. His enunciation was also poor – 'm's coming out almost as 'n's, 'b's as 'g's and so on (though many vents were far worse, leading to the old joke about 'a gottle of geer' when comics wanted to take a rise out of vents). Prince's voice and that of the dummy were also rather too similar – which was no help when he broadcast. On the credit side, the dummy had a strong character, and they worked at a fairly high speed, interrupting each other, so that the act was effective when not seen from too close.

Here Prince coaches the dummy for his naval examinations.

Arthur Prince and 'Jim'

PRINCE: Suppose I happen to be one of the admirals asking you a question. You'd march into the room and you'd stand to attention at the bottom of the table; I might see you and I might say to you, 'What are the equinox?'

JIM: You may say what?

PRINCE: I may say, 'What are the equinox?'

JIM: You *may* say that?

PRINCE: I *may* say that.

JIM: But you *wouldn't*, would you? I mean, you don't know me enough.

PRINCE: Now, you see, you've failed already.

JIM: Failed?

PRINCE: Failed – you didn't answer the question quick enough. Now come along . . . I'll ask again – 'What are the equinox?'

JIM: Lord lumme, he's thought of it again.

PRINCE: Come along!

JIM: They are people who live in Iceland . . . No? Not a bit like it?

PRINCE: Not a bit like it.

JIM: Not even related?

PRINCE: Not even related, no. 'People who live in Iceland!' Why Iceland?

JIM: God knows.

PRINCE: Come along – you must say something.

I said the equinox.

JIM: I thought you said the Esquimaux!

PRINCE: That's all right . . . that's a get-out, anyway. Now then, one more – what animals eat grass?

JIM: What?

PRINCE: What animals eat grass? Now there's the easiest question of the lot . . . Come along, surely you know what that is – what animals eat grass?

JIM: Animals!

PRINCE: Animals.

JIM: Lord lumme, sir – I thought you said *Admirals*![3]

Although most vents used the standard single dummy – most with fairly similar personalities – there were experimenters. Señor Wences reintroduced the old 'talking hand' technique at the 1937 Royal Variety Performance – the hand being covered by a glove, with the mouth being formed by the thumb and first finger, with two eyes placed just above the mouth; simple, but surprisingly effective. In the post-war period the French ventriloquist Robert Lamouret toured in Britain with his hand-dummy in the form of a duck, Dudule – Lamouret's arm formed the neck of the duck and his hand operated the beak; he worked at considerable speed and with much more flexibility than the standard dummy was capable of. Not all the experiments succeeded – Fred Russell, having pioneered the single small doll, reverted to the use of larger dummies around 1923; he and his wife presented a court scene with about twenty dummies – it was so realistic that many people thought he had several assistants and that the 'judge' was a real person; but it was never popular, and on one occasion when he reverted to 'Coster Joe' for a change, the theatre manager said, 'Why carry all those props about when you've got *that* act?'

The most popular vent acts used dummies with a very strong character. Although various vents had appeared in British radio Variety shows, it was Edgar Bergen in America who pioneered the use of ventriloquism in a radio series built round the dummy; *The Charlie McCarthy Show* was immensely popular for many years. Charlie McCarthy, a smartly dressed but obstreperous dummy, had a very distinct personality and a readily identifiable voice – much higher than Arthur Prince's 'Jim', for example. Similar voices were used by most vents from the 1930s onwards; the high pitch is produced not simply by 'singing' the voice to a higher note but by tightening the very back of the tongue against the roof of the mouth; this can be done with little visible sign, and can be changed to and from the normal voice more quickly and easily than singing the equivalent pitch change. It also changes the actual character of the voice as well as its pitch. (There is, of course, no question of the voice *actually* coming from somewhere else, despite popular belief – the ventriloquist uses the movements of the dummy to distract the audience's attention and thus confuse the ear's sound-location process.)

In Britain, the most popular ventriloquist from about 1945 onwards for some years was Peter Brough. His father, Arthur Brough, had also been a ventriloquist – his dummy 'Tim' was used in the episode in the film *Dead of Night* in which Michael Redgrave plays a vent whose dummy takes possession of him. Peter Brough, who was involved in the textile industry, worked as a vent for pleasure rather than to make a living; after some stage

Peter Brough and 'Archie Andrews' (1953)

appearances he made his name on radio, beginning in 1943 and going on to feature in *Navy Mixture*. Brough was never a top-class technician, and years of working on radio eventually eroded his ability to hide the lip movements; but what mattered on radio was the strong personality of the dummy, Archie Andrews.

Like Charlie McCarthy, Archie was obstreperous and badly-behaved; Brough's technique of letting the story of a trail of disaster emerge gradually as he questioned Archie was also similar to Bergen's; and Archie eventually took a strong hold on the public imagination (many people thought he was real) and had his own radio series (see Chapter 23).

In this 1945 broadcast example, Brough and Archie discussed Charlie Shadwell, the tall thin conductor of the BBC Variety Orchestra, who had been the butt of radio jokes going back to pre-war *Music Hall* and in *ITMA*.

BROUGH: You behaved very badly at Charlie
            Shadwell's party.
ARCHIE: Charlie Shadwell? *That's* whose party it
            was – now I know why the turkey was

stuffed with old band parts. It was a shocking turkey – and why do we always have to eat turkey at Christmas?

BROUGH: The turkey has been a symbol of thanksgiving ever since the Pilgrims landed on Plymouth Rock.

ARCHIE: No wonder it was so tough. And whatever happens, Brough, don't let Charlie Shadwell play Father Christmas again.

BROUGH: Why not?

ARCHIE: Well, he came down the wrong chimney, got mixed up in the gas-pipe, and we had to put seventeen-and-fourpence in the meter before we could get him out.

BROUGH: But Archie, Charlie Shadwell was our host – don't you remember, he was standing in the hall greeting all the guests as they arrived.

ARCHIE: He was standing in the hall when *we* arrived?

BROUGH: Of course he was.

ARCHIE: So *that's* what I hung my hat and coat on.

BROUGH: Oh, Archie, you're impossible. I just can't take you anywhere.

ARCHIE: I'm shocking, aren't I?

BROUGH: You are.

ARCHIE: Did I disgrace myself?

BROUGH: You most certainly did. Everyone in the room saw you sneak up to the table and steal all those legs of chicken – I'm ashamed of you.

ARCHIE: *You're* ashamed?

BROUGH: I am.

ARCHIE: Because I stole a few measly legs of chicken? Let me tell you I wasn't the only one pinching legs at that party.

BROUGH: Archie . . .

ARCHIE: And she was no chicken, either.

BROUGH: That's quite enough of that.

ARCHIE: I won't mention names, but there's a certain guy who talks out of the side of his mouth.[4]

Ventriloquists have never lost their popularity, and in recent years performers such as Ray Alan, with his dummy Lord Charles, have kept up the tradition. There has also been a resurgence of interest in illusionists, particularly on American television. However, with the closing of the Variety theatres and the disappearance of the bigger circuses, the other forms of Variety acts have found it more difficult to survive. Occasionally a juggler or acrobat may be used to fill out a television show, but there is no regular employment for most of the types of speciality acts who at one time were such a feature of Variety bills.

23 Falls – and decline
Acrobats: Two (knockabout and balancing acts)

Acrobats continued to be a staple part of Variety as supporting acts throughout the post-war boom years, although many of them felt that they needed to inject some comedy into their routines in order to maintain their appeal with the audiences. Ted Durante (family name: Aston) actually began as a small-time comic, doing a tramp clown act when he was in the army during the war. After he was demobbed, he joined a small acrobatic troupe as a 'bearer' (the one at the bottom when they all stood on each other's shoulders) and also did comedy turns with George Mooney, one of the other members of the troupe. Subsequently the two of them struck out on their own as an acrobatic double-act under the invented name of Ted and George Durante – the surname being picked almost at random off a bill featuring Jack Durant. (They pronounced their new surname as if it didn't have an 'e' on the end.)

Ted Durante: 'We did comedy acrobatic work – no patter, because we were supposed to be French; it's always been assumed that the continental acrobats were the best. The bill matter stayed with us for years – "Direct from the *Bal Tabre,* Paris" – I'd never been to Paris.'

They worked together for nine years, after which Ted teamed up with his wife Hilda – keeping the stage surname – to do a similar sort of act; they have continued to work, having expanded their original eight minutes to thirty-five. Whether or not acrobatics has to be 'in the blood', it may have been in his case; his father had been in the business.

'When my father was on the stage, the last thing he ever considered was his wife and children, who were left at home. I suppose in his lifetime I saw my father thirty, maybe forty times; so I have always put family first, and career second.'

With comedy an essential part of the act, acrobats needed to be able to execute comic falls as well as the more standard somersaults and balances. Various comic falls have themselves become standard, as Durante explains:

'A pratfall is when you fall on your bum; a one-oh-eight is when you go half forwards and land flat on your back – not many people do the one-oh-eight now, because it's a nasty one, it's half a front somersault and you actually take the fall on your shoulders; a butterfly is a cartwheel in mid-air without your hands touching the floor – a side somersault; a layout is when you go over backwards, and instead of curling up you keep straight – hollow back – and land on your feet; a roundel is like a forward somersault with a cartwheel – as you go forward you twist your back so that you land on your feet facing the way you came; flip-flaps are going forward onto your hands, then back to your feet – hands, feet, hands, feet. I've seen all-in wrestlers doing some of these falls – they're visual knockabout comedians, these fellows.'

Obviously all this takes a good deal of practice.

'What we tend to forget is the amount of work we did in the early days learning these things. Most top acrobats would be down at the theatre in the mornings, rehearsing, rehearsing. . . . The greatest fine-ness in physical work is juggling – and they've *got* to practise every day; with acrobatics, mostly once you've got the trick, you've got it. You start off learning with forward stuff – standing on your hands, then a flip onto your feet . . . it's progressive. Forward work is actually harder than backward work, because when you go over backwards you can at least see where you're going. Except that some stages used to have a matt black floor – so you wouldn't have the faintest idea whether you were twenty feet above it or two feet above it.'

An acrobat who added juggling to her routines, Suma Lamonte, also came from an acrobatic family. Her father, 'Masu', was Japanese, born in Tokyo and brought up in San Francisco. He toured the world with a Japanese acrobatic troupe for some years – he had actually been sold into it (this was around 1900 and such things were apparently legal) so he had to learn acrobatics whether he wanted to or not. Eventually he came to Britain and married an English girl who had been in another family troupe, the Jacksons; they toured as 'Masu and Yuri', specializing in hand-balancing (balancing on one hand on sticks, chairs, and so on).

Suma – the name was assumed, being an inversion of her father's stage-name, and the surname chosen simply for its sound – toured with her brother Johnny and also solo, combining balancing with juggling – a combination which not many acrobats tried.

Johnny and Suma Lamonte

She remembers: 'There was only one woman in England, when I was a child, doing stick-and-ball work – where you hold the stick in your mouth and balance a ball on the end of it – and there's been no-one else, only myself, since she retired. And my brother used to do one-hand balances on a pedestal, also balancing a stick and ball. We had a lot of material, but it was very exhausting, and in the theatres we only had to do about six to eight-and-a-half minutes. Today bookers require acts that do about forty minutes, so speciality acts are out unless you can pad them, because they're so tiring.'

Suma Lamonte poses an interesting paradox about balancers.

'A good hand-balancer can "take his own weight" – some balancers, their full body weight goes onto their hands, making them look very clumsy and heavy; whereas a good hand-balancer can take his own weight, which comes in useful if he is balancing on another person. Johnny and I used to do a trick where I did the splits, with a stick and ball in my mouth, and he balanced on my shoulders, also with a stick and ball, which put a lot of pressure on my back. Somehow he could lift his body away from me . . . when he wasn't well, with a pulled

muscle or something, I'd notice the difference because I could feel his weight much more.'

Now this suggestion – that a balancer can somehow actually *reduce* the downward pressure on his hands while stationary (as opposed to when springing up) is of course completely contrary to the laws of physics! Suma Lamonte could not offer any explanation, but was quite definite that it happened; Serge Ganjou was able to offer a partial explanation.

'If a person is lifting a heavy weight, it would be easier for him to lift, say, 100 lb if it's neat, and has got handles and so on . . . but take a 100 lb sack of flour or potatoes – this would be much harder to lift. If one acrobat is lifting another one, if the top fellow doesn't feel well the bottom fellow will know, because he is having to do more adjustment, and so the body will feel heavier.'

In this situation the man on top is failing to keep his centre of gravity exactly over the man beneath, who then has to adjust his position more often to keep them both in balance. This may be the answer . . . or perhaps acrobats know something that the rest of us don't about gravity.

While many acrobatic acts introduced an element of comedy, there were also knockabout comedy acts who – though they often used verbal comedy as well – relied heavily upon comic falls and business which was acrobatic in its technique if not its appearance. Jack Marks, who left his career as a tap-dancer to go into the RAF, teamed up after the war with Freddie Desmond – the brother of Florence Desmond – who had been with a knockabout act called The Three Jokers before the war. They used a wide range of business – including Desmond falling into the orchestra pit and making his way back under the stage and onto it to come up behind Marks, who was still haranguing the orchestra pit. (This went wrong on one occasion when they had failed to check that it was actually possible to get through under the stage.)

Jack Marks: 'Nearly all the gags that turned out to be any good started accidentally; neither of us is really a comedian – we have had to go on and crack gags, but it's not our forte – but the two of us had a chemistry, so that if we did something it could turn out to be funny – because of my trying to do something properly, and Freddie never doing anything properly but in the process doing very funny things. It's one of those things you can't explain – I would go on and fall down, and people would just go, "Oh"; Fred came on and fell down and the whole place would dissolve into laughter.'

Their act has been seen on television in recent years; there was relatively little logic to the knockabout comedy –

for example Marks started by tap-dancing while sitting on a kitchen-type chair, and Desmond came careering on and knocked the chair away from under him – but the act was lively and entertaining, and had one particularly spectacular fall where Desmond got his leg tangled up in the back of the chair and then did a complete forward somersault, taking the chair with him.

Bob Konyot changed from his springboard act to a knockabout act in the 1950s – he comments wryly, 'This is what happens to old acrobats' – although he had had previous experience of basic knockabout routines.

'In the old circus days in Europe we worked summer season in a show; we had a springboard act, but we had to do a second act, so this was a knockabout act. A lot of artists did this – the format was usually that there were some chairs and a table – you fall off the chairs, you fall off the table – and there were hundreds of acts doing this sort of thing. In those days you couldn't make money just with that sort of act, because there were so many of them – it was a *second* act.'

He built up a routine with his wife, Marion Olive – an American who had been brought up in Hollywood, and had been to the school run by the film studio with such people as Judy Garland and Mickey Rooney. Unlike the free-for-all knockabout of Desmond and Marks, they constructed a logical act in which they would appear to be attempting various standard tricks – her standing on his shoulders, and so on – which always go wildly wrong. The attempt to hoist her up merely results in her precariously doing the splits on his shoulders while he staggers about, blinded by her skirt; when she spins with her arms outstretched she inevitably clouts him in the face; and an attempt on his part to do a jump with her catching him results in a spectacular fall, sliding to the edge of the stage (and off it when the act is done in cabarets on a rostrum which is not too high off the ground). His movements look distinctly in the tradition of the European clowns such as Grock – although he himself does not see it this way.

'No, the act is very English, really – as you get older your movements get funnier and you start looking like a clown; that's the only resemblance there is.'

With the decline of both the Variety theatres and the circuses acrobatic acts have tended to die out; on the continent there is a stronger tradition, and a new generation is coming up, but in England increasing restrictions on the training of children were beginning to have an adverse effect even before the second World War. Faced with an almost total lack of anywhere to perform, there is little incentive for anyone to go through the rigorous

Bob and Marion Konyot

training necessary to produce a top acrobat. Philip Hindin, when putting together occasional stage shows, has sometimes booked such acts, but, as he comments:

'There is no reason for an act today to rehearse a hazardous routine, or one which requires great concentration or a lot of setting up – because there's no more money in it. You can sing a comic song and get the same money. And you can't do a hazardous act for eighteen minutes – you can only do six; and nobody will book a six-minute act. If you're doing a hazardous act and you want today's pay – say you're going to get £400 for a six-minute act – the producer can get one of the other acts to do two more songs and save himself £400.'

The lack of regular work is another factor.

Suma Lamonte: 'You need regular work to keep limbered up. There have not been enough shows – so when an odd show did come up, it would take us about a week rehearsing, just to do that one show; whereas in the earlier

Bob and Marion Konyot

days we were doing twelve shows a week, so we were always limbered up. When the theatres closed down, a lot of acts dropped out; the few that remained, like ourselves, had to adapt themselves to different conditions in cabaret. This was quite an adjustment – differences in props, because of low ceilings; people all the way round you instead of in front of you in an auditorium; waiters walking about; people talking; a small area in many places – difficult conditions, and no proper lighting facilities.'

Marée Authie found other hazards when doing her contortionist and dancing act in cabaret.

'I was doing decent places, but in nightclubs the men are just there to drink and chat up the hostesses, so you'd have the noise – and the majority of performers have learned their trade the hard way, and they want to be watched and listened to – and you might as well not be on the stage. And doing acrobatics on the floor, you're very vulnerable if drunks start coming on the floor trying to

shove a roll in your mouth or something like that. I had it down to a fine art, because if I did a back bend over, I had a very good left foot and I could knock them for six!'

Acrobatic acts can occasionally be seen on television – acting as supports in programmes such as *The Paul Daniels Show* for example – or in the very few circuses which are left; and there is another problem for acrobats – the extraordinarily spectacular routines performed by Olympic athletes. In the last decade or so, girls of fourteen and fifteen have been giving astounding demonstrations of skill in the Olympics, doing routines far beyond the abilities of most professional acrobats.

But there is a terrible price to pay: Olga Korbut, the darling of the 1972 Olympics, has finished up a little old woman before the age of thirty, her joints and ligaments ruined by arthritis caused by the strain of training for the Olympics while still growing.

Ted Durante comments: 'I predict that *all* these athletes are going to be little old people by the time they are in their twenties – their joints and ligaments will have gone; they will be stunted physically . . . I once worked with a child act called the Dunja Trio; they were about 15, 17 and 19, but they looked like 7-, 10- and 12-year-olds. The stuff they did acrobatically was fantastic, but already they had old bodies. You can't push a body like that – it's got to mature, it's got to grow.'

No professional acrobat would be prepared to train in this way while still growing, and so few could ever approach the phenomenal standards which misplaced national pride leads certain countries to encourage their athletes to achieve, at the cost of their health. In their time, Variety acrobats were a useful part of the supporting acts who gave the medium so much of its character; but more than other types of acts they have inevitably fallen into a decline.

24 'Look behind you!'
Variety and pantomime

Although Variety itself was slowly declining as the 1950s progressed, pantomime was still going strong (albeit in a reducing number of theatres) and provided a useful alternative source of work for Variety performers in the weeks after Christmas. By the end of the 1950s it was one of the few remaining stage outlets for their talents and one which reaffirmed their status as stars of what was left of Variety.

Pantomime is, of course, a major subject in itself, and one which cannot be dealt with in detail here; but the relationship between the two worlds of Variety and panto will be examined in this chapter. 'Traditional' pantomime is only just over a hundred years old. Before 1880 'pantomime' meant the mimed harlequinade which often followed serious productions, its standard characters – Harlequin the resourceful hero, Columbine the heroine, Pantaloon the old fool and so on – copied from the Italian *Commedia dell'arte* style which was several centuries old. It was a Victorian entrepreneur called Augustus Harris who began using stars of the music-hall in his Christmas productions, creating the more familiar style of 'panto' – the Principal Boy usually played by a woman, the Dame usually played by a man, with a traditional fairy tale told in a combination of spectacle and knockabout comedy. At this time panto was the only way the respectable middle classes ever got to see music-hall stars, since panto was acceptable (being theatrical) whereas music-hall was not.

Dan Leno was one of the leading pantomime comedians of his day, usually as the Dame, and usually working with Herbert Campbell, whose large size offset the smaller Leno – they were perhaps the Laurel and Hardy of panto. Leno died in 1904, but his son Herbert, working as 'Dan Leno Junior', continued starring in pantomimes well into the 1950s. Jan Harding, a stand-up comic with a northern background who came into the business just before the war, worked with Leno Jr in several pantomimes.

'He only did pantomimes – he never did anything else out of the panto season, except that he wrote pantomimes. He knew everything about pantomime – and he was a stickler for doing things properly, and not having any smut in it under any circumstances. He kept to the story all the way through.'

Throughout the period covered by this book panto would replace Variety in most theatres for the few weeks following Christmas.

As Jan Harding explains: 'If Variety people didn't want to go into pantomime they didn't work over Christmas – they just went on holiday or something – but most of them were booked for pantomime year after year. The same pantos would go round different towns from year to year; and they'd run for twelve weeks or more – six weeks was considered a short run – and all the major Variety theatres had pantomimes twice daily – they could make a lot of money.'

Most pantomimes would provide opportunities for a number of Variety acts – often a speciality act would be fitted into the show in some way – but the main parts were the Dame and the comic couple such as the broker's men, who would be played by a double-act such as the O'Gorman Brothers. In *Aladdin*, for example, the Dame part would be Widow Twankey, and as well as Abanazar and Wishee Washee – another good comedy part – there would be a couple of Chinese Policemen, so there were plenty of parts for comedians.

The script, or 'book', of the show was often based on one which had been going round for years, with suitable additions; it would cover the story and some of the comic scenes, and a printed version was often available for sale. For example, the pantomime of 1935–36 at the Lyceum, London – *Puss In Boots* – was published (price 3d); the book gives the text of the panto, and photographs of the principals – Clarkson Rose as Dame Tickle; the O'Gormans as Cackle and Crackle, the broker's men; and Jack Barty and 'Monsewer' Eddie Gray as further comic relief; the straight principals were Marjorie Sandford, Polly Ward, Eve Benson, Betty Bucknell, Molly Vyvyan and Noel Carey.

The comic scenes shown in the book are the usual rather obvious sort of material; but the most important comic sequences are not there, being covered by comments such as 'Cackle and Crackle take a list of all the furniture and china with rather calamitous results. Dame Tickle enters and gets a great surprise.' This is because the comedians were expected, as part of their contribution to the proceedings, to provide several comic scenes themselves; this meant that they could slot into the show routines which suited their own style. Any Variety comedian working in panto would have several such scenes to hand, which could be slotted into different pantomimes as the opportunity arose. At the end of the panto, the book simply announces 'Some entertainment is arranged for the King and his guests' – an opportunity for some speciality and comic acts straight out of Variety.

The most important part in the panto, from the point of view of Variety, was the Dame. On very rare occasions the Dame might be played by a woman – Nellie Wallace was one who did – but usually 'she' was a man. Famous dames over the years have included Dan Leno, George Robey,

Douglas Byng, George Jackley (Nat Jackley's father), George Lacey, Sandy Powell and Arthur Askey; Danny La Rue has played Dame, but as he is by profession a female impersonator the whole performance has a different aspect from the traditional panto Dame.

Douglas Byng brought his own particular style to panto.

'I was apparently the first to alter the style of the Dame from the old lady with the curlers and things – I made her smarter, and I was rather a snob – I never played the Nurse, always the Governess! And I wouldn't play the Cook, she was always the Housekeeper. But you have to play it seriously, you mustn't fiddle about – you can't send

George Robey

Douglas Byng

it up like Arthur Askey, you must play pantomime dead seriously. Of course, you don't play in profile, you play everything front on, straight out to the audience. You've got to maintain the illusion – I would never take my wig off at the end, for the walk-down; you must stay in character. When I was in *Sleeping Beauty* at Liverpool they asked me to go out in front in the interval to make an appeal for the VABF – I said, "I've just gone to sleep for a hundred years – nothing would induce me to go out there". I always liked it when a mother brought her children round afterwards because they wouldn't believe I was a man – I didn't want them to! I used to do one joke for the adults and then one for the children – and then the children would laugh at the one for the grown-ups, and vice versa!'

Not all Dames took Byng's view; Arthur Askey used to say, 'When they book me, they book Arthur Askey', and so he kept his glasses on and simply acted as himself, but in Dame costume.

Harry Secombe made no attempt to create an illusion:

'I was the world's worst Dame – terrible! I flouted the conventions – I put a big Groucho Marx moustache on. I never played Dame again.'

Few performers took things quite to Secombe's extreme; but Nat Jackley was one whose view of the Dame was quite different from Byng's.

'You've got to stay the man, really – let them know that inside that skirt is a man. You're not a female impersonator. I believe in the part I'm playing, but then I leave that alone and do audience participation – bringing the kids up on the stage and getting them to sing.'

Audience participation, which by the 1950s had become a major part of pantomime, was unheard of in Victorian panto, which was presented as a straight piece of theatre (albeit comic). It was Sandy Powell who pioneered the techniques of getting the audience to shout out 'Look behind you!' as the villain crept up behind him, or warned

Dickie Henderson (*left***) and Arthur Askey in 'Babes in the Wood' at the Bristol Hippodrome (1975)**

him as someone tried to steal the umbrella he had parked on the side of the stage and asked the audience to keep an eye on.

Arguments of the 'Oh yes it is – oh no it isn't' type, in which the audience could join, and chorus songs (with the words on a large sheet lowered from the flies so that the audience could join in with confidence) all became part of the fun of going to a panto. If the villain wasn't loudly booed, he was a failure.

Jan Harding: 'In the end you got the grown-ups doing it as well. If I was in a matinée towards the end of the run, when the kids were all back at school so that most of the audience were grown-ups, then I had to coach the audience by saying something like, "Look, when I come out again, could you all say 'Hello Simon' " . . . and the audience would look at you as if you were barmy . . . so I would say, "Look, *I* didn't want to come here either – but I'm here, and I've got to work, and I'm not going to work all on my own – you lot can't just sit there, so you'll all have to pretend you're kids . . . and I'm going to stay here until you do it!" And in the end you'd get a small audience enjoying the show more than a big one!'

Up to the early 1950s, pantos continued in the traditional way. They were often very spectacular; George Jackley was in the Lyceum pantos for fourteen years running, as his son, Nat, remembers:

'They used to start at 2 and finish at 6, and then at 7 and go on to 11 o'clock. They had about 100 people on stage, and they used to do a transformation scene with 30 cloths coming down and going up and people with all sorts of national costumes.'

Provincial pantomimes could rarely match this sort of extravagance, but even so the best of them were spectacular and well produced – they could after all use the same scenery year after year in different towns.

With the 1950s changes began to take place which made the 'traditional' pantomime a comparative rarity. Just as music-hall performers went into panto a hundred years earlier, radio and then television artists began to be necessary to the success of a panto. This could lead to some odd things happening, as Chris Wortman remembers.

'All they want today are television performers – it doesn't matter how good, bad or indifferent they are – it started with radio: I saw Issy Bonn as Buttons in *Cinderella* at the Brixton Empress; and when the Fairy Godmother gave Cinderella three wishes, her first was to go to the ball, the second was a lovely ball dress, and the third was to hear Issy Bonn sing "My Yiddisher Momma"!'

In more recent years some television performers have found themselves at a disadvantage on stage in panto, having been trained only for television; and the technique of having the Principal Boy played by a male pop singer has moved panto even further away from tradition.

Reg Dixon did regular panto work and maintained something of the old tradition.

'People know that you specialize, and have created original sketches that can be slotted into pantomime; I've got perhaps ten inserts into panto to offer as a choice. This way you can guarantee in advance all the laughs, because you know the material. It doesn't always happen that way – once, at the Belgrade Theatre Coventry, the producers hadn't had much experience of pantomime, and they had presented an original book, and they didn't want me to alter it in any way. I warned them in advance, "This is not going to get laughs – you're laughing a lot at rehearsal, but it's not going to get laughs on the night". As I'd said, they didn't get laughs, and gradually as the pantomime progressed it went home to them and they gave me a free hand. But I was dealing with actors and actresses as opposed to Variety artists – I could say to a Variety artist, "We'll put in the so-and-so gag", and they'd know what I was talking about; you could almost do it without a rehearsal. But actors and actresses want their lines – every line, carefully written, and it doesn't work like that. So I had to lay it all out in detail, even throwaway lines, so that it didn't upset the whole company.'

Nowadays there are relatively few theatres which can mount anything like the traditional pantomime; though pantomimes of various kinds are staged alongside other children's and family shows and some amateur dramatic societies do help to maintain the tradition; and occasionally television will present one of the pantos in something like the traditional format, with an audience of children and lots of participation (of course it cannot run to anything like the length of a stage show and inevitably much of the atmosphere is missing for viewers).

In its heyday pantomime was an important part of the year's work for Variety artists; it gave many of them a chance to do something different from the regular act which they toured round the halls, and to work to a quite different sort of audience.

25 Making the Grade
Running the business: Two (1940–1960)

As the 1950s progressed there was a considerable increase in the number of shows booked into theatres by agents, as opposed to the circuit bookers themselves. Eventually even Moss Empires, which had firmly resisted this trend before the war, allowed agents to book shows onto their circuit; from their point of view it saved a lot of work – all they had to do was to provide the theatre and leave the agent to manage the rest.

Foremost among the agents working in this way were Lew and Leslie Grade. Born Louis and Lazarus Winogradsky, they and their brother Boris came to Britain when still children. After winning a Charleston competition as a teenager, Lew teamed up with Alf Gold to form a professional dancing act; he shortened his surname to Grad, but a printing error turned it into Grade on one occasion and he kept to that version. Subsequently he worked with various girl dancers, also doing his Charleston on top of a table as part of the act. Boris meanwhile teamed with Albert Sutan and adopted the name Bernard Delfont to avoid clashing with Lew. Leslie, who was ten years younger than Lew, apparently had no ambition to go on the stage.

In 1935 Lew began working as an agent, in partnership with Joe Collins; Leslie, who had been working for Florence Leddington at the Syndicate Halls booking office, became an agent in 1939. Both were called up at the beginning of the war, although Leslie managed to go on taking bookings somehow. (Bernard was not called up because, unlike the others, he had not at that time taken British citizenship.)

As the war progressed, the Grades were among the first agents to take advantage of the circuits' new willingness to take package deals; Leslie was posted abroad, but Lew, who had been invalided out, left Collins and went into partnership with Leslie in 1943 and was able to keep the business going.

Bernard, who seems to have had a desire to be an impresario from the first, began taking over the leases of theatres and putting in his own musical shows, with varying degrees of success. In 1942 he brought Billy Marsh in to help him, and subsequently Marsh ran the agency while Delfont ran the shows.

Meanwhile the Grade brothers were consolidating their power. With Leslie back in the business at the end of the war, they began scouting round for artists to represent – they became adept at 'poaching' artists from other agents by offering them the hope of greener grass on the Grades' side of the fence – sometimes, having poached all an agent's best acts, they took on the agent himself.

Hunter Davies's book *The Grades*[1] mentions these activities, rather defensively pointing out that they were after all only 'normal business practices' – which is true enough; although it is not recorded what other agents thought about it. By these means the Grades became an extremely powerful agency, eventually representing most of the top stars in the business; other agents who might have their own artists found it difficult to place them because the Grades had obtained control of so many theatrical bookings.

Dennis Selinger, who started as an office-boy for the Monty Lyon agency in 1935 and had progressed to doing a few bookings just before the war, rejoined the agency in 1945. Shortly afterwards, Monty Lyon retired and asked Selinger whether he would like to take over the agency. Selinger, feeling that he was a bit young to be managing it on his own (he was then twenty-four), decided to go in with the Grades, and so merged his agency with them; he stayed with them for fourteen years, towards the end of which time he built up a section of the agency to deal with legitimate theatre – something in which the Grades had little interest. Subsequently he went off to work in his own business with various partners.

Even more than in the pre-war days, agents had to be salesmen.

Selinger: 'You can't learn to do deals – of course you can learn a bit by listening to other people and from experience – but it's something which is *in* you. If you're a good agent, it means you're a good salesman; the problem is, you're not selling a Rolls Royce or a can of beans – you're selling a human being to another human being. You have to be able to cope with all the problems that arise – you've really got to be the backroom boy. If you want publicity, don't be an agent. Lew Grade, who got all the publicity, was a marvellous agent – but he never wanted to remain an agent; he wanted to be Lew Grade – and he's proved that he could do it. Leslie, who did want to be an agent, was never really that well known. Lew was always the ideas guy – he was the one that went out and found the money to get the organization together; he is a deal-maker – and probably one of the world's greatest salesmen.'

Agents operated under controls, being licensed by the local authority. Norman Murray worked for Foster's agency and then for London Management, and remembers:

'The rules were quite strict – you weren't allowed to have a bed in your office; and you weren't allowed to use private premises for an agency unless there were extenuating circumstances – Dave Marks had special permission because he was a very sick man. You weren't allowed to enter into a contract with an artist unless he signed a commission note – which is an agreement that he would pay your commission – there had by law to be a commission note for every contract, and they were open for inspection at any time; someone used to come round without warning and go through them all.'

Some agents had an interesting little sideline; it was often possible to come to an arrangement with a commercial firm that their name could be worked into a performer's act for a consideration; this was not illegal or improper as it would have been on the BBC. Jack Marks first met this when he was working with Freddie Desmond.

'We did a gag about Singleton Snuff, because the firm – which was a very big one in Birmingham – had booked an entire performance of the panto we were in; so we put in a gag where Fred had a sniff of the snuff, sneezed, and did a back-somersault. The firm liked it so much that we went on doing it – they couldn't pay us because they would have had to declare it for tax, so we got 200 cigarettes a week for five or six years.'

Many comedians did this sort of thing.

'Sam Mayo did a Johnny Walker song, and he used to get a case of Johnny Walker a week. Douglas Wakefield had a car sketch in which he would blow up an inner tube from an India Tyre until it was huge – the whole scene was paid for by Indias. After the curtain went up, before the show started, there was a frontcloth which was covered in adverts – and that actually paid for the show. And somebody told me that nearly all Archie Pitt's productions were paid for by adverts before he even opened.'

Towards the end of the 1950s more and more promoters were mounting their own bills – some of them in a very small way. Keith Salberg first got into the business this way.

'I'd been running repertory companies, as a young man, and I'd lost so much money with it that I thought I would like to try putting on occasional Variety bills. The trouble was that they would only let you have a theatre if you were prepared to put on a bigger show than somebody else. So you'd book somewhere like Huddersfield or Rotherham, and not knowing the business you'd turn up and find out that it was Wakes Week and that's why they'd given you the date anyway. I lost a lot of money, but that's how I first came into it. I wasn't an agent, so I was dependent upon the result in percentage terms, and they were nearly all losing propositions – they were the sort of thing that anyone with any brains would never have done in the first place.'

Armed with this expensively gained experience Salberg went on to act as an agent and mount occasional – and more successful – small Variety shows.

With agents booking shows for their stars and obtaining support acts from other agents, the situation could get rather involved.

Norman Murray: 'Let's suppose that it wasn't the agent that put the show into the theatre, but the star himself. So he'd say to his agent, "Get me the acts", and the agent would ring other agents to get acts, and say "I need 5 per cent commission but I'm not getting anything out of the show." So he would split his commission with the other agent. The Foster Agency wouldn't split commissions, it wasn't their policy – I don't know whether they lost any business by doing that. But of course there was always the question, *was* it the star's show – or was the agent hiding behind the star, so that it was really his show – so he was geting the profit *and* half the commission – to which he might answer "Yes, but supposing I *lose* money that week?" '

Philip Hindin thinks that the business of agents acting as impresarios had a disastrous effect on Variety.

'Suppose I've got an artist who is top of the bill of that period – like Arthur Askey, or Elsie and Doris Waters – they're getting perhaps £500 a week; the phone never stops ringing for them; I book them with a management, the management puts the bill on, he shows a profit – and the manager stays in business. So I look at last week, we played to £3,000 takings, and my bloke was the draw – so I decide *I'll* put the bill in. So I get my man to do forty minutes instead of thirty; I put five acts on instead of eight and get some of them to do two spots; they probably come to £700, and I get the top of the bill for £400 because he's my mate and I book him; I'm in there for £1,100. I'm on 60 per cent of the takings, we play to the same £3,000, I get £1,800 and I've got £700 clear profit – what do I want to sell my act for commission for? Then because people are greedy, and don't have the long view of it, they put four acts in . . . now you're charging for ten or eleven, and what are they getting? – one act, and "wines and spirits". So when television came along and you could see top talent for free – why should you go out in the rain to see an indifferent bill?'

As the theatres began to close and things became more difficult, some agents – working on a much tighter margin than the old circuit managements, and in any case looking for a quick profit rather than the long-term future of the business – began to pare the bills down more and more. Copper McCormick was on the short end of this on many occasions.

'When they were trying to fix a fee they would find out if you were in digs, and if you went there by train – and they would work out the minimum that you could possibly survive on. They found out that we had a trailer caravan and a car, so they reckoned we could live on far less – they'd offer the fact that we could park at the back of the theatre. Then they were trying to find out if we smoked . . . and they'd pay us last thing on a Saturday night when we couldn't buy any food.'

Another factor about agents and performers running shows was that profit they made stayed out of the business in their pockets, whereas when the circuits had been running it the profits had been partly ploughed back to keep the business going. With agents running shows, the advantage to the circuits was that where there was a risk, they took less of it; and by the end of the 1950s television and other factors had made the business a risky one for anyone. As we shall see in Chapter 28, the Grades and Bernard Delfont were quicker than most to realize where the future lay and diversify into television; and when pressure began to be applied to the Government to allow commercial television the Grades were in the forefront of it.

26 Negotiation and amalgamation
The Variety Artistes' Federation, etc: Two (from 1945 onwards)

In the changing world of the post-war years, the Variety Artistes' Federation continued to do its best to represent its members' interests. Immediately following the war it successfully instituted a ban on 'ex-enemy aliens' playing in British halls, just as it had in 1918; this remained in operation until 1951. It also operated a service for its members whereby they could register their acts with the VAF – either written versions of spoken acts, or even written versions of purely visual speciality or acrobatic acts – in an attempt to reduce the prevalent problem of performers stealing other acts' material; by registering material in this way the originator could at least prove that he had performed the material earlier than the offending artist.

In the 1950s Reg Swinson was the general secretary of the VAF. He had started as an accountant, and as a member of his firm's auditing staff had been sent to the VAF to deal with their books on several occasions in the late 1940s; they asked him to join them as their accountant in 1949, and he subsequently became assistant general secretary, then general secretary in 1953.

One of the first problems he had to deal with was that of 'emergency contracts'.

'During the war years, when paper had been in short supply, the Award Contract was issued in an abridged form which merely said the particular appearances would be "subject to the Arbitrator's Award of 1919". I was a bit mystified by this, and there wasn't anybody on the staff at that time who was familiar with the original. In the end I tracked down all the details and started to insist that contracts should be issued in the full form. These emergency contracts had gone on after the war, and no-one was familiar with the 1919 contract; and some managers had been requiring artists to work thirteen performances in a week without paying the extra [as provided for in the 1919 contract]. I had one eminent gentleman apprehended for doing this . . . he was furious! – but he had to concede in the end that the contract *was* for only twelve performances and any additional ones had to be paid for.'

Recognizing that the 1919 contract did not cover modern conditions fully, the VAF, negotiating with the actors' union, Equity, and the managements, introduced a revised form of contract with various new provisions. The original had made no provision for arbitration in case of disputes, and this was introduced into the new contract, which allowed for arbitration by the Variety Council without prejudicing either party's right to have recourse to the law; the new contract also made provision for transportation to be paid for, and specified rehearsal requirements.

The VAF made a brave attempt to improve the position of Variety artists in the Welfare State when it began.

Reg Swinson: 'The Minister for National Insurance ruled that Variety artists were self-employed – which meant to say no sickness benefit, and no unemployment benefit. The VAF took the Minister to the High Court, but they lost; the Court ruled that the 1919 Award Contract was a contract *for services*, not a contract *of service*. And yet all the other contracts – such as actors, or even Variety artists in pantomime where they had to perform a part – came under the control of the manager and so became a contract *of service*.'

When Eurovision was first proposed in 1954, and the European Broadcasting Union (of television authorities) formed, the VAF, Equity and the Musicians' Union brought pressure to bear on them and won agreements about payments for international TV relays; the VAF also helped to win better protection for Variety artists of copyright in their material, both on gramophone records and as regards other countries.

One of the major problem areas for the VAF was that of the working-men's clubs which were in the 1950s becoming big business in the north of England – there had always been clubs, but at this time they were increasing in number and becoming much more expensively run. For a membership fee people could buy food and drink and get entertainment thrown in – in a way a throwback to the origins of music-hall. Unfortunately the working conditions they provided for artists were very unsatisfactory compared to the theatres. Vic Duncan, who was on the VAF Committee – and was appointed honorary treasurer in 1956 – had to help to deal with this sort of problem on numerous occasions.

'We used to hold arbitration "courts" where both the artist and the proprietors could have their say, and try to get them to agree – invariably it was the proprietors who were in the wrong. They would book an act for a week, and after the first show if they didn't like them, they would just sack them. If they'd booked an act "as known", then they were supposed to pay them, even if they got rid of them. And they would write to an artist three or four days before their booking and tell them that the engagement was off. This was something that they thought they had a perfect right to do. These clubs sprang up all over the place, and there were some very undesirable people running some of them.'

The VAF's attempts to get clubs to accept a standard contract, which would protect the artists against these abuses, ran into considerable opposition.

Reg Swinson: 'The VAF had only marginal success – later on Equity had greater success – with these working-men's clubs; I came across a greater omnipotence than capitalist employers could ever have arranged. They slammed the door in my face, and told me to push off – and other things. I found it a remarkable contradiction that, whereas ostensibly these clubs were linked with the Labour and Trades Unions movement, in practice they were very reluctant to allow artists an agreed contract. I noticed more recently that they were even reluctant to acknowledge legislation on racial equality and equal pay. We were dealing with the concert secretaries of the clubs; they were very powerful men, who gave out a lot of work – whatever they did in their normal jobs, this gave them a lot of responsibility which perhaps eroded their better natures.'

In more recent years, when many of the smaller and tattier clubs had closed, and the much larger surviving clubs were run on a more professional basis, the problem subsided and artists were able to get better treatment.

There were obvious disadvantages to having two unions – Equity and the VAF – operating in similar areas, and indeed overlapping from time to time. There was a long history of mistrust between the two unions – the Barrow-in-Furness incident detailed in Chapter 5 being a good example of it – which had to be overcome before the amalgamation between them, which eventually took place in 1967.

Reg Swinson: 'There were three abortive attempts before it finally happened even in my reign of office, and there had been earlier ones. When the VAF did finally amalgamate it was at a very strong point in its history – it had more standard contracts than it had ever had before, it was beginning to win its way back financially notwithstanding the savage closures of the theatres; and it had established a joint industrial negotiating machinery which Equity had never thought would work – it not only worked, but Equity is still using it.'

Serge Ganjou, who was on the VAF Committee, had thought for some time that there ought to be an amalgamation – not all that many members agreed with him – and lobbied for it.

'I had seen in America that the musicians' union, the stagehands' union, the electricians' union, were very strong – and the actual artists were the last to count in the theatre. So I thought the only thing to do was to make our union of artists as strong as the others; so instead of the VAF and Equity competing, I started to work – talking to our members – towards amalgamating our unions. It took more than ten years. There was a lot of opposition from our members – Equity had views which were more to the left, and the VAF was more to the right; now Equity has gone more to the right – I think thanks to us.'

What helped to bring matters to a head was Equity's exclusion of VAF members from some areas in which they were powerful.

Reg Swinson: 'From 1950 Equity were not recognizing the VAF card in films – they were the only people who had agreements with the film producers, and they wouldn't let us in in any way. We went to the TUC, and they wouldn't help; and then Equity said they wouldn't recognize our card in the West End of London – admittedly there was only the Palladium left, and the remaining theatres were straight theatre; but to say they wouldn't recognize our card was quite wrong. Equity came to an agreement with the Society of West End Theatre Managers which excluded the VAF, and they put this to the test when Jimmy Edwards was going to appear in pantomime at the London Palladium – he was chairman of the VAF, and they told him that they wouldn't recognize his card.

'Edwards said to the committee, "I'm prepared to make a stand if you back me"; but unfortunately the committee said in effect, "No, Jim, you're big enough to look after yourself" – and so he saw the futility of going on as two unions and favoured the amalgation. He didn't attempt to influence members when they voted, but employment opportunities were receding because the card wasn't recognized, so it made sense – and Equity wouldn't let go of their weapon.

'I would have been quite happy about the amalgamation

if Equity had absorbed Variety artists into the new union and not made a distinction between actors and Variety artists; but they have. I think it ought to have been called the Performers' Union – the VAF has been forgotten. Equity doesn't really understand Variety artists – this will take generations rather than just a few years – they're a different type of artist altogether. I've found a tendency for actors to be jealous of Variety artists, with their skill to go on cold and to perform their own material.'

With the amalgamation, Reg Swinson moved over to the Variety Artistes' Benevolent Fund, which continues to run Brinsworth, the retirement home, and which gets its main funds from the Royal Variety Performance each autumn: 'Without a name being announced, some 1,200 seats are asked for – this only leaves 1,500 for the general demand once the names are announced; we could normally have sold the house two or three times over. People still call it the Royal Command Performance, which of course it isn't, but we don't try to deter them.'

The income from these performances has put the Benevolent Fund in a strong position. Brinsworth, which had had a wing added to it in 1919, gained another in 1976 to house administration offices as well as some extra residents.

'We accommodate thirty-eight people here, and there are three hundred outside whom we help with pensions and paying bills and so on. The fund does a great deal more social work than it ever did; I go and see people in their homes and listen to their problems, and liaise with Social Services Departments and central Government. We formed a body, with other charities, called the Association of Charity Officers; the Government recognizes the rôle of voluntary organizations and accepts that even in the Welfare State it could not survive without them.'

Brinsworth itself is very well equipped with facilities and trained staff to look after elderly and often ill ex-members of the profession, and it is appropriate that the funds which make this possible should come largely from the Royal Variety Performance, itself one of the very few manifestations of the world of Variety which has survived into the modern age.

The Grand Order of Water Rats continues, and does general charitable work (not necessarily restricted to members of the profession); and another organization run by entertainers, the Variety Club of Great Britain, does charitable work for handicapped children – in particular providing the 'Sunshine Coaches' which enable them to have outings. Although the actual organizations have changed, the spirit of charitable work continues, having

direct historical links to the organizations run by music-hall artists in the last century – and in particular to the success of Jack Lotto's trotting pony in 1899.

THE 39th ANNUAL

GENERAL MEETING

OF THE

VARIETY ARTISTES' FEDERATION

WILL TAKE PLACE AT

THE HORSE SHOE HOTEL

(Adjoining Dominion Theatre)

TOTTENHAM COURT ROAD, LONDON, W.1

ON

Sunday Afternoon, Feb. 11, 1945
at 2.30 p.m. prompt

Chairman - - Mr. WILL HAY

AGENDA:

Appointment of Tellers and Scrutineers

The Report for 1944

The Balance Sheet for 1944

Election of Auditors

Proposed Partial Alterations to Rules

Rule 18. — Election of Officers and Committee.
  Section (6) Line (1) *Delete* " Two." *Substitute* " Three."

Rule 6.—Fees and Dues.
  Section (1) *Delete* " 5/- " *Substitute* " £1."

Rule 9. — Reinstatement of Members resigned or cancelled.
  Section (1) *Delete* " 5/- " *Substitute* " £1."

Foreign Question — Proposed Resolution:
  "That members of the V.A.F. pledge themselves for the immediate postwar period of five years not to appear in the programmes of any entertainments in Great Britain in which it is proposed to include such enemy aliens as German or Japanese performers."

By Order of the
EXECUTIVE COMMITTEE,
  A. VICTOR DREWE,
    General Secretary.

27 'Are you putting it around that I'm barmy?'
Sketch comics: Three (the 1940s and 1950s)

Whereas stand-up comics were, for the most part, restricted to working directly to the audience, sketch comics could draw the audience into their situations, or ignore them, as they chose. In the earlier days most sketches were firmly rooted into a situation – running an office, the Means Test Committee, and so on – even if the gags were usually added to the situation rather than growing out of it. By the post-war period, there was a tendency for the situations themselves to be less well defined, and for the jokes to be much more in the way of character jokes – arising out of the interplay of the participants – rather than actual one-line gags.

Nat Jackley had transferred from speciality dancing to sketches by this time, and usually worked in an almost unintelligible voice reminiscent of someone suffering from adenoids, a lisp, and a piece of toffee stuck to the roof of the mouth; he would make a feature of this to the point that it would infect the other participants in the sketch – in the end there would be five people on stage, all talking in the same way. (His punch line was to say, in a normal voice, 'Oh, I'm fed up with this – let's talk properly'.)

The feature of his act that made him famous, however, was arrived at purely by accident during a wartime performance at Aldershot Hippodrome. He agreed to take over the part played by a large fat man in a sketch.

'I learnt the sketch, and then forgot all about it! – I did my act, just before the sketch, and I was doing about ten minutes' hard dancing. I came off, exhausted, and I was taking my coat off when somebody shouted, "Nat! – You're on!". So I put the other chap's trousers on – they were very baggy on me – and the bowler hat; and I was wearing a singlet which was cut low and showed my chest. I was still putting the coat on as I made a dash onto the stage, and as I did so the coat slipped back over my shoulders – and there was a yell of laughter; then I jerked my neck, and got another laugh; and then I jerked my legs about, and the trousers slipped down on the elastic braces and then went – "Zip!", back up again . . . and as I was doing all this, my neck came into action – and the audience were screaming with laughter, and the man who was waiting for my line was in fits!'

This routine was so successful that he kept it in the act,

Nat Jackley

and later incorporated it into an army sketch (one of those sketches in which a number of idiotic soldiers cheek the sergeant-major for no very logical reason; very popular with servicemen). Part of the success of the movements lay in the unusual length of his neck, and his tall thin body; but the nickname 'rubberneck' – which he used as his bill matter – does not really describe the routine. If you imagine seeing a side view of a tall thin man, and imagine that he has a rod running from the centre-point of a line between his shoulders to a point one-third of the way down a rigid spine; then when the head moves forwards, so does this rod, whereas the base of the spine moves backwards and the shoulders stay where they are – and meanwhile the legs try to climb an imaginary staircase; then you will (perhaps) get some idea of what Jackley looked like.

Although he was born in Sunderland, Jackley was not really a specifically northern comedian; his appeal was wider than comics who relied upon a broad northern accent and characterization. Frank Randle, one of the most eccentric characters in Variety – off-stage as well as on – was very much a northern comic; he was a strange man in many ways. Roy Castle worked in Randle's touring show for a time.

He remembers: 'That was a real experience! He was a *very* strange character – they all said he was moon-mad, because every now and again he'd just go potty and disappear. He'd suddenly go out on his boat and not come back for three days. I was frightened of the man – he used to make everybody shake; I never saw him actually strike anybody, but he'd got a violent attitude all the time.'

Frank Randle stories are legion – how he disappeared for one performance and it turned out he'd been in the balcony watching the show; how he agreed to do a charity performance at a town hall and was so disgusted with the food provided for the company that he 'bought' it for five pounds and hurled it at portraits of ex-mayors decorating the room they were in; and he was frequently in trouble with Watch Committees for restoring cuts which they or the Lord Chamberlain's office had demanded.

One of his most famous acts was a monologue, which he usually performed at the end of his show – 'The Old Hiker'. Dressed like an octogenarian boy scout, and equipped with a huge bottle of beer, he described his adventures in an accent which a southern audience would find very difficult to follow.

Frank Randle

So this is Oswaldtwistle, is it? . . . By gum, there's a cheeky kid up theer, he just spotted me, he run to his mother, he says 'Come 'ere, Mother, there's a monkey oop a stick' . . . aye . . . Aye, well, I've walked through Europe, Arope, Sallop, Wallop, Jollop . . . me feet are red-hot. Aye . . . but, by gum, I've just had a bit of a narrow squeak. I was goo-in' across a field, it were a bull in it – it wasn't Barney's Bull, neither . . . in fact it was a hell of a long way off bein' Barney's Bull . . . Ooo, it was a fierce 'un . . . It 'ad a couple of prongs on it as long as this stick. Only they were a damn sight sharper than this, I'll tell you. Aye . . . it comes tuppin' away at me . . . I thought it was apologizin' the way it was bowin' and scrapin' . . . Aye, I shooed it away with me handkerchief . . . oh, it's a red 'un . . . made it a damn sight worse. By gum but did I pick 'em oop! I fairly sizzled . . . aye. I catched oop to a rabbit. I'd a' passed it, only it got between me legs. I said to it, I said, 'Hey, come on, hurry up or else get out of me road . . . ' I said 'Let somebody run as can.'[1]

Because of the broadness of both his accent and his humour he had relatively little success in the south of England; and indeed the films he made were never shown south of Birmingham at the time. Many years later *Somewhere in Camp* turned up at London's National Film Theatre (an event that probably marked the London debut of a Randle film) – it also starred Robby Vincent ('Enoch') and Harry Korris ('Mr Lovejoy'), so the humour was hardly subtle – and his last film, *It's A Grand Life* (made in 1953), has been shown on television. Both of them demonstrate his physical skill – his legs often seem to be made of jelly – and ability to project a character. Made, like all his films, cheaply and quickly in Manchester, they were directed by John Blakeley, who used the minimum of camera techniques such as tracking and panning, and could turn out a film in two weeks.

Both films suffer from idiotic plots, but *It's A Grand Life* in particular has hilarious sequences with Randle, who obviously wrote his own scenes – and towards the end of the film seems to be making them up as he goes along. What is most surprising is the sheer speed at which he works – unlike most northern comics, who worked at a fairly gentle pace, Randle's scenes in this film are taken at a breakneck speed; they demonstrate the relationship he could build up with his stooges, who are obviously quite as adept at this sort of thing as he is.

In his stage shows he worked with two or three stooges at a time in a similar way. One sketch from the 1941 version of his show *Randle's Scandals* derived most of its humour from Randle having his foot stepped on, and saying 'Get off my foot', at frequent intervals; in one of the sketches from *Randle's Scandals of 1952* he burlesqued an examination by an army medical orderly – a situation familiar to many of his audience. (The square backets indicate cuts demanded by the censor; whether Randle complied at all times is another matter.)

M.O.:	What's the idea of barging in like that?
RANDLE:	Well, we haven't been feeling so well, and the sergeant sent us down to see the M.O. (*Taps* M.O. *on head.*) I'm talking to you.
M.O.:	Don't do that – *I'm* the M.O.
RANDLE:	And he . . . we . . . they . . .
M.O.:	Quiet . . . quiet . . . quiet . . . (*business; quack, quack . . .*)
RANDLE:	He's a quack doctor.
M.O.:	Now pay attention.
RANDLE:	I'm paying nowt.
M.O.:	What do you want?
RANDLE:	What have you got?
[M.O.:	I'll show you what I've got.
RANDLE:	I don't want to see it.]
M.O.:	Quiet . . . quiet . . . quiet. . . . (*business as before*)
RANDLE:	He's got the fowl pest.
M.O.:	What's the matter with you?
[RANDLE:	I've been tampered with. (*Business with baggy part of trousers*) I've twisted myself . . . Eee, I'm back to front.]
M.O. (*to stooge*):	Number one forward. [You are one, aren't you?
RANDLE:	Oh, yes, he's one as well.] (*Sergeant walks round*) Do you want to go somewhere?
M.O.:	Stand to attention.
RANDLE:	It's my uniform that's at ease.
M.O.:	Look at the stains on your tunic – what are they?
RANDLE:	Canteen medals.
M.O.:	Through drinking beer, I suppose.
RANDLE:	No – through spilling it.[2]

Frank Randle

As long as Randle could still bring in audiences, his behaviour was tolerated by the managements; but when by 1953 he was beginning to lose his popularity with audiences who were finding the sort of act quoted above too old-fashioned, the clamp-down began.

Roy Castle: 'One of the first signs of people not putting up with his strange doings was at Wood Green Empire. We weren't doing very good business; and in the middle of the week, we had a singer called Jack Doyle – an Irish singer who used to be a boxer – and I think he'd had a few – he was leaning on the piano, anyway. The audience started giving him a hard time, and Randle heard about this – and this was late at night, his shows used to go on to midnight, sometimes – and he came out and started arguing with the audience – and they started shouting back – and he started swearing at them. The manager ordered the curtain down, and they kicked us out of the theatre that night. They wouldn't have done that to Frank Randle a few years earlier when he was packing the theatres – they'd have put up with it.'

As if this were not enough, the whole thing developed in a manner worthy of one of Randle's own sketches. Harry Harbour, as the bookings manager for Stoll (who owned the theatre), was called in.

'The manager, George Hoare, rang me up the next morning and said, "Frank Randle was calling the audience a lot of bastards – and the council were in!" I was afraid we'd lose our licence. I rang Randle's agents and told them that Randle couldn't go on that night – they quite agreed – and told George Hoare not to let him in the theatre. Then I heard that Randle had managed to get into the theatre and was on the stage with his whole company, rehearsing – they'd got in through a toilet window! I'd got an injunction against Randle, so I went down to the theatre with our solicitor. Eventually we got Randle off the stage – he was in pyjamas for some unknown reason – and served him with the injunction and told him he was not allowed to appear. He said, "*Me*, swear on the stage? What am I supposed to have said?" – I said, "You called the audience a lot of bastards" – he said, "Nothing of the sort – they were cheering so much I said 'basta, basta – enough, enough'!" – I said, "Frank, the house was practically empty!" '

In the end Randle was removed and Harbour had to get together a Variety bill in a hurry to play the rest of the week.

After Frank Randle, even relatively eccentric comics like Dave Morris seemed unremarkable. Another northern comic – for many years the uncrowned king of Blackpool, where he played in summer season – Morris's style was too aggressive for southern audiences, and, like Randle, he had only partial success in the south. Off-stage he was something of an eccentric, unable to resist a joke at any time.

Morris was born in Middlesbrough, and started in juvenile troupes and then as a black-face comic. In 1937 he began a nine-year run of summer seasons at Blackpool's north pier (he had extremely bad eye-sight and so was not called up), by now working as a northern comic in his famous straw hat and very thick glasses. After nine years, he refused to go on playing matinées and his contract was terminated; but despite predictions that he was finished in Blackpool he transferred to a long run at the Blackpool Palace for George and Alfred Black.

He worked as a sketch comic, also doing some stand-up material. In 1950 Joe Gladwin joined him as a 'feed' and

Dave Morris

stayed with him for twelve years. Gladwin – now well known as an actor in *The Last Of The Summer Wine* on television and as the little man in the Hovis TV advertisements – had been working as a comic and singing act up to that time. He remembers that working with Morris was a new experience.

'The first night I went on with him I was petrified, because he didn't write out a script for you to learn – he just went on and talked. After I'd worked with him for some years, it didn't worry me what we did. His comedy was scrupulously clean – even when we played stag nights he didn't do any different to what he did at the pier at Blackpool – and I've seen men falling off their seats laughing at him.'

Gladwin worked with Morris as 'Cedric', a weedy little man who could be the butt of Morris's jokes; they also did a routine in drag as a couple of Blackpool landladies, which did not so much depend on actual jokes as on observation of the characters and an ability to invest fairly ordinary concepts with a comic life of their own:

GLADWIN: How's your husband?
MORRIS: Oh, that dogsbody – I've got rid of him.
GLADWIN: You *haven't*?
MORRIS: Yes . . . oh, I couldn't stand it any longer – got me divorce through – didn't you see it in *The News of the*

World? . . . next to the unclaimed
money?

GLADWIN: No, no . . . I didn't see it.

MORRIS: Oh, you *must* have seen it – that was
me with the veil on.

GLADWIN: No, I'm sorry, I didn't see it, Shirley.

MORRIS: Oh, you must have done – it was next
to that bit where the boy scout attacked
the vicar.[3]

Another routine had 'Cedric' as a strong man – in a
leotard, long johns and a bowler hat – who was chained up
and was supposed to break loose; at intervals for the rest of
the show the audience could see (or just hear) Morris
desperately trying to get the chain off Gladwin with a
hammer and a cold chisel; and then, when they were
leaving the theatre after the show, the same thing would
still be going on – in the foyer.

Morris got a lot of mileage out of local jokes.

Joe Gladwin: 'We'd go to a town, and he'd use the
names of local people; every town we went to he knew – or
the audience thought he knew – everyone that mattered.
During the landladies act, talking about the divorce, he'd
say to me, "Don't go near that crowd in such-and-such
street" – and he'd name the biggest lawyer in the town.
And he used to like it! And he'd name the bookmaker,
or the poshest hairdressers. When we went to towns, he'd
ask the stage manager the names of the chief constable, the
mayor, the biggest pork butcher, and so on – then he'd
write them down and use them if any suitable opportunity
came up.'

His humour was, if not actually surreal, then certainly
individual; here he pokes fun at the restrictions in post-
war Britain where 'austerity' meant a lack of consumer
goods. The stooge on this occasion was another regular
sidekick, Billy Smith.

MORRIS: Have you ever tried to buy an alarm
clock?

SMITH: No.

MORRIS: Well, you're looking at one who has,
and suffered. Listen, and I will
describe it in detail. I went to the
jewellers for an alarm clock. The man
said, 'You'll need a form from the
Board of Trade.'

SMITH: There's nothing in that.

MORRIS: That's what I thought. It would have
been easier for me to employ a

knocker-up. I went to the Board of
Trade and found them all working.
That was a nasty blow for a start. They
gave me a form to fill in.

SMITH: The usual particulars, I suppose?

MORRIS: They were a little different. They
wanted my birth certificate, my
marriage lines, the wife's marriage
lines, a blood test, the lobes of my ears,
the day I was immunized, what won
the Grand National in 1891 and who
rode it. I filled it in and sent it to the
Board of Trade, Whitehall, London.
Back came a reply the same year – oh
yes, those boys are working day and
night down there, they don't clock on
like we do – no, they use a sundial.

SMITH: What about the reply?

MORRIS: The reply said, if I cared to send a
doctor's certificate I could have a pair
of corsets for the wife in eight weeks'
time.

SMITH: Why a pair of corsets?

MORRIS: Because I asked for an alarm clock.
You're dealing with the Government
now. A different race of people
altogether – they live in a world of their
own. They eat different food from us –
corrugated Spam tied with red tape. I
then wrote to the Preston telephone
exchange saying I was a ratepayer from
Huddersfield.

SMITH: Why Preston telephone exchange?

MORRIS: Because it had nothing to do with it. I
was making *them* suffer, now. Back
came the reply. I remember it well – it
was the week I got my orange. I put
my name down for some cigarettes in
the same week. And the reply said, if I
cared to send the size of the frame, I
could have a bicycle pump by return
provided I didn't take it out of the
country, owing to the War Weapons
Act of 1901.

SMITH: By now I suppose you were really fed
up?

MORRIS: Oh no, I kept my temper. I knew they
were busy on the demobilization. I then
sat down and wrote in triplicate to the

Ministry of Agriculture and Fisheries at Accrington.

SMITH: Why Accrington?

MORRIS: Because they've moved from Prestwich Asylum. The inmates couldn't stand the opposition. Back came a reply – I remember it well – the postman fell over his beard delivering it. When we started this correspondence he was a telegraph boy. The reply said, if I cared to send six penny stamps to cover postage, I could have an alarm clock, but it was austerity and the alarm wouldn't go off.

SMITH: Wouldn't go off?

MORRIS: No, only on a Sunday afternoon when I was on nights.[4]

He had his own touring stage show for some years, *The Dave Morris Show*, and a radio series called *Club Night* which ran for eight years on the BBC North of England Home Service (and after five years also got a placing on the Light Programme); there was also a television version The setting was a working-men's club, which allowed Morris to do what were in effect double-acts with a succession of stooges, including Gladwin as 'Cedric' and Geoffrey Banks as 'Pongo Bleasdale' – this last being a joke against the BBC's horror of advertising; they never realized that one of the biggest bookies in Blackpool was called Jack Bleasdale. (On one occasion the BBC remonstrated with him over the use of the name of Cammell Laird, the ship-builders; he said, 'Nobody's going to run out and order ships'.) The humour was in his individual style ('A fine regiment – always blanco their pyjamas before retiring'); the scripts were written by Morris himself, Frank Roscoe (who wrote many North Region shows) and 'Cass James' – James Casey in disguise.

Morris has been largely forgotten since his death in the early 1960s – partly because of his relative lack of appeal in the south, and also because no recordings seem to have survived of him; he was one of the finest northern comedians.

Comics who were born in the north tended, on the whole, to stay with their origins and work as northern comedians. It was less usual for comics born in the Midlands to be strongly regional – partly because the regional character of the Midlands is less well defined. Two comedians who were both born in the Birmingham area became very famous, but in styles which were uncon-

nected with the Midlands – Sid Field and Tony Hancock.

Sid Field was not really a Variety comedian in the strict sense; although he did do some work in Variety, he spent most of his time in revues where he could appear in a number of different sketches written by various different people – as opposed to touring the same one or two sketches for a lifetime. The legend has grown up that he never played in the West End of London until George Black discovered him; and that for years his agent prevented him from working in the south of England, keeping him working in touring revues in the Midlands and the north. Neither of these is true, although it is true that he spent many years touring in these areas, under contract to producers such as William Henshall, for whom he was principal comic from 1936 until 1942. In the course of this he gradually became better known as a comedian, and in 1942 he first worked with Jerry Desmonde, who made an

Sid Field

ideal straight man for him. His first major break-through came in George Black's show *Strike A New Note* in 1943, followed by *Strike It Again* and *Piccadilly Hayride*.

He worked in a style which was 'camp' (though not actually effeminate), creating a range of characters such as 'Slasher Green' the spiv, the tubular bell soloist, and the incompetent golfer taking instruction from a reluctant Jerry Desmonde (Desmonde: 'Get behind your ball' – Field: 'It's behind all the way round!').

He was not principally a verbal comic, and extracts from his material seen in print can give little idea of his style as he constantly tripped over invisible obstacles on the stage or wrestled with the recalcitrant bells, golf clubs or other impedimenta. In 'The Photographer', written for him by Basil Boothroyd (later editor of *Punch*), he played a singularly camp society photographer attempting to take a portrait of an old friend – Jerry Desmonde again – who is now a mayor.

FIELD: Now, how do you propose to be taken? How do you pro-*pose* to be taken?

DESMONDE: I know – all I want to be taken in is my regalia.

FIELD: . . . your *what*?

DESMONDE: In my regalia.

FIELD: Well, I'm flabbergasted! Absolutely flabbergasted! That's the second time this week my flabber's been gasted!

DESMONDE: No, no – I mean this – my chain of office.

FIELD: But that's just as bad as being taken in the . . . won't you find it draughty!

DESMONDE: But I shall be wearing other things as well!

FIELD: *What*, for instance?

DESMONDE: This – my mayor's hat.

FIELD: Ah – so that's a mayor's nest . . . a mayor's hat.

Before they proceed with the photographs, Field offers a little hospitality:

FIELD: Now, before we start to work, how would you like a nice cup of tea?

DESMONDE: Oh, I'd love it!

FIELD: You *would*? Oh, I'm *so* happy! (*Goes to fetch tea trolley*)

DESMONDE: I say, Sidney – can I come and help you?

FIELD: No, no, really, it's quite all right – it's *grand* of you to ask, though, thank you.

DESMONDE: I know – let me cut the bread and butter.

FIELD: No, really, it's already cut and the butter's wiped on and everything! (*Exits*)

DESMONDE: Well, it's so nice seeing old friends after all this long long time – looks quite well, too. (*Field re-enters with trolley*)

FIELD: There, now that didn't take very long, did it?

DESMONDE: Not long at all.

FIELD: I don't always do this for everyone, you know.

DESMONDE: I bet you don't.

FIELD (*sits down; sighs*): Ah, dear . . . hasn't it been cold?[5]

It is quite impossible in the printed text to convey Field's tone of voice on that last line in particular, which got a huge laugh. Several of his best sketches, including 'The Photographer', were included in the film *London Town* – an overblown and frankly very boring musical made in Britain in 1945. They come over quite well (except that it is over an hour into the film before the first one, by which time the stultifying effect of the rest of the film deadens their impact) and give some impression of his abilities; on-stage he was vastly more effective.

Tony Hancock was a great admirer of Field, and indeed there are distinct traces of Field's style audible in Hancock's early recordings before he reached his own distinctive style of faded gentility which made him famous. He worked as a stand-up comic for some years in Variety, doing an act which was not particularly good and to which he clung for far too long – he was still doing some parts of it in his stage appearances in the 1960s.

It was Hancock's radio work which demonstrated that his real ability was as a reaction comic – faced with idiots, his reactions to the situations they caused were hilarious. His radio and television work will be covered in the next chapter, and this is now so well remembered – a good selection of his radio work is still available on gramophone records – that it has tended to be forgotten that he also had a tremendous stage presence. Never at his best as a stand-up comic in Variety proper, his appearances in sketches with Jimmy Edwards in the Adelphi Theatre revues *London Laughs* (1952) and *The Talk Of The Town* (1954),

Sid Field and Jerry Desmonde in 'The Photographer' (film: *London Town*)

and in his own occasional touring shows, demonstrated his ability to project his complex characterization to the back of the largest auditorium.

This example – playing on the character he was already building up on radio, and originally intended for a performance at the Open Air Theatre, Regent's Park, London – dates from 1957. The setting is a park with a bench behind Hancock, who is attempting to give a Shakespearian recital. While he is in full poetic flight, a tramp comes on and lies down on the bench.

HANCOCK: . . . then lend the eye a terrible aspect . . . (*corner of mouth*) clear off.
(*The tramp unwraps a paper parcel with sandwiches in it and starts eating*)

HANCOCK: . . . let it pry through the portage of the head . . . hoppit . . . like the brass cannon; let the . . . er . . . let the . . . let . . .

TRAMP: Let the brow o'erwhelm it.

HANCOCK: Thank you. Let the brow o'erwhelm . . . do you mind? One singer one song, *if* you please. There's plenty of room in the park – find somewhere else.

TRAMP: But I live here. Leastways, I live upstairs. Jim's got the basement, underneath here (*points beneath bench*).

HANCOCK: I'm not interested in your domestic life, I'm trying to give a performance. If you're going to stay there, at least do me the honour of keeping quiet. Henry's speech before Agincourt. Once more into the breach, dear friends, once more . . .

TRAMP: Want a bite of me sandwich?

HANCOCK: No I do not . . . or close the wall up with our English . . . what are they?

TRAMP: Cheese and tomato.

HANCOCK: Oh, thank you. (*Takes it*) One does get a bit peckish during a heavy performance. Quite a nice bit of bunghole you got here.

TRAMP: Yes, I was lucky, finding them in the dustbin.[6]

Like most successful radio comics, Hancock was a superb reader of scripts – he could produce the ideal inflection to a sentence on the first read-through. However, he was hopeless at improvising; and he got the fright of his life in an edition of radio's *Star Bill*[7] when working with a comedian who was an expert improviser – Jimmy James (whose family name was James Casey).

James's son, James Casey, remembers the occasion: 'He had had to go round the back of the stage in the dark [the show came from the Garrick Theatre] and he had dropped his script. They were playing the music, so he came on anyway – and Hancock said, "Ah, Jimmy James" – and my father said, "Who are you?", and just ad-libbed the whole thing. Hancock didn't know what he was talking about – he talked about some fellow who got two bags of salt in his crisps by mistake, which meant that somebody had to go without. He said, "He won't enjoy them, anyway, they'll be too salty – it's not right!" Hancock was white in the face – and at the end the producer came down and said to him, "Don't tell me again that you can't ad-lib!"'

The producer was Dennis Main Wilson: 'This was live broadcasting . . . I rang presentation at Broadcasting House and said, "I'm sorry – we're going to over-run". They said, "Who cares?"'

Jimmy James was a comedian's comedian – one of the very few Variety artists whom other performers would

Jimmy James in his early days

take the trouble to watch from the wings during a performance. He started as a juvenile lead in touring shows, only becoming a comic when one day the show's comic absconded with the leading lady. Beginning with a grotesque costume, he gradually developed his own style based largely on an ability to create outlandish images. In a show for George Black at the London Hippodrome, called *Jenny Jones*, he was at first forbidden to alter lines.

James Casey: 'The critics panned it, and James Agate – who was a fan of my father's – said he was in the wrong vehicle. So George said to my father, "Well, you can do whatever you like with it". So he would walk on and just start ad-libbing – instead of delivering his one line, he suddenly started talking about his Uncle Joe's fried fish-and-chip shop – using the actor, Balliol Holloway, as an unwilling stooge . . . he didn't say anything, because he didn't know what to say!'

(One wonders how they got round the Lord Chamberlain's licence.)

This 'chipster' routine was later developed and used as part of his Variety act:

> You get hold of the potato between the forefinger and thumb, and you hold it sideways – now there's a reason for that, and the reason is that you get more chips, but the chips are shorter – but don't let on about that. That's something I learned from a landlady in Blackpool. You see, all you do is, you hold the potato, and you put it on the block, (*puts hand up and holds imaginary chopping handle*) and it's on, pull, chop – on, pull, chop . . . only, get your fingers out quick – otherwise you'll be thinking you've got more chips than you've chopped. Bad chipsters – you'll see them, hundreds, walking about like that (*holds up hand with two fingers 'missing'*) – too late in getting them out. You can always tell a bad chipster – he walks into a pub and says 'Four pints' – (*holding up index and little finger only*) – he forgets, you see.[8]

James developed two main routines which he used in Variety; in the first half he did one of several sketches as a drunk, and in the second he did his famous 'cardboard box' sketch. At the time he was better known for the latter; more recently he has become remembered for the drunk act, and an impression has grown up that the cardboard box sketch was also done as a drunk, which it was not.

James was a superb drunk comedian – one could almost see the stage altering its angle beneath him as he concentrated on staying upright and aimed vaguely at the cigarette in his mouth with two fingers; he always had to have several goes, before locating it.

James Casey: 'The main thing about his drunk, which was different from everybody else's, was that he was very polite; he never shouted; and he was always immaculately dressed.'

In one of the drunk routines, James has brought on a hurricane lamp and put it down, and is so busy talking to the stooge that he fails to hear a policeman (played by James Casey for a period) coming up behind him.

POLICEMAN (*holding hurricane lamp*): What's this here?
JAMES (*to stooge*): That was dam' good that – you said that without moving your lips! Do it again!
POLICEMAN: What's this here?
JAMES: That'sh fantashtic, that . . . you've got a fortune there, in your throat, if you can only . . . (*sees policeman*) How do, sailor . . . (*double take*) Oh hell, it's a copper.
POLICEMAN: What's the idea of this (*indicating the lamp*)?
JAMES: Oh, that – some damn fool left that in front of a hole – it might have fallen in.

Eventually, James and the policeman realize they were together in the army, and the policeman – noticing that James is clutching a bottle of whisky, becomes friendly.

POLICEMAN: Do you remember Ginger Dunn?
JAMES: Ginger Dunn? . . . Yes! . . . oh . . . the cook, the cook. We used to call him the Old Rissole Expert . . . or words to that effect.
POLICEMAN: Ginger's had it.
JAMES: Has he?
POLICEMAN: Yes, Ginger's had it . . . we'll drink to Ginger.
JAMES: What a lovely thought. You'll drink first, won't you? . . . (*To stooge*) 'cos he knew him better, you see.
POLICEMAN (*taking bottle*): Here's to Ginger Dunn. (*Drinks*) Do you remember Hookey Walker?

JAMES: D'you mind . . . just a minute . . . there's me and Charlie yet, if you don't mind, to do Ginger Dunn.
POLICEMAN: Where's yours?
JAMES: It's under yours if we can get *to* it.

James's timing was superb, and based on an understanding of how to use his material. The first time James Casey performed with him the script required him to whisper in his father's ear, so that his father could react with a line.

'When we came off, he said, "What the hell were you saying to me?" – I said, "Nothing – just rhubarb". He said, "Well, don't say bloody rhubarb! What are you supposed to be saying? . . . Well, say it! How the hell do I know what you're going to say until you say it?" At first I thought, "He's a nut." Then, I realized that he actually didn't react until he heard it – which is the sort of reason that everyone said he was a marvellous timer. If you get a performer who is a bad timer, the reason is they don't *listen* – they're ready to say their line, and they don't wait to hear you say your line and then react to it. He had great repose . . . that takes confidence, to *wait*, and then deliver your line. If you wait, and it dies, you've *really* died! My father was a great waiter . . . and his favourite comic was Robb Wilton, who was the greatest waiter of them all. And Robb Wilton's favourite comic was my father.'

The non-drunk act with the stooges – originally with one, then expanded to two later – depended entirely on idiot logic.

James Casey: 'He was involved with these two idiots, and he believed in them – it was clear to everybody else that he was madder than they were. He'd say he'd given up his job to put the first one on the stage.' The first stooge was usually played by Eli Woods – sometimes using the name Bretton Woods (after the site of an international conference) – a tall, thin, gloriously ugly man dressed in a tight jacket and a cloth cap. The second stooge – who was usually billed as 'Hutton Conyers' – was played by various people over the years, including Roy Castle and James Casey. He came on, interrupting the discussion of Eli's stage career – to perhaps the best entry line any stooge ever had.

CONYERS: Hey.
JAMES: How do you do?
CONYERS: Are you putting it around that I'm barmy?
JAMES: No.

Jimmy James and 'Hutton Conyers' (Dick Carlton) (1960)

CONYERS: Well is it him, then? (*Indicating Eli*)
ELI: I don't want any.
JAMES (*to Conyers*): He doesn't want any.
ELI: How much are they?
JAMES: How much . . . no . . . it's not him.
CONYERS: Well, somebody's putting it around that I'm barmy.
JAMES: Did you want to keep it a secret?

Conyers is dressed in a long coat and a daft hat, and is proudly carrying a shoe-box. It emerges that he has been to South Africa.

CONYERS: They gave me a present.
JAMES: What did they give you?
CONYERS: Two man-eating lions.
JAMES: Did they give you a few yards' start as well?
CONYERS: I brought them home.
JAMES: Well, of course. Where do you keep the lions, then?
CONYERS (*indicating shoe-box*): In the box.
JAMES: Are they in there now?
CONYERS: Yes.
JAMES: I thought I heard a rustling. (*To Eli*) Go and get two coffees; I'll try and keep him talking.
CONYERS: Are you telling him about the lions?
JAMES: Yes, I was just telling him about the lions. (*To Eli*) He's got two man-eating lions in there.
ELI: How much are they?
JAMES: How much are . . . he doesn't want to sell them! They're a sentimental gift from the African people.
CONYERS: I've been to Nyasaland as well.
JAMES: Oh, well . . . they're nice people, the Nyasas. I'll bet they gave you something.
CONYERS: Yes.
JAMES: What did they give you?
CONYERS: A giraffe.
JAMES: A giraffe. Did you bring it home?
CONYERS: Yes.
JAMES: Where do you keep the giraffe?
CONYERS: In the box.
JAMES (*To Eli*): Dial 999 – *somebody* must be looking for him.
CONYERS: Are you telling him about the giraffe?

JAMES: Yes – yes . . . he's got a giraffe in there.
ELI: Is it black or white?
JAMES: I don't know, I'll ask. (*To Conyers*) What colour is it, the giraffe?
ELI: No, the coffee, I mean.
JAMES: Your mother would have been better off with a set of spoons.[10]

Although he was never a top-line attraction, Jimmy James was one of the finest comics that Variety ever produced. He made television appearances, but he never made the adjustment entirely successfully and was always better on-stage. He was the last great sketch comic of the halls in a line that stretched back through Will Hay and Harry Tate; elements of his style can be seen in the work of later comics – particularly Eric Morecambe – but no-one since has combined his elliptical way of looking at the world with his superb timing.

28 The box in the corner
Broadcasting 1945–1960

Throughout the years between the end of the second World War and the end of the 1950s there was a gradual desertion of Variety by its audiences in favour of broadcasting – the box in the corner, either radio or television, which could provide entertainment without the need to go out to see what was beginning to seem an old-fashioned medium.

In the immediate post-war years, television was operating only in a very small way and it was radio which dominated. The Home Service, and its new sister network the Light Programme, established a changed pattern of broadcasting; though not as sharply differentiated as today's Radios 1, 2, 3 and 4, they did have a different style from each other. Variety programmes tended to appear on the Light Programme for the most part, although there were still a number which were originated on the Home Service (including those originated by a Region, such as North or Scotland); there were often repeats on the other network.

Michael Standing, who had been Director of Outside Broadcasts during the war (and done a brief spell as a war correspondent), was appointed Director of Variety at the end of the war; under his guidance radio Variety continued to move away from its pre-war dependence on theatrical Variety into a much wider range of programmes. Even apart from the 'Light Entertainment' programmes, radio comedy was increasingly creating its own original formats and styles, designed to exploit the particular advantages of a medium which spoke to individuals or families in their own homes rather than audiences of hundreds enjoying a night out in their local theatre.

Michael Standing: 'In those days I think we were filling 240 programme spots per week; we were trying to produce about 5 million words per annum of comedy! We were also responsible for cinema organ broadcasts, some light music, all dance music, all jazz, a number of gramophone record programmes – as well as the material which was scripted and performed. I had to create a context in which smaller groups could prosper – for example you could leave John Sharman [the producer of *Music Hall*] more or less on his own, but *ITMA* needed cosseting. And then of course new formats and new ideas needed to be hatched and developed . . . this I think was the most difficult thing of all.'

In the general expansion of ideas in the Variety output, the simple Variety or 'act' show was gradually replaced by different formats – although it never entirely disappeared, and there were always two or three such shows in important placings. John Sharman left the BBC in January 1949; *Music Hall,* the remaining major act programme, ended in 1952. Increasingly the format of act shows was expanded to increase their appeal to the radio audience. *Variety Bandbox* was one of the most important, mixing guest acts with resident comedians, who also appeared in sketches.

Because *Variety Bandbox* and similar programmes had sketches and special material in them, the writers of comedy material began for the first time to be important (in the profession – the public still rather imagined that the artists wrote it all, or made it up as they went along). Jimmy Grafton, an ex-army major who ran a pub in Victoria, took up writing as a sideline, and wrote for *Variety Bandbox*'s resident comedian, Derek Roy; he also wrote one of *Variety Bandbox*'s mini-series of sketches for Peter Sellers, Miriam Karlin and Bill Owen, which went over well.

'We indulged in pure radio, whereas people who came into radio from stage Variety had to rest to a great extent on their stage experience which usually had a strong visual element in it. But you also found that Variety artists who had a strong visual appeal could do well on radio – Gert and Daisy, for example – because they could project this visual image.'

If *Variety Bandbox* could reasonably be compared to the 'number one' theatres, then *Workers' Playtime*, which had started in 1941, could be compared to the 'number threes'; it was a lunch-time half-hour programme, which was relayed from a different factory on each occasion, in which the artists performed to the works audience during their lunch-hour. The audience was usually enthusiastic – mentioning the foreman's name was sometimes (but not always) a way to an easy laugh.

Some shows were based on the American 'personality show' model, featuring one particular performer in sketches and routines, but also bringing in guest artists who would work both with the principal artist and in their own act. *The Jack Buchanan Show* was a typical example; the sketches and linking material were written by Bob Monkhouse and Denis Goodwin.

Another series of programmes which mixed Variety with sketches by resident comics was *The Forces Show*, which was one of a 'family' of programmes which included *Calling All Forces, Forces All-Star Bill*, and finally – dropping the forces connotation – *Star Bill* in 1953. One of its producers was Trafford Whitlock, who had started in broadcasting in Australia and joined the BBC in 1951.

He remembers: 'We broadcast from a proper theatre, which helped a lot in establishing the Variety atmosphere on the air, because the artists were in the sort of surroundings they were used to. We used the Garrick, the Scala, and the King's, Hammersmith; it was done before members of the forces and the theatre was always packed to the rafters.'

With *Star Bill* the programme had become more an act show in disguise, relying heavily on resident comics – mostly Tony Hancock, supported by Graham Stark and Geraldine McEwan or Moira Lister. The producer for the second series was Dennis Main Wilson:

'It was live, Sunday nights – an important show; so I could book practically every top musical star in the country. I tried to book gag comics, as opposed to clowns – Hancock being a clown – like Ted Ray, rather than, say, Frankie Howerd.'

All these programmes were very glossy in their presentation; special choral arrangements for signature tunes, slick announcing and introductions, top artists – and a large and very well drilled orchestra. Recordings of programmes such as *Variety Bandbox,* when compared with the live recordings made in the Holborn Empire (and even some private ones made in the Palladium), show that the standard of playing was noticeably higher in the BBC orchestras (whose performance was by now much improved on the days of the pre-war *Music Halls*) – which were also rather bigger than the bands which could be crammed into the pit of an average theatre. This quality of music must have raised the expectations of audiences who, visiting the Variety theatres, would have found the pit band something of a let-down.

The wartime magazine-cum-Variety show *Navy Mixture* continued until 1947, with a regular cast of Dick Bentley, an Australian comedian; Joy Nichols, also an Australian, who sang and compèred the final series; and Jimmy Edwards. Edwards, who had been educated at Cambridge University (and had been in the Footlights

Club there), sported a huge moustache and a robust manner, and did a schoolmaster act on the halls ('Wake up at the back, there!'). When the series ended, the producer, Charles Maxwell, made plans for a new series featuring these three.

He remembers: 'Frank Muir, who had come out of the RAF, had been writing Jimmy Edwards's spots in *Navy Mixture*; so I asked Frank if he'd like to try to write a show to bring in Jimmy, and Dick Bentley and Joy Nichols. He knew Denis Norden – they both worked for Ted Kavanagh's writing agency – and we dreamed up the idea of *Take It From Here*. The idea was to do a show with a difference; it wasn't exactly satirical, and it wasn't exactly sophisticated, but it had elements of both.'

It was the quality of the writing which makes *Take It From Here* of importance in the history of radio Variety; it assumed a certain degree of intelligence on the part of the listener, while still remaining popular; it depended as much on the writers as on the performers; and Muir and Norden built much of the comedy round the actual personalities (if a little exaggerated) of their cast rather than dealing entirely in fantasy-grotesques.

All writers for radio had, of course, to work within the BBC's requirements; this meant avoiding trade names, vulgarity, and indeed any one of a wide number of forbidden subjects.

Peter Titheradge: 'There were five principal things we had to watch: religion, royalty, physical disability, colour [race], and homosexuality. Muir and Norden always said they wanted to start a script with " 'Christ,' said the Queen, 'that one-legged nigger's a poof' ".'

Michael Standing codified the restrictions – which look a bit silly now but were reasonable enough in the climate of 1949 – in the legendary 'Green Book' which has been reprinted *in toto* in Barry Took's book *Laughter in the Air*.[1] Banned subjects included lavatories, effeminacy in men, immorality of any kind, honeymoon couples, fig leaves, prostitution, commercial travellers, animal habits (e.g. rabbits), ladies' underwear (e.g. 'winter draws on'), brass monkeys and jokes about AD or BC (e.g. 'before Crosby'). Reading the complete text, one wonders how anyone ever found anything left to make jokes about; but they did.

There were many artists, of course, who did their best to bend the restrictions. Max Miller was banned on more than one occasion; there is some dispute about exactly what for (his BBC file is silent on the matter) but Allan Newman, then a BBC engineer, remembers him being banned for his optician joke ('That's funny – every time I see F, you see K').

The producers were responsible for making sure that nothing dubious was broadcast; sometimes this system had its weaknesses – Allan Newman remembers listening to playbacks of Suzette Tarri with producers Tom Ronald and Michael North, and having to explain her jokes to them – the jokes were then hurriedly cut from the recording before transmission. Most producers would hope to spot dubious jokes at rehearsal and cut them before transmission or recording; announcer Peter King outlines the basic rule at rehearsals: 'If the band laughs – cut it!'

Apart from actual Variety shows as such, there were more and more personality shows appearing. Peter Brough and his dummy Archie Andrews had a long-running success in *Educating Archie*. The shows consisted of sketches in which Archie took part – 'with' or 'without' Brough – separated by the usual two musical items.

This three-part structure was effective and widely used; the early editions of Ted Ray's *Ray's A Laugh* were divided into an opening monologue for Ray, in much the same style as his stage work; a domestic situation comedy sketch with Kitty Bluett as Ray's wife; and a playlet featuring Ray as 'George, the man with a conscience', the conscience being played by Leslie Perrins.

Although these sketches were quite well written, they were very much in the older tradition of radio comedy, and it was the central, less pretentious, domestic sketches that became the basis of the entire show from 1952. The musical interludes were dropped, and each show told a half-hour story. Although the show remained in the general robust tradition of Variety, Ray and Bluett – whose portrayal of Ray's long-suffering but affectionate wife was excellent – built up a genuine characterization of a married couple which had more depth to it than was usual in this sort of material.

Ray's A Laugh was unusual in that a change from a basic Variety format to a straight situation comedy took place within the life of the series; but it was merely reflecting a general trend away from formats rooted in theatrical Variety towards the supposedly more naturalistic situation comedy style which was eventually to dominate both radio and television comedy.

Although in many ways a much less satisfying programme, *Life With The Lyons* is of more importance in the development of broadcast comedy. Starting in 1950, and featuring the genuine family of American actor Ben Lyon – his wife, Bebe Daniels Lyon, and their teenage children Barbara and Richard – it presented a domestic situation comedy based firmly on the American model, written by Bebe Daniels, Bob Block and Bill Harding.

Radio's Variety Department, having successfully challenged the one-time dominance of theatrical Variety, was able to maintain a good standard of programmes until late in the 1950s, by which time it was itself being severely challenged by television. From its re-opening in the London area on 7 June 1946 its expansion was rapid, and outside broadcasts in particular became an important factor in building its popularity.

Television Variety was rather limited – many of the same objections were raised by performers and managements that had made life difficult for radio Variety in the 1920s – and entertainment programmes moved away from act shows into the fields of situation comedy, to which TV was more suited. Variety bills tended to be presented in some special setting or format – a good example was *Café Continental*, which staged the acts in a cabaret setting.

This particular programme was also presented in a stage version at the Chiswick Empire; but whereas stage versions of radio shows had been a reasonably sure thing, this idea flopped badly – audiences had after all already *seen* it on television, so why should they go out to the theatre and *pay* to see it?

Television Variety could never hope to compete with radio in terms of sheer output, but by the late 1950s the quality of radio Variety had gone into a decline (with a few honourable exceptions), while the public turned more and more to television.

The Coronation in June 1953 did much to increase television's popularity, as did the appearance of a rival to the BBC – Independent Television, which opened – after much acrimonious public debate – in September 1955.

It was Roy Thompson (later Lord Thompson of Fleet) who coined the famous phrase 'It's just like having a licence to print your own money' (in connection with the opening of Scottish commercial television), and this was obviously the view of the various consortia who fought to win the contracts. Lew and Leslie Grade, always quick to see an opportunity for expansion, were part of a consortium which also included Moss Empires, Harry Alan Towers (who had experience of commercial radio), Prince Littler and the commercial bankers Warburgs; the Independent Television Authority turned down their application, probably from a fear that they formed too powerful a combine. In the end the Grades went in with Norman Collins to form the Associated Television Company, servicing the Midlands. Lew Grade moved full-time to ATV in 1956.

Within a year or so things settled down, although the 'licence to print money' was not as secure as seemed likely; the audiences grew more slowly than had been hoped – people after all had to buy new television sets since ITV programmes were transmitted on a different waveband – and for several years the financial position of the companies was rocky. The two networks developed their own styles; the BBC tended to be better at drama, serious documentary and outside broadcasts – particularly royal occasions. Independent Television News maintained a high standard from the beginning, and there were some successful plays; but ITV's main strength lay in light entertainment programmes. Against the BBC's average of five such programmes a week, ITV usually offered about twelve.

The standard was variable; Associated-Rediffusion, who provided programmes for the London area, had entered into a contract with Jack Hylton (who had long since abandoned bandleading to become an impresario) to provide all their Variety programmes. Peter Black, in his book *The Mirror in the Corner*,[2] comments that most of Hylton's programmes were 'dire', although popular. ATV, having recourse to Lew Grade's experience and contacts in the Variety Industry, was able to provide a higher standard.

Since many Variety programmes were networked, viewers all over the country could see them, rather than their being confined to the area in which they were produced. Some of the shows were built round a personality, with guest artists; half-hour sketch shows built round a particular comic included *The Arthur Haynes Show* and *Alfred Marks Time*. There was a fairly high proportion of act shows in the early days, often billed under the name of the impresario producing them – Jack Hylton or Val Parnell; the most famous of ITV's act shows, Val Parnell's *Sunday Night at the London Palladium*, ran for an hour and featured top Variety stars. There were a few situation comedies, such as *My Wife's Sister* and *Joan and Leslie*, and several shows poached from BBC radio, including *Life With The Lyons* and *Educating Archie*.

ITV introduced a different way of producing programmes. The BBC always handled all aspects of production – bookings, technical facilities, arranging scripts where necessary, and so on. ITV tended to contract out most of the work, as Alfred Black explains.

'We were hired to do the *Arthur Haynes Show*, so we provided the script and obtained the artists, and ATV would pay the bill and provide the studios. The companies normally retained the rights on shows done in this way – except with Jack Hylton, who was very shrewd and didn't let go of many things.'

Hylton retained the rights on many shows, and indeed his company still holds the telerecordings of some of them, whereas much from this period has disappeared.

Jimmy Grafton wrote various television shows for both channels, including *The Dickie Henderson Show* on ITV for six years – Henderson, who had already established himself as a stand-up comic, played in situation sketches in this series – and material for *The Billy Cotton Band Show* on BBC-TV. Grafton found some differences between the two channels.

'ITV were less elastic than the BBC because of their commercial breaks; their timing was very tight. With the BBC you could go over or under a bit. Also, to a certain extent, the censorship on BBC was based generally on good taste; on ITV it was not only good taste, but also on excluding anything which might run counter to the interest of the advertisers.'

As the range of television comedy changed, artists whose style was unchangeably rooted in Variety found work more difficult to obtain. Those who survived were those who changed; and those who were best equipped to change were the younger ones, the NAAFI comedians, whose commitment had always been to comedy first and Variety second. The two shows which, moving in opposite directions, were the most significant of the 1950s used the more fully established medium of radio, and both starred NAAFI comedians: *The Goon Show*, with Harry Secombe, Peter Sellers, Spike Milligan, and (in its early days) Michael Bentine; and *Hancock's Half-Hour* which changed Tony Hancock from an indifferent stand-up comic to one of the greatest comic geniuses of our time.

Hancock's Half-Hour began on radio in 1954, following on from Hancock's success in *Star Bill*; the shows were written by Ray Galton and Alan Simpson, who had a perfect understanding of Hancock's needs. In the early shows the material was much like the sketches he had been performing in *Star Bill* – a better quality version of the sort of material that many artists were performing in various radio shows – tending to unreality and obvious comedy. The transition to a much more real and lifelike sort of comedy came as both Hancock and the writers worked towards a vision of humour which, at first incompletely realized, had by 1957–8 taken situation comedy to entirely new heights.

Tony Hancock with Bill Kerr and Sid James

Hancock's supporting artists were Sidney James, the archetypal cockney crook (even if he was in reality South African) and the Australian comic Bill Kerr, who was a very slow-witted Stan-Laurel-like character, so that Hancock could be in the middle; just as Will Hay had done with the boy and the old man, Hancock could be scored off by Sid but could score off Bill. Much of the comedy arose out of the interplay between Sid's cockney common sense and philistinism, and Hancock's faded gentility, dreams of grandeur, and aspirations as a connoisseur. The way the humour grew from the recognizable situations was a long

way from the rumbustious knockabout anything-for-a-laugh style of classic Variety.

SID: Every second we're getting older! Do
            you realize that as I'm talking this very
            minute, all your working parts are
            slowing down, wearing out, slowly
            falling to bits . . . grinding themselves
            to a standstill until one day . . . Phht!
HANCOCK: Thank you very much! I did enjoy that!
BILL: I didn't realize we were falling to bits.
HANCOCK: See what you've done, you've set *him*
            off now. He'll be holding his breath
            and looking in the mirror all day, now,
            waiting for something to drop off.
            You're all right, Bill – you're going like
            a bomb, mate – you're ticking away
            there like a mad thing! Don't worry,
            you've got . . . four or five years left in
            you yet.
BILL: Well, stop him talking like that, it
            worries me.
SID: Oh, blimey, you've got to face up to
            the truth some day. You can't bury
            yourself in your Mickey Mouse books
            all your life.
BILL: Oh, why can't you intellectuals leave us
            simple people alone?
HANCOCK: What, him? Sid? An intellectual? That
            thing, there – lying on the ottoman,
            scratching himself?[3]

Hancock's Half-Hour was also very successful in its television version, in which the basic character of Hancock and his 'East Cheam' surroundings were carried over, as was Sid James who made an ideal foil. But the increasingly subtle and complex aspects of television comedy left more and more of the old Variety comics out on a limb.

Jimmy Grafton: 'Variety comics as such are not considered to work so well in situation comedy, because they're slightly larger than life, and therefore they overproject. In a situation comedy you can't have that, because you have to suspend disbelief . . . so you have to have actors rather than comedians.

'I remember trying to confine Arthur Askey in terms of sketches, and it was impossible because he was always playing to the camera. Ethel Revnell, who was a very strong cockney character comedienne in Variety, was in

The Goon Show (1956)

an early Henderson show; we brought her in to play a character in a situation comedy, and she played it like a Variety sketch – expecting that she was going to get a laugh when she came on, and grimacing at the audience. She was so much larger than life that we had to scrap the show. That was an extreme example of the danger that Variety artists were always in on television. One or two have got round it – Jimmy Jewel is a very appealing actor on television; he's been able to go on in TV beyond his days as a comic, because he's also a very good comedy actor; and Alfred Marks is the same, another very good example of someone who started as a comedian and has gone into comedy acting. Those were the survivors.'

Where *Hancock's Half-Hour* took realistic comedy to a peak, *The Goon Show* took surrealistic comedy to a height which has never been matched. Milligan, performing and writing, Sellers, and Secombe created a gallery of exaggerated characters who acted out fantastic stories, making the fullest possible use of radio as a medium; the show did not so much push back the boundaries of radio comedy as trample them underfoot. Riotous use of sound effects and migraine-inducing logic added to the impact of a show which completed the long journey from radio comedy as pure Variety, to radio comedy as pure radio.

BLOODNOK:	Are you ready? Bugler – sound the elephant.
GRAMS:	INFURIATED HIGH-PITCHED TRUMPETING BY A SINGLE ELEPHANT.
BLOODNOK:	Oooh . . .
JYMPTON:	Here they come now, sir.
BLOODNOK:	Quick, me spoons and me music. I'll show 'em.
FX:	TWO SPOONS BUSKING IN TEMPO TO BLOODNOK SINGING 'GOODBYE DOLLY I MUST LEAVE YOU'.
BLOODNOK:	'Goodbye Dolly I must leave you.' (*shouts*) Come on you fools, there's more where that came from. (*Continues singing*) 'Off we go and fight the foe', (*shouts*) sing up, lads!
OMNES AND ORCHESTRA:	ALL JOIN IN SINGING AND RATTLING SPOONS.
GRAMS:	SHELLS START BURSTING IN THEIR MIDST, STARTING SLOWLY AND INCREASING IN INTENSITY. BLOODNOK CONTINUES TO SING BUT GRADUALLY HIS MORALE IS DESTROYED. HE BREAKS OFF.

BLOODNOK:	Run for it, lads – these songs aren't bullet-proof.
GRAMS:	WHOLE ARMY RUNS AWAY YELLING IN TERROR. SPEED UP AND FADE OUT. (*pause*)
GRAMS:	ARCTIC GALE HOWLING. OCCASIONAL WOLVES. THEN APPROACH OF RUNNING ARMY STILL YELLING AND PANTING.
BLOODNOK:	That's far enough, lads – where are we?
SEAGOON:	The South Pole, sir.
BLOODNOK:	No further, we don't want to back into them. Plant the Union Jack will you? . . . the national flag of the Union of Jacks. I claim the South Pole in the name of Gladys Pills of Sebastopol Villas, Sutton.
SEAGOON:	Who is she, sir?
BLOODNOK:	I don't know, but obviously we're doing her a big favour.[4]

(Bloodnok was played by Peter Sellers, Jympton by Spike Milligan and Seagoon by Harry Secombe.)

If *The Goon Show* took radio comedy to its limit, it also almost killed it off – nothing since then has expanded the field any further. The pressure from television caused a falling-off of radio comedy in the 1960s; having grown out of and sustained Variety, radio comedy now was dying itself. It has not disappeared entirely, of course; but simple economics mean that the best writers will almost always work for TV. Almost all surviving radio shows are comedy-team shows, and act shows have long since disappeared.

On television, the great expansion of comedy was only just beginning in 1960. The so-called 'satire boom' that started with *Beyond The Fringe* in the theatre and the magazine *Private Eye* led to *That Was The Week That Was*; and *Steptoe and Son*, *Till Death Do Us Part*, *Monty Python's Flying Circus* and *Yes Minister* have all been part of the long-term story in which television comedy has removed itself further and further from its origins – through radio – in Variety. The spirit of Variety sometimes shines momentarily, in the occasional speciality acts, in the recently-defunct *The Good Old Days* (an approximate reconstruction of Victorian music-hall), and in the work of a handful of performers, who will be examined in the final Interlude, p. 220.

29 Nudes and rock 'n' roll
Variety in decline 1953–1960

During the latter part of the 1950s, the post-war shortages and austerity gave way to a period of relative prosperity, with a new boom in consumer purchases as goods once again became generally available. This was the period of which Prime Minister Harold Macmillan supposedly said, 'You've never had it so good'[1]; and though this was not true of Variety in general, it was certainly true in some areas of it. Paul Raymond, from his small beginnings with two volunteer nudes in an otherwise straightforward show, was building a career as an entrepreneur in this field.

'In 1953 I had four touring revues; then six; the heyday was 1956, when I had ten going at one time. In 1957 I could see that the halls were closing – I had eight shows; and in 1958 when I started the Raymond Revuebar [in London's Soho] I still had four touring revues. They were mostly nude shows – not all, I did one called *Las Vegas After Dark* which had no nudes, *Hot From Harlem* with Shirley Bassey, and shows with people like Mike and Bernie Winters or the Dallas Boys. Previous nude shows had just been touring revues with nudes in them – models who stood still; I was the first person to do one where the whole show was built as a nude revue, and all my revues did very well and packed all the theatres out.'

The Lord Chamberlain's regulations specified that nudes must remain stock still; Raymond found a way to get round this and allow his girls to move.

'By not having any sketches in the show, but just a series of speciality acts, single comics, and with no talking in the scenes – we had song and dance scenes, but no talking – I didn't come under the jurisdiction of the Lord Chamberlain. We did have several occasions when we had to tell the local Watch Committee to contact the Lord Chamberlain's office to confirm that the Lord Chamberlain had no jurisdiction over the show. Then the local Watch Committee would do their own censorship – for example, we had a girl on a revolve, and in Manchester they wouldn't let it revolve showing her backside bare, and in Leeds they wouldn't let it revolve showing her front bare.'

There were many imitators of Raymond's success – some of them very sleazy, getting their girls practically off the street, much to the disgust of the established Variety performers who found themselves forced to work in these shows to make a living. Raymond himself – although many Variety performers viewed his shows with distaste – did at least provide a high standard and a range of gimmicks.

'We had nudes in a lion's cage, nudes *in* ice, the only Chinese nudes in Europe . . . but while the gimmicks were there to bring the audiences in, the entertainment was still there to keep them in and encourage them to tell their friends. It was very difficult for us to get onto the Moss and Stoll tours, but in the end we did, and we were playing to more money than many of the big stars.'

Even today many Variety performers of the period still complain that nude shows – whether well presented or not – were a death-blow to their business because they drove away the family audience. Certainly in the climate of the times few young men would feel they could take their girlfriends to a nude show, and few families would feel that these shows were suitable for their children; but in any case by the mid-1950s the family audiences were deserting the rapidly decreasing number of theatres.

Philip Hindin: 'Some theatres became bingo houses; the small theatres had only survived up to then because of the shortages of other things for people to spend money on, and by then what they were taking wasn't enough to pay for the visiting company. So visiting companies didn't go to these places, and they closed – places like Castleford, Stockport, Camberwell Palace, Hulme Hippodrome, the Pavilion Liverpool, Hippodrome Wigan . . . and there were some theatres which had fires, and through the smoke you could see the silver lining! – they were more profitable being burnt down than running shows.'

Paul Raymond feels that the nude shows in fact helped to extend the lives of many theatres for a few years; a view confirmed by Ted Gollop, who booked some of them onto Moss Empires.

'The strip shows were the only thing that did help to keep the theatres going. They did turn away family audiences – but what could we do? When the Finsbury Park Empire closed in 1960 there was an outcry – I had to go to an enquiry, and a member of the public stood up and said we were wrong to book strip shows because that was what had killed the theatre. I had to ask him what else he thought we could keep the theatre open with – people didn't want to see Variety or the ordinary revues, and there weren't enough of the big musicals, so you *had* to book strip shows.'

The non-nude Variety bills were increasingly dependent upon popular music stars for their main attractions. Pop music – as it was just beginning to be called – had always been an important part of Variety, but now it was becoming a major business in its own right and more and more was dominating Variety bills. Performers like the singer Vera Lynn, the black boogie-woogie pianist Winifred Atwell and the pianist who took over from her in popularity, Russ Conway, the jazz musician Humphrey Lyttelton, and Chris Barber, whose hit record 'Petite Fleur' helped to cause a short-lived boom in 'traditional' jazz, toured the halls. Joe Loss and Ted Heath toured with their bands; American singers Johnny Ray and Frankie Laine first toured in 1955. It was Laine who first pointed

up the connection between pop music and clothing that was to become such a feature of the pop scene as it increasingly became a teenage-dominated world; when he was appearing at the Palladium, a critic complained about his Italian-style suit – tight-fitting short jacket with wide shoulders – and pointed shoes. On his second night, Laine complained in his act about this – saying people could criticize his singing but not his tailor – and asked the audience if they approved of his suit. Their enthusiastic response started a whole new field of teenage interest.[2]

Johnny Ray – whose style consisted of weeping his way through sentimental songs such as 'Cry' and 'The Little White Cloud That Cried' – had been popular in America from 1952. On his first appearance in Britain in 1955 his audiences – composed largely of screaming and hysterical teenage girls – gave Britain its first taste of a new phenomenon that later manifested itself as 'Beatlemania' when the Beatles commanded a similar following.

There is of course a distinction between *pop* and *rock*

Johnny Ray

music. 'Rock-and-roll', as it was first called (then 'rock 'n' roll', then just 'rock') is generally held to have begun with the recording in April 1954 of 'Rock Around The Clock' by the American group Bill Haley and the Comets. This record became immensely popular in Britain, and together with the records of Elvis Presley laid the foundation for rock in this country; the field was American-dominated for several years.

Britain retaliated with skiffle – a slickened and simplified version of American fast blues which used homemade instruments such as tea-chest bass and washboard, and thus was more suitable to amateur performers than rock, which from the start demanded powerfully amplified electric guitars. Ken Colyer was among the first to bring skiffle to the public, but its most popular exponent was Lonnie Donegan, who recorded his version of the old Leadbelly number 'Rock Island Line' in 1955.

Lonnie Donegan

The following year saw a craze for skiffle, with amateur bands everywhere. Donegan himself appeared in Variety bills; indeed many of his records for the Pye label were actually recorded during live performances in Variety halls, and present him not only singing but interspersing his performances with one-line jokes. In 1960 he appeared in the Royal Variety Performance, singing his hit number 'My Old Man's a Dustman'. Skiffle was thus one of the last

contributions that Variety made to the world of light entertainment, by providing the appearances for performers like Donegan; these were as important to his popularity as his records, unlike later rock artists (many of whose performances were very much creations of the recording engineer's art).

In 1957 Bill Haley visited Britain, touring as a bill-topper in Variety. This proved not to be the happiest format for him; whereas skiffle was cheerful and acceptable to most adults, rock-and-roll was loud and subversive; adults found it raucous and felt threatened by it. Thus the audiences for the bills on which Haley appeared consisted of teenagers who sat in boredom through the usual supporting acts, and found that to their disgust Haley played only five numbers. In the following year one of Britain's first rock artists, Cliff Richard,[3] was discovered by George Ganjou (who with the break-up of the

Cliff Richard

act with his brothers in 1957 had become an agent). He arranged Richard's first recording session – including the hit number 'Move It' – and in 1958 Richard began touring with his backing group 'The Shadows'.

Philip Hindin was booking the Metropolitan Edgware Road at that time.

'We played Cliff Richard's very first Variety date. George Ganjou offered him to me – I'd never heard of him, and the only reason I booked him was that my twelve-year-old niece said he was very good – and I thought so little of Cliff Richard that I put twelve acts on the bill with him, in case he didn't succeed. And on the Monday night we played to reasonable business; on the Tuesday night it was *very* good; and on the Wednesday we had the police out. The rest of the week was a riot! There were kids fighting to get in, the theatre was packed – we did unheard-of business. We played Walthamstow with him on the Sunday and played to capacity; and he was offered to me for another few weeks but I said I didn't really want the responsibility of having the police out . . . I didn't want to be involved. I was of the old school, I wanted to see standard acts – and I couldn't be bothered with all the screaming kids, and an act that did twelve minutes and you couldn't hear a word he said.'

Despite Hindin's dislike of it, rock had arrived; Cliff Richard went on to tour the country (although Ganjou was unable to get him bookings because the Grades had control of so many theatres; in the end Ganjou sold Richard's contract to the Grades). The problem was that although a theatre could be packed when playing a rock star, when it reverted to a more normal bill the following week it attracted neither the teenage fans nor the older audiences, who had been to some extent frightened off by all the noise and hysteria associated with rock performers.

Ted Gollop: 'We were asked to go out to the Odeon St Albans to see Cliff Richard; I didn't know what rock-and-roll was – I didn't have any idea – but when all the kids tore down the aisle screaming the place down I decided to book him into Finsbury Park. He packed the place out. After that, unless you had a rock star, no-one wanted to know . . . it was all kids. It was not only the decline of the profession as a profession – it was the decline of the booking manager, too, because he didn't have to know his job . . . he could just go by what the kids liked. I'm not decrying rock-and-roll, but it was foreign to what *our* profession was.'

By the end of the 1950s the Variety business was pretty well dead. There had been various re-shuffles in the business management. In 1958 Val Parnell resigned as managing director of Moss Empires, while retaining an interest in the Palladium, to concentrate on television; he was succeeded by Leslie MacDonald and Prince Littler, working together. Six theatres were closed during the summer, and although plans were made to improve the comfort of theatres Variety was being phased out in favour of musical shows and revues.

More and more theatres closed; and in 1960 there was a battle for control of Moss Empires, with a bid from Stoll being followed by a bid from a company formed by Charles Clore, Jack Cotton and Bernard Delfont. Most of Moss's theatres were on prime sites in the middle of cities, and had this bid been successful the majority of them would probably have been promptly demolished to allow redevelopment; but in the end Stoll made a new bid and took over the company to form Stoll-Moss Theatres.

Television spin-offs such as *The Black and White Minstrel Show*, and appearances by pop and rock stars, kept the theatres going for a time; but the old world of Variety bills had vanished, and with it the opportunities for many acts. Some of them found a new field in the working-men's clubs which were becoming bigger, plusher and better run about this time; although few of them enjoyed the experience. They were expected to do about forty minutes, and often found that the audiences were not really very appreciative.

Sandy Powell: 'I worked at a club near Sheffield; I did the ventriloquist act in the first half, and didn't get one laugh. I was working away, dropping the doll . . . and it's agony to be on there, knowing you've got to be on for twenty minutes and they don't think you're funny. I went in the bar, and the barman said, "I've just had three fellows in here, and one of them said, 'Sandy Powell's not in the same street as Ray Alan' " . . . they thought I meant it, you see . . . Anyway, in the second half I did my conjuring routine – mucking up the tricks – and I went in the bar again afterwards and said, "Have your friends been in?" – the barman said, "Yes – they say you're a bloody sight worse as a conjurer". So I didn't work any more clubs.'

Another problem was that many of the clubs wanted their humour very dirty, with plenty of swear-words and what Dennis Main Wilson classes contemptuously as 'tit, bum, and wee-wee jokes'. Variety performers hated this, but there were plenty of younger comics who saw this as a way to an easy laugh. However, it was also of limited use outside clubland; and with the clubs providing the only training ground for young comics this sort of humour was of limited long-term value – as Reg Dixon said, 'You're only as funny as your last adjective'.

In recent years the few remaining clubs have been finding life extremely difficult – partly because of the high fees which their artists now expect; and this problem has also bedevilled the remaining theatres in their attempts to mount summer season shows, pantos, or revues. Many artists – particularly those trying to mount their own shows – have bemoaned the minimum wages imposed by the Musicians' Union for orchestra members and by Equity for dancing girls, which have tended to result in the orchestra being reduced to two or three and the number of dancing-girls from, say, a dozen to two in a typical show.

Norman Murray answers this: 'Of course, as soon as bottom-line artists want an improvement – Equity doesn't fight for the top-line artists, it doesn't have to – of course the managements get hurt. When the minimum rate goes up, of course we squeak – just as I squeak when my gas bill goes up. If you can't afford enough dancing-girls, tell the headliner to take less money . . . instead of taking £5,000 a week, tell him to take £4,000 – then you can have six girls instead of two. The same man who complains that he has to pay dancers £120 minimum or whatever, will have no compunction at all in asking you £8,000 a week for an artist. Some agents seem to have a death-wish – they want to show off how much they can get for their clients; they create monsters, they're stupid.'

The hard fact was that few theatres could take enough money to cover the cost of even a modest production; and competition from floodlit football, bingo, discos, and of course the wide range of entertainment available on television without the bother of leaving the house put the theatre very low on most people's list of interests. Louis Benjamin, as managing director of Stoll-Moss Theatres, has to attempt to keep the small number of theatres the company still runs in business.

'Today, people will not pay the money to see *good* acts; they will only pay to see superstars – the good acts are too easily available on television, and the novelty of seeing them live on stage has gone. The provinces don't need quite the size of star the West End of London does . . . but they will do – when the money's tight, summer shows and so on don't work.'

One result of all this is that new people have nowhere they can learn their trade; no longer can they work the 'number threes', then the 'number twos', polishing their acts over several years. As Bob Konyot says, 'There is nowhere they can be lousy'. On television, if they are not top-class to begin with, they are unlikely to make future appearances.

Jimmy Grafton: 'Success in show business today is dictated by television and the record industry; but video is going to distort all that, because most people, if you gave them a choice between a film they would like to see and a light entertainment programme, would opt for the film. Now video can give you all the films you want to see, and the specific programmes you don't want to miss on TV – half of which are going to be films anyway. So light entertainment is shrinking all the time, and so are the opportunities. There's still a market round the world for people who can only work in that sort of field; but it's not a market for young people who want to aim themselves towards records or television, and they tend to be singers or comics – not jugglers or whatever.'

So even the offshoots from Variety, which itself was dead by about 1960, may be withering away. There will always be *some* light entertainment shows on TV, and the stars to make them, and by the early nineeen-eighties a small-scale version of Variety had begun to emerge in small fringe theatres – and in pubs, thus echoing the beginnings of music-hall. Many of these entertainments were aimed at young audiences, and indeed were on the fringes of the pop and rock worlds; interestingly the actual label 'Variety' began to come back into use, as did 'Cabaret' to advertise them. But with video with us now and cable television on its way, the pattern of entertainment in the future is extremely uncertain. The only prediction that can be made with any assurance is that Variety itself, as it was in its heyday, can never return; and that though there will always be some light entertainment stars, there can never again be the tremendous range of entertainers at all levels that was once taken for granted when a night at the Variety theatre was the highlight of the week for so many people.

INTERLUDE

Indian Summer

Although Variety as a medium was dead by 1960, the following quarter of a century saw a small handful of acts who, though denied the format of Variety, were able to work within its spirit; by building their approach, each in their own individual way, on the basics of Variety they were able to rise to the top of the entertainment business. This Interlude examines the four most important acts who have managed this difficult transition.

Max Wall – born in 1908, family name Maxwell Lorimer – came to his greatest popularity after a career in Variety which started in the early 1920s. He began as a dancer, in particular doing eccentric dancing with a strong comedy effect; his bill matter was 'The Boy With The Educated Feet'. He was not at that time particularly well known by the public.

Max Wall

'I was known by head office as a good act – you can't fail with a ten-minute dancing act; but I wasn't well known in households until about 1945 when I was resident comedian with *Variety Bandbox*.' His first experience as a verbal comic was in the early 1930s when he was appearing with Will Fyffe's touring show; he progressed to work as a stand-up comic.

'I was just doing jokes, and guitar playing, and songs. I wrote all my own jokes – I've written my own stuff for years. Sometimes I used to use jokes from Orben's joke book – a lot of comedians used to take whole routines from it, whether it suited them or not – but I used to work out a structure and weave the jokes into it.'

After being invalided out of the RAF in the second World War (he had a nervous breakdown through combining too much entertaining with his normal duties) he became more widely known as a stand-up comic. At this stage, though competent, he was not in the top class, but he was able to continue expanding his style. He had a major break in 1955 when he appeared in the London version of the robust American musical *The Pajama Game*, making good use of both his singing and dancing abilities, and for the first time creating a character other than his usual stage persona.

His career might have taken off at that point but for the break-up of his marriage, which was followed by his romance with, and subsequent marriage to, a beauty queen. The press had a field day; page after page of fake outrage made him the scapegoat, with the result that his career went into a severe decline. He continued to work; with the death of Variety he played the northern clubs – with some success despite his refusal to pander to the audiences' usual taste for dirty jokes; but it was not until 1973 that he was 'rediscovered' with his one-man show, which he subsequently presented from time to time in London and the provinces, and which has also been televised.

In this show, unfettered by the limitations of time which Variety used to impose, he could work at a slow pace, building a relationship with the audience as he talked about his career and told jokes from which he kept digressing with odd remarks and comments. He would latch on to a word and pronounce it with relish, or break off to welcome latecomers ('Trouble with the bike? – the show hasn't started yet . . . I'm the compère') or simply to throw in silly one-liners (he coughs, and comments: 'I must get a room tonight . . . that joke's served me for twenty years').

Unlike some comics, the visible signs of age worked in Wall's favour; his lined face and a darker side to the humour – a type of comedy not usually acceptable in the days of Variety – added an extra dimension to the act. Sometimes he seemed almost to be repulsing the audience, daring them to like him – becoming almost aggressive, but then suddenly dropping back to his normal relaxed style, commenting, 'That's enough of that'.

He finished the show with a routine he had been developing since his wartime days: Professor Wallofski, the concert pianist. Attired in the style of Liszt as seen by Charles Addams, with a ridiculous wig and indecently tight black tights, he performed ('with the aid of an AA map and a spirit level') Rachmaninov's Prelude in C sharp minor and Liszt's Second Hungarian Rhapsody. To be accurate, his pianist, Bill Blezzard, did most of the performing while Wallofski (for the most part) mimed – when not arguing with an off-stage presence about the absence of the piano stool, or killing a flea by crushing it in the keyboard lid.

He finished with his trademark, the funny walk – a version of his old eccentric dance act, complete with high kicks (followed by an anguished clutch at the groin) and facial expressions reminiscent of a gorilla with toothache.

Although he has done television work (including *Waiting For Godot* with Leo McKern) and straight stage work (as Archie Rice in *The Entertainer*) it is this stage show which has brought him his greatest fame; he could work at his best with a real audience to play upon.

This need for a live audience is also true of another comic who has worked best in his own show – Ken Dodd. An eccentric stand-up comic – and one of the few in recent times to take the trouble to *look* funny – he was a Doddy-come-lately to Variety, making his debut in 1954. His big break came in 1965 with a forty-two week run at the Palladium; since then he has appeared in his own show on numerous occasions as well as in pantomime.

His career has not been restricted to stage; a one-off radio show in the series *Star Parade* in 1963 led to a radio series later that year and numerous subsequent ones. That first show was unusual in its construction; although not as far-out as *The Goon Show* (which finished in 1960) it was loosely constructed, poised between one-line gags and actual sketches; the ideas – almost mini-sketches – ran into each other in a stream-of-consciousness manner which, in a much more developed and aggressive form, was later to be made familiar by *Monty Python's Flying Circus*. Oddly, his later radio series settled into the more familiar format, building eight-minute sketches round inviting subjects such as Batman; well performed, but more restricted in style. On television he has made use of the 'Diddy people' style of humour, using children to represent the mythical population of the broken biscuit factory at Knotty Ash; but television has not proved as amenable to his style as it might have been.

Many comedians have also been singers, right back to Dick Henderson, but Dodd is unusual in having penetrated the Top Twenty; the song which later became his signature tune, 'Love is like a violin', made the Top Twenty in 1960, and in September 1965 his recording of 'Tears' reached number one in the charts.

But it is on stage that he really comes into his own. Like Max Wall, he uses length – over two hours – but, instead of quietly coaxing the audience along, he bludgeons them into submission with a string of gags and stories. Most of his gags conjure up strange images which make them funnier than they ought to be ('What a beautiful day – what a beautiful day for going up to the pick-'n-mix counter and mixing everything up with a pick'). Like Max Miller he can be blue *without* being blue, because the images are entirely in the mind of the audience.

Part of the secret of his success is a remorseless professionalism. It is by now an open secret that he maintains a log-book of every performance in which every joke he has used is noted down, together with the reaction to it; thus armed he knows better how to approach audiences in that part of the country next time he plays there.

Even when he was appearing on the request programme *Housewives' Choice* on radio in August 1965 he kept up his quest for perfection. The programme – a Monday-to-Friday morning request programme with a different host each week – might well have been seen as an easy lurk by most personalities; but not Dodd. First he tried to set up complicated jokes involving sound effects; this was sat on by the producer when it became apparent that it was going to get out of hand and eat up all the rehearsal time.

Then Dodd maintained a 'hot line' to his scriptwriter to obtain suitable gags to go with the requests; and even in this setting he had a secretary who noted down every gag used.[1] With this tireless approach to his business the apparent inconsequentiality of his act is backed by an exact knowledge of what he is doing and why he is doing it.

This example – which can only give a hint of the exhausting experience of seeing him in the flesh – comes from a performance in Liverpool's ornate Palace of Varieties for BBC Television's old-time music-hall show *The Good Old Days*.

Ken Dodd

What a thrill, ladies and gentlemen, to stand here this evening – here in this magnificent . . . shed – no, no, this *theatre*, this theatre of the imagination! Of course you have to use a lot of imagination . . . *I* have to – I have to imagine that you're enjoying yourselves. *You* have to imagine that I'm a comedian . . . you've got the biggest job. Now, ladies and gentlemen, one thing is very important – we all have to be out of here by ten thirty . . . yes . . . 'cos that's when they bring the trams in . . . I've really been looking forward to coming here – tonight I feel completely underwhelmed. I woke up this morning – I was up at the crack of noon.[2] This morning I thought, 'What a beautiful day – what a beautiful day for going up to Lady Smith and

saying "I hear you've been relieved" . . . What a beautiful day for going up to Count Zeppelin and saying "You'll never sell a sausage that size".'[3]

Dodd's impact tends to be muted on television, which needs a less extravagant approach. Les Dawson – a product not of Variety but of the northern clubs – has worked his way up to his own series on television, in which he shows a complete command both of the medium and of the background of Variety humour. He represents another link in the chain of northern humour that stretches right back to the downtrodden comedy of George Formby Sr; looking like a despondent dumpling, his quiet despair is completely convincing.

In the various sketch situations which he uses in his series, he builds effectively on the work of past comedians, incorporating some of their mannerisms (and occasionally some of their jokes) but most importantly the *ambience* of their acts. It is possible to detect traces of Jimmy James when he deals tiredly with idiot interruptions (an impression strengthened by the use of James's stooge Eli Woods); in some of his sketches the incompetence of Robb Wilton can be seen; and his regular spot in drag with Roy Barraclough – with Dawson as a slatternly depressed housewife and Barraclough as a rather more chic neighbour – combines the visual techniques of Norman Evans (heaving at an immense bosom or forming the mouth into a toothless expression) with the elliptical humour of Dave Morris's Blackpool landladies.

None of this is to imply that he steals material or has cobbled his act together from other people's mannerisms; what he has done is to build a style upon the achievements of the past, modifying them to create a personality which can communicate itself in the unsympathetic medium of a television studio.

His stand-up routines contain faint echoes of Dick Henderson – although where Henderson remained chirpy, Dawson faces his family situation with despair tempered with resignation. It is part of his particular gift that he can stand in a studio, smartly dressed and surrounded by a glossily coloured set, and tell convincing jokes about mothers-in-law.

Used to be a fellow lived near me used to sell horse manure for gardens. Colourful character – red nose, big hat . . . he used to go round going 'Get your manure from me – hand-picked manure' . . . somebody said to his wife, 'Why don't you get him to say fertilizer"?'. She said, 'It took me ten years to get him to say "manure".'

This morning I was just laying in bed playing a Hebridean lament on my euphonium – the wife hates it when I play in bed – it strips all the paint off her harp – and just then there was a knock at the door. I knew it was the wife's mother because the mice were throwing themselves on the traps. The wife said, 'How would you like to speak to Mummy?' – I said, 'Through a spiritualist.'

The wife said, 'What would you like for your breakfast?' – I said, 'I'll have beans on toast.' She came back ten minutes after, out of the kitchen – she said, 'You can't have that'. I said, 'Why?' – she said, 'The beans have clogged the toaster'. What a rotten cook – last year I bought her a pressure cooker – I don't know what she did but she put a sprout in orbit. I must have the only kids in the country who *want* to go to bed without supper.'[4]

Les Dawson in his television show (1984)

Where Les Dawson uses the medium of television, stamping it with his own personality, Morecambe and Wise, faced with the everlasting problems of Variety on television, solved the problem in a quite different way. The story of their career is by now fairly well known – the beginnings as teenagers in juvenile shows and in the tatty end of Variety; the disastrous 1954 BBC TV series *Running Wild*; the rather more successful series for ATV running from 1961 to 1968 (six series), and then the return to BBC Television for the vastly successful series of the next ten years.

Beginning with attempts to imitate the quick-fire style of Abbott and Costello, they gradually built their own style until by the ATV shows they were working in a manner which owed a good deal to their northern backgrounds. Their basic sketch plot was that Ernie Wise, the straight man, would set up some situation that exploited the relatively gormless Eric Morecambe; although this was not a rigid format, and even this early they were beginning to blur the sharp distinction between comic and straight man which had been observed by most previous double-acts.

Their writers for the ATV shows were Dick Hills and Sid Green, who produced many sketches successfully exploiting Morecambe and Wise's technique as it stood at that time; and when in 1968 the act returned to BBC Television Hills and Green continued to write for them. After that first series of eight programmes Eric Morecambe suffered a severe heart attack which kept them off television for ten months; when their new series eventually started in July 1969 – carefully rehearsed and recorded at a much slower pace to reduce the strain on Morecambe – Hills and Green had gone on to other work and were contractually unable to write for them.

Their new writer was Eddie Braben, a Liverpudlian who had been writing for Ken Dodd.

The producer of the series, John Ammonds, remembers: 'I knew he'd written gag material, but that he hadn't written sketches – which were what we needed; and Eddie said straight away, "I'm not a sketch man"; but the boys said, "It'll come". And it did, with the boys being creative in their ideas. We managed to get Eddie to inject gags into the sketches.'

Braben's Liverpudlian background added a new dimension of oddity to the act's style; it was also after he started writing for them that they reversed the previous roles of the straight man and the comic, blurring still further the distinction. Insofar as one of them was a straight man, it was Wise; but he came to play a stupid

self-satisfied character who was often the butt of Morecambe's schemes.

Morecambe usually emerged as the smarter of the two, although there were areas in which Wise could top him. Morecambe once said, 'The premise is, he's an idiot but I'm a bigger idiot'; but the relationship they built up was too complex for any single statement to describe it. In this example of their basic type of double-act routine, with which they normally opened their shows, it is Ernie Wise's birthday.

ERNIE: Is that a birthday present?

ERIC: I'm coming to that in a minute. Ernie – can I tell the ladies and gentlemen of the studio audience and your fan in Rotherham how old you are today?

ERNIE: No.

ERIC: Thank you . . . pardon?

ERNIE: No, you can't tell them.

ERIC: No?

ERNIE: Famous and popular stars of television don't go around telling everybody how old they are.

ERIC: I'm not asking a famous or a popular star – I'm asking you!

ERNIE: My age is *my* business!

ERIC: Oh! So then – it's by deduction, is it? Is it true to say that you are between twenty-four and a hundred-and-three?

ERNIE: I don't care how much you deduct, I'm not telling the ladies and gentlemen, or you, how old I am.

ERIC: Have you got a war-wound on your left shoulder – a scar left by the spear of a fuzzy-wuzzy? (I only just remembered that – true – it's all based on fear.)

ERNIE: No, and I'm not going to tell you how old I am, and that's that.

ERIC: Roll your trouser leg up.

ERNIE: What for?

ERIC: Go on – roll your trouser leg up. (*Ernie does so*)

ERNIE: What are you going to do?

ERIC: Find out how old you are.

ERNIE: How do you do that?

ERIC: You count the wrinkles and multiply by two!

ERNIE: I'm not a tree!

ERIC: I've found out how old you are – and I can tell the guests tonight, at your big surprise party at the big posh house.

ERNIE (*impressed*): A big surprise party at a big posh house?

ERIC: Hadn't you heard? *I'm* not going to tell

	you. All the drink and food you can consume.
ERNIE:	All laid on?
ERIC:	It could develop into one of those later on. You never really know – all depends if you play your cards right.
ERNIE:	A big posh party just for me?
ERIC:	Yes, if you will let me tell the ladies and gentlemen in the audience, and your fan in Rotherham, how old you are.
ERNIE:	You're joking.
ERIC:	Not with this material I'm not, no.
ERNIE:	All right then – you can tell the ladies and gentlemen, and my fan in Rotherham, how old I am.
ERIC:	Ladies and gentlemen in the audience – and your fan in Rotherham – Ernie today is sixty-three.
ERNIE:	No I'm *not* sixty-three!
ERIC (*handing him a paper*):	And that's the address for the big posh party in the big posh house. All the food and drink you can eat, free.
ERNIE:	That's *my* house? That's where *I* live!!
ERIC:	Well, I told you it was a surprise, didn't I?[5]

The television shows did not depend only upon this sort of cross-talk; the pair had famous guest stars off whom they could score, as well as unmolested musical guests; and periodically they retreated to their 'flat' for quieter sketches in which they reminisced about a fictitious past. This format should seem familiar – it is, very loosely, that of *Band Waggon*. A major feature of the show was the Ernie Wise 'plays' which for example starred Glenda Jackson as Cleopatra, or Frank Finlay as Casanova, with Eric Morecambe generally undermining the proceedings.

What is particularly interesting is the way they solved the problems of handling what for the most part is Variety-style material on television. Instead of fitting themselves into television's requirements, they deliberately created the illusion that the viewer was watching a stage performance.

John Ammonds: 'Since the ATV shows they always worked on a sort of stage in front of the audience, even though it's television. Everybody else works on the studio floor, but they had eighteen-inch rostra everywhere – which meant great problems because you have to build everything up and the cameras are working higher up. Eventually we had to raise the entire working area of the studio to avoid having to keep striking and resetting sets on the raised areas.'

Their insistence on the rostrum paid off in two ways; firstly, the cameras tended to work slightly lower than on other shows, and Morecambe and Wise could work *over* the cameras to the audience. (The central camera, covering the scene in medium long shot, was usually just below Wise's eye-level; the other two, one on each side, worked from distinctly below eye level. In ordinary shows, the tendency is for cameras to work at the eye-level of the shortest person, or, if one character is seated, at his eye-level.) On seeing the shows, this technique, aided by the use of 'wings' on the stage area and a curtain near the front of the stage in front of which they sometimes worked, gives the illusion that one is watching a stage performance from a seat in the stalls. (They worked almost exclusively to the studio audience, where most artists work to the camera.) The other function of the rostrum is less immediately obvious, but psychologically important: when Morecambe stamped on the stage it *sounded* like a wooden stage – studio floors are of course solid.

For most of the 1970s they were the top Light Entertainment team – Christmas Day would have seemed incomplete without their show – and they were at the height of their popularity when they did their last show for the BBC at Christmas 1977.

It had been a long-running joke that they were really a down-at-heel act who hired guests without paying them and performed rubbish (particularly the Ernie Wise plays). One of their exchanges sums it up neatly:

ERNIE:	You're making us look like a cheap music-hall act.
ERIC:	But we *are* a cheap music-hall act!

The BBC shows, although they had high production values, somehow managed not to undermine this premise; their subsequent ITV shows looked too glossy and were never quite so successful. In the BBC shows Morecambe and Wise succeeded brilliantly in capturing the spirit of the best in Variety and transferring it to the medium of television; just as Wall, Dodd and Dawson have, each in their own way, carried on the spirit of Variety.

Finale

In the course of this book we have seen how the Victorian music-hall grew out of the public houses to become a highly organized business, the main source of entertainment for the working classes; how the revision of the law broke music-hall away from food and drink to make it a purely theatrical entertainment – Variety; and how Variety itself survived for forty years against the competition from newer forms of entertainment.

In any survey of Variety the performers inevitably take first place, and here apologies are due to the many artists who could not be included because of lack of space. The people behind the scenes should not be forgotten; they played a vital part in making it the foremost form of popular entertainment in the beginning of the period, and keeping it going against the rival attractions.

However the performers, supported by the professional background created by the managers, were the essential part of Variety. They were a special breed; despite the rigours of touring and the hard work needed to reach any sort of position – let alone the top of the bill – they gave themselves wholeheartedly to their work. Most of them seem to have loved every minute of it – which is not so surprising when you consider that no-one in their right minds would pick a profession like that simply as a way to earn a living. Whether training animals, juggling, performing acrobatic tricks, singing, dancing or – most difficult of all – standing in cold blood in front of an audience and persuading it to laugh – they were all driven by a love of performing and an affection for their business.

For most of them it was all the world they knew, for it was necessarily an enclosed sort of life – performing, travelling, performing . . . and to many of them the anecdotes of their adventures on- and off-stage sum up their lives in the business. Having to create their own material, and ultimately being responsible to themselves for their own success or failure, they had perforce a strength of character which communicated itself over the footlights to the audiences for whom a weekly outing to this glamorous world of entertainment was an escape from drab and often depressing lives.

Television is the most usually named culprit when performers discuss the death of Variety; but the reasons why television (which in those days was black-and-white with nineteen-inch screens the maximum size) could overcome the attractions of live performances are more complex. Variety itself was by the end of the 1950s a tired format; at its peak it provided glamour within easy reach of those whose lives were hard and who had few luxuries. With the growth of general affluence and the increased availability of luxuries such as holidays in Spain and Greece the illusion of Variety lost its special magic.

By the return of depressed times and high unemployment in the 1980s, it would have been impossible for the old Variety halls to have continued even in the unlikely event that Variety could have appealed to the new generation who were victims of the cycle of history. The similarities between the 1980s and the 1930s are far less than the differences, and in the bitter atmosphere of modern times the particular happy-go-lucky appeal of Variety would have little place.

But though Variety as a major format can never return, its influence is widespread. Many of today's entertainers on television and the stage, and to a lesser extent on radio and in films, are the descendants in style of the top performers of the Variety period; and even though much modern comedy has sprung from other roots there runs through it the tradition of music-hall and Variety humour. Even the old jokes, when rested for long enough, become new to a new generation; and to the extent that much Variety humour grew out of the British character in its various regional manifestations, it will always be part and parcel of British comedy.

The final tribute to Variety performers is this: that the best of those whose acts survive on films and records are still effective – the humour as amusing, the songs as enjoyable, the sheer personality communicating itself across thirty-plus years. Because there were many artists who did not record or make films, the view obtained from these sources is necessarily unbalanced; but even so the appeal is sufficient to make original copies of music-hall and Variety records collectors' items, and there have been numerous re-issues on LP. Through this legacy it is possible to gain a glimpse of the past – the warmth, the vitality, and the popular appeal that characterized the best of Variety.

Variety was something special, run by and performed by special people; if the show really did 'go better second house' it was because of the eternal optimism and dedication of the performers who made it do so.

Glossary

The terms in this Glossary were sometimes used rather loosely within the Variety profession. My definitions reflect the usage of the period, but are often more precise than was normal in order to clarify the use of these terms throughout the book.

Act 1. The regular format of the performances given by a music-hall or Variety artist or group of artists. 2. An artist or group of artists when spoken of in relation to their performances.

Act show Term used principally in broadcasting to differentiate shows with a collection of unrelated acts from 'comedy-team shows' (sketches etc presented by a small regular team) and *situation comedies* (q.v.).

Adagio act An acrobatic act, usually without props such as bars, rings or trapezes etc, in which the movements are choreographed to music in a balletic style.

Bill 1. (noun) – a notice listing the performers in a theatrical show. 2. (abstract noun) – the running order of a Variety or similar show. 3. (verb) – to place a performer's name on a notice, placard or display.

Cabaret A small number of acts presented in a hotel, restaurant or *night-club* (q.v.), either on the floor or a small stage not usually having a proscenium or scenery; entrance was not usually charged in a hotel or restaurant, the cost of the performers being recovered from the sale of food and drink. Associated with a richer and more sophisticated audience than *Variety* or *Music-Hall*.

Cine-variety A small number of acts presented in a cinema as part of the supporting programme to the main film.

Circuit a number of theatres, usually in different towns, owned by one firm.

Concert party An unsophisticated, often genteel, type of show presented, often at seaside resorts and sometimes on the sands, by a small number of performers who would sing or appear in simple sketches in various groupings. The performers were usually dressed in pierrot costumes.

Double-act Two, usually comic, performers, who although one may be the evident leader and one the support, are equally important to the familiar presentation of the act and are usually billed equally.

House 1. The individual evening (as opposed to matinée) performance of a show on a particular day – e.g., first house, second house. 2. The audience, in terms of numbers rather than response.

Imitator / Impressionist A performer who imitates several other well known artists, or sometimes birds or animals.

Impersonator A performer who works in the clothes of the opposite sex.

Intimate Revue (Also 'Little Revue'); an unspectacular revue, with only a few performers, presenting sketches and songs aimed at an intelligent and educated audience.

Knockabout act A comic act, usually of two performers, dependent principally upon robust physical comedy with falls; also known as 'slapstick'.

Music-hall An entertainment consisting of a collection of disparate acts, usually presented in a hall with a small stage and facilities for serving food and drink to the audience; the term is often used interchangeably with *Variety* (q.v.) but in this book is used to mean this kind of theatrical 'act show' up to 1918.

Music Hall The theatre or premises where the above form of entertainment would take place.

Musical Comedy A theatrical presentation having a plot which provides the framework for a number of songs and musical items.

Night-club A restaurant, also presenting cabaret, which by theoretically limiting entrance to members and their guests is unrestricted by the licensing laws and can serve alcohol late at night and well into the small hours of the morning. Normally patronized by relatively rich clientele.

PA 'Public Address' – electronic amplification of the artists on a stage; the more rarely used term 'Sound Reinforcement' would be more accurate.

Patter Spoken comedy material.

Revue A theatrical show, either with or without a simple plot, consisting of a number of scenes in which the cast would perform in various groupings. Often more sophisticated and spectacular than *Variety*, but sometimes consisting of a show constructed like a Variety bill but graced with a title. Unlike Variety, revues always had titles.

Road show A theatrical entertainment, often similar to a normal Variety bill, which toured various theatres as a package – as opposed to the cast being split up and appearing in different locations each week – and had a title. Often mounted by the leading performer.

Routine A regular section of an act.

Situation Comedy A broadcast show, usually running half-an-hour, in which a familiar set of characters appear in more-or-less naturalistic – often domestic – situations which vary from week to week within a constant structure but are not usually serialized.

Speciality act An act, usually supporting rather than starring, not principally dependent on spoken comedy, songs (straight or comic), musical performance or straight dancing. Always a loosely defined category, it includes character dancers, magicians, acrobats and other physical performers, etc.

Sketch 1. (obsolete) – any short (up to one act) dramatic performance, whether comic or serious, the term usually being used in the context of a music-hall bill. 2. (from the 1920s) – a comic performance including dialogue involving three or more performers, or two where one is only an assistant to the main performer rather than being of equal importance (as in a *double-act*, q.v.).

Stand-up Comic A solo verbal comedian, performing either a monologue as a particular character, or simply telling a string of unrelated jokes.

Stooge Supporting performer to a comedian; usually presenting a dim character off whom the comedian can score; *cf straight man* (q.v.) who was usually at least as smart as the comic.

Straight Man Supporting performer to a comedian (see also *stooge*); also known as the 'feed' since he feeds the comic the lines to which the comic can respond.

Vaudeville Though strictly meaning a largely musical type of entertainment in the general manner of Variety, the term is occasionally used in Britain as interchangeable with *Variety*. In America the term is used almost exclusively instead of Variety or music-hall. Originally French, meaning a lighter type of song.

Variety A theatrical entertainment consisting of a collection of disparate acts; unlike *Music-Hall* (q.v.) Variety is not associated with the consumption of food and drink in the auditorium. Often used interchangeably with *Music-Hall*, but used in this book to mean this sort of entertainment after 1919.

Working-men's club A membership club, operated by and for members of the 'working classes', which provides entertainment, although this is often of secondary importance to the consumption of food and alcohol.

Notes

INTRODUCTION TO NOTES

As well as giving extra comments on the text, these notes indicate the origin of quoted material. The following abbreviations are used:

LCP: Lord Chamberlain's Archive: the material is taken from scripts submitted for a licence. The initials LCP ('Lord Chamberlain's Plays') are followed by the year and the box number in which the script is kept and by which it may be ordered: e.g. LCP 1936/25. This material is available to holders of the appropriate British Library Readers' Tickets.

BBC: BBC Radio transmission: the title of the programme and the transmission date will be given. Material quoted may be from either script or transcript.

Gram: indicates that the material is quoted from a gramophone record. The make and number will be quoted, where known. Recording date is given, where known. Only original catalogue numbers are given; most of this material has of course long since been deleted.

Principal sources for the research were: the author's interviews (listed in the acknowledgements); the magazine *The Performer*; *The Stage* Yearbooks; *Radio Times*; BBC Written Archives Centre at Caversham; and a wide range of published material such as books, films and records.

PROLOGUE

1. 10 Geo II c 28 (i.e., chapter 28 of the statutes passed during the 10th year of the reign of George II. All these statutes can be inspected at the Westminster Central Reference Library; the reference should be quoted.)
2. 6 and 7 Vict c 68.
3. The Disorderly Houses Act 1751 (25 Geo 2 c 36): 'An Act for the better preventing Thefts and Robberies, and for regulating Places of Public Entertainment, and Punishing Persons keeping Disorderly Houses.'
4. 41 and 42 Vict c 32.
5. Published in 1951 by W. H. Allen.

INTERLUDE

1. See *The Story of the Original Dixieland Jazz Band* by H. O. Brunn, published by Sidgwick and Jackson, 1961.
2. Gram: Columbia 870 (2-3-21).

CHAPTER 1

1. Alhambra, Balham Hippodrome, Battersea Palace, the Bedford, Bow Palace, Brixton Empress, Camberwell Empire, Camberwell Palace, Canning Town Imperial, Canterbury, Chelsea Palace, Chiswick Empire, Clapham Grand, Coliseum, Collins', Crouch End Hippodrome, Croydon Empire, Croydon Hippodrome, Ealing Hippodrome, East Ham Palace, Edmonton Empire, Empire Leicester Square, Euston, Finsbury Park Empire, Forester's, Golders Green Hippodrome, Greenwich Palace, Hackney Empire, Hammersmith Palace, London Hippodrome, Holborn Empire, Ilford Hippodrome, Islington Empire, Kilburn Empire, Kingston Empire, Lewisham Hippodrome, Metropolitan Edgware Road, Mile End Empire, New Cross Empire, Middlesex, Opera House, Oxford, Palace, Palladium, London Pavilion, Peckham Hippodrome, Penge Hippodrome, Poplar Hippodrome, Putney Hippodrome, Queen's Poplar, Richmond Hippodrome, Rotherhithe Hippodrome, Sadler's Wells, Shepherd's Bush Empire, Shoreditch Empire, Shoreditch Olympia, Stoke Newington, South London, Stratford Empire, Surrey, Tottenham Palace, Victoria Palace, Waltham Green Granville, Walthamstow Palace, Willesden Hippodrome, Wimbledon Theatre, Wood Green Empire, Woolwich Hippodrome, Theatre Royal Woolwich. (Information from an article by Fred Russell in *The Performer*, 1-7-43. By 1943 there were only 30.)

2. London Hippodrome, Finsbury Park Empire, New Cross Empire, Stratford Empire, Liverpool Empire, Liverpool Olympia, Glasgow Empire, Glasgow Coliseum, King's Theatre Southsea, Edinburgh Empire, Newcastle Empire, New Empire Cinema Newcastle, Leeds Empire, Nottingham Empire, Sheffield Empire, Birmingham Empire, Grand Theatre Birmingham, Summerhill Palace Birmingham, Cardiff Empire, Bradford Alhambra, Olympia Cardiff, Swansea Empire, Newport Empire, Hull Palace.

3. Coliseum, Alhambra, Stoll Picture Theatre Kingsway, Manchester Hippodrome, Shepherd's Bush Empire, Hackney Empire, Palace Leicester, Chatham Empire, Bristol Hippodrome, Chiswick Empire, Wood Green Empire, Ardwick Empire, Alexandra Stoke Newington, Bedminster Hippodrome, Floral Hall Leicester,

Picture House Chatham, Stoll
Picture Theatre Newcastle.
4. 15 and 16 Geo 5 c 50.
5. Reported in *The Performer*, 2-9-20;
she was not named.
6. 14 and 15 Geo 5 c 38.

CHAPTER 2
1. Gram: G&T GC2–2351 (1901).
2. Internal cut made here.
3. BBC: *The Old Town Hall*,
9-10-41.
4. Gram: HMV B 4264.
5. Although, interestingly, she looked
not so much like Davis actually did
by that time, but like the Bette
Davis of the 1940s, but aged
differently.
6. Gram: Zonophone 578 (1911).
7. Unidentified film.
8. Internal cut made at this point.
9. Gram: Columbia 5216/7 (1928).
10. Gram: Columbia 9205 (1926).
11. As above.
12. BBC: *Happidrome*, 13-8-41.
13. Gram: Imperial-Broadcast 4010
(1934).
14. Gram: Imperial 1559 (Feb. 1926).

CHAPTER 3
1. Internal cut made at this point.
2. Gram: HMV B 2120 (31-8-25).
3. In *The Golden Age Of Wireless*,
p. 80.
4. Gram: Broadcast X-6 (October
1928).

CHAPTER 4
1. Remembered by Ronnie Tate.
2. LCP 1931/28; *The Football Match*
by Fred Karno and Charles
Baldwin.
3. Gram: Regal-Zonophone MR 1120
(10-10-33).
4. LCP 1929/5; *Adventures of Parker
P.C.* (Austin and Ridgewell). (The
sketch dates back to at least 1910
and was *re*licensed in 1929.)
5. Gram: Broadcast 944 (1932).
6. This version is drawn from Gram:
Sterno 851 (24-9-31) and BBC:
Festival of Variety (6-5-51).
7. Three extracts, run together, from
a composite version based on the
original script, Gram: Columbia
DX 573 (25-9-36), a short film
version of the sketch (unidentified),
and BBC: *Music Hall*, 1941
(performed by Ronnie Tate).

8. Reconstructed from Ronnie Tate's
memory and his performance of
part of it in BBC: *Workers'
Playtime*, 11-10-41.

CHAPTER 5
1. Information given by the veteran
music-hall artist Fred Russell in the
BBC programme *Rats to You*,
5-12-38.
2. The early history of the VAF given
here is largely drawn from an
article by Fred Russell in *The
Performer*, 2-7-42.
3. History of the VABF from an
article by Albert Voyce in *The
Performer*, 21-4-26.
4. Reports in *The Performer*, 24-4-24,
7-5-24, 28-5-24, 7-1-25.
5. Article in *The Performer*, 21-4-27.

CHAPTER 6
1. Act 2 Sc. 2; and Act 3 Sc. 2.
2. Quoted in *The Performer*, 5-10-44.
3. Gram: Columbia 1804 (1911).
4. Gram: American Columbia 935-D
(14-3-27).
5. Gram: Broadcast 3275 (1932).
6. Internal cut made at this point.
7. This extract is combined from
BBC: *Music Hall*, 13-12-41 and
8-7-44: and Gram: Parlophone F
1023 (1937).
8. Gram: Piccadilly 575 (1930).
9. BBC: *Music Hall*, 1-10-43.
10. Gram: Parlophone E-6009 (1927).
11. BBC: *The Crazy Gang Story*,
3-11-81.
12. Internal cut made at this point.
13. Gram: Columbia DB 1042
(14-1-33).
14. Internal cut made at this point.
15. Internal cut made at this point.
16. Gram: Columbia FB 1226
(26-11-35).

CHAPTER 7
1. The family name was Parnell;
'Russell' was a stage name.
2. BBC: *Hoop-La*, 3-4-45.
3. Internal cut made at this point.
4. LCP 1934/20, *The 6th London
Palladium Crazy Show*. The
attribution of some of the lines is
not clear in the script, so I have
taken the liberty of guessing.
5. Information from the son of
Franklyn Davies, Kenney's stooge.

6. LCP 1936/36, *O-Kay For Sound*, by
Weston and Lee.
7. Thomas saw Buchanan in a
pantomime in Birmingham, not at
the Newport Empire.
8. Quoted in *Working The Halls* by
Peter Honri, published by Futura
in 1973.

CHAPTER 8
1. Gram: Zonophone 5997 (16-10-31).
2. Gram: Columbia 5034 (1-3-28)
(2nd verse, 1st chorus).
3. Gram: Zonophone 5407 (22-4-29).
4. Gram: Decca F 3287 (21-11-32).
5. Gram: Columbia DX 685 (29-3-35).
Mr Drage ran one of the first firms
to sell furniture by the then socially
unacceptable method of 'hire purchase'. The 'Polish Corridor', a
(relatively) narrow strip of land
between Germany and Danzig, was
Poland's only access to the sea; it
was a thorn in Germany's flesh.
Lady Oxford (Margot Tennant) was
the wife of H. H. Asquith, the
Prime Minister 1906–1916 and
Leader of the Liberal Party until
1926; she was well known as an
authoress and in society. Hore-
Belisha, the Minister for Transport
1934–1937, was responsible for the
first widespread pedestrian crossings, whose warning signs – orange
globes on striped poles – were
known as 'Belisha Beacons' at least
until the introduction of Zebra
Crossings in 1951 and flashing beacons in 1952.
6. Gram: Parlophone R 2391 (3-9-37).
7. Gram: HMV B 3683 (16-10-30).
8. Gram: Regal-Zonophone MR 2199
(27-9-36) (Last four lines from a different chorus to the rest.)
9. HMV C 2625/7 (issued on a long-
playing record on World Records
SH 170).

CHAPTER 9
1. *The Stage Yearbook*, 1921–5.
2. *The Performer*, 15-7-31.

CHAPTER 10
1. 'Randy': loud-tongued; boisterous;
disorderly: riotous (New English
Dictionary, 1932).
2. *The Performer*, 20-2-24.

CHAPTER 11

1. Details of the 1919 Contract – and most of the legal information in this chapter – from *The Law Relating to Theatres, Music-Halls, and other Public Entertainments* by Sidney C. Isaacs; published by Stevens and Sons Ltd, 1927.
2. 42 & 43 Vict c 34; as amended by the Dangerous Performances Act 1897 – 60 & 61 Vict c 52.
3. 11 & 12 Geo 5, c 51.
4. 11 & 12 Geo 5, c ciii.
5. Under the Local Government Act, 1888; 51 & 52 Vict c 41.
6. Under the Criminal Justice Act, 1925 (15 & 16 Geo 5, c 86) section 43.
7. Published by MacGibbon & Kee in 1967.
8. 'Barney's Bull'; Australian slang expression meaning 'exhausted' (but usually expressed in different words).
9. *First London Palladium Crazy Show*, LCP 1933/22.
10. *cf* the *Romans in Britain* row – a private prosecution brought against an uncensored play.
11. Reported in *The Performer*, 10--6-25.
12. See *Film Censorship* by Guy Phelps (Gollancz, 1975).
13. *'Appy 'Arf 'Our*, a revue by Leon Cortez and Hal Chrichton. LCP 1938/12.

CHAPTER 12

1. Gram: Brunswick 1106 (1931).
2. Internal cut made here.
3. Gram: Columbia DX 216 (11-12-30).
4. Story told by Billie Carlyle in her book *Claude Dampier, Mrs Gibson, and Me* (privately published).
5. BBC: *Garrison Theatre*, 2-11-40.
6. Gram: Broadcast 429 (*c.* May, 1929).
7. Unidentified broadcast.
8. LCP 1916/33; *Schoolmaster and Scholar* by Will Hay.
9. Nor on the records; Brian Rust's discography *British Music Hall on Record* credits them, but this is wrong. In any event, Moffat was nine, and his voice unbroken, when the first records were made. The records were Columbia 9689, 5695, (both 1929), and DX 558 (1933).

10. LCP 1938/63; *The Fourth Form at St Michael's*, or *On The Way To Cambridge*, by Will Hay.
11. Much of the biographical information is drawn from *Good Morning Boys – Will Hay* by Ray Seaton and Roy Martin (Barrie and Jenkins, 1978) which includes details of all of the films. The sketch quoted near the end of the book has been reconstructed from Cyril Platt's memory and is not accurate (*cf* LCP 1938–63, above). the book quotes Charles Hawtrey – who worked with Hay in several films and was later a regular member of the *Carry On* team – as describing the *Carry On* films as 'painfully slow' by comparison. Incidentally, *Ask A Policeman* was gruesomely remade in 1983, with Cannon and Ball, as *The Boys in Blue*.

CHAPTER 13

1. This quote from an article by Johnny Cooper in *Call Boy*, Spring 1981; all other quotes by Cooper from an interview with the author.

CHAPTER 14

1. Internal cut made here.
2. Unidentified film.
3. Gram: unidentified.
4. BBC: *Garrison Theatre*, 2-11-40.
5. Both routines remembered by George Bolton.
6. BBC: *Music Hall*, 3-9-43.
7. Internal cut made here.
8. Internal cut made here.
9. Gram: Regal-Zonophone MR 2837/8, live performance, August 1938.
10. Gram: Pye NPT 19026, live performance 30-11-57 at the Metropolitan Edgware Road.
11. Gram: Pye NPT 19026.
12. Gram: HMV BD 1022/3, live performance 12-10-42 at the Finsbury Park Empire.
13. Gram: HMV BD 980/1, live performance November 1941 for war workers.
14. Gram: HMV BD 883/5, live performance November 1940 for a forces audience.

CHAPTER 15

1. Liveing to D.P., 23-9-31. (BBC internal memo).

2. Controller (Programmes) to D.F.D., D.V., D.O.B. & Regional Directors, 3-2-37 (BBC internal memo).
3. Internal cut made here.
4. Internal cut made here.
5. Gram: Columbia 5067 (1-10-28).
6. Reported in *The Performer*, 20-1-38.
7. BBC: *Monday Night at Seven*, 2-5-38.
8. Excerpts from the last show of the first series were issued on HMV BD 693/5.
9. George Inns, the sound-effects man (Junior Programme Engineer); many years later producer of *The Black and White Minstrel Show* for BBC TV.
10. BBC: *Band Waggon*, 18-1-39.

CHAPTER 16

1. Gram: HMV BD 770/2, live performance, Finsbury Park Empire.
2. BBC: *Workers' Playtime*, 12-7-41.
3. Gram: Decca F 7320; live performance at the Argyle Birkenhead, 13-11-39.
4. Gram: Columbia FB 2960 (1943).
5. Published in 1978 by MacDonald and Jane's.
6. Report in *The Performer*, 18-4-40.

CHAPTER 17

1. ORBS recording, 1946/8.
2. LCP 1919/15; *Come Over* by Arthur Lucan.
3. LCP 1941/16; *Old Mother Riley and her daughter Kitty* by Lucan and McShane.
4. Unidentified film clip, remembered (perhaps approximately) by the author.
5. Quoted in *Radio Comedy* by Arthur Frank Wertheim, Oxford University Press (New York), 1979.
6. BBC: *Music Hall*, 22-8-42 (not the first appearance of this routine).
7. BBC: *Music Hall*, 21-6-42.
8. Gram: Parlophone R 789 (Sept. 1930).
9. Gram: Columbia FB 1827 (11-11-37).

CHAPTER 18

1. Memorandum from John Watt, 15-11-39.
2. Ted Kavanagh: *Tommy Handley* (Hodder and Stoughton, 1949).

3. T.T.F.N. = 'Ta-ta for now'.
4. BBC: *ITMA*, 24-6-43.
5. BBC: *Garrison Theatre*, 13-4-40.
6. Ibid.
7. Gram: Columbia FB 2717 (live recording of stage show, 1941).
8. Quoted in a memo from R. Macermot to D.P.P., 13-3-43.

CHAPTER 19
1. Published by Robson Books in 1974.

CHAPTER 20
1. BBC: *Music Hall*, 10-1-42.
2. BBC: *Garrison Theatre*, 20-4-40.
3. BBC: *Festival of Variety*, 6-5-51.
4. Internal cut made here.
5. BBC: *Variety Bandbox*, 5-2-50.
6. BBC: *Music Hall*, 31-5-51.
7. BBC: *Calling All Forces*, 31-12-51.
8. BBC: *Music Hall*, 11-5-46.
9. From a reconstruction of his act he performed in the ITV programme *Max*, 14-1-81.
10. BBC: *Music Hall*, 29-3-41.
11. BBC: *Music Hall*, 17-8-46.
12. BBC: *Variety Bandbox*, 29-1-50.

CHAPTER 21
1. Gram: Beltona 1923 (1933).
2. Internal cut made here.
3. Gram: Beltona 1440 (1929).

CHAPTER 22
1. Report in *The Performer*, 3-4-52.
2. LCP 1934-41; *Coram and Jerry*.
3. Short film *Arthur Prince and Jim in a Ventriloquial Sketch* made in 1935 for the Conservative and Unionist Films Association. The section quoted was a regular part of the act.
4. BBC: *Music Hall*, 29-12-45.

CHAPTER 25
1. Published by Weidenfeld and Nicolson, 1981.

CHAPTER 27
1. Gram: Regal-Zonophone MR 2861, live performance at the Feldman Theatre, Blackpool, August 1938.
2. LCP 1952/49; *Randle's Scandals*.
3. Remembered by Joe Gladwin.
4. BBC: *Music Hall*, 13-10-45 (based on a stage routine).
5. BBC: broadcast from a live performance of *Strike It Again*, recorded 28-12-44, broadcast 5-1-45.
6. LCP 1957/36; *The Tony Hancock Show*.
7. Broadcast 28-3-54.
8. Remembered by James Casey.
9. Remembered by James Casey.
10. From the act as performed by James Casey at the Royal Variety Performance, 14-11-82.

CHAPTER 28
1. Published in 1976 by Robson Books and the BBC.
2. Published by Hutchinson in 1972.
3. BBC: *Hancock's Half-Hour:* 'The Childhood Sweetheart', 6-10-59.
4. BBC: *The Goon Show:* 'The Battle of Spion Kop', 29-12-58.

CHAPTER 29
1. What he *actually* said was, 'Let's be frank about it, some of our people have never had it so good' (20 July 1957).
2. Story quoted in the book *Twenty Years of British Record Charts* edited by Tony Jasper; published by Queen Anne Press, 1976.
3. Rock fans regard Cliff Richard as having had early promise and betrayed it; pop fans regard him as having made great progress from his crude beginnings. Take your pick.

INTERLUDE
1. Story from Peter Copeland, who was playing the records on this occasion.
2. Internal cut made here.
3. BBC TV: *The Good Old Days*, 25-6-80.
4. BBC TV: *The Les Dawson Show*, 18-2-84.
5. BBC TV: *The Morecambe and Wise Show*, 2-3-73.

Appendix 1: Books

This appendix is not an attempt to compile a complete bibliography, but is a list of 'further reading' for those who would like to pursue particular aspects of the subject in more detail. Many of these books were used for background research on the present book. They are listed in a loose sort of subject order, with publishers, date and ISBN number where appropriate. They are hardback unless stated (pbk = paperback). Many of them are of course long since out of print, but are listed as they may be available from libraries or second-hand.

MUSIC-HALL AND VARIETY

The Melodies Linger On by W. McQueen-Pope. W. H. Allen 1951. *The classic textbook on Victorian and Edwardian music-hall.*

Idols of the Halls by H. Chance Newton. Heath Cranton 1928; facsimile reprint issued 1975, 0 7158 1047 2. *First-hand account of the Edwardian period, although heavily laden with unfunny anecdotes.*

The Northern Music Hall by G. J. Mellor. Frank Graham 1970. 0 900409 85 1. *Masses of fine detail, carefully researched.*

British Music Hall by Raymond Mander and Joe Mitchinson. Gentry Books 1974, 0 85614 036 8. *Many photographs and a brief review of the whole period.*

British Music Hall – An Illustrated Who's Who from 1850 to the Present Day by Roy Busby. Paul Elek 1976, 0 236 400533 3. *Useful encyclopaedia, although with some odd omissions and a number of mistakes.*

The Performer's Who's Who in Variety (*The Performer* magazine 1950) *Lists most performers in the profession in 1950; compiled as a professional directory. Very rare.*

Music Hall in Britain by David Cheshire. David and Charles 1974, 0 715 36212 7. *A review of the 'infrastructure' of the business. Includes plans of several famous halls.*

The Grand Order of Water Rats – A Legacy of Laughter by Charlie Chester. W. H. Allen 1984, 0 491 03251 X. *Heavily anecdotal but interesting review of performers who were members of the GOWR.*

The Good Auld Days by Gordon Irving. Jupiter 1977, 0 904041 72 7. *A study of Scottish music-hall and Variety up to television.*

The House That Stoll Built by Felix Barker. Frederick Muller 1957. *History of the London Coliseum.*

The Lyceum by A. E. Wilson. Dennis Yates 1952.

Every Night at the London Palladium by Patrick Pilton. Robson 1976, 0 903895 77 3.

Top of the Bill – The Story of the London Palladium by Ian Bevan. Frederick Muller 1952.

The Law Relating to Theatres, Music Halls, and Other Places of Entertainment by Sidney C. Isaacs, BA, LlB. Stevens and Sons 1927. *Definitive textbook on theatrical law of the period. Rare.*

Banned! – A Review of Theatrical Censorship in Britain by Richard Findlator. Macgibbon and Kee 1967. *Mostly concerned with legitimate theatre; a study of the theatres under the Lord Chamberlain.*

The Secrets of Houdini by J. C. Cannell. Hutchinson *c* 1931. *Explanations of many big illusions.*

The Illustrated History of Magic, by Milbourne Christopher. Robert Hale and Co 1975, 0 7091 4814 3. *Gives details of many stage illusionists.*

I Can See Your Lips Moving by Valentine Vox. Kaye Ward 1981, 0 7182 5870 3. *History of ventriloquism.*

Funny Way to be a Hero by John Fisher. Frederick Muller 1973, 0 584 10097 3, pbk Paladin 1976, 0 586 08240 9. *Pen-portraits of many comedians; with script extracts.*

Make 'Em Laugh by Eric Midwinter. Allen and Unwin 1979, 0 04 792011 4. *A study of several important comedians.*

They Made us Laugh by Geoff J. Mellor. George Kelsall 1982, 0 9505577 4 9. *Photos and brief biographies of many music-hall comics.*

Fighting for a Laugh by Richard Fawkes. Macdonald and Jane's 1978, 0 354 04201 7. *History of ENSA and other entertainment for the forces in World War Two.*

Sweet Saturday Night by Colin MacInnes. Macgibbon and Kee 1967. *Sociological examination of music-hall and popular songs.*

British Music Hall on Record by Brian Rust. General Gramophone Publications 1979, 0 902470 12 4. *Discography of many music-hall and Variety artists, giving dates and details of original 78s. Some odd omissions – but see next entry – and numerous tiny mistakes; but invaluable to the collector.*

London Musical Shows on Record 1897–1976 by Brian Rust. General Gramophone Publications 1977, 0 902470 07 8. *Includes discographies of numerous Variety performers who also took part in musical shows – including Tate, Askey, Flanagan and Allen, Robey.*

The Complete Entertainment Discography by Brian Rust with Allen G. Debus. Arlington House (USA) 1973, 0 87000 150 7. *Hardly 'complete' but includes several entries of interest, including Gracie Fields who is not in the previous two books listed here.*

Twenty Years of British Record Charts by Tony Jasper. Queen Anne Press 1976, 0 0362 00263 0. *Includes details of the early years of pop and rock.*

BROADCASTING

The History of Broadcasting in the United Kingdom by Asa Briggs. Vol 1: **The Birth of Broadcasting**, Oxford University Press 1961, 0 19 212926 0. Vol 2: **The Golden Age of Broadcasting**, O.U.P. 1965, 0 19 212930 9. Vol 3: **The War of Words**, O.U.P. 1970, 0 19 212956 2. Vol 4: **Sound and Vision**, O.U.P. 1979, 0 19 212967 8. *The definitive treatise on broadcasting up to 1955; very long and detailed; includes the history of Variety Department.*

Laughter in the Air by Barry Took. Robson/BBC 1976, 0 903895 78 1 and 0 563 17157 9. *'An informal history of radio comedy' – includes mention of all the important shows, with script extracts.*

Radio Comedy by Arthur Frank Wertheim. O.U.P. New York 1979, 0 19 502481 8. *History of American radio comedy; detailed, with script extracts.*

The Biggest Aspidistra in the World by Peter Black. BBC 1972, 0 563 12154 8. *History of early radio.*

The Mirror in the Corner by Peter Black. Hutchinson 1972, 0 09 110100 X. *History of television, particularly ITV, in 1950s and 1960s.*

The Goon Show Companion by Roger Wilmut and Jimmy Grafton. Robson 1976, 0 903 895 64 1; pbk Sphere 1977, 0 7221 9182 0 and 0 7221 9193 6. *History of the Goon Show, with complete list of all transmissions.*

ITMA 1939–1948 by Francis Worsely, Vox Mundi 1948. *The story of ITMA by its producer. See also 'Tommy Handley' below in biography section.*

for **Hancock's Half-Hour** see under 'Tony Hancock' below.

for **The Morecambe and Wise Show** see under 'Morecambe and Wise' below.

for radio and TV scripts see next section.

SCRIPTS

Frank Muir Presents the Book of Comedy Sketches, Elm Tree 1982, 0 241 10852 7; pbk 0 241 10870 5. *Includes Harry Tate's Motoring. The Will Hay sketch included is from one of the records and is not as performed on stage.*

I Scream for Ice Cream by Gyles Brandreth. Eyre Methuen 1974, 0 413 72340 4; pbk 0 413 32350. *Extracts from pantomime scripts.*

The ITMA Years, Woburn 1974, 0 7130 0101 1; pbk Woburn-Futura 0 86007 245 2. *Six complete ITMA scripts by Ted Kavanagh.*

Hancock – Four Scripts for Television by Alan Simpson and Ray Galton. André Deutsch 1961; pbk Corgi 1962.

Hancock's Half-hour Scripts by Alan Simpson and Ray Galton. Woburn 1974, 0 7130 0087 2; pbk Woburn-Futura 1975, 0 86997 246 0. *Six complete TV scripts with frame enlargements.*

The Goon Show Scripts, Woburn 1972, 0 7130 0076 7; pbk Sphere 1973, 0 7221 6079 8. *Selection of complete scripts by Spike Milligan.*

More Goon Show Scripts, Woburn 1973; pbk Sphere 1974, 0 7221 6077 1.

The Book of The Goons, Robson 1974, 0 903895 26 9. *More scripts plus ephemera.*

The Best of Morecambe and Wise by Eddie Braben. Woburn 1974, 0 7130 0133 X; pbk Futura 1975, 0 8600 7244 4. *Sketches from the BBC TV shows.*

Son of 'Curried Eggs' compiled by Roger Wilmut. Methuen 1984, 0 413 55170 9. *Includes a radio Hancock's Half-Hour, Hancock's Car'.*

BIOGRAPHY

Arthur Askey
  Before Your Very Eyes by Arthur Askey. Woburn 1975, 0 703 00134 8; pbk Coronet 1977, 0 340 21985 8.
Peter Brough
  Educating Archie by Peter Brough. Paul, 1955.
Douglas Byng
  As You Were by Douglas Byng. Duckworth 1970, 0 7156 0543 7.

Charlie Chester
  The World is Full of Charlies by Charlie Chester. New English Library 1974.
Claude Dampier
  Claude Dampier, Mrs Gibson and Me by Billie Carlyle. Privately published by Billie Carlyle 1978.
Florence Desmond
  Florence Desmond, by Herself, Harrap 1953.
Phyllis Dixey
  The One and Only Phyllis Dixey by Philip Purser and Jenny Wilkes. Futura 1978 (pbk) 0 7088 1436 0.
Ken Dodd
  How Tickled I Am – A Celebration of Ken Dodd by Michael Billington. Elm Tree/Hamish Hamilton 1977, 0 241 89345 3.
Sid Field
  What a Performance! – A Life of Sid Field by John Fisher. Seeley, Service and Co 1975, 0 85422 113 1.
Gracie Fields
  Sing as We Go by Gracie Fields. Frederick Muller 1960.
Bud Flanagan
  My Crazy Life by Bud Flanagan. Frederick Muller 1961.
Lew and Leslie Grade, Bernard Delfont
  The Grades by Hunter Davies. Weidenfeld and Nicolson 1981, 0 297 77953 2.
Tony Hancock
  Tony Hancock 'Artiste' by Roger Wilmut. Eyre Methuen 1978, 0 413 386805; pbk 1983, 0 413 50820 X.
Tommy Handley
  Tommy Handley by Ted Kavanagh. Hodder and Stoughton 1949.
  That Man – A Memory of Tommy Handley by Bill Grundy. Elm Tree/ Hamish Hamilton 1976, 0 241 89344 5.
Will Hay
  Good Morning Boys – Will Hay, Master of Comedy by Ray Seaton and Roy Martin. Barrie & Jenkins 1978, 0 214 20554 1.
B. C. Hilliam ('Flotsam')
  Flotsam's Follies by B. C. Hilliam. Arthur Barron 1948.

Stanley Holloway
Wiv a Little Bit o' Luck by Stanley Holloway, as told to Dick Richards. Leslie Frewin 1967.

Dan Leno
The Funniest Man on Earth by Gyles Brandreth. Hamish Hamilton 1977, 0 241 89810 2.

Harry Lauder
Great Scot! by Gordon Irving. Leslie Frewin 1968, 0 09 089070 1.

Morecambe and Wise
Eric and Ernie – The Autobiography of Morecambe and Wise, W. H. Allen 1973, 0 491 01211 X; pbk Star Books 1974, 0 352 30000 0.
There's No Answer to That!, Barker 1981, 0 2131 6803 3; pbk Coronet 1982, 0 340 28442 0.

Sandy Powell
Can You Hear Me, Mother?, as told to Harry Stanley. Jupiter 1975, 0 904041 387.

George Robey
Looking Back On Life by George Robey. Constable 1953.
Prime Minister of Mirth by A. E. Wilson. Odhams 1956.

Max Wall
The Fool on the Hill by Max Wall. Quartet 1975, 0 7043 2080 0.

Jack Warner
Jack of All Trades by Jack Warner. W. H. Allen 1975, 0 491 10952 1.

Appendix 2: Records

There would be little point in attempting to list original 78 r.p.m. records, as these are now collectors' items (although with luck it is still possible to obtain Variety artists on 78s in second-hand and specialist record shops). For details of 78s see the Brian Rust discographies listed in Appendix 1.

This appendix lists a selection of LP records featuring music-hall and Variety artists; this does not claim to be a complete list, but includes most of the important releases on LP. Many of these records are out of print, but second-hand copies are sometimes to be found. Lack of space precludes a complete contents listing.

The emphasis in LP re-issues has tended to be on Victorian and Edwardian music-hall, but there are some re-issues of items by later performers. A warning: transfers of pre-electric recordings (pre-1925) have very often been done at incorrect speeds; in one or two cases the error is quite serious and the resulting effect is ridiculous.

FIDELIO ATL 4010
Famous Stars of the Music Hall – includes Harry Lauder, Little Tich, Marie Lloyd, Florrie Forde, Dan Leno.

DELTA TQD 3030/RHAPSODY RHA 6014
The Golden Age of Music-Hall – includes Gus Elen, Marie Lloyd, Dan Leno, George Robey, Little Tich.

DECCA ACL 1077
Golden Voices of the Music-Hall – includes Ella Shields, Nellie Wallace, Gus Elen, Albert Whelan.

MUSIC FOR PLEASURE MFP 1146
Great Days of the Music Hall – includes Billy Merson, Vesta Victoria, Harry Champion, Florrie Forde.

ARGO ZSW 536/6 (double album)
Let's all go to the Music Hall – includes George Jackley, Leslie Sarony, Harry Champion, Gus Elen, George Formby Sr, Dan Leno ('Mrs Kelly'), Marie Lloyd, George Robey, Harry Lauder, Chirgwin.

WORLD RECORDS SH 145
Music Hall to Variety – Vol 1: Matinée – includes George Robey, Florrie Forde, George Formby Sr, Harry Champion, G. H. Elliott (transferred at a seriously incorrect speed), Ella Shields.

WORLD RECORDS SH 149
Music Hall to Variety – Vol 2: First House – includes Harry Tate ('Motoring'), Lily Morris, Flotsam and Jetsam, Layton and Johnstone, Will Hay, Leslie Sarony, Norah Blaney and Gwen Farrar, Tommy Handley ('The Disorderly Room'), Billy Bennett, Douglas Byng.

WORLD RECORDS SH 150
Music Hall to Variety – Vol 3: Second House – includes Horace Kenney, Gracie Fields, Ronald Frankau, The Crazy Gang, Nellie Wallace, Stanley Holloway, Elsie and Doris Waters, Max Miller, Florence Desmond ('A Hollywood Party'), The Western Brothers, Robb Wilton ('The Home Guard').

WORLD RECORD CLUB SHB 22 (two discs)
Music Hall – Top of the Bill – includes Gus Elen, Marie Lloyd, Fred Emney Sr, Harry Lauder, Whit Cunliffe, George Formby Sr, Dan Leno, George Robey.

WORLD RECORDS SH 350
Playing the Halls – includes Harry Champion, Marie Lloyd, Dan Leno.

DECCA ACL 1170
 Stars Who Made the Music Hall – includes Gus Elen, Hetty King, Florrie Forde, Charles Coborn, George Jackley, Lily Morris, George Formby Jr, Billy Bennett, Billy Russell.

DECCA PA 81
 The World of Music Hall – includes Max Miller, Leslie Sarony, Florrie Forde, George Robey.

ASV ASA 5004
 Your Own – Your Very Own – includes Harry Champion, Marie Lloyd, Dan Leno ('Mrs Kelly'), George Formby Sr, Chirgwin, Harry Lauder, Lily Morris, G. H. Elliott.

AUSTRALIAN COLUMBIA 330SX 7645
 Laughter Unlimited – import, long unavailable, but included here because it contains Harry Tate's 'Running an Office' plus Horace Kenney and Oliver Wakefield.

AUSTRALIAN HMV OCLP 7577
 Laughter Unlimited Vol 2 – import, long unavailable; includes Arthur Askey and Richard Murdoch in 'The Proposal'.

DECCA RFLD 23 (two discs)
 They Played The Empire – includes Elsie and Doris Waters, Tommy Handley, Suzette Tarri, Arthur Askey.

DECCA RFLD 30 (two discs)
 They Played The Palladium – includes Bing Crosby, Norman Wisdom, Reg Dixon.

BBC REC 138
 50 Years of Radio Comedy – includes Sandy Powell, Claude Dampier, Jack Warner, Max Miller, Mabel Constanduros, Murgatroyd and Winterbottom, Robb Wilton, Will Fyffe, Frankie Howerd and excerpts from *Band Waggon, Hi Gang, ITMA* and *Much-Binding-in-the-Marsh*.

BBC REC 151
 Great Radio Comedians – includes Suzette Tarri, Reg Dixon, Elsie and Doris Waters, Jewel and Warriss, Jeanne de Casalis, Lucan and McShane, Western Brothers, Gillie Potter.

BBC REC 134M
 Vintage Variety – includes Norman Evans, Max Wall, Will Hay, and excerpts from *ITMA* and *Take It From Here*.

ORIOLE MG 20032 (long deleted)
 Memories of ITMA – excerpts narrated by John Snagge.

FONTANA STFL 534/TFL 5103 (long deleted)
 Take It From Here – studio remakes of some sketches.

BBC REH 161
 The Glums – excerpts from *Take It From Here*.

TOPIC 12T 3876
 Billy Bennett.

TOPIC 12T 396
 You Have Made a Nice old Mess Of It – Gus Elen.

BBC REGL 380
 Gracie Fields – excerpts from broadcasts.

WORLD RECORDS SH 170
 Gracie Fields – Stage and Screen – includes the Holborn Empire live recording referred to in Chapter 8; essential listening.

WORLD RECORDS SH 126 and 151
 George Formby.

DECCA SPA 50
 The World of George Formby Vol 1.

DECCA SPA 446
 The World of George Formby Vol 2.

ARGO ZDA 170
There's Life in the Old Dog Yet – Stanley Holloway monologues, recorded in 1975.

STARLINE MRS 5104
 Stanley Holloway – Monologues – original recordings.

EMI ONCM 533
 Stanley Holloway – More Monologues and Songs.

EMI ONE-UP OU 2075
 Max Miller in the Theatre – live performances at the Holborn Empire, 24-10-38 (both houses). Essential listening.

NIXA NPT 19026/MARBLE ARCH MAL 740
 Max Miller – Max at the Met – live at the Metropolitan Edgware Road, 30-11-57; Miller at his best.

BBC RED 128M
 It's Morecambe and Wise – soundtrack excerpts from the 1975 BBC TV series.

BBC REB 210
 Morecambe and Wise – What Do You Think of the Show So Far? – excerpts from series on Radio 2 (re-worked TV material).

WORLD RECORDS SH 220
 Original Dixieland Jazz Band – The London Recordings – all the recordings made during their visit in 1919/20.

ASV AJA 5023
 Original Dixieland Jazz Band – includes some of the London recordings.

Tony Hancock: excerpts from *Hancock's Half-Hour*: BBC REB 150M; substantially complete shows issued on: NIXA PLP 1039/PYE GGL 0206/NPL 18045: and BBC REB 485/394/423/451.

The Goon Show – substantially complete shows issued on: BBC REB 177, 213, 246, 291, 339, 266, 392, 422, 444 and 481.

Index

Numbers in italics refer to illustrations

Ack-Ack, Beer-Beer (radio show), 155
acrobats, 15, 85, 86, 90–4, 95, 109, 138, 182–5
Actors' Association (AA), 49, 50, 52, 97
adagio' acts, 86, 90, 92, 93–4, 227
Adelphi Theatre, London, 202
Agate, James, 204
agents, 16, 82–3, 84, 89, 136, 157, 190–2, 219
Agents' Association, 83
Aladdin (pantomime), 186
Alan, Ray, and 'Lord Charles', 179, 181, 218
alcohol, 25, 135, 137
Aldershot Hippodrome, 196
Alfred Marks Time (TV), 211
All Alight at Oxford Circus, 66
Allen, Chesney *see* Flanagan and Allen
Allen, Gracie *see* Burns and Allen
Allen, Les, 128
Ambrose and His Orchestra, 72
American artists, 18, 53–4, 144, 157–8, 216–17
Ammonds, John, 223, 225
'Amos 'n Andy', 55
The Andrew Sisters, 157
animal acts, 15, 25, 87, 96, 113–15
animal imitations/effects, 177
Applesauce, 140
'*Appy 'Arf 'Our*, 98, 132
Arbitrator's Award, 193; 1907: 49; 1913: 49, 95; 1919 Contract, 18, 20, 49–50, 84, 95, 193
armed forces entertainment, 137–8; broadcasts, 151–2, 209
The Arthur Haynes Show (TV), 211
Ask A Policeman (film), 107
Askey, Arthur, 128, *130*, 130–1, 187, 188, *188*, 191, 212
Associated Rediffusion, 211
Associated Television Company, 211
Association of Charity Officers, 195
Aston, Ted *see* Durante, Ted and George
ATV 2, 223, 225
Atwell, Winifred, 216
Austin, Charles, 'Parker, PC', 41–2
Authie, Marée, 90, 95, 96, 185
Averard and Lawson, *109*

Babes In The Wood (pantomime), *188*
Baird, John Logie, 132
Band Waggon (BBC series), *130*, 130–2, 152, 154, 225
bands/orchestras, 133–4; on-stage, 72, 157
Banks, Geoffrey, 201
Barber, Chris, 216
Bare Ideas, 138
Barker, Eric, 155
Barraclough, Roy, 222
Barton, Sam, 19
Barty, Jack, 186
BBC radio, 101, 136, 137, 150, 164, 169; Forces Programme, 151, 155; General Overseas Service (now World Service), 155; Home Service, 208; in the 20s, 36–9; in the 30s, 126–32; Light Programme, 155, 201, 208; National and Regional Programmes, 39; 1945–60: 208–10, 211–14; North Region, 208; OBs, 38, 39, 126–7, 129, 130, 152; Scottish Region, 174, 208; wartime, 151–5
BBC Television, 132, *151*, 151, 153, 210, 211–12, 214, 223–5
BBC Variety Orchestra, 128

Beasley, Harry, 44
The Beatles, 216
Beerbohm, Max, 14
The Bells Go Down (film), 120
Ben-Hur, 22
Benjamin, Louis, 84, 87, 219
Bennett, Bill, *32*, 33–4, 118, 120; 'The League of Nations', 34; 'No Power on Earth", 33
Benny, Jack, 157
Benson, Eve, 186
Bentine, Michael, 211
Bentley, Dick, 209
Bentley, Walter, agent, 21–2
Bergen, Edgar, and 'Charlie McCarthy', 157, 180
Berkeley, Busby, 68
Beyond The Fringe, 75, 214
The Billy Cotton Band Show (BBC-TV), 211
The Bing Boys Are Here, 19, 23
Bits and Pieces, 27
Black, Alfred, 64, 199
Black, Alfred (junior), 64, 65, 67
Black, Edward, 64
Black, George, 38, *63*, 63–7, 71, 89, 97, 104, 118, 119, 129, 140, 141, 156, 157, 199, 201, 202, 211
Black and White Minstrel Show, The, 113, 218
Blackbirds, 70
'black-face' acts, 53, 55, 113
Blackpool Palace, 199
Blakeley, John, 197
Blaney, Norah, 23, 37, 46, 70
Block, Bob, 210
Blore, Eric, 117
Bluett, Kitty, 210
Bolton, George, 117–18, 135
Bonn, Issy, 167, *167*, 189
bookings managers, 83–4
Boothroyd, Basil, 202
Boswell Sisters, 68
box-office cards, 86
Boys Will Be Boys (film), *106*
Braben, Eddie, 223
Bradford Alhambra, 169
Briggs, Asa, 38, 126
Brinsworth House, 50, 195
Bristol Hippodrome, *47*, 132, 158, *188*
Britannia Theatre, Hoxton, 13
Brixton Empress, 110, 189
'Broadcast' records, 102–3
broadcasting *see* radio; television
Broadhead circuit, 22, 63, 68, 71
Brough, Arthur, and 'Tim', 180
Brough, Peter, and 'Archie Andrews'. *180*, 180–1, 210
Brown, Teddy, 38, 82, 126
Bucknell, Betty, 186
Burdon, Albert, 41
Burke-and-Head, 109–10
Burke, Bill, 109
Burns and Allen (George Burns and Gracie Allen), 38, 144
Butterworth circuit, 140, 157
Byng, Douglas, 74–5, *187*, 187–8

cabaret, 74, 227
Café Continental (TV show), 210
Cagney, Peter, 118
Calling All Forces (radio), 209
Cambridge Footlights, 136
Campbell, Herbert, 186
Campbell, Connelly, music publisher, 110
Canterbury Hall, London, 13, 14
Capra, Jean, *152*
Carey, Noel, 186

Carlyle, Billie, 100
Carr, Jean, 123
Caryll, Billy, 64, 173
Casalis, Jeanne de ('Mrs Feather'), 161, *161*, 162, 165
Casanova, 69, 110
Casey, James, Senior *see* James, Jimmy
Casey, James ('Cass James'), 169, 201, 204, 205
Casey's Court, 44, 119
Casson, Peter, 177
Castle, Roy, 133, 197, 205
Cavanagh, Peter, 162
censorship, 14, 15, 96–8, 112, 138–9, 166, 173, 198, 211
Chamberlain, Neville, 132, 136
Champagne Charlie (film), 120
Champion, Harry, 139, *139*
Chaplin, Charlie, 40, 109
The Charlie McCarthy Show (radio), 155, 180
Charlot, André, 70, 74
Chase, Chaz, *23*
Chester, Charlie, 155
Children, legal restrictions on employment of, 94, 95–6
Children's Dangerous Performances Act (1879), 95
Chiswick Empire, 114, 135, 210
A Chorus Line, 69
Church, Harry *see* Murray and Mooney
Cinderella (pantomime), 189
cine-variety, 21, 52, 68, 110, 159, 227
Clapham and Dwyer (Charlie Clapham and Bill Dwyer), 38, 58–9, *59*
Clark, John, *107*
Clitheroe, Jimmy, 42
Club Night (radio series), 201
Cochran, C. B., 74
Cock, Gerald, 38
Cole, Walter, 178
Collins, Fred, circuit of, 63, 140, 157
Collins, Horace, 137
Collins, Joe, 89, 157, 190
Collins, Norman, 211
Collinson and Breen, 56
Collinson and Dean, 55–6
Colyer, Ken, 217
comic songs, 72–81
concert parties, 24–5, 37, 112, 117, 227–8
Connolly, Billy, 174
Constanduros, Mabel, 38–9, 126, 147; 'Mrs Buggins Makes the Christmas Pudding', 38–9
contracts, 16, 52, 84, 95, 193, 194; and arbitration, 193, 194; barring clauses, 95; emergency, 193
Convict 99 (film), 107
Conway, Russ, 216
'Conyers, Hutton', 205, *206*, 207
Coogan, Jackie, 38
Cook, Peter, 164
'coon' acts, 113
Cooper, Johnny (Johnny Lawson), *109*, 109–10, 176, 177
Cooper, Tommy, 176
The Co-Optimists, *24*, 24–5, 74
Coram (Thomas Whittaker) and 'Jerry Fisher', *178*, *178*
Cortez, Leon, 97, 98, 132, 166
Cotton, Billy, and His Band, 72, 128, 158
Cotton, Jack, 218
The Court Jester (film), 157
Coventry, Belgrade Theatre, 189
Coward, Noel, 28, 96
Cowley, Frank, 162

Crazy Gang, 62, 64–7, 69, 97, 119, 140, 167
Cromer, Lord, 97
Cunliffe, Whit, 113

Dalziel, May, 172
'the Dame', in pantomimes, 186, 187–8
Dampier, Claude, *100*, 100–1
Dance Cabaret (BBC), 132
dancing acts, speciality, *109*, 109–12, 113
'Dancing Daughters', 128
Danger, Men at Work (BBC radio), 155
Daniels, Bebe, 155, 210
Daniels, Paul, 176
Dante (Harry Hansen), 175
The Dave Morris Show, 201
Davies, Hunter, *The Grades*, 190
Davis, Bette, 28, *28*
Dawson, Les, 170, 222–3, *223*, 225
Day, Elsie, 128
Day, Nat, 157
Dead of Night (film), 180
Dean, Basil, 137–8
'Del Oro', 90, *91*
Delfont, Bernard (Boris Winogradsky), 140, 157, 190, 192, 218
Desmond, Florence (*née* Dawson), 21, 24, *28*, 28–9, 96, 126
Desmond, Freddie, 183–4, 191
Desmonde, Jerry, 201–2, *203*
Devant, David, 175, *175*
Diaghilev, 22
Diamond, Rex, 108
Diary of a Schoolmaster (radio series), 108
The Dickie Henderson Show (ITV), 211
Dixey, Phyllis, 113, 138, *139*, 159
Dixon, Reg, *168*, 169–70, 189, 218
Dixon of Dock Green (TV series), 153
Dodd, Ken, 170, 221–2, *222*, 223, 225
Doncaster Grand Theatre, 126
Donegan, Lonny, 217, *217*
Dorchester Follies, 132
double-acts, 228; 1920s and 1930s, 53–62; 1930s and 1940s, 141–50
Doyle, Jack, 198
The Dramatic, Equestrian and Musical Sick Fund, 49
Drury Lane, 14, 69
Duncanson, Jack, 37
Duncan, Vic ('Duncan's Collies'), *114*, 114–15, *115*, 133, 194
Dunja Trio, 185
Dunville, T. E., 22
Durante, Jimmy, 158
Durante, Ted and George (Ted Aston and George Mooney), 182, 185
Durante, Ted and Hilda, 182
Dwyer, Bill *see* Clapham and Dwyer

Edgar, Marriot, 29, 107
Edinburgh, Theatre Royal, 137
Educating Archie (radio), 210
Educating Archie (TV), 211
Education Act (1921), 95
Edwards, Jimmy, 156, 194, 202, 209
Edwards, Percy, 177
Eight Lancashire Lads, 109, 110
Ellington, Duke, 157
Elliott, G. H., 113
Elstree Calling (film), 68, 77
Elvin, Joe, 49
Elwes, Gervase, 23
Emery, Dick, 138, 160, 169
Empire, Leicester Square, 159
English, Arthur, 166–7

ENSA (Entertainments National Service Association), 138, 152
ENSA Half-Hour, 152
The Entertainer, 221
Entertainment Tax, 88, 140
Entertainments Federal Council, 50, 52
Equity, 49, 50, 193, 194, 219; amalgamation of VAF with, 194–5
The Establishment, 164
European Broadcasting Union, 193
Eurovision, 193
Evans, Norman, 31, *31*, 222; 'Auntie Doleful', 31; 'Over the Garden Wall', 31, *31*
Eve Takes a Bow, 138

Farrar, Gwen, 23, 70
Fawkes, Richard, *Fighting for a Laugh*, 138
fees/salaries, 88, 95, 136, 218–19
Festival of Nudes, 160
Field, Sid, *201*, 201–2; 'The Photographer', 202, *203*
Fields, Gracie (Grace Stansfield), 29, 38, 67, 78, 79, *80*, 81, 86, 103, 120, 123, 129, 136, 139
Fig Leaves, 138
films (cinema), 21, 52, 63, 67–8, 79, 81, 96, 107, 108, 113, 120, 123, 140, 142–3, 157, 197
Findlater, Richard, 97
Finlay, Frank, 225
Finney, Jimmy, 53
Finsbury Park Empire, 83, 87, 88, 215
fire regulations, 96
Fitzgerald, Ella, 157
Flanagan and Allen (Bud Flanagan and Chesney Allen), 60–2, 65–7, 128, 141, 142, 146, 150
The Flying Banvards, 19
Forces All-Star Bill (radio), 209
The Forces Show (radio), 209
Forde, Florrie, 60, 126
The Foreman Went to France (film), 120
Formby, George, Senior, 30, 222
Formby, George, 67, 78, 78–9, 120, 129
Foster Agency, 82, 191
The Four Astounderz, 90
Fox, Roy, and His Band, 72, 132
Foy, Tom, 30, *30*, 35, 169
Francis Day and Hunter, 110
Frankau, Ronald, 75–6, 101, 130
Frederick, Cecil, 154–5
Freeman, Denis, 39
Fryer, Bertram, 39
Fun at St Fanny's (film), 165
A Funny Thing Happened On The Way To The Forum, 164
Fyffe, Will, 68, 171–2, *172*, 220

Gadbin, 92
gag books, 118
Gainsborough pictures, 67, 107
Galton, Ray, 212
'Gang Show', RAF, 138, 156, 165, 169
Ganjou Brothers (Serge, George and Bob) and Juanita, 92–3, 92–4
Ganjou, George, 217, 218
Ganjou, Serge, 183, 194
Garrison Theatre (BBC), 153–4, *154*
Gaston and Andrée, 98
Gatti's music hall, 14
Gaumont-British Picture Corporation, 23, 63
General Artists Corporation of America, 158
General Theatres Corporation (GTC), 23, 38, 39, 56, 63, 64, 69, 82–8, 140, Moss Empires takes over theatres, 156–7
'Gert and Daisy' *see* Waters, Elsie and Doris
Gibbons, Walter, 22, 49
Gideon, Melville, 74
Gielgud, Val, 39, 126, 128
Gladwin, Joe, 199–200, 201
Glasgow Empire, 171
Gold, Alf, 190

Gold, Jimmy *see* Naughton and Gold
Golden, illusionist, 175
Gollop, Ted, 83, 97, 215–16, 218
The Good Companions (Priestley), 24
The Good Old Days (BBC-TV), 214, 222
Goodchild, Harry *see* Murray and Mooney
Goodwin, Denis, 209
The Goon Show (radio), 211, *213*, 213–14, 221
Gordon, Harry, *173*, 173–4
Gourley, Ronald, 37
Grade, Leslie (Louis Winogradsky), 157, 158, 160, 190–1, 192, 211, 218
Grade, Lew (Lazarus Winogradsky), 89, 110, 140, 157, 158, 160, 190–1, 192, 211, 218
Grafton, Jimmy, 208, 211, 212, 219
Grand Order of the Water Rats, 49, 195
Gray, 'Monsewer' Eddie, 65–7, 186
Green, Sid, 223
Griffiths Brothers, 53
Grock, clown, 19
Guest, Val, 107
Gulliver, Charles, 22, 63

Haley, Bill, and the Comets, 217
Half-Past Eight, 173
Hall, Adelaide, 70, *70*
Hancock, Tony, 138, 150, 160, 169, 201, 202–4, 209, 211–12, 212
Hancock's Half-Hour (radio), 211–12, 213
Hancock's Half-Hour (TV), 212
Handley, Tommy, 38, 68, 117, 130, 132, 151, *152*, 152–3
Hansen, Harry *see* Dante
Happidrome (BBC), 154–5
'The Happiness Boys' (Billy Jones and Ernest Hare), 55
Happy and Glorious, 140
Harbin, Robert (Ned Williams), 176
Harbour, Harry, 114, 135, 158, 199
Harbour, Sam, 87, 114
Harding, Bill, 210
Harding, Jan, 186, 189
Hare, Ernest *see* 'The Happiness Boys'
Harmer, Dolly, 42
Harris, Augustus, 186
Harris, Vernon, 130, 131, 151
Harvey, Charlie, 106
Hastings, Ernest, 19, 29
Hatton, Pat, 176
Hawtrey, Charles, *107*
Hay, Will, 67, 105–8, 116, 120, 128, 134
Hay, Will, Junior, 108
Hayes, Alex, 108
Hazell, Rupert, 128
Heath, Ted and His Band, 216
Hemsley, Harry, 116–17
Henderson, Dick, *34*, 34–5, 68, 86, 116, 118, 122, 129, 221, 222
Henderson, Dickie, 34–5, 68, 153, *188*
Henlere, Herschel, 72
Henry, John, 37
Henshall, William, 201
Henson, Leslie, 29
Hibberd, Stuart, 131
Hi, Gang! (radio), 155
Hill, Benny, 158
Hilliam, B. C. *see* 'Mr Flotsam and Mr Jetsam'
Hills, Dick, 223
Hillyard, Pat, 132, 151, *151*, 155
Hindin, Philip, 82, 88, 157–8, 184, 191–2, 215, 218
Hoare, George, 199
Hogan, Michael, 38
Holborn Empire (formerly Royal Holborn), *12*, 14, 22, 25, 63, 81, 89, 103, 110, *122*, 123, 129, 134, 140, 209
Holloway, Balliol, 204
Holloway, Jimmy *see* Nervo and Knox
Holloway, Stanley, 24, 24–5, 29, 29–30, 68, 74, 77, 87, 120; 'Albert' monologues, 29; 'Old Sam', 29, *29*

Hollywood Revue of 1929 (film), 93
Holmes, Leslie, *see* The Two Leslies
Honri, Peter, 69
Hopkins, Ted and May, 31
'Horace and Edna', 112, *112*, 113
Horne, Kenneth, 155
Houdini, Harry, 175–6
Housewives' Choice (radio), 221
Howard and Wyndham, 22, 63, 140, 173
Howerd, Frankie, 72, 163–5, *164*, 209
Hoxton Varieties, 14
Hulbert, Jack, 156
Hutchinson, Ronald *see* Tate, Harry
Hutton, Betty, 157
hypnotists, 109, 177
Hylton, Jack, 211
Hylton, Jack, Orchestra of, 72, 73

illusionists, 175–6, 181
imitators, 177, 228
impressionists, *28*, 28–9, 162, 228
'The Indefinites' (radio), 37
Independent Television, 210–11
ITMA (*It's That Man Again*: BBC), 117, 132, *152*, 152–3, 154, 208
It's A Grand Life (film), 197
ITV, 211, 225

The Jack Benny Show (radio), 155
The Jack Buchanan Show (radio), 209
Jackley, George, 110, 187, 189
Jackley, Joy, 110
Jackley, Nat, 110, 188, 189, *196*, 196–7
Jackson, Glenda, 225
Jackson, Jack, 132
'James, Cass' *see* Casey, James
James, Jimmy (James Casey senior), 169, *204*, 204–5, *206*, 207, 222
James, Sid, 212, *212*
'Jane', strip cartoon, 159–60
Jay, Mannie, 157
The Jazz Singer, 25
Jeffrey, R. E., 36, 39
Jenny Jones, 204
Jewel and Warriss (Jimmy Jewel and Ben Warriss), *141*, 141–2, 150, 213; 'The Boxing Match', 141–2
Jewish comedians, 31, 167, *167*
Joan and Leslie (TV), 211
The Johnny Lawson Trio, 110
Jones, Billy *see* 'The Happiness Boys'
Joy Bells, 18
jugglers, 85, 86, 109, 126, 177, 181, 182

Kalanag, illusionist, 175
Karlin, Miriam, 208
Karno, Fred, 40, 41, 65, 99, 105, 112; 'The Football Match', 40, 41; 'Mumming Birds', 40
Kavanagh, Ted, 152, 209
Kaye, Danny, 157, *157*
Kenney, Horace, 66, 99, 99–100; 'Almost A Film Star', 99
Kenway and Young (Nan Kenway and Douglas Young), 144
Keppel, Joe *see* Wilson, Keppel and Betty
Kerr, Bill, 212, *212*
Kester, Max, 108, 151
Keys, Nelson, 132
Kilburn Empire, 83
The Killing of Sister George, 165
King, Nosmo (Vernon Watson), 87
King, Peter, 210
Kingston Empire, *23*, *94*
Kitchen Front (BBC), 150
Knock On Wood (film), 157
Knox, Betty, 111
Knox, Patsy, 111
Knox, Teddy *see* Nervo and Knox
Konyot, Bob, 91–2, 139, 177, 184, *184*, *185*, 219
Konyot, Marion (Marion Olive), 184, *184*, *185*
Koringa, 113
Korris, Harry, 154–5, 197

La Rue, Danny, 74, 187
Lacey, George, 187
'Lady Syncopators', 22
Laine, Frankie, 216
Lamonte, Johnny, 182–3, *183*
Lamonte, Suma, 162, 182–3, *183*, 184–5
Lamouret, Robert, and 'Dudule', 180
landladies, theatrical, 133, 134
Lane, Samuel Haycroft, 13
The Last Of The Summer Wine (TV), 199
Lauder, Sir Harry, 133, 171, *171*
Lawson, Johnny *see* Cooper, Johnny
Layton and Johnstone, 70–1
Leddington, Florence, 83, 146, 190
Leicester Palace of Varieties, 22
Leighton-Porter, Christabel ('Jane'), 159–60
Leno, Dan, *26*, 26–7, 35, 186, 187
Leno, Dan, Junior (Herbert Leno), 186
Lester, Claude, 135
Levante (Leslie George Cole), 175
Lewis, Shari, 179
Licensing Act (1737), 14
licensing regulations, 14, 16, 95–8, 173
Life Begins at Oxford Circus, 66
A Life of Bliss, 177
Life With The Lyons (Radio), 210
Lister, Moira, 209
The Little Dog Laughed, 66, *140*
Littler, Prince, 140, 211, 218
Liveing, E. W., 126
Liverpool Empire, 44
Liverpool Palace of Varieties, 222
Lloyd, Marie, 16, *16*, 72
Local Government Act (1888), 98
Lodge, David, 169
Logan, Jimmy, 172, *173*, 174
London Alhambra, 22, 37, 38, 63, 64, 69, 87, 140, 148
London Casino, 157
London Coliseum, 15, 22, 38, 63, 68, 69, 87, 88, 89, 110, 140, 148
London County Council (General Powers) Act (1921), 96
London Hippodrome, 18, 23, 44, 63
London Laughs, 202
London Management (agency), 191
London Palladium, 18, 22, 29, 38, 56, 63, 64, *64*, 66, 68, 69, 89, 102, 118, 119, 140, 148, 157–8, 172, 174, 194, 204, 216, 218
London Pavilion, 22, 140
London Rhapsody, 66
London Theatres of Variety Ltd (LTV), 22
London Town (film), 202, *203*
Lorimer, Maxwell *see* Wall, Max
Lorraine, Violet, 19
Loss, Joe, and his band, 216
Lotinga, Ernie, 99
Lotto, Jack, 49, 195
Lowe and Webster, 56
Lucan and McShane (Arthur Lucan and Kitty McShane), 'Old Mother Riley', 142–4, *143*
Lyceum, London, 186, 189
Lynn, Vera, 216
Lyon, Ben, 155, 210
Lyon, Monte, agent, 190
Lyttelton, Humphrey, 216

Maccabe, Frederic, 178
MacCauley, Bobbie *see* Mills, Nat and Bobbie
McCormick, Richard, 90
McCormick, Rikki and Copper ('Del Oro'), 90, *91*, 96, 138, 156, 192
MacDonald, Leslie, 218
McEachern, Malcolm *see* 'Mr Flotsam and Mr Jetsam'
McEwan, Geraldine, 209
Mack, Charles E. *see* Moran and Mack
McKern, Louis, 221
Macmillan, Harold, 215
MacNaghten circuit, 22, 63, 71
MacPherson, Sandy, 151

Macqueen-Pope, W., 17
McShane, Kitty *see* Lucan and McShane
magicians and illusionists, 109, 175–6, 181
Make and Mend (radio), 155
Marks, Alfred, 213
Marks, Dave, 191
Marks, Jack, 110, 158, 183–4
Marlowe, Joy, 93–4
Marriott, Moore, 107, 108
Marsh, Billy, 82, 136, 162, 190
Martin, Tony, 157
Marx, Harpo and Chico, 157
Maschwitz, Eric, 128
Mashford, Horace and Edna, *112*, 112–13
Maskelyne, Jasper, 175
Maskelyne, John Nevil, 175
Maskelyne, Nevil, 175
'Masu and Yuri', 182
Masters, Kitty, 128
Matcham, Frank, 88
Maxwell, Charles, 129, 209
Mayne, Clarice, 19
Mayo, Sam, 110, 191
Merry-Go-Round (radio), 155
Metropolis Management Act (1878), 15
Metropolitan, Edgware Road, 14, 22, 56, 63, 83, *83*, 89, 89, 123, 146, 218
microphones, 68–9, 123
Middlemiss, Philip, 37
Miller, Max, 87, *122*, 122–5, 134, 136, 140, 161, 169, 209
Milligan, Spike, 138, 211, 213, 214
Mills, Nat, and Bobbie, 97, 144, *145*, 146–7
minstrel shows, 53, 55, 113
Miranda, Carmen, 157
Modley, Albert, 169
Moffatt, Graham, 107, 108
Monday Night at Seven (BBC), 130
Monkhouse, Bob, 209
Monty Python's Flying Circus, 54, 214, 221
Mooney, George *see* Durante, Ted and George
Mooney, Harry *see* Murray and Mooney
Moran and Mack (Charles Moran and George Mack), 55
Mordaunt, Frank, 178
Morecambe and Wise (Eric Morecambe and Ernie Wise), 150, 171, 207, 223–5, *224*
Moreton, Robert, 138
Morgan, Tommy, 173, 174
Morris, Dave, *199*, 199–201, 222; 'Blackpool Landladies', 199–200; 'Buying an Alarm Clock', 200–1
Morris, Harry, 162
Morris, Lily, 68, 77–8, *78*, 128
Morton, Charles, 14, 15–16
Moss, Sir Edward, 15, 16, 22
Moss Empires, 15, 22, 25, 38, 49, 63, 69, 70, 72, 82, 83, 95, 110, 119, 136, 140, 148, 211, 215, 218; GTC merges with (1932), 63; GTC theatre circuit taken over by (Moss GTC: 1946), 156–7; running the business, 83–9, 190; taken over by Stoll (1960), 218
'Mr Flotsam and Mr Jetsam' (B. C. Hilliam and Malcolm McEachern), 73–4, 132
Mr Skitch (film), 28
Mr Tower of London, 79
'Mrs Feather' *see* Casalis, Jeanne de
Much Binding in the Marsh (BBC), 155
Muir, Frank, 156, 209
Mundy, Hilda, 64, 173
Murdoch, Richard, *130*, 131, 152, 155
Murray, Norman (agent), 82, 84, 109, 191, 219
Murray and Mooney (Harry Church and Harry Goodchild), *56*, 56–7; 'The Stake', 56–7
music-hall, Victorian, 13–17, 21, 26, 28, 112, 120, 134, 136, 178, 186, 226, 228

Music Hall (BBC radio), 127, 128, 155, 208, 209
Music Hall Artists' Railway Association, 49, 50, 135, 158
The Music Hall Benevolent Fund, 49
The Music Hall Provident Society and Sick Fund, 49
Music Hall Strike (1907), 16, 95
musical acts, 70–81
musical comedy, 17, 23, 69, 228
Musical Director (MD), 88, 94
Musicians' Union, 133, 193, 219
My Wife's Sister (TV), 211

NAAFI comedians, 156, 158, 162, 163, 211
National Film Theatre, London, 197
National Insurance Act (1948), 159, 193
National Vaudeville Corporation, 63
Natova, Natasha, 93
Naughton and Gold (Charlie Naughton and Jimmy Gold), 38, 58, *58*, 64–7
Naughty Girls of 1940, 138
Navy Mixture (radio), 180, 209
'Nedlo the Gypsy Violinist', 118
Nervo and Knox (Jimmy Nervo and Teddy Knox), 22
Newcastle Empire, 72, 104, 169
New Cross Empire, 87
Newman, Alan, 209–10
Newport Empire, 69, 114
Nicholls, Billy, *107*
Nichols, Joy, 209
A Night at the Show (film), 40
Norden, Denis, 156, 209
Norman and Forman, *25*
North, Michael, 151, 210
northern comedians, 30–1, 169–70, 197–201, 222
Nottingham Empire, 68
nude shows, 138–9, 159–60, 215–16

Odeon Cinemas, 68
Odeon Leicester Square, 69
O'Farrell, Talbot, 146
O'Gorman, Joe (father), 53, 57
O'Gorman Brothers (Joe and Dave), *57*, 57–8, 186
Oh, Mr Porter (film), 107
O-Kay for Sound, 66, 67
Old Bones of the River (film), 107
Olden, George *see* Ray, Ted
Oliver, Vic, 155
Olivier, Laurence, 69, 123
The Optimists of Nine Elms (film), 162
Orben, Robert, 118, 220
Original Dixieland Jazz Band (ODJB), 18, *19*, 20, 27
Owen, Bill, 208
Oxford music-hall, London, 14

PA (public address), 68–9, 81, 123, 228
The Pajama Game, 220
Palace of Varieties (BBC), 128
Palace Theatre, London, 16
Palace Theatre, Manchester, 169
Palmer, Florence, 42–4
Palmer, Gaston, 177
pantomimes, 24, 75, 186–7, 193
'Parks, Aerbert', 37
Parlophone records, 148
Parnell, Val, 56, 63, 64, 65, 83, 85, 89, 104, 140, 156, *156*, 157, 158, 211, 218
Pathé Gazette, 68
The Paul Daniels Show (TV), 185
Pearson, Bob and Alf, 71, 71–2, 82, 134, 135, 137
Penge Empire, 87
Pepper, Harry S., 128
The Performer, 49, 50, *51*, 68, 94, 110; 'Next Week's Calls', 50, *85*
Performing Animals (Regulation) Act (1925), 25
Perrins, Leslie, 210
Petts, Norman, 159
Phono films, 25
Piccadilly Hayride, 202

Pink, Wal, 44–5
Pitt, Archie, 79, 191
Pitts, Zasu, 28
Platt, Bert and Cyril, 106
Poluski Brothers (Sam and Will), 54, 54–5
pop music, 216, 218
poster billings, 86–7
Potter, Gillie, 128–9, 173
Powell, Kay, 104
Powell, Lily, 101
Powell, Sandy, 101–4, *132*, 136, *187*, 188, 218; 'The Lost Policeman', *102*, 102–3; spoof ventriloquist act, 104
Presley, Elvis, 217
Prince, Arthur, and 'Jim', 19, 126, 179, *179*, 180
Private Eye, 214
Puss In Boots (pantomime), 186

Queens Park Hippodrome, Manchester, 160

Radcliffe, Jack, 173
radio Variety, 21, 58, 64, 69, 71, 108, 117, 142, 144, 146, 150, 159, 164, 165, 169–70, 177, 180–1, 202–3, 221; American programmes, 155, 180; in the 20s, 36–9; in the 30s, 126–32; 1945–60: 208–10, 211–14; wartime, 151–5; *see also* BBC radio; television
Radio-Keith-Orpheum circuit, USA, 111
Radio Luxembourg, 129
Radio Normandie, 129
Radio Times, 37, 127, 129, 130, 152
Randle, Frank, 97, 197–9, *197*, *198*
Randle's Scandals, 198
Ray, Johnny, 158, *216*, 216
Ray, Ted (George Olden), 118–19, *119*, 135, 157, 161, 209, 210
Raye, Martha, 157
Raymond, Paul, 160, 215
Raymond Revuebar, 215
Ray's A Laugh (radio show), 210
Rebler, juggler, 177
records, recordings, 101–4, 106–7, 123, 148; live theatre, 79, 81, 86, 103–4, 123, 129
Redgrave, Michael, 180
Reeves and Lamport, agents, 82, 148
Reid, Beryl ('Marlene'), 165
Reith, John, 36, 151
Revnell, Ethel, 212–13
revues, 17, 23, 25, 228; intimate, 136, 228; nude, 215; wartime, 136, 138, 140
Richards, Cliff, and The Shadows, *217*, 217–18
Richards and Marks, agents, 82–3
Ristori, Harry and Marjorie, 111, 113
Roberts Brothers Circus, 114
Robey, George (George Wade), 18, 19, 23, 27, *27*, 35, 87, 96, 118, 133, 164, 187, *187*
Robinson, Cardew ('Cardew the Cad'), 165–6, 169
rock music, 216–18
'A Romance in Porcelain', 93
Ronald, Tom, 210
Rooney, Mickey, 157
The Roosters (radio), 37
Roscoe, Frank, 201
Rose, Clarkson, 97, 186
Rose, Julian, 31, 167
Round About Regent Street, 66
Roy, Derek, 208
Royal Command Variety Performance, 1912: 16, 18, 44; 1919: 18–20, 23, 44
Royal Variety Performances, 18, 50, 56, 119, 195; 1933: 93; 1937: 180; 1960: 217; 1978: 81
Royalty, London, 24
Royce, Sidney, 71
running order for Variety bills, 84–6
Running Wild (BBC-TV), 223
Russell, Billy, 120–2, *121*, 137

Russell, Fred, 18, 63, 180; and 'Coster Joe', 178, *178*, 180
Russian Ballet, 22
Ryder, Slim, 177

St Albans Odeon, 218
St George's Hall, 175
Salberg, Keith, 191
Salter, Ralph, 177
Sandford, Marjorie, 186
Sandy Powell's Road Show, 104
Sarony, Leslie, 72–3, *73*, 85, 126
Saturday Spotlight (radio), 155
Saunders, Scott, 134
Savoy Follies (Savoy Theatre), 28
Savoy Orpheans, 18
Saxotet, J. Thomas, 38
Scottish comedians, 31, 171–4
Seaforth, Victor, 162
seat prices, 88, 140
Secombe, Harry, 133–4, 138, 156, 163, *163*, 169, 188, 211, 213, 214; *Twice Brightly*, 158
second-spot comics, 84–5, 119, 163
Second World War (1939–45), 132, 136–40, 150, 151–5
Selbit, illusionist, 175
self-employed artists, 159, 193
Selinger, Dennis, 190–1
Sellers, Peter, 138, 162, 169, 208, 211, 213, 214
Shadwell, Charles, 180–1
Sharman, John, 39, 127, 146, 208
Shaw, George Bernard, 136
Sheffield Empire, 50
Shields, Ella, 14, 38
Shipmates Ashore (radio), 155
Shore, Dinah, 157
Short, Jack, 172
Sim Bala Bim, 175
Simpson, Alan, 212
Sinatra, Frank, 158, 164
Sing As We Go (film), 81
sketch comics, 228; 1920s, 40–8; 1930s, 99–108; 1940s and 1950s, 196–207
skiffle, 217
Sky High, 136
Sleeping Beauty (pantomime), 188
Smith, Billy, 200–1
Society of West End Managers, 194
Somewhere in Camp (film), 197
speciality acts, 15, 82, 109–15, 138, 175–81, 228
Spencer, Fred, 36–7
The Squire's Party, 162
The Stage, 49, 50, 84
Stand Easy (radio), 156
Standing, Michael, 127, *127*, 137–8, 152, 208, 209
stand-up comics, 77, 81, 84, 220, 221, 228; 1920s, 26–35; 1930s, 116–25; 1940s and 1950s, 161–70
Stanford and Allen, 60
Stansfield, Grace *see* Fields, Gracie
Star Bill (radio), 204, 209, 212
Star Parade (radio), 221
Stark, Graham, 169, 209
'Stars in Battledress', 138
Steptoe and Son (TV), 214
Stetson, Juggler, 177
Stoll, Sir Oswald, 15, *15*, 16, 22, 38, 63, 87, 140
Stoll circuit, 22, 25, 38, 63, 64, 140, 157, 158, 199, 218
Stoll-Moss Theatres, 218, 219
Stoll Picture Theatre, 22
Stone, Christopher, 64, 69
Strike A New Note, 202
Strike It Again, 202
Strip Strip Hooray, 138
The Stuff To Give The Troops (radio), 155
summer-season shows, Scottish, 172–3, 174
Summers, Dorothy, *152*, 152–3
Sunday Night at the London Palladium, 211
Sunderland Empire, 169
Sutan, Albert, 190

Sweeney and Ryland, 53–4
Sweet and Low, 136
Swinson, Reg, 193, 194, 195
Syndicate Halls, 22, 63, 83, 140, 146, 157, 190

Take It From Here (BBC radio), 209
The Talk Of The Town, 202
Tarri, Suzette, 161–2, 210
Tate, Harry (Ronald Hutchinson), 19–20, 23, 40, 44–8, 87, 126, 128; 'Going Round the World', *47*, 47–8; 'Golfing', 20, 44; 'Motoring', 44, 45; 'Peacehaven', *45*; 'Running an Office', 45–6; 'Selling a Car', 19–20, 44
Tate, Ronnie (Harry Tate Junior), 44–5, 46–8, 53, 68, 134
Tauber, Richard, 68
Taylor, Harold, 176
Taylor, Tom, 90
Ten Thousand Jokes, Toasts, Stories, 118
television, 31, 113, 132, 159, 160, 164, 170, 183, 189, 192, 193, 201, 202, 208, 210–14, 219, 222–5, 226
Tennens, Nat, 157
Tennyson, Joe, 53
Terence Byron Ltd, 69
That Was The Week That Was (TV), 214
theatre managers, 15–16, 87–8, 96
Theatres Act (1843), 14, 96, 97, 98
Theatres of Variety (BBC), 132
Theatrical Employers Registration Act (1925), 25, 52
Theatrical Managers Association, 16
These Foolish Things, 66
This Is The Show, 139
This Year of Grace, 28
Thomas, Brenda, 84, 86
Thomas, Wally, 21, 68–9, 114, 134
Thompson, Roy (later Lord Thompson), 210

Thornton, Richard, 49
Those Were The Days (film), 68
'The Three Jokers', 183
Till Death Do Us Part (TV), 214
Tilley, John, 69
Titheradge, Peter, 209
Took, Barry, *Laughter in the Air*, 209
'top of the bill', 15, 86
Top of the Bill (radio), 155
Top of the World, 66, 140
Towers, Harry Alan, 211
Trinder, Tommy, 60, 119–20, *120*, 132, 138, 140, 155
Tucker, Charlie, 82
Tweedly, Tommy, 19–20, 44
Twinkle, 97
The Two Leslies (Leslie Sarony and Leslie Holmes), 73, *73*, 85, 128

Under Your Tin Hat (radio), 155
Underneath the Arches, 60
Up In Arms (film), 157
Up Pompeii (TV), 164
Up The Pole (radio), 142
Up With The Curtain (BBC), 132

vacancy cards, 83
'The Valve Set' (radio), 37
Van, Sammy, 110
Van Damm, Vivian, 160
Variety Artists' Benevolent Fund (VABF), 37, 50, 52, 188, 195
Variety Artistes' Federation (VAF), 18, 37, 63, 68, 94, 129, 134, 135, 140; amalgamation with Equity (1967), 194–5; Barrow-in-Furness incident, 150, 152, 194; from 1945 onwards, 193–5; 1906–39: 49–52
Variety Bandbox (BBC radio), 164, 169, 208, 209, 220
Variety Club of Great Britain, 195
Variety Council, 193
Variety Fanfare (radio), 165

Variety Half-Hour (BBC), 132
Variety Jubilee (film), 93
Variety Theatres Controlling Co. Ltd, 22
vaudeville, 38, 228
Vaudeville (BBC), 38, 126
Vaughan, Norman, 163
ventriloquists, 19, 104, 109, 126, 177–81, 218
Very Tasty, Very Sweet (radio), 144, 155
Victoria Palace theatre, 73, 140
video, 219
Vincent, Robbie, 154–5, 197
Vocalian Gramophone Company, 71
Vyvyan, Molly, 186

Wade, George *see* Robey, George
Waiting For Godot, 221
Wakefield, Douglas, 191
Wakefield, Oliver, 116
Wall, Max (Maxwell Lorimer), *220*, 220–1, 225
Wallace, Nellie, 77, *77*, 87, 137, 187
Wallendas, 92
Ward, Hilda, 22
Ward, Polly, 186
'Wardle and Olden', 118
Warner, Jack, 153–4, *154*
Warriss, Ben *see* Jewel and Warriss
Watch Committees, 96, 97, 98, 118, 138–9, 150, 166, 173, 197, 215
Waterlogged Spa (radio), 155
Waters, Elsie and Doris ('Gert and Daisy'), 147–50, 191, 208
Waters, Jack *see* Warner, Jack
Watson, Vernon *see* King, Nosmo
Watt, John, 39, 128, 151, *151*
Webster, M. C., 127
Weinthrop, Reuben *see* Flanagan and Allen
Weldon, Harry, 40, 101
Welfare State, 156, 158–9, 193, 195
Wences, Senor, 179–80

Western Brothers (Kenneth and George), *75*, 76
Weston and Lee, 79
Whelan, Albert, 69
White Horse Inn, 69
Whitlock, Trafford, 209
Whittaker, Thomas *see* Coram
'Will Hay and his Scholars' (record), 106–7
The Will Hay Programme, (radio) *107*
Williams, Cissie, 63, 83–4
Williams, Ned *see* Harbin, Robert
Willis, Dave, 173
Wilson, Dennis Main, 204, 209, 218
Wilson, Keppel and Betty (Jack Wilson, Joe Keppel), 82, *111*, 112, 113
Wilton, Robb, *42*, 42–4, 90, 102, 137, 222; 'The Fire Chief', 43–4
Wilton's Music Hall Trust, 69
Windmill Theatre, London, 138, 160, 163, 166
Winogradsky *see* Delfont, Bernard: Grade, Leslie and Lew
Wintergarten Theatre, Berlin, 68
Winters, Joan, 153, *154*
Wise, Ernie *see* Morecambe and Wise
Wood, Wee Georgie, 42, 126
Wood Green Empire, 198
Woods, Eli, 205, 207, 222
Workers' Playtime (radio), 208
working-men's clubs, 112, 193–4, 218, 228
Worth, Harry, 160
Wortman, Chris, 113, 189
Wright, Lawrence, music publisher, 110

Yes Minister (TV), 214
Young, Douglas, 144
Young Bloods of Variety, 64
Yule, Fred, 151